Elites and the Wealthy in
Modern British History

Elites and the Wealthy in Modern British History

Essays in Social and Economic History

W.D. Rubinstein

Associate Professor, School of Social Sciences
Deakin University, Australia

THE HARVESTER PRESS · SUSSEX
ST. MARTIN'S PRESS · NEW YORK

First published in Great Britain in 1987 by
THE HARVESTER PRESS LIMITED
Publisher: John Spiers
16 Ship Street, Brighton, Sussex
and in the USA by
ST. MARTIN'S PRESS, INC
175 Fifth Avenue, New York, NY 10010

British Library Cataloguing in Publication Data
Rubinstein, W. D.
   Elites and the wealthy in modern British
   history: essays in social and economic
   history.
   1. Great Britain—Social conditions
   I. Title
   941.07   HN385

ISBN 0–7108–1173–X

Library of Congress Cataloging-in-Publication Data

Rubinstein, W. D.
   Elites and the wealthy in modern British history.
   Bibliography: p.
   Includes index.
   1. Elite (Social sciences)—Great Britain—History.
2. Great Britain—Social conditions. 3. Great Britain—
Economic conditions. I. Title.
HN400.E4R8 1987   305.5'2'0941   87–9879
ISBN 0–312–00947–X

Typeset in 10/12pt Plantin by
C. R. Barber & Partners (Highlands) Ltd,
Fort William, Scotland
Printed and bound in Great Britain
by Billings & Sons Limited, Worcester.

To my parents

Contents

Contents

SURVIVALS

List of Tables

1

Introduction

I

This volume is a collection of eleven of my essays on modern British economic and social history, six of which have been previously published between 1977 and 1986, and five of which are new to this work.

They may be divided—the division being somewhat arbitrary—into three sections. The first primarily discusses wealth-holding, although its essays also trace the evolution of Britain's elite structure in a way which I would not wish basically to revise. Chapter 2, reprinted from the *Economic History Review* (1977) provides the main statistical evidence for the nature and evolution of top wealth-holding in Britain, while Chapter 3, reprinted from *Past and Present* (1977) reiterates some of this and extends its conclusions and implications to the whole of British society from before industrialization to the present.[1]

The main points which emerge from Chapter 2 are that the bulk of Britain's wealthiest businessmen were situated in London and other commercial towns, that the importance of industrialists and manufacturers in Britain's wealth structure was much less important than was previously almost universally supposed, and that industrialization *per se* was probably much less significant to Britain's middle classes, and even to the whole population, than was previously imagined. Chapter 3 extends this to present a view of the evolution of modern British society based upon the development of its elites as revealed primarily, but not exclusively, by the evidence on wealth-holding: the unified elite, in which landowners and landed society were joined, to a considerable and surprising extent, by much of the (especially) Anglican middle classes, broke down around 1832 into three elites: those of the landowners, the London-based commercial elite, and the northern industrialists who had quite different bases, economies, assumptions and relationships to the working classes; these in turn increasingly merged after the 1880s and probably decisively after World War One, when British politics was realigned almost exclusively along class lines.

Both of these articles seem to me as sound today as a decade ago; all of the factual evidence which I have collected since abundantly supports the view of the greater significance of commercial wealth, while I am equally convinced that my overarching schema of the development of modern British history is heuristically correct, in so far as a theory at this level of generality can be termed 'correct' or not. Although my research on wealth-holding has been cited very many times by economic and social historians since it first appeared, far less has been made of my schema of the evolution of modern British history, in part because I have never followed it up with the fully-developed study which it obviously requires. However, I am currently at work on a book on the Victorian middle classes which will certainly use this schema as its backbone to a large extent.

Part of the further evidence which has come to light about the significance of London and of commercial wealth is presented in my previously unpublished essay on 'The Geographical Distribution of Middle-class Income in Britain, 1800–1914' (Chapter 4). The two previous chapters focus on *wealth* and wealth-holding, while this presents further statistics on middle-class *incomes* as evidenced by a detailed study of the income tax records. The trends demonstrated by these two quite separate types of data are broadly very similar and reinforce one another, with a number of interesting differences spelled out in Chapter 4. In particular, the share of middle-class London income, which constituted nearly one-half of all middle-class British income during the Napoleonic period, declined to about one-third by mid-century; this was paralleled by a steep rise in middle-class incomes in the major industrial countries of Lancashire and Yorkshire. Yet there was never a decisive breakthrough to a middle class in which this type or locale of income was predominant, and, especially after 1880, there was a distinct swing back to London, whose share of the cake of middle-class income was almost fully restored to what it had been during the Napoleonic period by the outbreak of World War One. These shifts in income distribution were of profound importance for the type of society Britain became.[2]

Chapter 5, originally published in *Business History*, places British wealth-holding in a comparative framework by comparing the peak British fortunes with those found in the United States and Australia. The most striking feature here is the extraordinary size of the largest American fortunes compared with those in Britain (or anywhere else), a size differential which cannot, in my view, be readily explained. This differential was seemingly not the result of any failure on the part of British entrepreneurs, and must be a product of factors inherent in and specific to the two national economies, but it is remarkably difficult to state cogently what these were.[3] These *inherent* national differences have profound implications for the ways in which we should, in my opinion, view entrepreneurial success, especially as to whether the success allegedly brought about by effort and ability are not entirely contextual to the particular national economy in which the entrepreneur's career took place.

Three further chapters deal with British elite groups, covering, respectively, the propensity or otherwise of wealthy businessmen to purchase land in large quantities during the nineteenth century, the extent of genuine social mobility among British elite groups, and the evolution of the British honours system since 1780, especially peerage creations, and especially the manner and degree in which it evolved to cover new forms of economic activity and distinguished conduct.

'New Men of Wealth and the Purchase of Land in Nineteenth-Century Britain', reprinted from *Past and Present* (1981) questions the long-standing assumption that wealthy businessmen and professionals used their wealth to obtain high status by the purchase of land on a large scale. There is remarkably little evidence that they did, once the statistics of wealth-holding and land ownership are examined objectively and systematically. My first rule for giving a seminar paper, one which I have found to be true by repeated experience, is that one never is asked the questions one expects to hear, and a similar rule seems to be the case in the publication of articles and books as well—the point which is taken up and debated is simply not the one which, in advance, seemed most contentious. When I wrote 'New Men of Wealth', I regarded the conclusions as well-founded and quite unobjectionable and never expected to find the subject discussed again, but in the mysterious ways of academe, this article has, it would seem, aroused more genuine controversy than anything I have ever written. The major reason for this was the publication, soon afterwards, by the celebrated historian Lawrence Stone, and Jeanne C. Fawtier Stone, of *An Open Elite?* which arrives at fairly similar conclusions for a much longer period although using the much narrower data base of three countries rather than the whole of Britain, as I do. The Stones (and, more briefly myself) have been attacked by Professor David and Eileen Spring, on other grounds as well as the issue of land purchase, while I am informed that Professor F. M. L. Thompson, Director of the Institute of Historical Research (to whom I have always been close) will soon have in print a major attack upon my conclusions, based upon his research using the Succession Duty Registers, which he has kindly let me see in typescript. It would be premature to comment upon his forthcoming article, except to make the point that he has not convinced me that my article was erroneous in its conclusions, however matters of detail may have to be revised; I hope to set out the reasons for this at length in due course, and generally to enter into the debate which has emerged.

Another widely-held myth or rather (as is so often the case) untested and unverified assumption, especially among sociologists and social critics of 'privilege' in Britain, forms the subject of 'Education and the Social Origins of British Elites, 1880–1970', reprinted from *Past and Present* (1986). The aim of this chapter is to identify the egregious circularity which one encounters time and again in analyses of social mobility and elite groups in Britain, wherein education of an 'elite' public school or university is taken *ipso facto* as evidence of a background of wealth or privilege, and to show that, on the contrary, when the question of social origins of these groups is directly addressed with cogent and comprehensive evidence, many and probably most elite position-holders in modern Britain came, and increasingly come, from surprisingly meagre backgrounds, above all from the lower part of the established middle class, and were in no real sense associated with wealth and privilege in the way which those who criticize Britain's class structure plainly mean to imply; furthermore, merit and ability has played far more of a role in the selection and promotion process than is often acknowledged. The irony here, about which the chapter reflects only momentarily, is that this talented elite may have been consistently responsible for public policy choices in Britain which were regrettable and deleterious to Britain's prospects.

The highest mark of public esteem throughout British history has been the formal honours system of titles, especially peerages. Since it has survived so long, virtually intact, despite all the economic, social and political changes which have come to Britain over the past two hundred years, it must have altered fundamentally in its bases and underlying assumptions, and 'The Evolution of the British Honours System since the Mid-Nineteenth Century' traces the development of the bases and underlying assumptions of the system, especially of peerage creations, in some detail. Essentially, a system in which land ownership was king, and in which there was a close nexus between wealth, status and power, gave way to a system in which business wealth mimicked, but never really replaced, the old system; in this century this, too, has given way to a status system which is again sharply, fundamentally and, I would argue, genuinely altered, in which wealth or economic power is of only minor importance and in which the notion of an 'honour' has been immensely broadened. A number of other topics, for instance the myth of Lloyd George's peerage creations, are also discussed here and, hopefully, placed in their proper historical context.

To those familiar with my publications on wealth-holding and elites, the essays in the third section of this book, under the general heading of 'Survivals', will doubtless seem a departure, but they represent one of my major interests—what might be termed 'hidden' themes or modes of thought in modern British history, 'hidden' because they are outside or apart from the normal conceptualization of British history. In these three cases that which is 'hidden' are anomalous and out-of-place survivals from the past, which 'shouldn't' be where they are or occur when they did and which, hence, are regularly unnoticed or unobserved. As a foreigner to Britain, a natural-born Tory and conservative, and someone with a keen interest in the arcane and unusual, I think it fair to say that I am especially sensitive to these 'survivals', particularly when they occur in an urban, rather than the more anticipated rural milieu, and one of the themes running through these three chapters is just that the chief *locus* of conservative survivals may well be in urban rather than rural Britain, and especially in London. 'The End of "Old Corruption" in Britain, 1780–1860,' republished from *Past and Present* (1983), discusses the system of perquisites, sinecures and the like which was so important to eighteenth-century British politics, and argues that it persisted far later, and far more pervasively than is commonly allowed, up to the end of the British *ancien régime* or afterwards, remaining a remarkably lucrative source of income for much of the Tory (as opposed to Whig) aristocracy and for many others, in the unified elite structure which existed at the time. Its continuing existence, moreover, was 'pre-modern' and indicative of a pre-modern mode of mentality which has to be accepted at least in part at face value; this system and its ambience were genuinely swept away in the second and third quarter of the nineteenth century, replaced by the qualitatively different sensibility of 'Victorianism'.[4]

Chapters 10 and 11 extend this theme of 'survivals' to different areas. In 'Charles Dickens, R. Austin Freeman and the Spirit of London' I trace the central concern of Dickens (as well, as a number of his contemporaries) with London and its unique survivals. Dickens' attitude to London, it is argued, was highly ambiguous but included, besides his often-noted personal loathings, a substantial measure of appreciation, admiration, and even nostalgia for what I term the *urban non-dynamic* backwaters which still existed there. The conservative, anti-modernist implications of this mode of appreciation were continued, in my view, by R. Austin Freeman (1862–1943), a now-forgotten writer, remembered if at all for quite different things, who presented a twentieth-century continuation of Dickens' insights, stripped of their equivocation and ambiguity.

The final chapter in this collection, 'British Radicalism and the "Dark Side" of Populism', discusses the affinities between a significant, but largely unnoticed strand in British radicalism, and the bundle of ideas and attitudes normally termed 'populism' found over and over again in similar historical contexts around the world; in particular, the affinities between this strand of British radicalism and American and Australian populism are analyzed. Among the populist *gestalt* are ideas unexpected and extremely unpleasant and (see, for instance, notes 6 and 50, pp. 366 and 371) we not merely approach the lunatic fringe but actually go beyond it. Although the historian may wish to 'rescue' these ideas from total obscurity, no sensible person would wish to revive them for, as it is argued, the contemporary system of knowledge and information in the twentieth-century English-speaking world, especially among the elite of the well-educated and opinion-makers, has precluded and excluded what were once ubiquitous facets of the populist ideology. As with 'Old Corruption', it is argued that nothing or virtually nothing survives today (in the mainstream) of these assumptions or attitudes; hence—together with the like-minded historian's wish to see only good in his intellectual forbears—the difficulty of noticing it and the infrequency with which it is discussed, or even encountered, among today's scholars.

II

In order to fit these essays into their proper background and context, it will be necessary for me to say something, however brief, about myself. I was born in New York in 1946 and was educated in New York, at Swarthmore College and at Johns Hopkins University where I worked under Professor David Spring, the expert on English landed society, and an excellent teacher.[5] From earliest youth I had an affinity for things English—highly peculiar in my social setting—which I attribute to the influence of my maternal grandfather, a Russian Jew who lived in London for some years prior to settling in New York just before World War One. My mother, in particular, was always on anglophile and, although a New Yorker, did much war work for Britain before Pearl Harbor.

Although I never set foot in England until 1966, I always, as noted, felt an affinity with Englishmen, and especially with the rationality and wise but suppressed intuition of the English middle classes—as unpopular an object of affection as its source is improbable. As an undergraduate and post-graduate student I gradually drifted, but ever more certainly, into modern British history—I had always wanted to be an historian—and it has been the main preoccupation of my professional life ever since.

When I began at Johns Hopkins, it was my aim to write a dissertation on political history, especially on right-wing politics and on the Conservative party in the Edwardian period.[6] However, in 1969, by sheer accident while browsing, I discovered on the shelves of the Johns Hopkins University library some volumes of a publication entitled *The Daily Mail Yearbook* from the early part of the century, and within its pages noticed annual lists, apparently complete, of all persons leaving £500,000 in Britain within the previous year. This information was both obviously important and, so far as I knew, totally novel in the sense that no historian, so far as I could ascertain, had ever used it. I quickly discovered that the Library of Congress in Washington D.C. had a complete run of *The Daily Mail Yearbook* from its origins in 1901 to the present issue, and that every issue of this publication contained a similar list of top wealth-holders deceased during the previous year, with the exception of some wartime years in the 1940s, which could be supplemented by the daily lists of 'Large Wills' in *The Times* and other newspapers. Tracing these twentieth-century wealth-holders' occupations, social origins, family connections and so on became a hobby and a preoccupation, more and more driving out my 'legitimate' scholarly interest in political history.

Upon arriving in Britain to do research in the time-honoured way of graduate students, I managed to persuade my somewhat bemused supervisor that the subject was sufficiently important to warrant full-time research toward a doctoral dissertation. Given the fact that twentieth-century lists of top wealth-holders were available in published sources, the main immediate task before me was literally to go through *every* probate calendar for nineteenth-century Britain and abstract, literally by turning over every page, the identities of all large estates and the basic information given about each wealth-leaver. There were simply no substitute methods and no printed sources.[7] I spent the summer and autumn of 1972 looking through every significant probate index of the nineteenth century, containing several million names at least: I have often toyed with recording this in *The Guinness Book of Records*.[8] The pre-1858 probate records are scattered throughout a variety of sources, especially Prob. 8 at the PRO and in record offices in York, Preston and Edinburgh, while the printed indexes at Somerset House, which cover all of England and Wales (Scotland and Ireland have separate indexes), begin from January 1858. The number of deceased persons recorded in these indexes, considerable to begin with, of course increases markedly as the century proceeds, but the task, to the keen historian, is far from tedious and finding a very large estate is its own reward. In the process I compiled complete lists of everyone leaving £100,000 or more in the nineteenth century. Since in the printed indexes valuation figures are printed one below another, the student can scan a whole page almost instantaneously to look for estates with six digits; in 1892, some genius at the Principal Probate Registry altered the format so that valuation figures were no longer printed in a column, tripling the time required for a search; this change, which allowed far more names to appear on a page, doubtless earned him a minor place in the honours list, but my posthumous curses. The next year or two were spent happily tracing the identities of everyone leaving £500,000 or more (with two groups of 'lesser wealthy', as noted in

Chapter 1 in this collection.) The bulk of the biographical research was done in the Institute of Historical Research in London University's Senate House, probably the best open-shelf historical library, especially for the tracing of elites, in the world.[9] The Institute has been my base of operations ever since, and any visit to London will normally find me there much of the time. In the preface to *Men of Property*, my book on the wealthy, I described it as 'the best club in London'; astonishingly, this phrase was noticed and is used by the Institute in descriptions of itself and in Negley Harte's official history of London University. Although the Institute has a rather dreadful reputation as a place of Dickensian gloom and a prop to 'reactionary' history among many radical historians and Young Turks, I have always found it delightful and memorable in other ways, with its obscure, seldom-visited upper-floor rooms (Dutch History, Latin American History) virtually crying out for a genteel murder mystery to take place therein; and what in this vale of tears compares with the sheer unalloyed pleasure of lying back in an armchair in the Local English History room, reading bound inter-war issues of *Notes and Queries*?

In March 1973 I gave a paper at a conference on British elites at Cambridge, an event of great significance to any future career, apart from its intrinsic importance.[10] The first significant thing which happened to me there was that Professor Colin Harbury, the economist who specializes in the inheritance of wealth, suggested that I rearrange my wealth-holders by the Standard Industrial Classification, the schema which separates commercial from industrial activities. I had done something of the sort previously, but when I did so in a rigorous way the scales fell from my eyes. Few historians, perhaps, experience the blinding flash of insight proverbially associated with scientific discovery, but I did so in that moment: in a flash, I saw the entire pattern of modern British history with which much of my work deals and which has underlain my historical perspective ever since. I have had such an uncanny and exhilarating experience only a few other times, and never in such a way as to equal that one. Secondly, Harold Perkin, the distinguished social historian, suggested out of the blue that I participate as Research Associate in a research project on British elites from 1880–1970 which he intended to propose to the SSRC, Britain's chief academic research grant body. Needless to say I was flabbergasted and delighted and, when the grant was indeed funded, there followed two splendid years of research into elites which entailed much hard work but whose new information and interesting results immeasurably strengthened my knowledge of Britain's upper classes.[11]

In early 1976 I was offered a Research Fellowship in Sociology at the Australian National University, and moved to Australia, where I have lived ever since. A move of such distance for someone of my background may seem bizarre, but it is by no means unusual for a British academic, and the opportunity to do research in ivory-tower conditions for three more years at least, at twice my British salary, was compelling. My time at the Research School of Australia's most prestigious university was mainly spent in research on Australian wealth-holding, some of which is noted in the comparative article included in this collection. The many friends and colleagues I met in Canberra have been a lasting influence, and I thoroughly enjoyed myself, despite Canberra's somewhat anodyne, artificial character. Although 'semi-peripheral' and remote, Australia is very similar to America in its ambience and prosperity, but without its extremes of wealth or social conflict. Australia is said to have a notorious intellectual inferiority complex, its 'culture cringe', and a pervasive anti-intellectualism, but it possesses a respect for genuine learning and academic life which often, oddly often, goes with such an attitude. A New York Jewish academic would be so common as to sink without trace in America or England but, armed with prestigious credentials from America and Britain, in Australia is sufficiently exotic to stand out, while the 'culture cringe' has regularly endowed me with an unwonted degree of respect, via what is termed the 'halo effect' which has benefitted my career clearly and persistently.

In early 1978 I was appointed to a tenured lectureship in the School of Social Sciences at Deakin University, Australia's newest university, the equivalent of Britain's Open University. Deakin is located in Geelong, an industrial city of 150,000. About forty-five miles away is Melbourne, where I have lived for most of the period and participated fully in aspects of the life of that interesting city of three million. The structure of Deakin in this field has allowed me maximum time for research and, at a time of ever-increasing scarcity, I have been generously treated in terms of promotion and research grants.[12] Australia's libraries of course have extensive collections of modern British material—Melbourne's resources are probably about as good as, say, Birmingham's—better than is the case in America, and there is an excellent inter-library loan system.

Australia also has a lively community of scholars in modern British history, although of course any scholar engaged in continuing research in this field must regularly return to England.

III

These essays speak for themselves and it would, perhaps, be redundant to add anything further to them but it is probably necessary to say something about their overall methodology and thrust. It is evident that what chiefly animates the essays on wealth and elites in this collection is a strict insistence on the painstaking and comprehensive collection of salient data, and an absolute refusal to take for granted any accepted opinion, no matter how seemingly well-founded, which lacks compelling evidence. Indeed it is regularly the case that an application of searching data to a commonly-received opinion reveals it to be unsustainable, often based upon quite confused thinking and incorrect tacit assumptions, as well as upon quite inadequate evidence. This is not inconsistent, in my view, with the identification or suggestion that underlying patterns exist in the evolution of British society, patterns which are in all likelihood broader and more wide-ranging than some historians would like to believe. There is no contradiction whatever in these two approaches, and it is the massing of far-reaching evidence in a cogent way which alone makes useful generalization possible. Much that is revealed is 'obvious' once it is clearly presented—but no one has ever done this, for 'the world is full of obvious things which no one by chance ever observes'.

Most of all, these essays reveal a Britain which was much more 'conservative' in its evolution than many historians would credit, and my essays have often been seen as part of a conservative 'backlash' against the exaggerated importance given to Britain's industrialization in the past. The concern for elites and wealth is intended as an antidote to the neglect of these obviously vital areas by social historians in the past and is, frankly, a result of my own relative lack of interest in working-class and trade union history, which in any case has its large vanguard of practitioners.

It seems absolutely clear to me that the course of modern British history can best be understood by, first and foremost, attempting to delineate and identify society's elites and the socio-economic dimensions in which they were able to occupy their positions of authority—at almost all times with the consent of the governed. To look at British history the other way round, from the bottom up, is virtually to invite distortion, as we are left in the dark about both the peaks and the framework. Clearly, a comprehensive socio-economic history must research society at all levels. Regrettably, however, the social history which has emerged in Britain during the past twenty-five years, especially in the wake of E. P. Thompson, has completely reversed its traditional direction and subject-matter. Academic writing on historical elites is now surprisingly rare, and there have been remarkably few attempts comprehensively to account for the emergence of modern British society as a whole—Harold Perkin's *The Origins of Modern British Society* (1969) still standing as a landmark—nor have the traditional frameworks of our understanding of modern British history received the systematic revisionist questioning—a questioning, that is, both of the traditional Whig and contemporary Marxist historiography—that eighteenth-century history has recently received in J. C. D. Clark's *English Society 1688–1832* and his *Revolution and Rebellion*. There is much to do; this book may, hopefully, show something of the way and suggest new avenues, but it does nothing more.

W. D. Rubinstein
Deakin University
Victoria, Australia
1987

NOTES

1. 'The Victorian Middle Classes: Wealth, Occupation, and Geography', (Chapter 2 of this collection) was joint winner of the T. H. Ashton Prize of the Economic History Society for that year, and was recently reprinted in Pat Thane and Anthony Sutcliffe (eds), *Essays In Social History, Volume 2* (Oxford, 1986).
2. Students of this subject might also wish to take note of my article—not included in this collection—on 'The Size and Distribution of the English Middle Classes in 1860', (*Historical Research*, 1987), which employs a unique return in the Parliamentary Papers to ascertain the percentage of income tax payers in all English parliamentary boroughs in 1859–60; the results here also show the importance of London in a striking manner.

3. Against this pattern must be set the extraordinary and anomalous success of Sir John R. Ellerman, 1st Bt. (1862–1933), Britain's richest-ever man in real terms, whose fortune was probably a match for virtually any American centi-millionaire. On Ellerman's career, see my biographical notice of him in David Jeremy (ed.), *Dictionary of Business Biography*, Vol. II (London, 1984).

4. Although much 'irrational' patronage undoubtedly remained, more, perhaps, than ever I had thought. See J. M. Bourne, *Patronage and Society in Nineteenth-Century England* (London, 1986).

5. Although nothing 'dramatic' has ever happened to me, and despite the blandness of the facts set out here, other aspects of my autobiography are strikingly unusual and would be interesting to relate. I should also perhaps note that I am probably better known in Australia and in Europe as a writer on politics and Jewish affairs. Anyone who wants to know 'my complete views on everything' should read my book *The Left, the Right, and the Jews* (Croom Helm, London; Universe Books, New York, 1982).

6. My MA dissertation was on the extreme right-wing politician Henry Page Croft. See my 'Henry Page Croft and the National Party of 1917–22', *Journal of Contemporary History* Vol. 9, no. 1 (January 1974).

7. Quite a few of these large estates were recorded in the *Illustrated London News*, which also gave details about the size of each legacy, and in Boase's *Modern English Biography* (privately printed Truro, Cornwall 1892–1921; repr. Cass, London, 1965) but these lists are incomplete.

8. I received much assistance from my wife Hilary, and also owe much information about the nature of these sources to my fellow post-graduate at Johns Hopkins, the late Dan Duman, who wrote two important books on the nineteenth-century English judiciary before his tragic death in Israel of a brain tumour at the age of thirty-five, in January 1984. Duman was at the time of his death collaborating with me on the study of the Victorian middle classes, and was methodologically and conceptually closer to me than any historian I have encountered.

9. The Library of the Genealogical Society, presently in Charterhouse Buildings, may run it a close second. The point is that the library must be open-shelved, allowing the historian free access, unless the time taken to identify each figure is not to become excessively and annoyingly long.

10. See Philip Stanworth and Anthony Giddens (eds), *Elites and Power In British Society* (Cambridge, 1974), which contains the edited essays of this conference, including one of mine not included here.

11. I am somewhat concerned that this *précis* makes my career sound a bed of roses. Nothing whatever could be further from the truth. Until I was appointed to a tenured lectureship, when I was thirty-one, and indeed until my tenure was officially confirmed several years later, there hung over me constantly, as an obsessive, almost diabolical Sword of Damocles, the necessity to find a tenured academic job, a form of

torture which most young academics in a time of greatly diminished opportunities will know only too well. I have no private means, and could probably not have survived at all without my wife's income; I had no training in any other area and no desire to do anything else with my life. I was of course, unknown, and applied unsuccessfully for a staggering number of jobs.

12. For much of this period I was awarded research grants by the Australian Research Grants Scheme or Deakin University, sufficient to allow me to employ a research assistant in London. All of these assistants are acknowledged in the chapters in this work, with the exception of my most recent researcher Carole Taylor, the most excellent of all, who has worked on my most recent projects. Without them, serious research cannot easily be done from Australia, certainly not of the kind I do. Of course research assistants merely carry out one's instructions. They do not think for you, and if they do this fact should clearly be punctiliously acknowledged.

Wealth

2

The Victorian Middle Classes: Wealth, Occupation and Geography[1] *

The question of who earned the largest personal fortunes in Britain during the nineteenth century is one which has hitherto been neither asked nor answered. More surprisingly, neither has the larger question of which elements, occupational and geographical, predominated within the Victorian middle class been subject to serious research. Both of these are of considerable importance to the social and economic historian, for our common perception of British history during the nineteenth century rests upon several tacit assumptions which remain untested and which may or may not be correct. The chief among these are that the wealthiest men of nineteenth-century England, apart from the great landowners, were engaged in industry and manufacturing, in trades which were a direct part of the Industrial Revolution; that the nineteenth-century middle class consisted primarily of industrialists and manufacturers; and that the new towns of the north of England brought into existence a group of middle-class industrialists sufficient in wealth and numbers to constitute the dominant element in Victorian society. None of these assumptions, it will be suggested here, is correct, and any view of Victorian society which subscribes to them must stand in need of revision.[2]

This article emerges from research undertaken on the top wealth-holders of Britain deceased between the early nineteenth century and 1939, based upon the valuation figures in the probate records at Somerset House, the Public Record Office, in Edinburgh, York, and Preston.[3] In the course of this research, a catalogue of all

---

* This chapter was published in *Economic History Review*, Vol. XXX, No. 4, November, 1977.

persons leaving £100,000 or more in Britain since 1809, when these
sources begin in a usable form,[4] was compiled, although most
attention centred on those wealth-holders leaving £500,000 or more
between 1809 and 1939, and on two groups of lesser wealthy, those
leaving between £160,000 and £500,000 between 1809 and 1829,
and those with estates worth between £250,000 and £500,000 in the
period 1850–69.[5] During the nineteenth century until 1898 the
probate calendars recorded the global value of the gross unsettled
personalty of all persons, testate or intestate, leaving property in
Britain (or within the jurisdiction of that probate court), while
between 1898 and 1925 the valuation figure consisted of gross
unsettled personalty and settled land.[6] Although imperfect in
several respects, the probate calendars contain comprehensive and
objective information on the personal wealth of the entire British
population, and the purposes to which they may be put are
manifold.[7]

Several methodological problems are involved in identifying
personal wealth-holding with estates left at death. Among these are
the problem of gifts *inter vivos* or of deliberate estate duty
avoidance; and the comparability of valuation conventions when
applied to different types of assets, especially limited liability
companies compared with private partnerships. There is an
obvious possibility that either or both of these factors may have
affected the findings of this article in the sense that, compared with
other businessmen, manufacturers may, during their lifetime, have
passed a significantly larger fraction of their business assets to
relatives in the interests of their firm's continuity.

It must be realized that there is no precise way in which the
accuracy of any of these contentions may be established, since the
identity of wealth-holders escaping the death duty net cannot be
comprehensively traced from other sources. From 1881 account duty
was levied on gifts *inter vivos* made three (later twelve) months or
less before death; its yield was described as 'trifling' by Sydney
Buxton and George Stapylton Barnes in *A Handbook to the Death
Duties* (1890), p. 13. Although the accuracy of valuation
conventions would surely have been affected by the spread of
limited liability, in fact the final cohorts of wealth-holders show the
lead of commerce over manufacturing much as do those of the mid-
century, a picture confirmed as well by the income-tax figures,
which are derived from entirely different sources. If any group of
wealth-holders was likely to be under-represented here, it is not the

manufacturers but the merchants and merchant bankers of London, whose businesses remain private partnerships or private limited companies to this day.

I

The first section of this chapter examines the occupational structure and geographical venues of Britain's wealth-holders deceased between the early nineteenth century and 1914.

Between 1809 and 1914, the total of deceased male British wealth-holders at each level of wealth discussed here and by period of death was:[8]

	1809–58	1858–70	1880–99	1900–14
Millionares	12	34	69	89
Half-millionaires	62	120	177	206

	1809–29	1850–69
Less wealthy	192	186

The occupational distribution of these estates was not an even one, but clustered primarily among a limited number of fields. Ranked according to the Orders of the Standard Industrial Classification,[9] the distribution of the occupations in which these fortunes were earned[10] appears in the shape of a capital 'E', with Orders I, II and III—agriculture, mining, and the production of food, drink, and tobacco—and Orders XIX, XX and XXI—transport, distribution, and finance—containing the bulk of the wealth-holders, and Order X—textiles—forming the crossbar. Yet even among these well-represented trades it is clear that the wealthy earned their fortunes disproportionately in commerce, finance, and transport—that is, as merchants, bankers, shipowners, merchant bankers, and stock and insurance brokers—rather than as manufacturers and industrialists. This is apparent in Tables 2.1–2.3, which record the occupations of the wealth-holders according to the Standard Industrial Classification. To make this point more concisely, it would help to assimilate the various Orders into a more convenient form. In Table 2.4, Orders II and IV–XVII (except for newspaper proprietors and publishers, classed according to the SIC with paper manufacturers in Order XV) are termed 'industrial'; the 'food and drink' category here includes the brewers, distillers, foodstuff, and tobacco manufacturers of Order III, to distinguish them from the more strictly industrial categories.[11] Those wealth-holders engaged in trades in Orders XIX–XXI are numbered in the 'commercial' category. Among the 'professional, public administration, and defence' wealth-holders have been classed the newspaper proprietors and publishers.

Table 2.1: Distribution of Millionaires by SIC (position of known, non-landed total in brackets)

Order		1809–58	Deceased 1858–79	1880–99	1900–14
I.	Agriculture	3	4	10	14
II.	Mining	—	2 (6.7)	2 (3.4)	2 (2.7)
III.	Food, drink, tobacco	—	1 (3.3)	14 (23.7)	14 (19.2)
IV.	Chemicals	—	—	3 (5.1)	2 (2.7)
V.	Metals	1 (11.1)	5 (16.7)	3 (5.1)	1 (1.4)
VI.	Engineering	—	—	1 (1.7)	3 (4.1)
VII.	Shipbuilding	—	1 (3.3)	2 (3.4)	2 (2.7)
VIII.	Vehicles	—	—	1 (1.7)	1 (1.4)
IX.	Miscellaneous metals	1 (11.1)	—	1 (1.7)	—
X.	Textiles	2 (22.2)	4 (13.3)	5 (8.5)	8 (11.0)
XI.	Leather	—	—	—	—
XII.	Clothing	—	—	—	—
XIII.	Bricks, glass, pottery	—	—	—	—
XIV.	Timber, furniture	—	—	—	—
XV.	Paper, publishing	—	—	1 (1.7)	—
XVI.	Miscellaneous manufacturing	—	—	—	—
XVII.	Construction	1 (11.1)	1 (3.3)	3 (5.1)	1 (1.4)
XVIII.	Gas, water	—	—	—	—
XIX.	Transport	1 (11.1)	1 (3.3)	3 (5.1)	7 (9.6)
XX.	Distribution	—	3 (10.0)	7 (11.9)	9 (12.3)
XXI.	Finance	2 (22.2)	12 (40.0)	13 (22.0)	22 (30.1)
XXII.	Professionals	—	—	—	1 (1.4)
XXIII.	Other services	—	—	—	—
XXIV.	Government, defence	1 (11.1)	—	—	—
	Miscellaneous, unknown	—	—	—	2
	Total categorized non-landed	9	30	59	73

It is evident from Table 2.4 that fortunes earned in commerce and finance were either the majority or the plurality of Britain's non-landed wealth among most of the cohorts in this study: indeed, of all the cohorts except among the nine millionaires deceased prior to 1858 and among the millionaire and half-millionaire groups deceased in 1880–99. Moreover, except among the first millionaire cohort, at no time did manufacturing in the strict sense lead

Table 2.2: *Distribution of Half-Millionaires by SIC (position of known, non-landed total in brackets)*

Order	Deceased			
	1809–58	*1858–79*	*1880–99*	*1900–14*
I. Agriculture	11	16	15	22
II. Mining	—	1 (1.0)	7 (4.4)	11 (6.1)
III. Food, drink, tobacco	1	3 (2.9)	23 (14.6)	21 (11.6)
IV. Chemicals	1	—	8 (5.1)	5 (2.8)
V. Metals	5 (10.6)	12 (11.8)	7 (4.4)	13 (7.2)
VI. Engineering	—	1	4 (2.5)	4 (2.2)
VII. Shipbuilding	—	—	1 (0.6)	
VIII. Vehicles	—	—	1 (0.6)	2 (1.1)
IX. Miscellaneous metals	1 (2.1)	1 (1.0)	2 (1.3)	2 (1.1)
X. Textiles	2 (8.5)	12 (11.8)	23 (14.6)	11 (6.1)
XI. Leather	—	—	—	1 (0.6)
XII. Clothing	—	—	—	—
XIII. Bricks, glass, pottery	—	—	2 (1.3)	2 (1.1)
XIV. Timber, furniture	—	—	—	1 (0.6)
XV. Paper, publishing	1 (2.1)	4 (3.9)	4 (2.5)	7 (3.9)
XVI. Miscellaneous manufacturing	—	—	—	—
XVII. Construction	—	3 (2.9)	6 (3.8)	3 (1.7)
XVIII. Gas, water	—	—	—	1 (0.6)
XIX. Transport	2 (4.3)	5 (4.9)	9 (5.1)	13 (7.2)
XX. Distribution	15 (31.9)	25 (24.5)	23 (14.6)	44 (24.3)
XXI. Finance	10 (21.3)	30 (29.4)	34 (21.5)	34 (18.8)
XXII. Professionals	1 (2.1)	5 (4.9)	4 (2.5)	4 (2.2)
XXIII. Other services	1 (2.1)	—	1 (0.6)	—
XXIV. Government, defence	5 (10.6)	—	—	1 (0.6)
Miscellaneous, unknown	3	2	4	3
Total categorized non-landed	47	102	158	181

commerce as the origin of great fortunes, even in the 1880–99 period. Although the proportion of commercial wealth-holders declined to as low as 39 per cent of the 1880–99 millionaire cohort, in the early twentieth century the significance of commerce in the wealth structure again increased and once more supplied the majority of top fortunes. Despite the Industrial Revolution, the most important element in Britain's wealth structure during the nineteenth century, apart from landed wealth, was commerce and finance.

Two aspects of the distribution outlined above require some special comments. One is the place of industrialists among the wealthy. There are numerous examples of immensely wealthy nineteenth-century manufacturers and industrialists—millionaires like Richard Crawshay (1739–1810), the Cyfarthfa ironmasters, Sir

Table 2.3: Distribution of Lesser Wealthy by SIC (position of known, non-landed total in brackets)

			Deceased	
Order		1809–20	1850–69	
I.	Agriculture	32	32	
II.	Mining	1 (0.7)	3	(2.2)
III.	Food, drink, tobacco	8 (6.0)	10	(7.2)
IV.	Chemicals	3 (2.5)	4	(2.9)
V.	Metals	2 (1.5)	4	(2.9)
VI.	Engineering	1 (0.7)	4	(2.9)
VII.	Shipbuilding	1 (0.7)	—	
VIII.	Vehicles	—	2	(1.4)
IX.	Miscellaneous metals	—	3	(2.2)
X.	Textiles	5 (3.7)	17	(12.3)
XI.	Leather	—	—	
XII.	Clothing	—	—	
XIII.	Bricks, glass, pottery	1 (0.7)	1	(0.7)
XIV.	Timber, furniture	—	1	(0.7)
XV.	Paper, publishing	1 (0.7)	2	(1.4)
XVI.	Miscellaneous manufacturing	—	2	(1.4)
XVII.	Construction	1 (0.7)	3	(2.2)
XVIII.	Gas, water	1 (0.7)	—	
XIX.	Transport	3 (2.5)	4	(2.9)
XX.	Distribution	35 (26.1)	37	(26.8)
XXI.	Finance	28 (20.9)	32	(23.2)
XXII.	Professionals	17 (12.7)	3	(2.2)
XXIII.	Other services	4 (3.0)	—	
XXIV.	Public admin., defence	22 (16.4)	6	(4.3)
	Miscellaneous, unknown	1	1	
	Unknown	25	15	
	Total categorized non-landed	134	138	

Table 2.4: Occupations of Wealth-holders, Concise Ranking (percentage of known non-landed total in brackets)

Millionaires

	1809–58	1858–79	1880–99	1900–14
I. Manufacturing	5 (55.5)	13 (43.3)	22 (37.3)	20 (27.4)
Food, drink, tobacco	0	1 (3.3)	14 (23.7)	14 (19.2)
II. Commercial	3 (33.3)	16 (53.3)	23 (39.0)	38 (52.1)
III. Professional, public administration, defence	1 (11.1)	—	—	1 (1.4)

Half-Millionaires

	1809–58	1858–79	1880–99	1900–14
I. Manufacturing	11 (22.9)	32 (31.7)	60 (38.0)	59 (32.6)
Food, drink, tobacco	1 (2.0)	2 (2.0)	23 (14.6)	22 (12.2)
II. Commercial	28 (58.3)	60 (59.4)	66 (41.8)	91 (50.3)
III. Professional, public adminstration, defence	8 (18.7)	7 (6.9)	9 (5.7)	9 (5.0)

Less Wealthy

	1809–29	1850–69
I. Manufacturing	17 (12.7)	44 (31.9)
Food, drink, tobacco	8 (5.8)	12 (8.7)
II. Commercial	66 (49.3)	73 (52.9)
III. Professional, public administration, defence	43 (32.1)	9 (6.5)

Robert Peel, 1st Bt (1750–1830), or Richard Arkwright (1755–1843)—but the typical successful manufacturer appears to have left an estate in the range of £100,000 after the mid-century, and rather less before. Among the well-known politico-industrialists at or around this level were William E. Forster (1818–86), who left £81,574; John Bright (1811–89), £86,289; Charles T. Ritchie, first Baron Ritchie of Dundee (1838–1906), £116,245; and Joseph Chamberlain (1836–1914), £125,495, as did the various members of the Ashworth cotton family deceased in this period.[12] Many successful industrialists left far less—for example, Anthony J. Mundella (1825–97), who left £42,619, or the Manchester umbrella-cloth manufacturer Frederick Engels (1820–95), who left £25,000. The level of wealth required to place a manufacturer firmly within the servant-keeping middle class was lower still, perhaps as low as a few thousand pounds.

The extraordinarily high percentage of early wealth-holders, particularly those among the lesser wealthy deceased in 1809–29, engaged in the professions, public administration, and defence, also requires some comment. It will be seen that the percentage among these groups declined considerably between 1829 and 1850. This was 'Old Corruption', the beneficiaries of government contract and holders of government place, and their significance in the wealth structure virtually ceased after about 1840. Men like John, first Earl of Eldon (1751–1838), the celebrated Lord Chancellor, who left £700,000; the government provision contractor Sir Charles Flower (1763–1834), worth £500,000; or the army agent Alexander Adair (1739–1834), whose estate totalled £700,000, were as typical a part of the British wealth structure at this time as Hargreaves or Stephenson.

If it was on the commercial or financial side of the Victorian business world that the great fortunes were disproportionately to be found, it would seem to be a corollary that the centre of wealth-making in nineteenth-century Britain was London rather than the industrial towns of the north of England. This was, indeed, the case, although it would evidently be a gross oversimplification merely to identify London with commerce and the north with industry. Nevertheless, most top London fortunes were left by those in commerce and finance, while most of the fortunes of the north were earned in manufacturing, despite the wealth of merchants in provincial trade centres like Liverpool, Glasgow, Leeds, and elsewhere. Assigning each non-landed wealth-holder to the locality or conurbation in which his fortune was earned—where his bank, factory, mine, or ships were located—a pattern of geographical distribution is indicated as favourable to London as the occupational distribution demonstrated the lead of commerce.[13] This is indicated in Tables 2.5–2.8.

Among millionaires, London was the venue for between about 39 and 63 per cent of the total number of each cohort; among half-millionaires, for between 38 and 64 per cent; while among the lesser wealthy London's lead was even clearer. The six conurbations making up the heart of industrial England in Lancashire and the West Riding accounted for no more than some 25 per cent of the most favourable millionaire cohort, and for between 18 and 27 per cent of the half-millionaire groups. As with the place of commerce in the occupational distribution, London's lead, although less marked at the close of the nineteenth century, was never lost.

At the centre of London's wealth was the City, which was by itself in every period, and at every level of wealth, in these tables the single most important geographical unit, generally by several orders of magnitude over its nearest rival. Nearly all of the City

Table 2.5: Number of Millionaires, by Geographical Origin and Date of Death

Area	1809–58	1858–79	1880–99	1900–14
1. City of London	4	14	11	24
2. Other London	1	2	9	15
3. Outer London	—	—	1	1
4. Greater Manchester	—	2	2	2
5. Merseyside	—	1	8	2
6. West Yorkshire	—	2	2	4
7. South Yorkshire	—	—	—	—
8. West Midlands	—	—	2	—
9. Tyneside	—	1	1	4
10. Clydeside	—	2	4	8
11. East Anglia	—	1	1	—
12. Bristol	—	—	1	5
13. South-west England	—	—	—	—
14. Other Southern England	—	—	—	—
15. Ribblesdale	1	—	1	—
16. Mid-Lancashire	—	—	1	—
17. Notts.–Derby–Burton	1	1	4	1
18. Other Midlands	—	—	2	—
19. South Wales	1	2	2	1
20. Tees-side	—	—	1	1
21. Humberside	—	—	—	—
22. Other Northern England	—	—	—	—
23. Edinburgh	—	—	—	1
24. Other Scotland	—	1	—	—
25. Belfast	—	—	—	1
26. Dublin	—	1	—	—
27. Other Ireland	—	—	1	—
Total	8	30	54	70

wealth-holders were engaged in commerce: only five City millionaires, for example, cannot be readily assigned to a commercial Order among the SICs. Many of the City's wealth-holders obviously belonged to such celebrated financial or mercantile dynasties as the Rothschilds, Barings, Rallis, Sassoons, Gibbses, Montefiores, *et al.* But many others remain virtually unknown, and one important reason for the failure of economic historians to grasp the central importance of the City has been its

Table 2.6: *Number of Half-Millionaires, by Geographical Origin and Date of Death*

Area	1809–58	1858–79	1880–99	1900–14
1. City of London	15	37	40	40
2. Other London	9	9	19	22
3. Outer London	1	1	3	3
4. Greater Manchester	1	11	15	12
5. Merseyside	2	10	8	13
6. West Yorkshire	2	4	3	12
7. South Yorkshire	—	3	3	5
8. West Midlands	2	2	3	3
9. Tyneside	—	3	7	12
10. Clydeside	1	6	11	13
11. East Anglia	—	1	2	2
12. Bristol	1	1	2	1
13. South-west England	—	1	3	—
14. Other Southern England	—	—	1	2
15. Ribblesdale	2	—	2	2
16. Mid-Lancashire	—	—	1	2
17. Notts.–Derby–Burton	—	3	3	7
18. Other Midlands	—	—	6	3
19. South Wales	3	2	—	4
20. Tees-side	—	2	2	2
21. Humberside	—	—	—	3
22. Other Northern England	—	—	—	—
23. Edinburgh	—	—	3	3
24. Other Scotland	—	—	2	2
25. Belfast	—	—	1	1
26. Dublin	—	—	1	1
27. Other Ireland	—	—	—	—
Total	39	96	141	170

relative neglect in business histories and industrial biographies. While everyone knows of the major figures of the Industrial Revolution, little attention has been paid to the careers of many of the City's wealthy men. It is likely that the richest commoner of the nineteenth century was the self-made textile warehouseman and merchant banker James Morrison (1789–1857), who left between £4 million and £6 million at his death, in addition to more than 100,000 acres of land. His eldest son Charles (1817–1909), a financier, left nearly £11 million, and was probably the second wealthiest man in Britain at his death; while eight other members of this family have also left fortunes of £500,000 or more. Yet the family remains unchronicled and largely unknown.[14] Unnoticed, too, are the vast, and typical, City fortunes of such men as Richard Thornton (1776–1865), an insurance broker and Baltic merchant

Table 2.7: Number of Less Wealthy, by Geographical Origin and Date of Death

Area	1809–29	1850–69
1. City of London	59	43
2. Other London	31	21
3. Outer London	2	1
4. Greater Manchester	6	14
5. Merseyside	2	5
6. West Yorkshire	2	—
7. South Yorkshire	—	—
8. West Midlands	4	4
9. Tyneside	2	3
10. Clydeside	—	3
11. East Anglia	4	1
12. Bristol	3	5
13. South-west England	3	1
14. Other Southern England	—	2
15. Ribblesdale	—	1
16. Mid-Lancashire	—	—
17. Notts.–Derby–Burton	3	7
18. Other Midlands	2	1
19. South Wales	—	1
20. Tees-side	—	—
21. Humberside	—	—
22. Other Northern England	—	—
23. Edinburgh	—	2
24. Other Scotland	—	—
25. Belfast	—	—
26. Dublin	—	—
27. Other Ireland	—	—
Unknown	22	13
Total	123	115

who boasted that his signature was 'good for three million' and left £2,800,000;[15] Hugh McCalmont (1809–87), a stockbroker and foreign merchant worth £3,122,000; and Giles Loder (1786–1871), a Russia merchant who left £2,900,000. Such men were among the very wealthiest in the country, wealthier by several dozen times than the majority of successful industrialists. G. K. Chesterton's shrewd observation that the wise man hides a pebble on a beach, a leaf in a forest, is perhaps best illustrated by the visibility of many of the City's richest men.[16]

London consisted of far more than the City, and its predominance in the British wealth structure was to a large extent the product of the variety and number of fortunes in its outlying districts. It is impossible to characterize these quickly. Brewing, retailing, and shipping fortunes were the most numerous, including among them dynasties like the Watneys and Charringtons, department-store owners like William Whiteley (1831–1907) and James Marshall (1806–93), art dealers like Sir Joseph J. Duveen (1843–1908), and shipowners like the Scruttons and Harrisons. Industrial fortunes were a minority, heavy industry represented by engineers and shipbuilders like John Penn (1805–78) of Greenwich, chemical manufacturers like Frank C. Hills (1808–92), and builders like Thomas Cubitt (1788–1855) and Edward Yates (1838–1907). Most of the remaining London wealth-holders were government placemen or London bankers.

Beside London, Manchester appears very much like the dog which did nothing in the night-time. Manchester will always remain a symbol and synonym for many things, from the doctrine of *laissez-faire* to the 'immizeration of the working-class', but its importance as a centre of British wealth is simply belied by the available facts. This may seem difficult to credit, but in the entire period between 1809 and 1914 only one Manchester cotton manufacturer left a millionaire estate, while only two others left fortunes in the half-millionaire class.[17] Of all the Manchester wealth-holders deceased in the span of this study, only six were manufacturers or industrialists, while the remainder included seven cotton merchants, three bankers, a number of brewers, and a newspaper proprietor. It is to the outlying towns of Greater Manchester that one must look to find the textile manufacturing and industrial fortunes in this conurbation. Such wealth was to be found in the smaller towns like Oldham, with its nine cotton-spinners and three machinery manufacturers among the wealth-holders, or among families like the Fieldens in Todmorden, the Peels in Blackburn, or the Bulloughs in Accrington. In these smaller outlying towns, every wealth-holder without exception was a manufacturer or industrialist.

Liverpool, as the greatest of northern commercial cities, followed the London pattern in producing more wealth-holders than Manchester. Here only two of the local fortunes were earned in industry—both in soap manufacturing—and the bulk of Merseyside fortunes were earned by its foreign trades, shipowners, and commodity merchants of various types. The West Yorkshire wealth-holders were mainly in the industrial SICs, among them such families as the Fosters, worsted manufacturers at the Black Dyke Mills, and the Cunliffe-Listers, Barons Masham, silk-plush manufacturers. But the commercial life of the area was dominated by several old Anglican families based in Leeds, like the Fabers, Becketts, and Oxleys.

Each of the remaining centres of wealth requires some comment. The west Midlands had not by 1914 become of the first importance as the home of top fortunes; such as there were here were largely earned by ironmasters and colliery owners in the Black Country rather than by Birmingham men. On Tyneside the most lucrative sources of wealth were the coalfields of Durham and Northumberland and the engineering and shipping trades of Newcastle and Jarrow. Similarly, Clydeside rose to its leading place as a venue of wealth only among the cohorts deceased from 1880 onwards, on the basis of Glasgow's shipping and engineering, the nearby coal and iron seams, and the sewing-thread families of Coats and Clarks in Paisley. The situation in Bristol was unusual in that nearly all of its wealth-holders belonged to two families, the tobacco-manufacturing Willses and the Frys, the Quaker sweets makers. There were virtually no fortunes here whose origins lay in the slaving and mercantile past of that town. Among the smaller towns and geographical areas, a considerable number of manufacturing and industrial fortunes were earned in much smaller localities, among families like the Claytons and Shuttleworths, the agricultural machinery manufacturers of Lincoln, the Arkwrights and Strutts in Derbyshire, or the Patons and Thomsons, who made woollens in Alloa, Clackmannanshire. With the exception of East Anglia, where dissenters provided a number of local banking dynasties of great wealth, it was a rarity for a merchant or banker not trading in a large conurbation to accumulate a vast fortune, while in smaller towns the leading manufacturer was likely to be its wealthiest man.

To turn from the general to the individual, an appreciation of the points made here may be gleaned from Table 2.8, which lists the

Table 2.8: Largest British Fortunes (£2m. or more), 1809–1914

Name, occupation, venue	Valuation (000)
1. George, first Duke of Sutherland (1758–1833), landowner	'Upper Value'*
2. Nathan M. Rothschild (1777–1836), merchant banker in London	'Upper Value'†
3. James Morrison (1789–1857), warehouseman and merchant banker in London	c. £4,000–6,000‡
4. Sir Isaac L. Goldsmid, 1st Bt (1778–1859), bullion broker and merchant banker in London	c. £2,000§
5. William Baird (1796–1864), ironmaster in Lanarkshire, etc.	£2,000
6. Richard Thornton (1776–1865), insurance broker and Baltic merchant in London	£2,800
7. William Crawshay (1788–1867), ironmaster in South Wales	£2,000
8. Thomas Braseay (1805–70), railway contractor	£3,200
9. Giles Loder (1786–1871), Russia merchant in London	£2,900
10. Baron Mayer A. de Rothschild (1818–74), merchant banker in London	£2,100
11. Lionel N. de Rothschild (1808–74), merchant banker in London	£2,700
12. Samuel J. Loyd, first Baron Overstone (1796–1883), banker in London	£2,119‖
13. Herman, Baron de Stern (1815–87), merchant banker in London	£3,545
14. Hugh McCalmont (1809–87), stockbroker and foreign merchant in London	£3,122
15. John Rylands (1801–88), cotton manufacturer in Wigan	£2,575
16. Sir Andrew B. Walker, 1st Bt (1824–93), brewer in Liverpool	£2,877

* Sutherland left a personal estate proved in the Canterbury Prerogative Court at 'Upper Value' in addition to a personal estate of £77,499 in Scotland. The precise value of his personalty, including the Bridgewater property he inherited is not known, but Eric Richards, his recent biographer recalls Greville's comment, 'I believe [he was] the richest individual who ever died'.—*The Leviathan of Wealth* (1973), p. 12. In 1883, the two heirs to his landed wealth, the Duke of Sutherland and the Earl of Ellesmere, were in receipt of a gross annual income of £213,000.

† Rothschild's fortune was estimated by contemporaries at up to £5 million.

‡ Sworn at 'Above £1 million'; this estimate was given by contemporary writers and in obituaries.

§ Sworn at 'Above £1 million', and estimated at this figure in the *Illustrated London News* of 11 June 1859.

‖ Overstone also owned land costing over £1,500,000 to purchase.

Table 2.8: Largest British Fortunes (£2m. or more), 1809–1914—cont.

Name, occupation, venue	Valuation (000)
17. Andrew Montagu (1815–95), landowner	£2,005
18. John Gretton (1833–99), brewer in Burton	£2,883
19. William Orme Foster (1814–99), ironmaster in Stourbridge	2,588
20. William R. Sutton (1836–1900), carrier in London	£2,119
21. John, third Marquis of Bute (1847–1900), landowner	£2,067
22. Samuel Lewis (1837–1901), money-lender in London¶	£2,671
23. William, sixth Earl FitzWilliam (1815–1902), landowner	£2,882
24. Harry L. B. McCalmont (1861–1902), stockbroker (not in trade)**	£2,279
25. Sir John B. Maple, 1st Bt (1845–1903), furniture retailer in London	£2,153
26. Edward Brook (1825–1904), sewing-thread manufacturer in Huddersfield	£2,181
27. Edmund D. Beckett, first Baron Grimthorpe (1816–1905), barrister in London; banking family in Leeds and Doncaster	£2,127
28. Sir Charles Tennant, 1st Bt (1823–1906), chemical manufacturer in Glasgow	£3,146
29. Wentworth Blackett Beaumont, first Baron Allendale (1829–1907), landowner	£3,189
30. John S. Schillizzi (1840–1908), foreign merchant in London	£2,089
31. Charles Morrison (1817–1909), financier and warehouseman in London	£10,939
32. Sir Frederick Wills, 1st Bt (1838–1909), tobacco manufacturer in Bristol	£3,051
33. Sir Donald Currie (1825–1909), shipbuilder in London and Liverpool	£2,433
34. Sir Edward P. Wills, 1st Bt (1834–1910), tobacco manufacturer in Bristol	£2,635
35. Baron Sir John Schroeder (1825–1910), merchant banker in London	£2,131

¶ Lewis, who began life as a traveller in pen and watch materials, was a money-lender to the wealthy at Cork Street in Mayfair. 'Undoubtedly his terms were high,' commented an obituary, 'but probably no member of his profession possessed a larger number of clients among the upper classes of society.'—The Times, 4 Jan. 1901.

** McCalmont inherited the bulk of the fortune of his great-uncle Hugh McCalmont (d. 1887), which had been left to gather interest for seven years after his death.

Table 2.8: Largest British Fortunes (£2m. or more), 1809–1914—cont.

Name, occupation, venue	Valuation (000)
36. Henry Overton Wills (1828–1911), tobacco manufacturer in Bristol	£5,215
37. William H. Wills, first Baron Winterstoke (1830–1911), tobacco manufacturer in Bristol	£2,548
38. Peter Coats (1842–1913), sewing-thread manufacturer in Paisley	£2,562
39. Sir James Coats, 1st Bt (1834–1913), sewing-thread manufacturer in Paisley	£2,548
40. William Wier (1826–1913), ironmaster and colliery owner in Lanarkshire, etc.	£2,220

largest individual fortunes—those of £2 million or more[18]—left between 1809 and 1914.

Of the 40 male British fortunes[19] at or above this level, four belonged to landowners and one to the railway contractor Thomas Brassey (1805–70), who cannot be assigned to a specific geographical venue. Of the remaining 35, however, no fewer than 20 were Londoners—16 from the City alone—while five were Clydesiders, four Bristolians, and the remainder spread among six other geographical areas. None was a Manchester man. Apart from Brassey and the ironmasters William Baird and William Crawshay, all of the non-landed millionaires listed here deceased prior to 1888 were Londoners, and it is only in the late Victorian period that provincial fortunes appear of a size sufficient to rival the largest among Londoners. Eighteen of these fortunes were commercial, only ten industrial, and six of these were left in the last fifteen years of the study. Thus, nor merely were large fortunes earned more readily in London, but the highest peaks of wealth were reached by Londoners, and especially by City men. In contrast, the fortunes earned in industrial Britain were fewer in number and relatively less lucrative.

II

The key question which must be asked of the occupational and geographical distributions outlined above is whether they were characteristic only of a handful of millionaires, or an important fact about the whole of Victorian middle-class society. In this section it will be contended that the geographical—and, by implication, the occupational—statistics offered above are the tip of an iceberg whose composition beneath the water is very largely similar to the visible portion, that the income of the Victorian middle class as a whole came as disproportionately from London as did the wealth of Victoria's millionaires.

Although the individual returns of nineteenth-century income-tax payers have almost certainly been destroyed,[20] there exists an immense variety of manuscript records in the Public Record Office of the assessment of the nineteenth-century income tax by schedule, by range of income, and by geographical area for every year during which the income tax was levied between 1799 and 1815, and from 1842 to 1911.[21] In addition, there are several remarkable returns in the Parliamentary Papers which have previously received no attention. Two of these will form the basis of the discussion in this section. The first is a county breakdown of Schedule D assessments in 1812,[22] the second, printed in April 1882, a listing of assessments under Schedules A, B, D and E, as well as the amount of taxation paid under each of these schedules in each *parliamentary constituency* in the United Kingdom in 1879–80.[23] A comparison of these sources demonstrates the lead of London over the rest of the country, despite the growth of the great provincial towns after the Napoleonic Wars. A consideration of the geographical distribution of income-tax assessments is particularly useful in shedding light on the composition of the middle class, as the liability for payment of income tax was practically coextensive with the middle class as commonly understood, the minimum level of income being £50 or £60 p.a. in the period 1799–1815, and £150 p.a. at the time the 1879–80 return was compiled. In Table 2.9 are given the county assessments under Schedule D in 1812, and the assessments in 1879–80 of the London boroughs and all provincial boroughs with a population in excess of 100,000.

In 1812 of the United Kingdom total of £34,384,000 assessed under Schedule D, £13,349,000 or 38.8 per cent of the national total, was assessed in London, Westminster or Middlesex. In contrast, no more than £4,046,000, or 11.8 per cent of the national total, was assessed in the six industrial counties of Lancashire, Yorkshire, Warwickshire, Staffordshire, Northumberland and Glamorgan.[24] The place of London in these figures, moreover, is almost certainly understated in several important ways. First, the assessment in the Home Counties of Essex, Kent and Surrey amounted to £3,883,000, or 11.3 per cent of the national total, and evidently the bulk of the income here represented industries located within the future municipal boundaries of London, or of London businessmen living and paying taxes there. This alone is sufficient to bring the London total to just under half of the national total assessed under Schedule D.

Furthermore, since only Schedule D is included in this table, no account is taken of income earned by owners of London ground-rents assessed under Schedule A, of the income from government funds, assessed under Schedule C,[25] which in the main probably accrued to wealthy brokers or *rentiers* located disproportionately in London, or of the income of office-holders under Schedule E. Practically all of this last category was paid in London. In 1814, the 'charge' (assessment) under Schedule E amounted to only £9,092 in the counties of Lancashire, Yorkshire, Durham, Northumberland, Staffordshire and Warwickshire, while the charge in London, Westminster and Middlesex totalled £915,310.[26] Finally, at this time the staffs of the Admiralty Court, the College of Arms, Court of Arches, Prerogative Court of Canterbury, and several other government offices in London were assessed under Schedule A at between £85,000 and £153,000 p.a.[27]

Table 2.9: (a) *Schedule D Assessments, by Counties, 1812*

County	Assess-ment (£000)	County	Assess-ment (£000)	County	Assess-ment (£000)
Bedfordshire	96	Huntingdonshire	101	Suffolk	440
Berkshire	291	Kent	1,625	Surrey	1,660
Buckinghamshire	220	Lancashire	1,539	Sussex	365
Cambridgeshire	235	Leicestershire	300	Warwickshire	592
Cheshire	274	Lincolnshire	366	Westmorland	45
Cornwall	238	Norfolk	505	Wiltshire	366
Cumberland	164	Northampton	181	Worcestershire	258
Derbyshire	196	Northumberland	474	Yorkshire	1,763
Devonshire	702	Nottinghamshire	293		
Dorset	203	Oxfordshire	305	Wales	419
Durham	238	Rutland	32	Scotland	2,314
Essex	598	Shropshire	279		
Gloucestershire	352	Somerset	1,223	City of London	6,697
Herefordshire	62	Southampton*	903	Westminster	2,678
Hertfordshire	256	Staffordshire	525	Middlesex	3,974

* The county of Hampshire.

Table 2.9: (b) *Schedule D Assessments of Largest British Provincial Towns and the London Boroughs, 1879–80*

Borough	Popula-tion 1881 (000)	Assess-ment (£000)	Borough	Popula-tion 1881 (000)	Assess-ment (£000)
Birmingham	401	4,016	Swansea	106	628
Blackburn	101	384			
Bolton	106	682	Aberdeen	105	974
Bradford	180	1,921	Glasgow	488	8,148
Brighton	128	1,156	Dundee	140	1,182
Bristol	207	2,310	Edinburgh	228	4,807
Hull	162	1,218			
Leeds	309	2,480	Belfast	174	1,1464
Leicester	122	909	Dublin	273	4,296
Liverpool	552	11,104			
Manchester	394	9,819	*London*		
Newcastle-			*Boroughs*		
upon-Tyne	145	1,851	Chelsea	367	1,844
Nottingham	112	1,155	Finsbury	524	7,925
Oldham	153	799	Greenwich	207	933
Portsmouth	128	536	Hackney	417	1,898
Salford	176	859	Lambeth	379	3,317
Sheffield	284	2,020	London, City	51	41,237
Stoke-on-Trent	152	1.075	Marylebone	498	12,297
Sunderland	125	869	Southwark	222	4,857
Wednesbury	117	500	Tower Hamlets	439	3,063
Wolverhampton	164	436	Westminster	229	10,302

It is probably not surprising that more than half of Britain's middle-class income in 1812 should represent the income of Londoners. What is perhaps more remarkable is that the lead of London over Britain's other major urban areas persisted throughout the nineteenth century. This is demonstrated in the other geographical distribution offered in Table 2.9. In 1879–80, the 28 provincial towns with populations in excess of 100,000, whose combined population was 5,773,000, were assessed under Schedule D for £67,508,000, while the ten London boroughs, whose population totalled 3,453,000, were assessed for £87,674,000.[28] The place of commercial as opposed to manufacturing wealth at this time may be seen more clearly if the provincial trading centres like Liverpool—assessed at £11,014,000, more than any provincial city—Bristol, Edinburgh and Dublin are considered apart from the manufacturing towns. There is evidently no definitive distinction between commercial and industrial towns, but were the predominantly commercial cities excluded, it seems likely that the assessment of the major provincial towns would be decreased by approximately three-sevenths. Moreover, as with the 1812 data, exclusive reliance on Schedule D excludes those portions of the middle class assessed under Schedules A, C and E, and found more frequently in London than in the provincial towns. The amount for which tax was assessed under Schedule E in 1879–80, *apart from* public office-holders (including the military and naval forces), was £5,934,000 for the ten London boroughs and £4,788,000 for the 28 leading provincial towns.[29] This income would largely consist of that of limited corporations and their employees, as well as non-business corporations such as churches.[30]

London's place among the leading British towns in 1879–80 was the more remarkable in view of the fact that the provincial cities examined here were 67 per cent more populous than the London boroughs in 1881. Thus it seems a plausible inference not merely that London possessed a larger total business income than all of the chief provincial towns combined, but that its middle class was richer *per capita* and almost certainly more numerous than that in the provincial towns.[31] The expansion of Britain's industrial base in the post-Napoleonic War period made London relatively less important than it had been, but it still remained considerably wealthier than the remainder of Britain's leading towns combined. The assessment of the City of London alone was nearly twice that of Manchester and Liverpool combined.

An important question which must be asked here is whether the predominance of London is merely a reflection of the fact that some provincial businesses were assessed there. Since the names of individual taxpayers remain unknown, the question cannot be answered definitively, but it is unlikely that even in 1879–80 many provincial businesses maintained their corporate headquarters in London, and possibly the major provincial towns would have attracted the assessments of outlying businesses in the same way. The 1860 return by parish (see note 23) detailed the place of assessment of the mines, railways, quarries, etc. which were listed separately. At that time no income from mineral deposits was assessed in London, and the total of railways assessed in Middlesex was £3,475,000, of a total assessment of railways in England of £10,603,000. Further, the amalgamation of provincial banks into the 'big five' did not get under way until the 1890s. It is also the case that the income-tax and probate data are wholly independent of one another, yet support the same conclusion.

Another interesting question raised by these data is whether an analysis of those worth below £150,000 but above, say, £25,000, would show a similar distribution, either occupationally or geographically, to those at the very top. The Manchester cotton-lords and their kind must be found *somewhere* on the wealth scale, and if not at the very top, necessarily this was at a lower level. As suggested above, it seems likely that most successful manufacturers left around £100,000 after mid-century. Yet one should not really assume that there were not also a great many businessmen in commerce, or in commercial towns, at a similar level of wealth, perhaps plentiful enough to make the distribution at the lower wealth levels similar to that at the top. Some light is thrown on this matter by the income-tax records, where numbers of assessed income units (as noted above, not necessarily individuals) can be traced down to the lowest limits of tax liability. Table 2.10 indicates the regional and income distribution of individual units assessed for taxation under Schedule D in 1879–80.

Table 2.10: Distribution of Individual Units Assessed for Taxation under Schedule D, 1879–80

| | Income range | | | | |
	£3–4,000	£4–5,000	£5–10,000	£10–50,000	£50,000+
Lancashire (total for county)	264	155	281	168	8
Liverpool	128	75	129	69	2
Manchester	90	56	94	61	3
Yorkshire	111	70	127	52	5
Warwickshire	54	16	36	16	0
Staffordshire	24	7	32	14	2
Northumberland	23	4	18	10	2
Middlesex, Metropolitan portion of	583	336	630	353	38
Surrey and Kent, Metropolitan portions of	51	32	53	32	4
Total Metropolis	634	368	783	385	42
City of London	318	181	373	232	25

Source: PRO, IR, 16, 51.

Although it would be quite fallacious to infer more than a cautious minimum concerning the occupational distribution of Londoners from the bald figures for their assessed incomes, it can with considerable truth be asserted that where there was commerce, finance or trade, money was made more readily than where there was manufacturing or industry. And standing above everything else there was London, the fixed point around which the Victorian middle classes revolved.

III

If it may now be accepted that commercial-based wealth and income exceeded that earned in manufacturing and industry during the nineteenth century, the central question which must flow from this is whether the distinction between the two forms of property is an artificial one, or whether it constituted a basic dichotomy in the nineteenth-century middle class as a whole. Might it not be useful to accept the possibility that two middle classes existed, quite distinct not merely in source of income but in attitudes and behaviour as well? This topic is a large one, and any suggestions must clearly be tentative; it ranges far beyond the scope of economic history. But in the space at hand it might not be irrelevant to the concerns of the economic historian to explore this question in light of the above data.[32]

In economic terms, the chief distinction between the London- and provincial-based middle classes was that one was largely capital- and the other largely labour-intensive. There were, of course, commercial industries which employed vast armies of workers, from the railways to the large retail shops, but even the largest bank or mercentile house employed only dozens where a factory or mine might employ thousands. Furthermore, although many employers in commerce or finance provided working conditions as bad or worse than anything in the north of England—merchant seamen and shop assistants were bywords for exploited labour—one may agree that what sociologists of labour term 'occupational ideology' was quite distinct in commerce and manufacturing. Even a menial clerk in the City was still a member of the middle class in some sense and enjoyed an income considerably higher than that of a skilled labourer. He worked fewer hours and could depend upon more fringe benefits.[33]

The chief social distinction between the two middle classes lay in their contrasting relationship with the traditional landed society. The London-based middle class was far closer to the old society than its provincial counterpart. Indeed, a not unimportant reason for the invisibility of this class was its failure to join in reform agitation, which, from Wyvill in the 1780s to the Jarrow hunger marchers, has typically possessed a provincial base: down the years a section, as well as an economic class, has felt itself aggrieved.[34]

The ties between London's middle class and the old society were many and varied. Two of the more important were in religion and in the education secured for its sons. Most London-based businessmen who were not aliens were Anglicans, and few were Protestant dissenters—a quite different profile from their northern counterparts. The Anglicanism of London's business class, together with its wealth, made its members far readier to send its sons to a major public school and Oxbridge than were the manufacturers. Most of the major public schools were located in London or the Home Counties and were of Anglican foundation. The leading historical study of public school alumni—that of Winchester, by Bishop and Wilkinson[35]—found that among 8,187 Wykehamists born between 1820 and 1922, the percentage of fathers engaged in finance or commerce was more than twice that of fathers engaged in manufacturing, a ratio which remained virtually constant throughout the nineteenth century. Similarly, down to 1914 more than twice as many of the Wykehamists themselves entered commerce rather than manufacturing.

In politics the picture is similar, with London's middle class returning Conservative members earlier and with greater consistency than its counterpart in the industrial areas. By 1895 finance had replaced land as the most important single business interest among Unionists MPs,[36] while Liberals relied primarily upon industrialists and manufacturers, especially those with non-Anglican backgrounds. Much of the history of late Victorian Conservatism—for instance, the Liberal-Unionist split of 1886—may be interpreted as the movement of commercial wealth into the Conservative Party. Along with this movement went a parallel shift towards participation in City business life on the part of landed society. Society's opposition to the underworld of City life—to the Baron Grants and Jabez Balfours—vanished in the late nineteenth century, and with it vanished all reluctance to join the boards of public companies or the Stock Exchange. As early as 1866 the

Saturday Review concluded that 'the City is rapidly becoming another branch of that system of relief for the aristocracy which Mr Bright denounces.'[37] In contrast, British industry possessed few such attractions for the aristocracy, and the number of aristocrats directly concerned with industry or manufacturing, apart from membership on boards of companies exploiting the minerals on their own land, was probably nil.

These social distinctions between elites were part of the larger dichotomy between finance and industry in Britain during the nineteenth century. The role of the City during the nineteenth century was largely to finance foreign and government loans. It did not act as a capital market for British industry until the very end of the Victorian period, if then. Manufacturing industry was either self-financed or financed by local banks whose directors had few City connexions. This was of the utmost importance to Britain's economic development: to no small degree the chronic underinvestment in British industry has been caused by the City's traditional role of financing foreign and government loans rather than domestic manufacturing. It was probably only in the 1930s that the merchant banks, driven by the lack of investment opportunities abroad, revised their attitudes towards financing home investment.[38] Even by 1914, as Professor Payne has demonstrated, the role of the merchant banks as issuing houses was limited by the extremely patchy development of limited liability among major industrial firms in Britain.[39]

Obviously, economic historians are well aware of the central importance of London and, indeed, of finance and commerce in nineteenth-century Britain. Yet it is simultaneously true that the very dimensions of our common view of Britain's economic development in the past two hundred years have invariably been fixed by the central importance of the Industrial Revolution and the growth of those areas of the country where industry flourished. There is a common notion, held so deeply as to be almost subconscious, that British economic history in modern times has been about the growth of industry, and therefore about industrialists. It is doubtless easy to overlook or underrate the importance of any line of business which does not leave a hole in the ground, or make a noise, and to forget that a warehouse or mercantile office could prove as great a source of profits as a mine or a factory.

Several culprits have been at work here. The first in point of time has probably been Marxism. It is a tribute to the power of an idea, even of a dubious one, that the view of history embodied in dialectical materialism should have been tacitly accepted by many whose own politics are far removed from Marxism. Although in many of his writings Marx gave full weight to the importance of bankers and large-scale merchants as an element in the post-industrial bourgeoisie,[40] it can hardly be doubted that the interaction of industrial capitalists with their employees *per necessitum* constitutes the focal point of the class struggle; it is here that revolutions are made or aborted. This may be true, but it is surely a logical fallacy to infer from the central importance of industrial capitalism in the dialectical process the central importance of industrial capitalism for the bourgeoisie. Marx viewed mercantile capitalism as characteristic of an earlier and inferior stage of society than industrialism,[41] and by nature as being inherently representative of a more primitive state of society.

The effect of macroeconomics must also be noted. No *lése-majesté* is implied in asserting that macroeconomic history is basically inappropriate to assessing the role of the middle class. The reason for this is simple: the statistical indexes of macroeconomics are influenced far more by labour-intensive than by capital-intensive industries. One has merely to compare the role of banking in the occupational distribution of the wealthy with its place in the net national product to appreciate this. The manufacturing, mining and building sectors of the economy accounted for between 33.4 and 40.2 per cent of the total national income during each decade between 1831 and 1901, while the share of the trade and transport sector ranged between 17.3 and 23.3 per cent.[42] The difference between the lead of manufacturing over commerce evidenced in these figures, and the lead of commerce over manufacturing in the statistics of the wealth-holders reflects the distribution of working-class incomes in the whole population. National employment statistics demonstrate that the difference at the top was made up at the bottom: 'commercial occupations' accounted for only 1.4 per cent of all employed males in 1841, while the various census categories of industrial and manufacturing trades were the fields of employment of 43 per cent of the total; in 1911 while commercial occupations still amounted to only 5.7 per cent of the male labour force, industry and manufacturing rose to 48.6 per cent.[43]

Quite clearly, no discussion of the middle class in Victorian society can be accurate which fails to take notice of the importance of London and of commerce, or which emphasizes the place of industrialists or manufacturers. The net effect of viewing the development of British society in the way suggested here is surely to make the fundamental break which the Industrial Revolution undoubtedly represented less important, and to make the continuities at the top of society between the Old Society and the New stronger and more tenacious. It may be that in viewing the middle class we have missed the woods for the trees, and the woods were traditionalist, Anglican and, in a very real sense, conservative.[44]

NOTES

1. In writing this chapter, I was greatly indebted to Professors E. J. Hobsbawm, Harold Perkin, and David Spring, and to Dr Stanley Chapman, M. Didier Lancien, Miss Mary Chadwick, and Mr John Mercer for their helpful criticisms. Needless to say, none is responsible for its errors or inelegances.
2. A typical exposition of these assumptions was made by G. D. H. Cole. He noted that: [Great Britain] became capitalist in a new sense by the rise of the factory system . . . A new class of aristocrats—cotton-lords, coal-lords, iron-lords—grew up . . . It has often been suggested that the fear caused by the French Revolution put back the Reform movement for a generation. It did more than that: it made inevitable the final alliance between the old and the new lords of land and factory which is the basis of the English oligarchy of today.—*Life of William Cobbett* (1924), p. 4.
    In this chapter, it will be seen, the assumption is made that there is a direct relation between 'importance', business success, and personal wealth. There are evidently many other senses in which a businessman, or a business elite, may be 'important' for his society or for economic development. Among these are: control of the labour force, contribution to technological innovation, to investment, or to the dominant ideology of the age. In several of these senses, Victorian manufacturers were more 'important' than financiers or merchants. But it is quite incorrectly inferred that they were also wealthier, more numerous and more powerful.
3. All property passing at death in Britain must be sworn for probate by the executor or administrator of the estate, and an inventory of property drawn up as part of the probate process. Since the mid-eighteenth century this has taken the form of a cash valuation. Prior to the establishment of the Principal Probate Registry in 1858 (located until 1874 at Doctor's Commons, London, and since then at Somerset House) estates might have been proved in any one of several dozen

ecclesiastical courts in England and Wales, although the estate of a person leaving property to the value of £5 or more in two separate dioceses had to be sworn in either of the two Prerogative courts (York and Canterbury). The Bank of England required all funds in a testator's portfolio to be proved in the Canterbury court, and hence the great bulk—90 per cent or more—of the pre-1858 estates valued at over £100,000 were proved in the Canterbury court (which was located at Doctor's Commons). For this research, the Act Books of the Canterbury court (PRO Prob. 8), and the indexes of the York Prerogative court, and the Chester Consistory court (containing those Lancashire estates not proved in a Prerogative court) were examined, as well as the printed probate calendars 1858–99 at Somerset House, the Scottish Calendars of Confirmation 1876–99, and the manuscript Scottish indexes 1824–75 (I.R. 9) at the Scottish Record Office, and the Irish Calendars 1858–99. The largest twentieth-century wills have been printed annually since 1901 in the *Daily Mail Yearbook* and in newspapers like *The Times*. The authoritative guide to the probate records is Anthony J. Camp, *Wills and their Whereabouts* (rev. edn, 1974). On this topic see also W. D. Rubinstein and D. H. Duman, 'The Probate Records as a Tool of the Historian', *Local Historian*, XI (1974), and C. D. Harbury, 'Inheritance and the Distribution of Personal Wealth in Britain', *Economic Journal*, LXXII (1962).

4. Prior to 1809 estates valued at above £100,000 (£10,000 before 1803) were sworn in the Canterbury court records as 'Upper Value' rather than at a cash figure. It was only in that year that very large estates were given an approximate cash value. Estates at this level continued to be sworn to the nearest £50,000 or £100,000, rather than to a precise sum, until 1881 in England and Wales.

5. This was done primarily because of the dearth of very large estates in the early nineteenth century: only 12 millionaire estates were proved during the period 1809–58, for instance.

6. In Scotland, however, real property was not included in the probate valuations until 1964. It should be kept in mind that the personalty of landowners (and unsettled land in the period 1898–1925) has always been valued for probate, and numerous very large estates were left during the nineteenth century by landowners, consisting of their personalty. The percentage of wealth-holders engaged in Agriculture in Tables 2.1–2.3 thus greatly understates the actual place of landowning in the British wealth structure.

7. Previous research taking the probate data as its basis has focused primarily on intergenerational social mobility, comparing the valuation of father and son. See Josiah Wedgwood, *The Economics of Inheritance* (1929); C. D. Harbury and P. C. MacMahon, 'Intergenerational Wealth Transmission and the Characteristics of Top Wealth Leavers in Britain', *Economic Journal* LXXXIII (1973). It should be noted that the figures in the probate calendars differ from those published since 1894 in the *Annual Report* of the Inland Revenue, which largely form the basis of the debate on the contemporary distribution of wealth in Britain. The Inland Revenue's

figures are anonymous, generally make use of the net rather than the gross valuation, and have always included both personalty and realty, as well as certain types of property not included in the probate calendar valuations, e.g. *inter vivos* gifts passed on before the three- or seven-year period prior to death had elapsed.

8. Women and foreigners leaving large estates in Britain have been excluded from all tables. Virtually all of the foreigners were engaged in commerce and had business interests in London. Of the 29 women wealth-holders above the £500,000 level, the origins of the fortunes of 15 were in commerce or finance, only two in industry or manufacturing.

9. *Standard Industrial Classification* (HMSO 1958) has been used. (Henceforth SIC).

10. Each wealth-holder was assigned to the main field in which his fortune was earned, based upon biographical evidence. In only a handful of cases was there any ambiguity; here, the wealth-holder was assigned to the trade in which he appeared to have possessed the larger interest, again based upon biographical evidence. Several groups of trades, especially shipbuilding/shipowning and iron/coalmastery, commonly produced wealth-holders with overlapping interests within each group. But there was in particular virtually no overlap whatever between the classical City financier and the classical north of England industrialist. Descendants of businessmen were assigned to the field in which their family fortune originated, even if they were not actively engaged in trade, or if indeed no part of their portfolios appeared to be invested in their family firm. Conceptually it might be argued that such men ought to be classified elsewhere, but the aim of these tables is to identify the source of wealth of each wealth-holder, not the occupation (or lack of occupation) he may incidentally have held. There is in addition the problem that many wealthy heirs continued to hold partnerships or directorships in their family firm which were largely nominal.

11. Socially, brewers, and especially the London brewers (e.g. the Whitbreads or Hoares, or, further afield,the Walkers in Liverpool or the Guinnesses in Dublin), were close to traditional society and readily accepted by businessmen as something higher than tradesmen.

12. See Rhodes Boyson, *The Ashworth Cotton Dynasty* (Oxford, 1970), family trees, facing p. 270. Dr John Foster regards a probate valuation of £25,000 as a convenient bench-mark to distinguish the capitalist elite *c.* 1851 in the industrial towns (Oldham, South Shields, Northampton) he has studied. See his *Class Struggle and the Industrial Revolution* (1974), pp. 161ff. In 1830 the compiler of a Warwickshire directory estimated that in Birmingham there was at the time one individual worth £400,000, two worth £300,000, 12 between £100,000 and £300,000, and no more than 66 worth between £20,000 and £100,000.—William West, *The History, Topography, and Directory of Warwickshire* (Birmingham, 1830). This was a considerable increase on 1783, when William Hutton believed that only three Birmingham men were worth more than £100,000, only seven worth £50,000—

History of Birmingham (1781), cited in Asa Briggs, *The Making of Modern England, 1784–1867* (New York, 1959), p. 64. Among the more famous industrial dynasties, no Wedgwood, Kenrick, Marshall or Greg ever left £500,000 or anything like it, in the period surveyed in this article.

13. I have been guided in this division of Britain into geographical units by T. W. Freeman's *The Conurbations of Great Britain* (Manchester, 1959). Most of these divisions are self-explanatory, but some require comment. 'Outer London' and 'Other London' correspond to the LCC and GLC areas respectively. 'Clydeside' includes the mineral fields in Lanarkshire, Renfrewshire and Ayrshire, as well as Greenock. 'Mid-Lancashire' chiefly consists of Wigan and St Helens and the surrounding mineral areas. 'Ribblesdale' comprises Preston, Accrington, Blackburn and Burnley. 'Nottingham–Derby–Burton' also includes the outlying mineral deposits and local cotton works. As with the assignment of wealth-holders by occupation, much in these tables is necessarily arbitrary. Nevertheless, in the great majority of cases there was no question of the wealth-holder's proper venue. Several types of wealth-holders, however, could not be assigned to a particular locality and are excluded from this set of tables, most importantly foreign merchants trading abroad, multiple retailers with branches across the country, and contractors and builders not exclusively in local trade; landowners are also excluded. Thus the number of wealth-holders in these tables is lower than in Tables 2.1–2.3. There is a time-honoured pattern of a family beginning in a small way in the provinces and then transferring its business to London as it grew in size. With few exceptions this is not reflected in the data in these tables. Most families experiencing this pattern had moved to London at least a generation before they produced a wealth-holder; such wealth-holders were Londoners, maintaining few if any links with their place of origin. Previous research on the geographical distribution of personal wealth or income in Britain is remarkably sparse. E. J. Buckatzsch, 'The Geographical Distribution of Wealth in England, 1086–1843', *Economic History Review*, 2nd ser. III (1950–1), used only Schedule A (the tax on rents) of the income tax for the nineteenth century. A. D. M. Phillips and J. R. Walton, 'The Distribution of Personal Wealth in English Towns in the Mid-Nineteenth Century,' *Transactions of the Institute of British Geographers*, 2nd ser. LXIV (1975), make use of Assessed Taxes (which fell on windows, carriages, armorial bearings, men-servants, horses for riding, game duties, etc.) and reach the same broad conclusions as this article. But it is open to the serious objection that men of wealth who chose not to possess some of the taxed items would be under-represented and that this would disproportionately affect the dissenting, manufacturing new men of wealth. This is an objection which cannot be raised against income tax of probate figures.

14. This is not for lack of surviving documents. Vast quantities of family and business papers survive, in the possession of a descendant, Mr

Richard Gatty, JP of Pepper Arden, Northallerton, and in the London Guildhall Library.

15. See W. G. Hoskins, 'Richard Thornton: A Victorian Millionaire', *History Today* (1962), p. 578. Prof. Hoskins discovered Thornton and his immense fortune 'by pure chance in the official index of wills [at Somerset House] for 1865, while looking for an impecunious artist'.

16. The largest fortune ever left in Britain (until 1973, when his son left £52,200,000) was that of Sir John Ellerman, 1st Bt (1863–1933), the City financier and shipowner, whose estate, left at the bottom of the Depression, totalled £36,700,000.

17. The sole Manchester cotton millionaire was Edward R. Langworthy (1796–1874), who served as mayor of Salford 1848–9 and 1850–1. At the half-millionaire level were Thomas Worthington (d. 1840) and Thomas Ashton (1818–98).

18. No distinction is drawn here between non-landed fortunes and those left by landowners in personalty or unsettled realty. It is worth repeating that since settled land is excluded, successors to, e.g. the dukedoms of Westminster, Bedford, Northumberland and Portland, and to the earldom of Derby, who were undoubtedly worth far more than £2 million, are often excluded. For a full list of millionaire fortunes left between 1809 and 1949, see W. D. Rubinstein, 'British Millionaires, 1809–1949', *Bulletin of the Institute of Historical Research*, XLVIII (1974). A perusal of this list raises several important questions related to inheritance and to the distinction between 'old' and 'new' wealth, as several families account for more than one top fortune. But the distinction drawn in this article between commercial and manufacturing wealth would not seem to be much affected: both commercial dynasties, like the Rothschilds and the Morrisons, and manufacturing ones, like the Coatses and Willses, appear. It may well have been true, however, that there was a lower risk involved in maintaining an inherited financial than an inherited manufacturing fortune, which entailed continued entrepreneurial ability in subsequent generations, and it is maintained below that for sociological reasons commercial heirs were less likely to leave business than those inheriting a fortune in manufacturing.

19. Aside from those listed in Table 2.7, several foreigners and women left fortunes at this level. They were the three 'Randlords' Barnett I. Barnato (d. 1900), £2,300,000; Alfred Beit (1853–1906), £8 million; and Sir Julius Werhner (1850–1912), £10 million; the French merchant banker Baron A. C. de Rothschild (d. 1900), £2,300,000; and the Canadian railway magnate Donald Smith, first Baron Strathcona (1820–1914), £4,700,000. Millionairesses at this level: Mrs Enriquetta Rylands (d. 1908), widow of John Rylands, £3,600,000; and Ellen Morrison (d. 1909), daughter of James Morrison, £2,400,000.

20. As is well known, the system of schedules in force after 1803 prevents any knowledge of the number of individuals paying income tax, or of the size of individual incomes, until the super-tax of 1911. A single individual would have been assessed under several or all of the five

schedules if he received sufficient income from the requisite sources; 'individuals' included firms and businesses (except corporations, assessed under Schedule E). On this complicated matter, and on all other questions of the scope of the nineteenth-century income tax, see Josiah C. Stamp's peerless *British Incomes and Property* (1916). Briefly, Schedule A taxed the profits arising from ownership of lands, houses, and other realty, Schedule B was the tax upon 'the occupier [of land] on the profits made by the occupier . . . from husbandry', i.e. upon farmers (*ibid.* p. 81), Schedule C taxed profits arising from government securities and funds, Schedule D was the tax upon the profits arising from business and the professions, while under Schedule E were taxed the salaries of public officials and the employees of any public corporation, including limited liability companies: thus in the late nineteenth century there was a constant 'drift' of assessed income from Schedule D to E. (*ibid.* p. 266). Until 1867–8, profits arising from mines, quarries, ironworks, gasworks, waterworks, canals, docks, railways, market and fair rights, tolls etc. were anomalously assessed under Schedule A rather than D. (*ibid* p. 37). It is well known that the individual returns of the first income tax were assiduously destroyed. See Arthur Hope-Jones, *Income Tax in the Napoleonic Wars* (Cambridge, 1939), p. 4. It is more than likely that post-1842 returns were destroyed when no longer current. In 1857 a scandal occurred when it was discovered that London tax returns were sold as waste paper to wrap fish. (Parl. Papers, 1857–8, XXXIV). However, it appears that the names of individuals and amounts assessed during the first income tax survive for many Scottish parishes. See Hope-Jones, *op. cit.* pp. 128–30. There is a 150-year time limit on the examination of confidential documents held by the Inland Revenue.

21. These include the hundreds of enormous sacks, containing records of defaulters and county and half-county assessments, which were sent to the King's Remembrancer in 1798–1815, and which are presently to be found at the Public Record Office (E. 182), and the manuscript books containing the details of the number, size, and venue of assessments by schedule (PRO, I.R. 16), running from 1845–6—1847–8 through to 1911–12.

22. *Accounts of Duty Arising From Profits* (PP 1814–15, X).

23. *Parliamentary Constituencies (Population)* (PP 1882, LII). An even more valuable return is that of April 1860, *Property and Income Tax* (PP 1860, XXXIX, PT II) detailing the gross value of property assessed under Schedules A and B, and the net amount of profits assessed under Schedule D in 1859–60 in every *parish* in Great Britain. Moreover, the income arising from railways, mines, quarries, *et al.* which were anomalously assessed under Schedule A until 1867 (when transferred to Schedule D) are each given separately by parish.

24. The assessment of Glamorgan was £109,474.

25. So far as I am aware, no survey of the geography of Schedule C taxpayers exists. Assessments were made through the Bank of England or the Bank of Ireland, not through individual taxpayers.

26. PRO King's Remembrancer Manuscript, E. 181, No. 42.
27. Hope-Jones, *Income Tax, op. cit.*, pp. 131–3.
28. The total of Schedule D tax assessed in that year in England and Wales was £209,318,000, and £249,489,000 in the United Kingdom. Apart from the London assessment £6,581,000 was assessed under Schedule D in eight county constituencies near London. Much of this would have been income earned in London.
29. It is unfortunately not possible to establish separately the geographical distribution of the Schedule E income of public office-holders, which would quite plainly add still further to the lead of London. The 1882 return only details at the end of each of its country divisions a global figure for all public office-holders not distinguishing between military and civilian offices. For England and Wales this amounted to £13,983,000; for Scotland to £292,000; for Ireland to £896,000.
30. See Stamp *British Incomes, op. cit.* pp. 263–71, for an explanation of these distinctions. A thorough comparison of the business incomes assessed under Schedules D and E after mid-century would be useful in ascertaining the growth of limited liability.
31. Among the manuscript sources referred to in p. 47, n. 21 are Schedule D assessments by range of income, arranged by the taxation districts employed by the Inland Revenue. In 1879–80 (PRO I.R. 16, Nos. 49–51), 385 individuals or business units reported a net income of £10,000–50,000 under Schedule D, and 42 others an income of £50,000 or more within the Metropolitan taxation districts, of which 232 and 25, respectively, were in City of London districts. The respective totals for some leading provincial taxation districts: Liverpool, 69 and 2; Manchester, 41 and 3; Birmingham, 13 and zero; Leeds, 11 and 1; Bradford, 8 and 1. In the United Kingdom there were 939 incomes in the range £10,000–50,000, and 82 of £50,000 or more. These figures are slightly at variance with those in Leone Levi, *Wages and Earnings of the Working Classes* (1885), p. 58.
32. In this section we are speaking of both the 'super-rich' wealth-holders studied from the probate material and the middle class as commonly understood, including all businessmen liable to income tax. Yet it is here contended that the central occupational and geographical distinctions described above apply to all income or wealth levels considered here, and that both the 'super-rich' and the middle class can profitably be discussed together in this section.
33. On 'occupational ideology', see Theodore Caplow, *The Sociology of Work* (Minneapolis, 1954); J. A. Banks, *Marxist Sociology in Action* (1970), p. 159. There are few books, apart from George and Weedon Grossmith's *The Diary of a Nobody* (1894), describing the world of the City clerk. One of the most entertaining is the autobiography of H. G. de Fraine, *Servant of this House* (1960), who entered the Bank of England in 1886 as a sixteen-year-old clerk in the bank-note department and retired as principal of the printing department. De Fraine began on £42 p.a. rising to £80 p.a. after the second year. When Lord Cunliffe, known as the 'Terror of the City', became Governor of the Bank of England in 1913, he raised the hours of work for employees

in the Bank's printing department from 39 per week to 48, to bring it more nearly in line with the 52 hours prevailing in the printing trade. In the private drawing room, a department of bored and underworked staff performing menial secretarial work for which they were too intelligent, absurd practical jokes flourished, and 'jokes shouted from one end of the office to the other, the singing of a line from some popular song, winding up with "Amen" in a solemn cadence of about one hundred voices'. Everyone here had a nickname: de Fraine's was 'Duck' since his home was in Aylesbury, and he was 'greeted with a chorus of quacks' whenever he returned to his old office in later years. (*ibid.*, pp. 161. 85, 88). On the paternalism of N. M. Rothschild & Co. see Ronald Palin, *Rothschild Relish* (1970), esp. pp. 42ff. Palin rose from junior clerk to Secretary.

34. See Donald Read, *The English Provinces c. 1760–1960: A Study in Influence* (1964). Cf. Francis Place's celebrated explanation of London's idiosyncrasies to Cobden in 1840: 'London differs very widely . . . from every other place on the face of the earth. It has . . . a working population . . . who . . . are a quiescent, inactive race as far as public matters are concerned.' (G. Wallas, *Life of Francis Place, 1771–1854* (1898), pp. 393–4. I discuss the class structure of Victorian Britain in light of this interpretation more fully in Chapter 3.
35. T. J. Bishop and Rupert Wilkinson, *Winchester and the Public School Elite* (1967), Table 5, pp. 104–8.
36. J. A. Thomas, *The House of Commons, 1832–1910: A Study of its Economic and Functional Character* (Cardiff, 1939), p. 25.
37. *Saturday Review*, 5 May 1866.
38. William M. Clarke, *The City in the World Economy* (1967), p. 129. On the Rothschilds' movement into domestic finance at this time, see Palin, *Rothschild, op. cit.* p. 104. An exception to this dichotomy has been insurance, where London houses dominated the field and contributed an important element to the stability and success of provincial industry.
39. P. L. Payne, 'The Emergence of the Large-Scale Company in Britain', *Economic History Review*, 2nd ser. XX (1967). A considerable literature exists in Marxist and quasi-Marxist sources on the development of 'finance capital' and the dichotomy between manufacturing and finance, generally in the context of *fin-de-siècle* imperialism. The classical works are R. Hilferding, *Das Finanzkapital* (Vienna, 1910), which has never been fully translated into English, and Lenin's *Imperialism: The Highest Stage of Capitalism* (1916; English trans. 1933). Among contemporary elaborations, see Michael Barratt Brown, *After Imperialism* (rev. edn, 1970) and 'The Controllers of British Industry', in K. Coates, *Can the Workers Run Industry?* (1968); Andrew Glyn and Bob Sutcliffe, *British Capitalism, Workers, and the Profit Squeeze* (1969); and S. Aaronovitch, *The Ruling Class* (1961). It is especially unfortunate that this viewpoint has never been systematically applied to the whole of the British experience. There appear to be two reasons for this: the preoccupation with imperialism, and the fact that Britain was unique among industrial powers in that

there was no merger between industry and finance until after World War One. In my opinion the most salient feature of British elite group structure since 1918 has been the absorption of the manufacturing middle class and the landowners—the other elite hierarchies of the nineteenth century—by the City and finance.

40. E.g. Ch. 6 of *The Eighteenth Brumaire of Louis Bonaparte*, in Karl Marx and Frederick Engels, *Selected Works in One Volume* (1968), p. 157.

41. George Lichtheim, *Marxism, A Historical and Critical Study* (1961), Pt IV, Ch. 3, 'Bourgeois Society', especially pp. 155–9. The importance of 'finance capital' is, to be sure, fully recognized by Marx's successors.

42. Phyllis Deane and W. A. Cole, *British Economic Growth, 1688–1959* (Cambridge, 1969), Table 37, p. 166.

43. B. R. Mitchell and Phyllis Deane, *Abstract of British Historical Statistics* (Cambridge, 1962), p. 60.

44. Little has been said thus far of the place of landowning in the nineteenth-century wealth structure. Until the 1880s, half of the wealthiest men in Britain were landowners; earlier in the century the percentage was far higher. At the time of the Napoleonic Wars, perhaps seven-eighths of all persons worth £100,000 or more in Britain were landowners. It is now widely accepted, thanks chiefly to Norman Gash and D. C. Moore, that the 1832 Reform Bill did not fundamentally alter the balance of power between the landed and middle classes. In so far as wealth transmuted itself into political power, this corresponded to the realities of the day. Indeed, when the change did come later in the century, the political decline of the landowners may have preceded their decline in relative wealth.

3

Wealth, Elites and the Class Structure of Modern Britain*

Those who write about class structure must avoid equally the Scylla of over-simplification and the Charybdis of excessive complication. Successful interpretations of class structure must be sweeping, digestible, à propos, and rooted in firm statistical evidence. The failure of any but Marx's theory of class to meet these criteria is a major reason why the Marxist view of class structure has survived so long and so successfully: there are few challengers. Marx's theory of class structure and its evolution is, of course, largely an extrapolation from the British experience and, to no small extent, must stand or fall with the accuracy of Britain as the test case. In this chapter something of an alternative theory of the growth and evolution of class structure in Britain will be offered, taking as its focus the changes in and behaviour of those elites which have dominated Britain politically and economically in the modern period. Briefly, it is suggested that mid-Victorian Britain contained two middle classes, by far the larger and wealthier based on commerce and London, the other on manufacturing and the north of England. Together with the landed elite, these contested for the

* Much of the statistical portion of this article recapitulates what is presented more fully in Chapter 2. This is unavoidable, given that the evidence is original, and that the arguments which follow derive from it, and are largely unsupported without it. Earlier versions of this chapter were read to Professor E. J. Hobsbawm's Seminar at the Institute of Historical Research, University of London, to that of Professor A. H. John and Dr Charlotte Erickson at the London School of Economics, and to the History Seminar at the Research School of Social Sciences, Australian National University, Canberra. I am most grateful for the helpful comments received at each. For criticism of a later version of this paper I acknowledge the help of Professor Oliver MacDonagh, Dr F. B. Smith and Mr M. E. J. Krygier, all of the Australian National University, of Professor R. S. Neale, of the University of New England, and of Dr Paul Robertson, University of Melbourne.

benefits of wealth, status and power, and evolved separate means of social control. These separate elites replaced the unified eighteenth-century world of 'Old Corruption' and themselves merged, by a gradual process, into a single elite, finally formed in the period 1918–25.

In the first part of the chapter is an exposition of what is hoped is the firm statistical evidence underlining the later inferences.

I

'Wealthy men as a specific group have been studied very little up to this time'.[1] Unfortunately Pitirim Sorokin's remark, true fifty years ago, has remained largely so until today, at least for Britain.[2] The evidence advanced here derives from my research on the top British wealth-holders, mainly those persons leaving £500,000 or more between 1809 and 1939, based upon the probate records at Somerset House, the Public Record Office, and in Edinburgh, York and Preston. In the course of this work full lists were compiled of all persons leaving estates of £100,000 or more in Britain since 1809, when these sources began in a usable form. Research on the careers of individuals was restricted to those wealth-holders leaving £500,000 or more in this period, and to two groups of 'lesser wealthy'—those leaving between £160,000 and £500,000 between 1809 and 1829, and those with estates between £250,000 and £500,000 left in the years 1850–69.[3]

The salient legal and technical conditions and problems associated with the British probate material may be summarized: all property passing at death in Britain must be sworn for probate by the executor or administrator of the estate, and an inventory of property drawn up as part of the probate process. The valuation figures have always consisted of a single sum[4] comprising, during the nineteenth century until 1898, the gross unsettled personalty of all persons, testate or intestate, leaving property in Britain; between 1898 and 1925 unsettled realty was included and from 1926 both settled and unsettled realty. The major omission during the nineteenth century was thus real property, whose absence may be compensated for to a very large extent by the income figures in the *Return of Owners of Land* (1871–6) and Bateman's *Great Landowners of Great Britain and Ireland* (1883 edition).[5] Foreign holdings were included with the home asssets if they were tradeable in Britain. The valuation figures record the gross rather than the net value of the estate, the difference consisting of personal debts and funeral expenses. Valuations were sworn to an approximate rather than to an exact figure before 1881—in the case of the wealthiest, generally to the nearest £50,000 or £100,000. Prior to the establishment of the Principal Probate Registry in 1858 (at Somerset House from 1874) English and Welsh estates could be proved in any one of dozens of ecclesiastical courts; in the case of a testator with property in two or more dioceses, however, the estate had to be proved in either of the Prerogative Courts at York and Canterbury (the latter located at Doctor's Commons, London) with jurisdiction in their respective archbishoprics. It was a requirement that any estate including as a component government funds had to be proved in the Canterbury Prerogative Court, and in fact more than 90 per cent of pre-1858 estates in excess of £100,000 were proved there.[6]

Although imperfect in several respects[7] the probate valuations offer comprehensive and objective information on the personal wealth of the entire British population in the modern period. They are, moreover, probably unique among advanced industrial nations in presenting probate valuations for the whole population, readily available (for England and Wales in the period from 1858 at any rate) at a single record office in printed alphabetical volumes, and are evidently among the most important single sources available to the social historian. It is a mystery why so little use has been made of them.

The analysis offered here, and indeed the structure of the argument which follows, derive from examinating the wealth-holders in terms of their occupational and geographical distribution and from additional confirmatory evidence from income-tax statistics. Each of these matrices points to the same conclusion and demonstrates the lead in number and wealth of commerce and finance over industry and manufacturing, and of London and provincial entrepôts like Liverpool over manufacturing towns, both among the very wealthy and among the tax-paying middle class.

Ranking each wealth-holder according to the Order of the Standard Industrial Classification[8] in which his fortune was earned the point emerges that the wealthy of nineteenth-century Britain earned their fortunes disproportionately in commerce, finance and transport, as merchants, bankers, shipowners, merchant bankers, and stock and insurance brokers, rather than as manufacturers and industrialists. Table 2.4 shows clearly the lead of the commercial trades as a source of wealth.[9] This lead persists among all of the cohorts in this study with the exception of the early millionaires and the two 1880–99 groups. Moreover, except among the first millionaire cohort, at no time did manufacturing in the strict sense lead commerce as a source of wealth, even in the 1880–99 period. Although the percentage of commercial wealth-holders declined to as low as 40 per cent of the 1880–99 millionaire cohort, the predominance of commerce in the wealth structure returned in the early twentieth century. Despite the Industrial Revolution the most important element in Britain's business wealth structure during the nineteenth century was commerce and finance.

The numerically largest group of wealth-holders, however, was neither industrialists nor bankers, but the great landowners; and Table 2.4 indicates in an approximate way the phenomenally high percentage of landowners among Britain's wealth elite.[10] These figures are the product of multiplying the number of landowners above an appropriate income level in Bateman's *Great Landowners* (£33,000 p.a. in the case of millionaires) by the year's rental required to ascertain the capital value of their land, which varied with the economic health of British agriculture. These figures record the worth of the great landowners' real property alone, and exclude all of their personalty, which was very substantial indeed in many cases. Among the 1880–99 cohort, for example, ten landowners left millionaire estates consisting of their personalty alone, for instance, William, seventh Duke of Devonshire (d. 1891), who left £1,864,000 besides land yielding £180,750 p.a., or George, third Duke of Sutherland (d. 1892), whose personal fortune totalled £1,378,000 in addition to his land, worth £141,667 p.a. Until the 1880s more than half of Britain's wealthiest men were landowners; at earlier periods of the century the percentage was far higher. At the time of the Napoleonic Wars perhaps seven-eighths of all persons worth £100,000 or more were landowners. Indeed the political decline of landowning which began in 1832 may have *preceded* their decline in relative worth by a quite considerable stretch.[11] Moreover the richest landowners were far richer than the wealthiest British businessmen until this century. The richest landowner of all during the late nineteenth century, the Duke of Westminster, was reliably said to have been worth £14 million in 1895 on the basis of his London estates alone; in addition he left £950,000 in personalty and other land. Such aristocrats as the

Dukes of Bedford, Northumberland, Portland, Devonshire, and Buccleuch, or Lords Derby and Lansdowne, were nearly as wealthy. In contrast, the richest British businessman of the nineteenth century left no more than £6 million, while it is not until the 1920s that business millionaires began to leave estates exceeding that of Westminster.

What of the industrialists? Although there are numerous examples of immensely wealthy nineteenth-century manufacturers and industrialists, from Richard Crawshay (d. 1810), the Cyfarthfa ironmaster, or the textile manufacturers Sir Robert Peel (d. 1830) and Richard Arkwright (d. 1843)—millionaires all—the typical successful manufacturer appears to have left an estate in the range of £100,000 after mid-century, and rather less before; Joseph Chamberlain's (d. 1914) £125,000, or John Bright's (d. 1889) £86,000, are typical. John Foster[12] takes £25,000 as a convenient bench-mark to distinguish his industrial elite *c.* 1851 from the rest: this seems right, although the figure is probably lower in the provinces than in London: Frederick Engels's (d. 1895) £25,000 possibly went as far as Macaulay's (d. 1859) £70,000 or Disraeli's (d. 1881) £84,000.[13]

If it was on the commercial or financial side of the Victorian business world that the great fortunes were disproportionately to be found, it would seem to be a corollary that the centre of wealth-making in nineteenth-century Britain was London rather than the industrial towns of the north of England. This was indeed the case, although it would evidently be a gross oversimplification merely to identify London with commerce and the North with industry. Nevertheless most top London fortunes were left by those in commerce and finance, while most in the north were earned in manufacturing, despite the great wealth of merchants in provincial entrepôts like Liverpool, Glasgow and Leeds. Assigning each non-landed wealth-holder to the locality or conurbation in which his fortune was earned—where his factory, mine or ships were located—a pattern of geographical distribution is indicated as favourable to London, in just such a way as the occupational distribution demonstrated the lead of commerce. This is partially indicated in Table 2.5, which details information on the business venues of non-landed millionaires.[14] It must be stated clearly that Table 2.5 omits all landowners, all merchants trading abroad, and certain other occupational categories not readily assignable to a precise venue.

Among millionaires London accounted for between 39 and 63 per cent of the total number in each cohort and, among half-millionaires, for between 38 and 64 per cent. The six conurbations making up the heart of industrial England in Lancashire and the West Riding accounted for no more than 25 per cent of the most numerous millionaire group. As with the place of commerce in the occupational structure, London's lead, although less marked at the close of the nineteenth century, was never lost.

London's centre was the City, sufficient by itself in every period and at every level of wealth in this study to constitute the single most important geographical unit, generally by several orders of magnitude over its nearest rivals. Commerce and finance predominated here, of course; all but five city millionaires, for example, can be readily assigned to a commercial Order among the *Standard Industrial Classification* listings. Many of the City's wealth-holders belonged to the celebrated financial and mercantile dynasties like the Rothschilds, Barings, Sassoons and Montefiores, but many others remain virtually unknown, and one important reason for the failure of economic historians to grasp the central importance of the City of London has been its relative neglect in business histories and industrial biographies, in contrast to the attention paid to the Industrial Revolution and its major figures. Typical of such City millionaires were James Morrison (d. 1857), a textile warehouseman and merchant banker, who left between £4 million and £6 million and was probably the richest commoner of the nineteenth century; Richard Thornton (d. 1865), an insurance broker and Baltic merchant who left £2,800,000; Herman, Baron de Stern (d. 1887), the merchant banker and financier who left £3,545,000;[15] and Hugh McCalmont (d. 1887), a stockbroker and foreign merchant who left £3,122,000. Such men were among the very wealthiest in the country, wealthier by several dozen times than the majority of successful industrialists; their invisibility is perhaps the product of their very number.

London apart from the City was nearly as productive of large fortunes, and London's predominance in the British wealth structure was equally a result of these outlying fortunes. Those of the brewing families (like the Charringtons, Watneys and Combes), together with those in retailing, whether from general merchandise in a department store like William Whiteley (d. 1907) and James Marshall (d. 1893), or from speciality products for the wealthy like the art dealer Sir Joseph J. Duveen (d. 1908), and in shipping (such as those of the Harrisons or Scruttons), were the most numerous, but heavy industry was represented by wealthy engineers, shipbuilders, chemical manufacturers and builders. Manchester stands in stark contrast to London. Manchester's symbolic importance, which will always be great, is belied at every turn by the statistics of wealth-holding there. Only *one* Manchester cotton manufacturer left a millionaire estate during the entire period 1809–1914; only two others left fortunes in the half-million class. Of all the Manchester wealth-holders deceased in the span of this study, only six were industrialists or manufacturers, while among the remainder were seven cotton merchants, three bankers, and a number of brewers and newspaper owners. It is to the outlying towns of Greater Manchester that one must look to find the textile-manufacturing and industrial fortunes in this conurbation— to the smaller towns like Oldham, with its nine cotton-spinners and three machinery manufacturers among the wealth-holders, or to families like the Fieldens in Todmorden, the Peels in Blackburn, or the Bulloughs in Accrington. In these smaller towns every wealth-holder without exception was a manufacturer or industrialist. The true 'captains of industry' may have existed in their pure form almost exclusively in towns where, relatively isolated and insulated, there was to be found, besides themselves, only an industrial work-force, with all the potential here either for revolt or control.[16]

Space does not here permit an examination of the other leading provincial towns, but in passing it might be noted that Merseyside—the Liverpool conurbation—produced considerably more fortunes than Greater Manchester, and these largely among the local commercial magnates—its shipowners, merchants and bankers.[17]

As well as being relatively more numerous than industrial fortunes, those earned in commerce or in London were, on the whole, larger in size. Of the 40 male British fortunes worth £2 million or more left between 1809 and 1914,[18] four belonged to landowners, and one to the railway contractor Thomas Brassey (d. 1870), who cannot be assigned to a specific venue. Of the remaining 36, however, no fewer than 20 were Londoners (16 from the City alone) while five were from Clydeside, four from Bristol (all members of the Wills tobacco family), and the remainder spread among six other geographical areas. None was a Manchester man. Apart from Brassey and the ironmasters William Baird (d. 1864) and William Crawshay (d. 1867) all of the ten non-landed multi-millionaires deceased prior to 1888 were Londoners, and it is only in the late Victorian period that provincial fortunes appear of a size sufficient to rival the largest in London. Eighteen of the largest fortunes were commercial, only ten industrial, and six of these were left in the last fifteen years before 1914. It would thus appear that not merely were larger fortunes earned more readily in London, but the highest peaks of wealth were reached by Londoners, and especially by City men. In contrast, the fortunes earned in industrial Britain were fewer in number and relatively smaller in size.

It is one thing if this pattern applies merely to the handful of British millionaires; it is another, and vastly more important, if the type of distribution found here represents an important fact about the whole of Victorian middle-class society. In fact it does: the geographical—and, by implication, the occupational—statistics offered here are similar for the entire middle class. The income of the Victorian middle class came as disproportionately from London as did the wealth of Victorian millionaires. The evidence here comes from the surviving assessment figures of the nineteenth-century income tax—an immensely valuable and relatively accessible source, and one, like the probate records, virtually never used by the social or economic historian. Although the individual returns of the nineteenth-century income tax have almost certainly been destroyed,[19] there exists an immense variety of manuscript records in the Public Record Office concerning the assessment of the nineteenth-century income tax by schedule, by range of income, and by geographical area for every year the income tax was levied down to 1911; there are, in addition, several remarkable returns in the Parliamentary Papers which have previously attracted no attention.[20] Perhaps the most useful for our purposes here is that of April 1882, listing assessment under Schedules A, B, C and E, as well as the amount of taxation paid under each of these schedules in each parliamentary constituency in the United Kingdom in 1879–80.[21] The minimum liability for income tax in 1879–80 was an income of £150 p.a., making the tax-paying class virtually identical with the middle class as commonly understood.

In 1879–80 London incomes formed as predominant a share of all taxable business and professional incomes as did London's wealth among the very wealthy, a fact made clear in Table 2.9b.[22] The 28 provincial towns with populations in excess of 100,000, and with a combined population of 5,773,000, were assessed under Schedule

D for £67,508,000, while the ten London boroughs, whose populations totalled 3,453,000, were assessed for £87,674,000. No less than £41,237,000 was assessed in the City of London alone, £12,297,000 in Marylebone, and £10,302,000 in Westminster; by contrast, Liverpool, the wealthiest provincial town, was assessed for £11,014,000, Manchester and Salford together for £10,678,000, Birmingham for £4,016,000, and so on. Moreover, obviously many provincial cities like Liverpool, Bristol or Edinburgh were primarily commercial or governmental rather than industrial in their primary roles and, again, as with the 1812 data, Schedule D does not include any income arising from ground-rents, from the profits of the public funds, or from any government employees' salaries, all of which would evidently add still further to the lead of London. Since the combined population of the leading provincial towns was two-thirds higher than the London total, it is a plausible inference that London not merely possessed a larger total business income than all of the chief provincial towns combined, but that its middle class was richer *per capita* and almost certainly more numerous than in the provincial towns.

It might be contended that the income-tax figures produced here distort reality in so far as the lead of London is a product of a handful of enormous incomes at the top. After all, as with wealth and the wealthy, if the Manchester cotton-lords and their kind are not to be found at the very top, they most be somewhere else, and necessarily that can only be at a lower level. Indeed it is the case that the very largest incomes were disproportionately found in London[23] but, perhaps surprisingly, it is not true that further down the income scale the provincial tax-paying class is in a numerical majority.

At the income range of £3–10,000, probably equivalent to the smaller type of successful enterprise, the number of individual units assessed in 1879–80 was as shown in Table 3.1. Although we cannot safely infer more than a cautious minimum concerning occupational distribution from these bald figures of assessed income, it does seem clear that where there was commerce, finance or trade, money was made more readily than where there was manufacturing or industry. England's role as 'Clearing-house of the World' preceded its emergence as 'Workshop of the World': it has outlived it and, even during the midday of Victorian prosperity, it predominated over it.

Table 3.1: Assessed Incomes under Schedule D, £3,000–£10,000, in 1879–80

	£3–4,000	£4–5,000	£5–10,000
Lancashire (total for county)	264	155	281
Liverpool	128	75	129
Manchester	90	56	94
Yorkshire	111	70	127
Warwickshire and Staffordshire together	78	23	57
Total Metropolis (Metropolitan			
Middlesex plus London)	634	368	783
City of London alone	318	181	373

Source: PRO, IR 16, 49–51.

II

It is contended in this section that the distinction between commercial wealth, based largely in London, and manufacturing wealth, based in the provinces, is not an artificial product of geography but a basic dichotomy within the nineteenth-century middle class as a whole. Indeed, the elements in the dichotomy are so strong that it might be useful to examine the possibility that two middle classes existed, quite distinct not merely in sources of income but in attitudes and behaviour as well.

The chief economic distinction between the London- and provincial-based middle classes was that one was largely capital- and the other largely labour-intensive. There were, of course, commercial industries which employed vast armies of employees, from the railways to the large retail shops, but even the largest bank or mercantile house employed dozens where a factory or mine might employ thousands. Furthermore, although many employers in commerce or finance provided working conditions as bad or worse than anything in the north of England, one must agree that what sociologists of labour term 'the occupational ideology' was quite distinct in commerce and manufacturing. Even a menial clerk in the City was still a member of the middle class in some sense and enjoyed an income considerably higher than that of a skilled manual labourer. He worked fewer hours and could depend upon more fringe benefits and higher status. Indeed, while the world of industry revolved around income distinctions, that of London was concerned with status distinctions—a fact making generalizations from one to the other inappropriate.[24] The period of near-insurrection in the north, broadly from 1790 to 1845, which Foster convincingly demonstrates was most fully and radically developed in Oldham where the novel features of the industrial labour structure were most manifest[25] (and which I believe represented a failure of the new capitalist class to develop convincing authority structures), was largely missing from London, or took a different form. Conversely, there was no necessity on the part of commercial employers in London to develop such an authority structure, and there was perhaps no fundamental change in this field until women clerks replaced men after 1914.[26]

The economic distinctions between the two middle classes were not so important, however, as the social distinctions. The most important of these, perhaps, was the contrasting relationship between the two middle classes and the traditional landed society—a separate and distinct elite, which competed with them for the benefits of wealth, status and power. The London-based middle class was far closer to the old society than its provincial counterpart: indeed, a not unimportant reason for the invisibility of this class was its failure to join in and reform agitation which from Wyvill in the 1780s to the Jarrow hunger-marchers, has typically possessed a provincial base: down the years a section as well as a class has felt itself aggrieved.

Two of the more important ties between London's middle class and the old society were in religion and in education. Many of the great nineteenth-century industrialists were Anglicans, such as Arkwright, Peel, Stephenson, Cunliffe-Lister, Brassey and Armstrong, and although a very large proportion of London's wealth was foreign in origin—the numerous Jewish families of the 'Cousinhood', the Greek mercantile network of the intermarried Rallis, Schillizzis and Vlastos, Germans like Goschen and Kleinwort, or the Danish Barings—nevertheless most London-based businessmen were also Anglicans, and only a few were Protestant dissenters. The predominance of London within the British wealth structure was one of the main reasons why the dissenting portion of the non-landed wealth-holders whose religion, or ancestral religion, could be traced, amounted to under 20 per cent of the total, while a majority among virtually every cohort was Anglican.[27] The Anglicanism of London's business (and professional) class, together with its wealth, made its members far readier to send its sons to a major public school and Oxbridge, than were the manufacturers. Most of the great public schools were, of course, located in London or the Home Counties—three of the Clarendon schools were actually located in the City of London at the time of the 1859 Report—and almost all were of Anglican foundation. Bishop and Wilkinson, in their extremely detailed study of Winchester College, found that among 8,187 Wykehamists born between 1820 and 1922, the percentage of fathers engaged in commerce or finance was more than twice that of fathers engaged in manufacturing, a ratio which remained virtually constant throughout the nineteenth century.[28] Similarly, down to World War One, more than twice as many of the Wykehamists themselves entered commerce as manufacturing.

Coincident with these changing social preferences on the part of London's middle class went a parallel and equally important change of attitude towards participation in City business life on the part of landed society. The attitude of landed society towards the City had long been ambivalent. On one hand, a wealthy banker or East India Company director would seldom have found himself shut out by society and, indeed, several aristocratic families, like the Earls of Jersey, who succeeded to the ownership of Child's Bank, or the Earls of Leven and Melville, who were bankers and merchant bankers, were directly concerned in City life. Thomas Coutts (1735–1822), who left £600,000, married his daughters to a marquess, an earl and a baronet; his widow married a duke.[29] On the other hand, the underworld of the City, with its alien financiers, its swindlers and speculators, its fictional Auguste Melmottes and living Baron Grants and Jabez Balfours, found no welcome in the old aristocracy.[30] It was society's opposition to this side of City life which vanished in the late nineteenth century, as younger sons eagerly acquired directorships or seats on the Stock Exchange while their fathers agreed to lend their names to the letter-heads of new issues. As early as 1866 the *Saturday Review* concluded that 'the City is rapidly becoming another branch of that system of relief for the aristocracy which Mr. Bright denounces'.[31] In contrast, British industry possessed few such attractions for the aristocracy. Despite the fact that the pioneering industrialists were seldom bona fide 'self-made men'—many dated their families' ascendance into respectability and status from Puritan times[32]—the number of aristocrats, or even minor landed gentry, who were directly concerned with industry or manufacturing (apart from membership on boards of companies exploiting the minerals on their own land) was surely nil.

The higher status of commercial wealth mirrored an important difference between the entrepreneurial behaviour of dynasties engaged in commerce and manufacturing. Hitherto the voluminous debate on the secular decline of British entrepreneurship has focused almost exclusively on the performance of industrialists, particularly those in the mining and metal industries and in engineering, to the virtual exclusion from the discussion of businessmen engaged in commerce or finance.[33] It would, indeed, be hazardous to argue that finance and commerce in Britain, and especially the financial role of the City of London, underwent such a decline, since in the period 1870–1914, when Britain's industrial output was outstripped by her leading rivals, the City's position as world's entrepôt was at its zenith, while the transfer of much of the City's traditional role to New York after 1914 has quite clearly been an exogenous result of World War One. Those who argue that sociological factors were of primary importance in explaining the decline of British entrepreneurship—the *Buddenbrooks* phenomenon; the 'haemorrhage of talent' as industrial dynasties move into the gentry; the baneful effect of the public schools—must explain why this failed to affect Britain's commercial and financial dynasties, especially as many of the City families originated earlier than their industrial counterparts and were socially closer to the aristocracy.

The reasons for this are many, but surely at the end of the day it must be conceded that in high-prestige commercial and financial undertakings, the 'haemorrhage of talent' has largely failed to apply—families like the Rothschilds, Barings, Barclays or Smiths have never severed their connexions with business life and continue to head apparently flourishing undertakings, despite the acquisition of great wealth and high status and attendance for several generations at a public school and university. Part of the explanation for this may lie in the greater openness of the City and commerce to new men. It is a striking fact that most of the famous 'self-made men' of the past century, from Whiteley, Selfridge, Lipton, Marks and Sieff to Clore, Wolfson, Hyams and Slater were engaged in commerce and finance rather than manufacturing, and commerce may remain an area where an individual or small family unit may actually rise from humble origin to great wealth. Thus there has been a continuous refreshment of entrepreneurial life from below. But this is surely not the whole story, and a residue remains of essential differences between status groups with similar economic interests. Ironically the price which dynasties in prestigious fields like merchant banking and brewing had to pay to gain acceptability from society was far less than that required of industrialists. There is, after all, less difference between what a *rentier* or landowner does in managing his portfolio, than between a gentleman and an industrialist. The efforts of a banker or merchant require less hard work and are unquestionably more gentlemanly than the work of the 'captain of industry'. It is only among industrialists that the 'haemorrhage of talent' is alleged to occur, and one may indeed point to numerous examples of industrial dynasties which have withdrawn from business life, like the Peels, Bairds, Arkwrights, Strutts or Morleys. The excellent question posed by Professor Coleman—what does it matter to entrepreneurial performance if the entrepreneur has been to Eton?[34]—suggests the reply that it mattered far more for some types of businesses than for others. For manufacturers and industrialists the road from wealth to status was a one-way street.

Finally, it cannot be denied that there really was a dichotomy between finance and industry in Britain during the nineteenth century. The role of the City during the nineteenth century was of course largely to finance foreign and government loans, and it did not act as a capital market for British industry until the very end of the century; British industry in this period was either self-financed or financed by local banks whose directors had few City connexions. This was—and again, surely no restatement of this can be termed a novelty—of the utmost importance to Britain's economic development, and it has been a major factor in the chronic underinvestment of British industry which continues to this day; it meant that Britain, anomalously among advanced industrial countries, would see the development of what the Marxists term 'finance capital' postponed until after World War One. It was probably only in the 1930s that the British merchant banks, driven by the lack of investment opportunities abroad, revised their attitudes towards financing home investment.[35] Even by 1914 the role of the merchant banks as issuing houses was limited by the extremely patchy development of limited liability among major industrial firms in Britain.[36]

III

The main features of Victorian society have thus far been presented statistically; all the developmental aspects of this view of British social structure have been omitted. It would be incorrect to assert that the two middle classes of Victorian Britain always existed, or that they have remained unaltered in this century. The rest of this chapter will outline the salient features of a developmental view of British class structure during the past century and a half—a large order, to be sure, and one which the author is only too conscious of doing inadequately.[37]

Broadly, it would be best to divide modern British history into four main periods—approximately 1783–1832, 1832–86, 1886–1922 and 1922–60. As to the first period, we may accept that in one sense the old pre-industrial society in Britain was what Peter Laslett has termed a 'one-class society'[38]—not, obviously, in the sense of possessing no sharp differences of status, wealth or power, which would, of course, be an absurd claim, but in the sense that one status system was universally recognized throughout society with the exception, perhaps, of the urban dissenters. At its uppermost levels the desideratum of this status system was the familiar one of eighteenth-century society: wealth transformed into landed acreage, into seats and influence in Parliament and the Court, and eventually into a peerage, with marriage of one's eligible sons and daughters into an older titled family. It was the deference society of the English *ancien régime*. Yet the fact that land and landed wealth were the focal points of this society should not blind us to the realization that it was, as it were, a society with both an urban and a rural face, not in sharp distinction to one another but as part and parcel of the same society, accepting the same notions of status. As well as an upper-class society, it was also a middle-class society, though not one drawn from the modern middle classes. Rather, it was the middle class of what is often termed 'Old Corruption', the world of patronage and place of the older professionals, particularly the Law and the Church, and the older type of merchant and financier (though no less wealthy for that). This is the meaning of the extraordinarily high percentage of early wealth-holders, particularly those among the 'lesser wealthy' deceased in 1809–29, engaged in the professions, public administration and the military.[39] Men like John, first Earl of Eldon (d. 1830), the celebrated Lord Chancellor, who left £707,000 in addition to much

land, and his brother, Lord Stowell, also a judge, who left £200,000
or George, first Baron Arden (d. 1840), brother of Spencer Perceval
and Registrar of the Court of Admiralty for fifty years, who left
£700,000; the government provision contractor Sir Charles Flower
(d. 1834), worth £500,000 or the first Duke of Wellington (d. 1852),
recipient of some £600,000 from the British government for his
military services, who left £500,000 in personalty—all were as
typical of the British wealth structure at this time as Hargreaves or
Arkwright. It will be seen from Table 2.4 that the percentage
among these groups declined considerably between 1829 and 1850,
apparently, it might be noted, as a result of that rarest of all reforms,
one affecting the wealthy which really worked.[40] The main
contemporary chroniclers of Old Corruption were its opponents
William Cobbett and John Wade, author of *The Extraordinary
Black Book* and *The Black Book, or Corruption Unmasked*, and other
similar works.[41] Wade was an advocate of middle-class, not radical
reform, as many statements in *The Black Book* make clear: 'on the
middling classes the revenue laws are peculiarly oppressive', 'the
embarrassment of the commercial and manufacturing classes, the
stagnation of industry, the emigration of capital', and the like, all
unfortunate consequences of the funding system which he
attacked.[42] Yet Wade was attacking in his works not merely the
sinecures of the aristocracy but the middle-class professions and
businesses which were a part of the old society: for this section of
reformism, at any rate, the old society consisted of far more than the
landed aristocracy. Of the Law, for instance, Wade noted that:

> It is impossible to give a correct estimate of the immense sums drawn
> out of the pockets of the people by this rapacious profession . . . perhaps
> £7,600,000. . . . Such is the immense number of law books, and their
> ponderous size, that it would require the age of patriarchs to acquire a
> knowledge of them. They are literally Ossa piled on Pelion, a huge
> uniformed mass, which no man can fathom. Lord Stanhope mentions a
> little pocket compilation, *Viner's Abridgement* in twenty volumes folio,
> which is considered necessary for every lawyer almost to know by
> heart. . . . This is English law, the perfection of human wisdom! The
> people are expected to know, to worship, and to obey this great
> absurdity.[43]

Wade also has much to say about the Bank of England:

> It is not merely the Bank of England, but nearly the whole banking
> system of the country that is indebted for its origins and prosperity to

the War ... the whole system of these classes [private bankers, stockbrokers, loan-contractors, speculators] owe their origin to the Pitt system, or, to ascend a generation higher, to the Borough System.[44]

Of the political influence of these institutions, Wade was clear:

The Bank of England and the East India Company form the two strong outworks of the Government, and, by their various connections and interests, add greatly to that mass of influence by which the latter is supported.[45]

Thus, to Wade, and to his sympathetic contemporaries like Cobbett, there was a close association between the Tory government which was in power almost continuously between 1783 and 1830, and this section of the middle class. Although the bulk of the Tories' strength came from a part of landed society, it was perhaps equally reliant on the world of pensions, sinecures, and emoluments of Old Corruption, and on its associated supporters in the Bank of England, East India Company, and the like. Wade points out that the members of the Tory Cabinet serving in 1816 received collectively £124,000 p.a. from sinecures of various types—Lord Liverpool for instance obtaining about £9,600 as Constable of Dover Castle, Clerk of the Pells in Ireland, and Commissioner for the Affairs of India.[46]

The close association between the various elements in Old Corruption came under increasing attack from the time of Burke onwards and broke down in the wake of the reforms of 1832–5. The following period saw the three elites increasingly going their separate ways, as each discovered its distinctive economic role and its approach to the control of power, status and wealth. Each, as it were, became more self-sufficient. In the economic sphere a sharper differentiation of roles became apparent. The old type of capitalist, who often acted as both merchant and manufacturer, give rise to a distinctive manufacturing elite and to a distinctive commercial elite, based in different parts of the country. Landowning on a large scale ceased to be socially attractive to the new men of wealth created since the Industrial Revolution—although purchase of land in a more limited way remained socially necessary for full acceptance by society until 1914.[47] Only four business and professional millionaires deceased up to 1914 acquired landed estates of 25,000 acres or more; only six in the half-millionaire class, according to the statistics in Bateman's *Great Landowners*; more

than two-thirds of these millionaires and nearly 80 per cent of the
half-millionaires are simply unlisted in Bateman, they or their
successors owning under 3,000 acres in 1883. On the other side, the
political effects of the Industrial Revolution removed the necessity
for the landed elite to form a close alliance with the older forms of
middle-class capitalism and professionalism, as a much wealthier
variety of landowner, the Whig grandee, with rent-rolls of
£100,000 or more, replaced the Tory squire. Ironically the
Industrial Revolution fortified the wealth—and isolated position—
of such men by giving them vast mineral royalties and the proceeds
of urban ground-rents and railway-building. But direct
participation in technology or the direction of industry, in the style
of the Duke of Bridgewater (d. 1803), became an anachronism as a
new category of professional estate managers, colliery-owners and
viewers, large-scale builders, and the like, grew up: to the great
landowner, such things need no longer be visible.[48]

The industrial elite was much the weakest of the three, less
wealthy either collectively or individually, as we have seen, than the
commercial elite and vastly less influential than the landowners.
Nor, until very late in the Victorian period, was the majority of the
working population engaged in manufacturing: although the figures
are well-known, the thinness of the population in the new industrial
centres can still startle: Manchester with Salford and other outlying
districts held 235,000 people in 1831; Birmingham 144,000; a town
like Blackburn only 27,000—and not all, needless to say, were
proletarians.[49] The history of the northern working class does
present a problem because of the period of acute unrest from 1790 to
1845: whether this represented the birth-cry of a working class or
the death-pangs of an artisan class is another matter.[50] What
emerged in the later half of the nineteenth century was a kind of
deference: it would be interesting to know to what extent this was a
continuation, however tenuous, of their agricultural past:

> . . . in a large concern of old standing, where perhaps one thousand to
> two thousand persons are employed, there has grown up a strong 'esprit
> de corps' among the hands. Each individual operative comes to identify
> with the mill at which he works and if he be not troubled with
> convictions of his own, readily accepts its political shibboleths. At a
> contested election in a Lancashire borough, one may see the entire body
> of workers at two rival factories pitted against each other, like hostile
> armies.[51]

The late nineteenth-century structure of authority in the classic mill towns, Patrick Joyce assures us in his brilliant article, was 'fed by dependency and the experience of authority, though it was only marginally a product of coercive "illegitimate" influence'.[52] This may be demonstrated by the non-effect of the Ballot Act of 1872: if inside this deference politics there was a class politics waiting to get out, surely the secret ballot would have had *some* effect. But it had none. The change came only after 1918, as always, as much as anything else, from an 'abdication on the part of the governors', as the local industrial elites abandoned their old leadership positions. The change, however, was real:

> One felt the new awareness that men had brought back with them from war. Not only the poor but the working class as a whole had somehow grown far bolder and more articulate. A street discussion took progressively a more intelligent political turn; labourers were no longer grateful to their masters. At intervals ILP speakers gathered attentive audiencies—not five yards from our shop doorway where the old SDF speakers had preached in vain.[53]

London's elite, as we have seen, was rich but silent. The voices of London were not those of its commercial elite but of its reformers and intellectuals, at best tenuously connected with the business world, yet separate from the new world of poverty in the north; their writings reflect a curious lack of depth and realism about factory poverty.[54] The real problem for the City wealth-holders was finding a source of investment as lucrative as the funding system had been: the total Funded Debt charges had risen from £3,991,000 in 1776 to £28,000,000 in 1817, then levelled off at around £21,000,000 for the rest of the century.[55] That they succeeded is obvious, profiting from peace and free trade no less than from war, and far more than did the cotton-spinners.

Among the most important features of the next phase, that lasting from 1886 to 1922, was the movement of commercial wealth into the Conservative party. Although between 1832 and 1874 London's middle class was largely Liberal—as was much of the aristocracy— it returned Conservative MPs earlier, and with greater consistency, than its counterpart in the industrial areas, particularly that on Tyneside, the West Riding, and in Lancashire after the free trade split of 1903.[56] Both of the main parties drew their parliamentary contingent from among the wealthy, but Conservatives tended to recruit wealthy bankers and merchants with City connexions. By 1895 finance had replaced land as the most important single

business interest among Unionist MPs,[57] while the Liberals relied
primarily upon industrialists and manufacturers, especially those
with non-Anglican backgrounds. An important element in the
defection of the Liberal Unionists in 1886 was the movement of
commercial wealth away from the Liberal party: among the original
93 Liberal Unionist MPs were George Goschen (whose father, a
merchant banker, had left £500,000) a Rothschild, a Mildmay of
Baring Bros, a Goldsmid, a Jardine, a Morrison, and a Brown of
Brown, Shipley. By 1906, when the City's economic interests
clearly lay with free trade against tariff reform, its Conservatism was
sufficiently deep-rooted to ensure that it remained firmly
Conservative.[58] In contrast, Lancashire and the West Riding
reverted to their traditional Liberalism in the wake of tariff
reform—which was designed to benefit British manufacturing. No
middle-class seat in Manchester, Bradford, Leeds or Newcastle,
among other large towns, returned a Unionist in 1906. The heavy
reliance of post-1886 Liberalism upon industry and manufacturing,
coupled with the habit of industrial towns of returning its richest
man, and largest employer of labour, to Parliament, would cost it
dear when the industrial working class turned to socialism after
1920.[59]

The period of 1886–1922 thus saw two of the nineteenth-century
elites, those of commerce and land, associated ever more closely in
politics and in social life. The period following World War One
witnessed what was in effect the completion of this revolution, as
the manufacturing elite finally deserted the Liberal party for
Conservatism. In addition, this period witnessed a thorough change
in the economic and social structure as well, a coincident series of
events which completely transformed the way the British elite
structure stood in relation to the rest of society. First, there was the
realignment of politics along class lines for the first time, with the
emergence of a working-class party first as opposition and then as
government; and secondly, the decline of the northern industrial
elite—socially in the sense that for the first time it was fully
acceptable to the old society; politically as a cohesive group; and,
more important, in the economic sphere, as large-scale
corporations, headed by managers with few local ties, replaced the
older paternalistic type of industry. Thirdly, there took place the
collapse of the three old elites and their merger into one elite,
dominated by the south of England and finance, with its London-
based associates of great influence in twentieth-century society, like

the Civil Service and the professions—the familiar 'Establishment' of fact and fiction. It could be argued that the effectiveness of the 'Establishment' had to await both the disappearance of the provincial elite and the growth of state responsibility and power, and that this did not occur until the twentieth century.[60] Fourthly, and most important, perhaps, was the emergence of 'finance capital' in Britain for the first time, as the banks, particularly the merchant banks, began to interest themselves on a large scale in British industry. Apparently, a considerable change in the relationship of the merchant banks to British industry occurred very rapidly in the years 1929–32 as foreign investment opportunities declined.[61] One might note as well the growth of the newer type of consumer durable industry, large-scale retailers and large-scale building contractors, heavily centred in the south of England and the Midlands rather than in the north of England.[62]

This sketch returns us, no doubt by a circuitous route, to the question raised briefly at the outset and so far left unanswered—namely, the accuracy of a Marxist view of class structure and its notions of the relationship of elites to the rest of society. The evidence presented here suggests that the Marxist view largely fails, in the British case at any rate, not for the usual reason put forward against Marxism—typically, some recital of the 'managerialist' thesis—but for its failure to comprehend the complexity and diversity of the capitalist elite. Although in many of his writings Marx gave full weight to the importance of bankers and large-scale merchants as an element in the industrial bourgeoisie,[63] what can hardly be doubted is that first, Marx's view of class was too heavily drawn from Ricardo's schema, in which the three classes of landowners, capitalists and workers were distinguished by the varying way in which they took their incomes, respectively from rents, profits and wages; and secondly, in his view, the interaction of *industrial* capitalists with their employees *per necessitum* constitutes the focal point of the class struggle, and hence lends industrialism an intrinsic importance almost in a metaphysical sense. Nothing could be more explicit than Engels's view of the forces arrayed within the bourgeoisie in nineteenth-century Britain:

The Reform Bill of 1831 [*sic*] had been the victory of the whole capitalist class over the landed aristocracy. The repeal of the Corn Laws was the victory of the manufacturing capitalist not only over the landed aristocracy, but over those sections of capitalists too whose interests were more or less bound up with the landed interest—bankers, stockjobbers, fund-holders, etc. Free Trade meant the readjustment of the whole policy of England in accordance with the interests of the manufacturing capitalists—the class which now represented the nation.[64]

Yes, but surely it is a logical fallacy to infer from the central importance of industrial capitalism in the dialectical process the central importance of industrial capitalism for the bourgeoisie. The notion of the pre-eminent importance of industrialism and the Industrial Revolution has, moreover, affected our view of nineteenth-century British history totally, and in so insidious a way as to be accepted virtually without thought. A typical exposition of this view is found in G. D. H. Cole's biography of Cobbett:

> [Great Britain] became capitalist in a new sense by the rise of the factory system. . . . A new class of aristocrats—cotton-lords, coal-lords, iron-lords—grew up. . . . It has often been said that the fear caused by the French Revolution put back the Reform movement for a generation. It did more than that: it made inevitable the final alliance, between the old and new lords of land and factory, which is the basis of the English oligarchy of today.[65]

If one were to search for a more relevant and accurate Marxist tradition, one could do worse than go to the later generation of Marxists—to the schools of Hilferding's *Finanzkapital* and Lenin's *Imperialism*, which at least took into account the importance of finance capital, even if they were too ready to assume that Britain's evolution neatly dove-tailed with that of other advanced countries, which it did not. However, their work, one might argue, has until very recently seldom entered into the mainstream of British Marxist historiography nor, manifestly, into the way in which historians, whatever their politics, have viewed British society. Since the concept of finance capital would be difficult to apply to Britain until after 1918, this is perhaps no bad thing. In so many ways Britain is an anomalous country: the first with a bourgeois revolution, the last with an aristocracy; the earliest with a modern working class, yet manifesting the least working-class consciousness; the earliest with industrialization, yet the last among the advanced countries to witness a merger of finance and industry, and so on. Britain is always an exceptional case, and too often its being first has been confused with its being the norm. Marx himself would, one suspects, have been better employed in the Library of Congress than in the British Museum.[66]

NOTES

1. Pitirim Sorokin, 'American Millionaires and Multi-Millionaires', *Social Forces*, III (1924–5), p. 627.
2. On Britain, however, see Wedgwood, *The Economics of Inheritance, op. cit.* and C. D. Harbury, 'Inheritance and the Distribution of Personal Wealth in Britain', *Economic Journal*, LXXIII (1962), pp. 845–68.
3. The total number of individual wealth-holders in this study was:

	1809–58	*1858–79*	*1880–99*	*1900–14*	*Total*
Millionaires	12	34	69	89	204
Half-Millionaires	62	120	177	206	565

	1809–29	*1850–69*	
Less Wealthy	192	186	378

The Principal Probate Registry replaced the old ecclesiastical courts from 9 Jan. 1858; the division in 1858 occurs at that date. The wealth-holders deceased 1915–39 are not brought into this discussion.
4. Except that from 1926 onwards settled land is entered separately. The inventory of the estate, detailing, for example, the stocks and bonds held by the deceased, may be seen by researchers in the case of estates proved in Scotland but not, however, in England and Wales. Settled land was not included in the Scottish valuation figures until 1964.
5. *Return for 1872–3 . . .* [of Every Owner of Land in England and Wales], Parliamentary Papers (hereafter PP), 1874 [c.1097], LXXII, Pts. 1–2; *Return for 1872–3 . . . of Every Owner of Land . . .* [in Scotland], PP, 1874 [c.899], LXXII, Pts. 1–2; *Return of Owners of Land . . . in Ireland*, PP, 1876 [c.1492], LXXX; John Bateman, *The Great Landowners of Great Britain and Ireland*, (4th edn, London, 1883; repr. Leicester, 1971).
6. W. D. Rubinstein and D. H. Duman, 'The Probate Valuations as a Tool of the Historian', *Local Historian*, XI (1974), p. 69. I systematically went through the Canterbury and York Prerogative court records as well as those of the Episcopal Consistory court of Chester and other Lancashire court records held at the Lancashire Record Office. On various aspects of this complicated subject, see especially Camp, *Wills and Their Whereabouts, op. cit.*, Wedgwood, *The Economics*; *op. cit.*, esp. Ch. 6; Harbury, *loc. cit.*
7 Among the most important methodological problems involved in identifying personal wealth-holding with estates left at death are those of gifts *inter vivos* or estate duty avoidance, and the question of the comparability of limited liability companies with private partnerships in ascertaining valuation. These are both very complicated matters, to which this note cannot do justice. During the nineteenth century, rates of estate duty were minimal (contrary to popular belief, estate duty originated in 1694, not as a result of the Harcourt duties of 1894), and it is unlikely that substantial amounts of duty avoidance occurred until this century. Even if *inter vivos* giving occurred widely, there is no *a priori* reason to suppose that it is any other than randomly distributed

among the different types of wealth-holders, who each have equally
weighty motives to avoid estate duties. Thus, in a study of this kind,
where one is attempting to infer the percentage of, for example, bankers
or Londoners, the actual and recorded percentages should not be
greatly different, given a sample of sufficient size.

8. Central Statistical Office, *Standard Industrial Classification* (London,
   HMSO 1958). There proved to be little difficulty in assigning each
   wealth-holder to an occupational category. In only a handful of cases
   was there any ambiguity. Each wealth-holder was assigned to the trade
   in which he appeared to have possessed the larger interest, based on
   biographical evidence. Descendants of businessmen who were
   themselves *rentiers* were assigned to the category in which the family
   fortune had originally been made. The relative lack of overlap in
   business interests among British businessmen sharply distinguished
   them from, for example, Americans or Australians, among whom a
   wide spread of business interests, as evidenced by directorships, is far
   more common. From 1880 it is possible to trace most British
   directorships from T. Skinner, *The Directory of Directors, 1880. A List
   of the Directors of the Joint Stock Companies of the United Kingdom*
   (London, 1880), and subsequent annual editions to 1914. It was
   extremely uncommon for a British wealth-holder to hold more than
   eight directorships, and most held no more than three. Those holding
   numerous directorships were mainly concerned either in subsidiaries
   of their main company, or in local firms actively seeking (or compelled
   to take) the services of a local notable, and seldom if ever in firms of
   national size.

9. In the 'Manufacturing' category are Orders II, IV-XIV, and XVI-
   XVIII, with the paper manufacturers among Order XV (Paper,
   Publishing); 'Food, Drink and Tobacco' is identical with Order III;
   the 'Commercial' group consists of Orders XIX-XXI; 'Professionals,
   Public Administration and Defence' contains Orders XXII and
   XXIV, as well as Order XXIII, and newspaper proprietors and
   publishers among Order XV: Central Statistical Office, *Standard
   Industrial Classification, passim.*

   A number of miscellaneous and unknown individuals remain
   unclassified; two among the millionaires, 12 among the half-
   millionaires and, unfortunately, no fewer than 42 among the 'lesser
   wealthy' cohorts. To judge by their addresses the bulk of these were
   almost certainly London merchants.

10. These figures have been calculated only for millionaires and half-
    millionaires. They exclude a certain number of landowners holding
    valuable London properties (London was excluded from the
    parliamentary survey on which Bateman's *Great Landowners* was
    based).

11. The gross assessments arising under Schedule A of the income tax, the
    tax on landowners' rentals, was £91,900,000 in 1851; that under
    Schedule D (profits of trades and the professions) was then
    £65,700,000. Schedule A was concentrated in the hands of a few
    thousand landowners; Schedule D fell on incomes down to £150 p.a.

Mitchell and Deane, *Abstract of British Historical Statistics, op. cit.*, p. 430.

12. John Foster, *Class Struggle, op. cit.*, pp. 161ff.

13. The surprisingly small valuation of cotton and other factories for insurance purposes is well known. See Stanley D. Chapman, *The Early Factory Masters* (Newton Abbot, 1967), pp. 125–45. R. S. Neale has pointed out that the expense of building the town of Bath during the eighteenth century was 'roughly equivalent to the fixed capital invested in the cotton industry by the end of the eighteenth century': R. S. Neale, ' "The Bourgeoisie, Historically, has Played a Most Revolutionary Part" ', in Eugene Kamenka and R. S. Neale (eds), *Feudalism, Capitalism and Beyond* (London, 1975), p. 93.

14. The venues of half-millionaires and the 'lesser wealthy' groups are not included here; full tables for these may be found in Chapter 2. The geographical distribution of these groups, particularly the earlier (1809–29) cohort of 'lesser wealthy', is more *favourable* to London than that of the millionaires, with 59 wealth-holders in the City and 33 from other London venues, compared with only six in Greater Manchester and two in Merseyside of a total of 123 of the 1809–29 group whose venue could be traced.

15. Baron de Stern (he was created a Baron of Portugal in 1864), one of 12 children of a Jewish banker in Frankfurt, founded the London branch of the family banking business in 1848 with his brothers David (d. 1872), later Viscount de Stern, who left £1 million, and James (d. 1901), who left £1,114,000. David was the father of Sydney James Stern (d. 1912), a Liberal MP who was created Baron Wandsworth in 1895 and left £1,556,000, and of Sir Edward, 1st Bt (d. 1933), who left £555,000; Herman was the father of Herbert (d. 1919), created Baron Michelham in 1905, who left £2 million. This might be seen in its proper perspective if it is realized that George Stephenson (d. 1848), the great locomotive builder, left £140,000.

16. Foster, *Class Struggle, op. cit.*, pp. 74–84.

17. For a fuller discussion of provincial wealth, see Chapter 2.

18. A full list of millionaire estates may be found in my article, 'British Millionaires, 1809–1949', *Bulletin Inst. Hist. Research*, XLVIII (1974), pp. 202–23. The richest landowners, it is worth repeating, are not included among these unless they left personalty (or, from 1898, unsettled realty) at this level; five foreigners (including the South Africans Barney Barnato, Werhner and Beit, and the Canadian Lord Strathcona), as well as two women, left British fortunes at this level. Ten of these fortunes were in excess of £3 million.

19. Income tax was levied from 1798–1815 and again from 1842. The system of schedules in force after 1803 prevents any knowledge of the number of individuals paying income tax, or the size of individual incomes, until the coming of the super-tax under Asquith. A single individual would have been assessed under several or all of the five schedules if he received sufficient income from the requisite sources. The five schedules comprised: A, taxing the profits arising from the ownership of lands, houses and other realty; B, taxing 'the occupiers [of

land] on the profits made by the occupier . . . from husbandry', i.e., farmers; C, taxing profits arising from government securities and funds; D, taxing profits arising from business and the professions, as well as profits not taxed elsewhere; and E, taxing the salaries of public officials and employees of any public corporation, including limited liability companies.

Three important points to be kept in mind in using the income tax returns: 'individuals' included firms and businesses, and the total number of 'individuals' taxed is thus (entirely apart from the fact that one man might appear under several schedules) not the number of persons taxed; until 1867–8 profits arising from mines, quarries, ironworks, gasworks, waterworks, canals, docks, railways, market and fair sites, tolls, etc., were anomalously assessed under Schedule A rather than D (this is adjusted for in note 11 above); and because of the growth of limited liability, there is a constant drift of assessed income from Schedule D to E in the late nineteenth century.

The authoritative guide to the Victorian income tax, and one of the most astonishing works ever published on modern British economic history, is Josiah C. Stamp's *British Incomes and Property, op. cit.* On the first income tax, see Hope-Jones's very useful *Income Tax in the Napoleonic Wars, op. cit.* There is an ingenious attempt to calculate the number of individual taxpayers in the early twentieth century in L. G. Chiozza Money, *Riches and Poverty, 1910* (London, 1911), esp. Ch. 3.

20. At the Public Record Office (PRO) may be found: (1) the records of defaulters, county and half-county assessments, which were sent to the King's Remembrancer in 1798–1815; these are in hundreds of sacks, and are difficult to use: PRO, E.182; (2) the manuscript books containing the details of number, size and venue of assessment by schedule from 1845–6—1847–8 up to 1911–12: PRO, I.R.16; and (3) returns by *parish* for 1857, 1864, 1874, and every tenth year thereafter up to 1904: PRO, I.R.2. Among the most valuable returns to be found in the Parliamentary Papers are: (1) a breakdown of Schedule D by county for 1812: *Account of Duty Arising from Profits* (PP, 1814–15) X (238, 249, 250, 251); and (2) details of the gross value of property assessed under Schedules A and B, and the net amount of profits assessed under Schedule D in 1859–60 in every *parish* in Great Britain, moreover distinguishing individually the income arising from railways, mines, quarries, etc., which were anomalously assessed under Schedule A until 1867–8: *Property and Income Tax*, (PP, 1860 (546), XXXIX, Pt. II). Several other returns detail Schedule A figures by parish at other dates.

21. *Parliamentary Constituencies (Population)* (PP, 1882 (149), LII).

22. At an earlier time London's lead was greater still, as might be expected. In 1812, for instance, of a United Kingdom total of £34,384,000 assessed under Schedule D, some £13,349,000 (38.8 per cent of the national total) was assessed in London, Westminster or Middlesex; in addition, £3,883,000 (11.3 per cent of the total) was assessed in the Home Counties of Essex, Kent and Surrey, and clearly largely represented London businessmen resident there or industries well

within London's future municipal boundaries. In contrast, only £4,046,000 (11.8 per cent of the national total) was assessed in the six counties of Lancashire, Yorkshire, Warwickshire, Staffordshire, Northumberland and Glamorgan. *Account of Duty Arising from Profits* (PP, 1814–15 (251), X).

23. In 1879–80 the number of individual units assessed for taxation under Schedule D, by range of income and relevant county or local origin, was as follows (*Source*: PRO, I.R.16, 51):

	£5–10,000	£10–50,000	Over £50,000
Lancashire (total for county)	281	168	8
Liverpool	129	69	2
Manchester	94	61	3
Yorkshire	127	52	5
Warwickshire and Staffordshire together	57	30	2
Total Metropolis (Metropolitan Middlesex plus London)	783	385	42
City of London alone	373	232	25

It should be kept in mind that these figures refer to individual tax-paying units, not to persons, and that the substantial London income assessed under Schedule E, etc., is excluded.

By comparison, the number of units assessed for taxation under Schedule E (which included, besides limited liability companies, public corporations of all kinds—for instance, the Inns of Court, colleges, churches, etc.) was as follows (Source: PRO, I.R.16, 51):

	£5–10,000	£10–50,000	Over £50,000
Lancashire (total for county)	46	48	19
Liverpool	17	21	11
Manchester	9	14	6
Yorkshire	12	33	5
Warwickshire and Staffordshire together	7	21	2
Total Metropolis (Metropolitan Middlesex plus London)	87	151	64
City of London alone	58	120	60

24. For example, Dickens, who was of course writing about London and *not* the north—his one venture into industrial territory, in *Hard Times*, excepted—can be misunderstood unless this distinction is clear. See the perceptive essay on 'Charles Dickens' by George Orwell, in *The Collected Essays, Journalism and Letters of George Orwell*, ed. Sonia Orwell and Ian Angus, 4 Vols (Harmondsworth, 1968–70 edn.), Vol. I, esp. pp. 469, 487. 'In nearly all of his books one has a curious feeling that one is living in the first quarter of the nineteenth century': *ibid.*, p. 487. Orwell means Regency London, of course, not the world of Peterloo.

25. Foster, *Class Struggle, op. cit.* esp. Chs. 3–4.

26. On the *sui generis* nature of poverty in London, see Gareth Stedman

Jones, *Outcast London: A Study in the Relationship between Classes in Victorian Society* (London, 1973).

27. Thus the dissenting portion among the wealth-holders amounted to almost precisely the same percentage as their apparent proportion in the 1851 Religious Census: a random result. The entire question of the 'WeberThesis' and its application to modern British entrepreneurial performance is overripe, in my opinion, for a critical re-examination. The high percentage of non-landed Anglican wealth-holders is particularly striking in that the ladders of opportunity for bright but poor Anglican boys led invariably, by way of the remaining scholarships to public and grammar schools and universities, into professional and governmental fields, into the Church, Civil Service, teaching, imperial and military service and the like, rather than into business life.

28. Bishop and Wilkinson, *Winchester and the Public School Elite, op. cit.*, Table 5, pp. 104–8.

29. Entry for 'Duke of St. Albans': *Complete Peerage*, Vol. XI (1949), pp. 292–3; entry for 'Thomas Coutts': *Dictionary of National Biography*, Vol. IV, p. 1,279.

30. Macaulay attended a party given by the Rothschilds in the early 1830s: 'I did not see one peer, or even one star, except a foreign order or two, which I generally consider as an intimation to look to my pockets': G. O. Trevelyan, *The Life and Letters of Lord Macaulay* (London, 1881 edn.), p. 160. By 1891, when the teenage Winston Churchill faced the possibility of failing his army examination, Lord Randolph Churchill thought a City career an attractive alternative: 'I could get him something very good either thro' Natty [Rothschild] or Horace [Farquharson (*sic*)] or Cassel': Randolph S. Churchill, *Winston S. Churchill*, Vol. I, *Youth, 1874–1900* (London, 1966), p. 182. Winston Churchill's little-known younger brother John (1880–1947) was a stockbroker.

31. *Saturday Review*, 5 May 1866. I owe these quotations to Professor David Spring, to whom I am greatly indebted.

32. Harold Perkin, *The Origins of Modern English Society* (London, 1969), pp. 225–6; Foster, *Class Struggle, op. cit.*, pp. 177ff.

33. P. L. Payne, *British Entrepreneurship in the Nineteenth Century* (London, 1974), contains a critical summary of the debate, with a full bibliography.

34. D. C. Coleman, 'Gentlemen and Players', *Economic History Review*, 2nd ser., XXVI (1973), pp. 109ff.

35. Clarke, *The City in the World Economy, op. cit.*, p. 129.

36. P. L. Payne, 'The Emergence of the Large-Scale Company in Britain', *Economic History Review*, 2nd ser. XX (1967), pp. 519–42.

37. Because, one imagines, of the famous empiricist tradition and (perhaps) because of the dichotomy at the university level between economic and political history, there have been curiously few efforts to explain the whole development of modern British social structure in novel terms. The chief exceptions known to me are Harold Perkin's *Origins of Modern British Society* and, in a much more limited way, the

essays of R. S. Neale, collected as *Class and Ideology in the Nineteenth Century* (London, 1972), and Perry Anderson's essay, 'The Origins of the Present Crisis', in P. Anderson and R. Blackburn (eds), *Towards Socialism* (London 1966). Each of these works, though not without their separate excellences, ultimately accepts what might be termed the 'geological metaphor'—the primary importance of three (or more) horizontal classes following the Industrial Revolution. This, I think, is the essential distinction between the view of the development of British class structure presented here and the other views. In the nineteenth century the geographical/occupational paradigms were the primary reference groups; these cut vertically instead of horizontally; 'class' in the Marxist sense was not salient until after 1918.

38. Peter Laslett, *The World We Have Lost* (London, 1965), pp. 22ff. Laslett himself states that in pre-industrial England 'there were a large number of status groups but only one body of persons capable of concerted action over the whole area of society . . .': *ibid.*, p. 22.

39. See Table 3.1. A great many of those engaged in commerce had at least some connection with the East India Company, the Bank of England (as director), or as a government contractor.

40. So far as I am aware, the decline of 'Old Corruption' awaits serious historical study. Those whose conception of the 'Age of Reform' omits this important element in reform agitation seriously distort its dimensions. A fairly typical example of a recent general work on reform agitation, J. T. Ward, *Popular Movements, c. 1830–1850* (London, 1970), fails altogether to mention 'economical reform' amid other chapters on Chartism, parliamentary reform, the Factory Acts, etc.—this is par for the course. A full account of Old Corruption and its decline would certainly address the following questions: (1) To what extent was Old Corruption a continuation of court and political patronage, the time-honoured pattern of the seventeenth century, and to what extent a novel outgrowth of the expansion of the system at the time of the French wars? (2) How true was it to say that the Tories were beneficiaries of sinecures and place money, while the Whigs were not— a point continuously made by Whig reformers? (3) To what extent is Old Corruption at the national level to be linked with the old closed borough system at the local level? What economic and social forces did the Tory and largely Anglican hierarchies in the pre-1835 chartered towns represent? What became of them in the new order? (4) What took the place of Old Corruption? What became of the sons, distant relatives and hangers-on of the Tory aristocracy who were unable, after the 1830s, to succeed to pensions and sinecures? Service in the Empire? In the City? Genteel poverty?

41. [John Wade], *The Black Book: or, Corruption Unmasked* (London, 1820); [John Wade], *The Extraordinary Black Book* . . . (London, 1831); see also 'A Commoner', *A List of the Principal Places, Pensions and Sinecures held under the British Government, Extracted from the Extraordinary Red Book* (Newcastle-upon-Tyne, 1817). One is bound to record that Wade, who lived until 1875, ended his days as the recipient of a Civil List pension, awarded by Lord Palmerston. *The*

Black Book, etc., were all published anonymously.

42. *The Black Book: or, Corruption Unmasked,* pp. 210, 447.
43. *Ibid.,* p. 206.
44. *Ibid.,* pp. 240ff.
45. *Ibid.,* p. 344.
46. *Ibid.,* p. 22.
47. F. M. L. Thompson, *English Landed Society in the Nineteenth Century* (London, 1963), esp. pp. 60–1, 292–326.
48. *Ibid.,* esp. Chs. 6 and 9; David Spring, *The English Landed Estate in the Nineteenth Century: Its Administration* (Baltimore, 1963); J. T. Ward and R. G. Wilson, *Land and Industry* (Newton Abbot, 1971), esp. Chs. 1–2. It is frequently pointed out that landowners were the first proprietors in Britain to employ managers. So far as my statistics indicate, no great landowner drew the *majority* of his income from non-landed sources in 1883.
49. Mitchell and Deane, *Abstract, op. cit.,* pp. 24ff.
50. One way that this was accomplished was political: at the local level there was a substantial narrowing of access points to power, by a decrease in the number of local offices and elections, and by a tidying-up and narrowing of the local franchise after about 1844. '[F]rom at least 1844–59 any search for the location of power is unlikely to have to go beyond the ranks of property owners': John Garrard, *Leaders and Politics in Nineteenth Century Salford: A Historical Analysis of Urban Political Power* (Univ. of Salford, research ser. monograph, Salford City Politics, Salford, 1976), p. 62.
51. W. A. Abram, 'Social Conditions and Political Prospects of the Lancashire Workman', *Fortnightly Review,* new ser. XXII (Oct. 1868), p. 437; quoted in Patrick Joyce, 'The Factory Politics of Lancashire in the Later Nineteenth Century', *Historical Journal,* XVIII (1975), pp. 525–53, at p. 526.
52. *Ibid.,* p. 527.
53. Robert Roberts, *The Classic Slum: Salford Life in the First Quarter of the Century* (London, 1973), p. 228. On the insignificance of the Labour party prior to 1914, see Roy Douglas, 'Labour in Decline', in Kenneth D. Brown (ed.), *Essays in Anti-Labour History* (London, 1974), pp. 104–25. Needless to say, there were other reasons for this change, most importantly the increase in the working-class vote after 1918.
54. The City of London failed to develop a distinctive ideology or continuing viewpoint, in contrast to 'Manchester Liberalism'. See S. G. Checkland, 'The Mind of the City, 1870–1914', *Oxford Economic Papers,* IX (1957), pp. 261–78. The problem of professionals and intellectuals is one of the most difficult of all those facing the analyst of class structure. It is the gammy leg of class theory. Marx was notoriously unable to deal successfully with them; modern writers, like Harold Perkin in his *Origins of Modern British Society,* esp. pp. 252–70, are more ingenious but not, I think, ultimately satisfying. Intellectuals are not an independent 'class'—they may be members of any other class; they may be spokesmen for any or every interest.

Professionals are servants; they are the servants of their fee-payers and, in this sense, are *hors concours* in the class war. Yet they also, needless to say, acquire an independent existence with a life and ethos of their own. In so far as the incorporated professionals may be assigned anywhere, it is invariably with the most conservative elements in society, to the pre-industrial urban elite or even to the aristocracy. This is obviously so with the Church and the bar, and no less true of medicine, civil engineering or accountancy—in Britain at any rate. The process of incorporation, acquisition of an expensive and palatial headquarters in central London, establishment of an apprenticeship system, limitations on entries, and scheduling of fees, are all manifestly designed to 'gentrify' the profession and make it acceptable to society. This aspect of professionalization is profoundly anti-capitalist, and hence at odds with much of the rest of nineteenth-century British society. Nor is it true that professional rewards have increased: there has been a steady decline in the probate valuations of many top professionals from roughly 1840 in the case of the older professions, and from about 1900 among the newer ones. The enormous wealth of the bishops and judges of Old Corruption is well-known, but the process has also occurred among, for example, civil engineers. Of the 16 presidents of the Institution of Civil Engineers serving in the period 1880–99, one (Lord Armstrong) left £1 million, and six others left £100,000 or more; the average probate valuation (omitting Lord Armstrong) was over £95,000. Of the ten presidents of this institution serving in 1950–69 who are deceased, the average valuation is under £50,000 (in real terms worth one-fifth or less of the earlier group), with only one estate exceeding £100,000. This pattern is similar to that of the other leading professions.

55. Mitchell and Deane, *Abstract, op. cit.*, pp. 390–1, 396–7.
56. Henry Pelling, *Social Geography of British Elections, 1885–1910* (London, 1967); J. Vincent and M. Stenton (eds), *McCalmont's Parliamentary Poll Book, 1832–1918* (Brighton, 1971).
57. J. A. Thomas, *The House of Commons, 1832–1901, op. cit.*, p. 25.
58. Richard A. Rempel, *Unionists Divided* (Newton Abbot, 1972), esp. Ch. 6. *Vide* the remarks of Andrew Glyn and Bob Sutcliffe, who perceptively notice 'the rivalry of finance and industry' in their *British Capitalism, op. cit.*, p. 41: 'At times finance has preferred free trade (because it coexisted with the free movement of capital) when protection would have been beneficial for industry. This was certainly true in the years between 1880 and 1913 . . .': *ibid.* Note also the remark of the well-known Marxist economist Michael Barratt Brown: 'What defeated Chamberlain in the last analysis was the City of London, which still dominated the British economy, and whose wealth did not derive any longer [!] from manufacturing at the time of the first decade of the twentieth century': Brown, *After Imperialism, op. cit.*, p. 106. The behaviour of the City and other commercial groups when the Chamberlainite programme was mooted is exceedingly interesting: it is surely an example of status rising above economic interests, and the radical commentary cited here is historically incorrect. Although much

free trade sentiment came from the City, this did *not* defeat tariff reform (which *had* captured the Tory party, at least in a sense, after 1904); it was its rejection by the Liberals and nonconformists (based in industrial areas or reliant upon heavy industry) which did so. Would that the past was always easy to read.

59. On Lancashire, see P. F. Clarke, *Lancashire and the New Liberalism* (Cambridge, 1971), and Pelling, *Social Geography, op. cit., passim*.

60. On the role of the state in modern Britain, see, for example, Ralph Miliband, *The State in Capitalist Society* (London, 1973). On the career patterns of civil servants, nothing has improved on H. E. Dale, *The Higher Civil Service of Great Britain* (Oxford, 1941), esp. pp. 42ff. Dale points out, profoundly, that public school education is not *prima facie* evidence of wealth—quite the opposite is true of the social origins of higher civil servants.

61. Clarke, *The City in the World Economy, op. cit.*, Ch. 8.

62. As Stedman Jones has pointed out, labour relations among this element of the new working class remain neglected by historians: Gareth Stedman Jones, 'History in One Dimension', *New Left Review*, XXXVI (1966), pp. 50ff.

63. For example, Karl Marx and Frederick Engels, *The Eighteenth Brumaire of Louis Bonaparte*, Ch. 6, in Marx and Engels, *Selected Works, op. cit.*, p. 157. On a theoretical level and late in his life, Marx postulated 'the separation of money-capitalists and industrial-capitalists', in the context of the differing necessity of the two to charge interest: Marx, *Capital*, 3 Vols. (English trans., Moscow, 1959), Vol. III, p. 370. These were 'as persons playing entirely different roles in the reproductive process': *ibid.*, p. 375. But almost everywhere else in his writings he assumes the essential unity of the bourgeoisie. There are numerous examples in Ralf Dahrendorf, *Class and Class Conflict in Industrial Society* (London, 1959), pp. 9–18.

64. Frederick Engels, 'England in 1845 and 1855', *London Commonweal*, 7 March 1885, cited in the 'Preface to the English Edition of the 1892 Edition', of his *The Condition of the Working Class in England* (London, 1969), p. 28.

65. Cole, *William Cobbett, op. cit.*, p. 4.

66. 'Intrinsically, it is not a question of the higher or lower degree of development of the social antagonism that results from the natural laws of capitalist production. It is a question of these laws themselves, of these tendencies working with iron necessity towards inevitable results. The country that is more developed industrially only shows, to the less developed, the image of its own future': Karl Marx, 'Preface to the First German Edition of the First Volume of *Capital*', in Marx and Engels, *Selected Works*, p. 228.

4

The Geographical Distribution of Middle-class Income in Britain, 1800–1914*

I

In two articles originally published in 1977—which are reprinted as Chapters 1 and 2 of this volume—attention was drawn to the seeming fact that the wealthiest businessmen of Edwardian Britain were disproportionately to be found in London rather than in the northern industrial towns.[1] The bulk of the data on which this conclusion was based was drawn from the probate records of individual wealth left at death by the largest wealth-holders deceased in Britain between 1809 and 1939, and from an analysis of their individual biographies and careers. It was also suggested in a very preliminary way that evidence also existed in the surviving income-tax data for the nineteenth century which pointed to precisely the same general conclusion, that middle-class business and professional incomes are earned disproportionately in London rather than in the northern industrial areas, and (as is the case among wealth-holders) disproportionately within the largely industrial area of the north and Celtic Britain, in commercial towns such as Liverpool rather than in manufacturing towns like Manchester.

Much of the confidence I held then, and still retain, in this conclusion stemmed from the fact that the two separate types of

* An earlier version of this chapter was read at the Modern British History Seminar at Cambridge University in October 1984. I am most grateful for the comments and suggestions I received on that occasion. The research for this paper was sponsored by a grant from the Australian Research Grants Council in 1982. My research assistant, Mrs Rosemary Nixon, carried out laborious work of copying out the extremely detailed statistics from the manuscript returns of I.R.16 at the Public Record Office, Kew, in an exemplary fashion.

statistical evidence from which this conclusion was inferred—the
probate statistics of wealth at death and the income-tax statistics of
middle-class   taxpayers—are   absolutely   distinct,   measuring
different but complementary and obviously related tests of affluence
compiled by different branches of the government at differing times
for differing purposes. Each set of data has certain advantages and
disadvantages to the economic and social historian. The probate
data possesses the all-important advantage of allowing the historian
to name and identify the wealthiest businessman (or anyone else
leaving wealth at death), as well as the size of his fortune at death,
enabling   a   good   many   conclusions   to   be   drawn   about
entrepreneurship, social mobility, the connexion between religion
and business success, inheritance patterns and many other similar
questions in something like a precise rather than an anecdotal
fashion. There are also disadvantages to the historian's use of the
probate records, as no one denies. To research the careers of more
than a handful of the wealthiest millionaires entails an enormous
research agenda and implies substantial funding for its success,
while the probate records of course measure only wealth left at
death, with all the considerations obvious in the use of this data for
this purpose: those who make and lose a fortune are excluded, there
may be substantial *inter vivos* giving for estate duty avoidance or
other purposes, while the probate statistics are highly age-specific
to the elderly and, among other things, may measure social or
enterpreneurial patterns and opportunities which existed many
decades before.

The advantages of employing income tax statistics to cast light on
these questions is also clear. The income tax was assessed on all
middle- and upper-class incomes and was levied in such a way that
the types of incomes earned—whether obtained from landed
rentals, farming, business or professional life—may be gauged in at
least a very general way. Income tax was, obviously, levied
annually, and for a very long period of time—from 1798 to 1815 and
again from 1842 onward. Because of the existence of the manuscript
sources which are examined in this paper, the geographical
distribution of middle-class incomes can be measured and
analyzed.

The disadvantages of the income tax for illuminating the nature
of the Victorian middle classes are also significant and are, in a
sense, the opposite side of the coin of the probate data. The statistics
are anonymous. No individual income-tax returns from the pre-

1914 period survive in any systematic way,[2] and it is impossible to learn how much income a particular man or company earned in a particular year. More crucially, it is impossible to learn the individual income of any particular *person*, for two important reasons. First, income tax was assessed using a series of five schedules according to the type of income earned—rents, farm incomes, profits of companies and so on—rather than assessed upon the whole of an individual's annual income. Secondly, both individual persons and companies or corporations, including non-business corporations such as Oxford colleges, were counted as 'individuals' in the eyes of the Inland Revenue and its predecessors. Even in the confidential and internal manuscript records which form the basis of the evidence presented in this chapter it is seemingly impossible to ascertain how many individual persons were liable to income tax for nearly all of the period surveyed here. Only at the very beginning of the first income tax, between 1798 and 1802, do some national figures survive, and again only after 1911, in the wake of Lloyd George's super-tax legislation of 1909, is it once more possible to ascertain the number of individual taxpayers with very high incomes.[3] Between these two periods, with one partial exception (referred to in Chapter 1) no statistics whatever exist, and this must surely make the data less valuable than the historian would obviously desire.

Nevertheless, the very considerable value of the surviving income-tax data for the economic and social historian of modern Britain is to be found at a very basic level indeed and is very wide indeed, and in this chapter one facet of this will be explored, namely, the geographical distribution of middle-class incomes. As noted, I have previously drawn attention to the great importance of the distinction between London, with its largely commercial and financial middle class, and the northern cities, with their largely industrial and manufacturing base. It was further suggested that London and the commercial and financial middle classes and their very wealthy were more important and consistently successful economically than the north and the industrial middle class, and that this division was of considerable importance to our understanding of the development of modern British society. However, nothing could be offered in the way of comprehensive evidence for the whole of the middle classes below the tiny class of millionaires. It is this comprehensive evidence which is offered and analyzed here, in the form of a detailed examination of the

geographical distribution of the business and professional portions
of the income tax normally at five-year intervals between 1806 and
1911–12. The relevant surviving evidence, I.R. (for 'Inland
Revenue') 16, since the early 1970s deposited at the Public Record
Office (and now at Kew), consists of the enormous manuscript
books, generally three for each year, detailing the county, and often
sub-county, totals of the assessments made under each Schedule of
the income tax, between the reinstitution of the income tax in 1842
and the last such volume to be declassified, that of 1911–12. The
series is immensely and extremely detailed, varying in its precise
and small-scale categories (though not in its major ones) without
explanation, and contains much other information not employed
here, for example the taxes paid under each Schedule of the income
tax as well as the amount of tax assessed. The primary concern of
nearly all of the manuscript tables in I.R.16 is to detail the
geographical distribution of the income tax in a variety of ways, and
it is in its important evidence about the subject analyzed here that
the great value of the series lies.[4] Additionally, for the first income
tax, that levied between 1798 and 1815, there are numerous printed
summaries of the geographical distribution of the tax in the
Parliamentary Papers, enabling us to compensate for the lack of a
usable manuscript source like I.R.16 for the earlier period.[5] In
particular, printed returns exist for most years detailing the
individual county assessments and payments under each Schedule
of the income tax, with the London area divided into the City of
London, Middlesex, and Westminster. These printed sources do
not, however, detail the assessments of provincial cities, while
Scotland is treated as a whole, and it would seem that no Scottish
county figures were printed.[6]

It is important to reiterate that the income tax was levied only on
what might fairly be termed the incomes of the middle and upper
classes, and probably entirely excluded the working classes
throughout the whole period these taxes were levied, with the
possible exception of the period 1853–76 when the limit for liability
for the tax was lowered from £150 p.a. to £100 p.a. and again prior
to World War One, when some skilled workmen might have earned
more than the £160 exemption limit. No one with an annual income
of less than £50 or £60 between 1798 and 1815, and £150–£160 for
most of the period from 1842 until the inter-war period, was liable
to pay income tax.[7] It is possible that these lower limits affect the
data when they were lowered still further to £100 between 1853 and

1876, but the conclusions to be drawn from it throughout this chapter are those for the middle classes only. The geographical distribution suggested here would thus, presumably, differ markedly from a similar analysis of a national income (or of the distribution of the population as a whole from the census) which includes working-class incomes. A comparison of the two would be quite interesting; this would seemingly require an enormous and perhaps impossible research effort as there are no comparable geographical statistics relating to working-class incomes, and a comparison of middle-class income distribution with the geographical distribution of the whole population would probably have to suffice.

As well, during the nineteenth century several returns were printed in the Parliamentary Papers, and these provided an extremely detailed geographical breakdown of the income tax, in one case for every parish in the United Kingdom for Schedules A, B and D in 1859–60, and in another for Schedules A, B, D and E for each parliamentary constituency as they existed in 1879–80.[8] Regrettably, however, neither of these sources is as inclusive for our purposes as the manuscript returns I.R.16, since both exclude the assessments made under a relevant schedule: in the former, Schedule E, the tax on the incomes of corporations and employees of corporations, and in the latter the business portions of Schedule A. (Table 4.1 includes the 1879–80 return for comparison purposes.)

Lord Palmerston noted of the Schleswig-Holstein situation of the 1860s that only three men in Europe understood it, one of whom was dead, one of whom was insane, while he, the third, had forgotten all about it, and the intricacies of the nineteenth-century income tax undeniably bear a resemblance to the Schleswig-Holstein crisis. To be sure, a number of excellent guides to the income tax do exist, especially Arthur Hope-Jones' *Income Tax in the Napoleonic Wars* and Josiah Stamp's *British Incomes and Property*, but the details of the tax are often so bewildering and complex, and the surviving historical evidence so often given in a generalized manner, without the complete explanation as to its precise meaning for the questions asked here, that it is surely extremely easy for any historian to lose his way rather quickly. I do not believe that I have done so in this chapter or in any other of my writings which employ the income tax data, but the hazards which exist for any economic historian attempting to use nearly any data base from the past certainly exist in abundance with this series; equally, however, its value is immense if it is employed cogently.

As noted, the nineteenth-century income tax was levied not simply on the total income of every liable taxpayer, but was divided into five schedules, termed A, B, C, D and E. Schedule A, according to Stamp, assessed the 'profits from the ownership of lands, houses, etc., and every description of property in the nature of realty'.[9] Often termed the 'Property Tax', it thus assessed incomes arising from landed rentals and real estate. However, and most anomalously, from 1798 until 1865–6 it also included incomes arising from certain types of industrial or business activities, namely from quarries, mines, ironworks,[10] fisheries, canals, docks, railways, waterworks, gasworks, market tolls, cemeteries, salt springs or works and alum works.[11] In 1865–6 these categories were transferred to Schedule D, where of course they rightly belong. However, in both the manuscript source I.R.16 up until 1911–12 and in a number of printed returns of the income tax in the Parliamentary Papers, statistics for these anomalous returns are given separately and individually. These enable the historian to ascertain, for example, the assessments made for railways by each individual county, and thus serve as a test of the accuracy of the geographical distribution of the income tax data as a whole—a matter which will be discussed below. The existence of this peculiarity would also enable the historian to investigate such topics as the profitability or location of specific industries, and as in so much in this material, in this chapter the surface of its value has probably only been scratched.

Schedule B was 'the tax . . . chargeable in respect of the occupation of all lands . . . a charge on the profits made by the occupier from the exercise of his capital and skill in husbandry'.[12] It was, in other words, the tax on the income of farmers. Schedule C was the tax 'in respect of all profits arising from interest, annuities, dividends, and shares of annuities payable to any person, body politic or corporate . . . out of any public revenue'.[13] Schedule C was thus a tax on income from government securities. Schedule C was almost invariably assessed as from the Banks of England or Ireland and to the best of my knowledge no other geographical statistics of its assessment was included in I.R.16.

Under Schedule D, for our purposes by far the most important schedule, were taxed all profits arising from all businesses (except those clearly denoted elsewhere), professions, foreign and colonial securities and possessions except those assessed under Schedule C, and all other profits not assessed elsewhere.[14]

Finally, Schedule E taxed all incomes or pensions from 'public offices or employment of profit', and 'every other public office or employment of profit of a public character', by which was meant the salaries of any employee of a corporation or public company.[15] By World War One corporate salaries comprised four-fifths of the income assessed under this schedule. 'Corporations' included non-business corporations in Law, including such bodies as Oxbridge colleges and churches. There was a 'constant drain' from Schedule D to E as incorporations grew.[16]

This chapter considers the changing geographical assessment of the middle-class portion of the income tax, that is, Schedules D, E and the business (quarries, mines, railways, ironworks, etc.) portions of Schedule A, according to the evidence for this provided in the Parliamentary Papers and in I.R.16. A case can also be made for additionally considering Schedule C, but there are no consistent geographical breakdowns for this series and consols were as likely to have been owned by landowners as by businessmen. Income arising from landed and urban rents, taxed under Schedule A, are not discussed or included here, nor are farmers' incomes assessed under Schedule B. Conceptually, although the exclusion of both seems an obvious enough matter, some would argue that since farmers normally had incomes in the middle-class range, they ought to be included here, while much urban property was owned not by the Westminsters and Bedfords, but by small-scale *rentiers* whose incomes came into the middle-class range and who might also be included in a wider definition of the middle class. However, there appears to be no way fully to distinguish this type of small urban *rentier* from his large-scale brother, the bona fide landed magnate, and both this type of income-earner and the middle-income farmer have been excluded from the discussion here. A satisfactory definition or delineation of the boundaries of the middle classes is a notoriously difficult and contentious matter. This chapter has adopted a quasi-Ricardean definition based upon the type of income received, with all taxpayers receiving incomes from profits, fees or salaries included, and the recipients of rentals or farmers' incomes excluded (together with the working classes). It should be noted that there are no upper income boundaries to this definition, although this matter will be examined in more detail below: the Rothschilds and Barings are middle-class by our definition, so long as their incomes were assessed under Schedules D, E, or the business portions of A. The landed incomes of such men would, however, be totally excluded from this survey. The delineation here may well be imperfect or arguable, but the arrangement of the income tax data will not allow any other.

What this study attempts to trace is the evolution of the distribution of middle-class business and professional incomes in terms of geography, especially and above all in terms of the changing respective shares of London on one hand and the major industrial counties of the north on the other.[17] Although the aim of this study is straightforward enough, it must be realized that the series I.R.16 exists only in manuscripts with numerous emendations and little or nothing in the way of a definitive key as to its use. If any such keys or maps to the use of I.R.16 are still held by the Inland Revenue, they ought certainly to be made available to researchers as quickly as possible. For most years, however, the process of addition of the county totals for the three middle-class portions of the income tax is straightforward enough. Because of the manuscript nature of most of the sources, however, there is probably a small margin of error concealed in the seeming exactitude of the figures, and changes of less than, say, 3 per cent in the basic comparison of London *vs* the north should probably be discounted.

Although the I.R.16 returns present comprehensive information on the geographical distribution of the middle-class portions of the income tax on an annual basis, this study analyzes the changing breakdown generally on a five-year basis. In Tables 4.1 and 4.2, the county percentages of middle-class income from 1806 to 1911–12 are given. Table 4.1 presents this data for all English counties, together with national data for Scotland and Wales, in addition to some separate statistics for Ireland. Table 4.2 highlights these findings for Greater London and for the most important industrial counties; the information in Table 4.2 is also presented in graph form (see Figure 4.1). It should be emphasized that the percentages in these tables are *relative* ones—the relative position of one county in the national totals—and of course even a fall in a county's percentage could well be consistent, and often was, with an absolute rise in middle-class incomes assessed there. The overall British totals for incomes assessed, according to the statistics handwritten in I.R.16, are also given at the base of each column, and absolute county assessments may be recalculated from these. It must also be

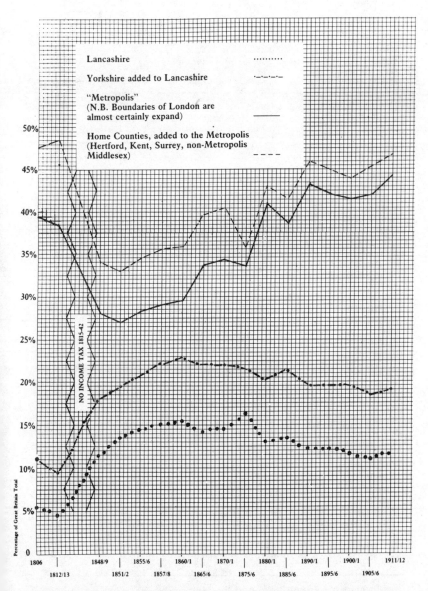

Figure 4.1: Percentage of Business and Professional Incomes (Schedules D and E, and Business Portions of A) of £100-£150 or more, by London and Leading Industrial Counties, 1806-1911/12.

Table 4.1: Middle-class Income Tax Assessed, 1806–1911/12
(percentages, by county)

	1806	1812–13	1848–9	1851–2
Bedford.	0.28	0.26	0.31	0.34
Berkshire	0.74	0.81	0.54	0.53
Buckingham.	0.61	0.60	0.36	0.35
Cambridge.	0.61	0.65	0.53	0.61
Cheshire	0.90	0.82	1.13	1.06
Cornwall	1.09	0.86	0.79	0.62
Cumberland	0.53	0.57	0.43	0.42
Derby.	0.79	0.68	1.71	1.70
Devon	1.90	1.02	1.20	1.00
Dorset	0.53	0.59	0.43	0.45
Durham	0.95	0.79	1.84	1.63
Essex	1.58	1.64	0.82	0.66
Gloucester.	1.11	0.99	1.37	1.30
Hereford.	0.17	0.17	0.20	0.20
Hertford.	0.70	0.72	0.53	0.42
Huntingdon.	0.23	0.28	0.18	0.16
Kent	3.36	4.45	1.85	1.76
Lancashire	5.52	4.71	11.56	13.66
Leicester.	0.78	0.83	0.70	0.62
Lincoln.	1.04	1.02	1.20	1.13
Monmouth.	— (in Wales) —		0.52	0.45
Norfolk	1.58	1.39	1.24	1.08
Northants.	0.42	0.50	0.80	0.81
Northumb.	1.50	1.45	1.23	1.71
Nottingham.	0.89	0.81	0.77	0.85
Oxford.	0.77	0.84	0.55	0.53
Rutland	0.09	0.09	0.07	0.07
Salop.	0.83	0.84	0.88	0.76
Somerset	3.97	3.40	2.00	2.02
Southants.	2.31	2.49	1.07	1.00
Stafford.	1.38	1.58	2.37	2.58
Suffolk	1.38	1.58	2.37	2.58
Surrey	4.59	4.50	3.75	4.13
Sussex	1.02	0.99	0.95	0.94
Warwick.	1.68	1.83	2.44	2.42
Westmorland	0.19	0.13	0.12	0.14
Wiltshire	0.87	0.99	0.63	0.48
Worcester.	0.80	0.71	0.97	0.85
Yorkshire	5.42	4.99	6.41	5.69
⎧ London	19.63	20.67	11.90	11.10
⎨ Westminster	7.39	7.35	4.55	4.36
⎩ Middlesex	12.22	10.86	11.56	11.46
Total Metropolis	39.24	38.88	28.01	26.92
Wales*	1.54	1.41	1.79	1.69
Scotland	6.39	7.49	14.93	15.73
GB	100.00	100.00	100.00	100.00
TOTAL	£36,678,215	£37,025,451	£81,661,924	£78,269,375

* Includes Monmouth 1806 and 1812–13.

1855–6	1857–8	1860–1	1865–6	1870–1
0.25	0.24	0.25	0.20	0.20
0.47	0.46	0.45	0.39	0.44
0.31	0.30	0.29	0.23	0.23
0.54	0.52	0.48	0.35	0.36
1.53	1.49	1.44	0.99	1.04
0.76	0.84	0.83	0.59	0.47
0.43	0.47	0.47	0.51	0.57
1.49	1.57	1.77	1.57	1.91
1.22	1.15	1.19	0.99	1.04
0.33	0.34	0.34	0.26	0.24
1.59	1.91	1.76	1.75	1.88
0.61	0.67	0.71	0.64	0.70
1.19	1.10	1.08	0.86	0.95
0.16	0.15	0.71	0.64	0.70
0.44	0.43	0.39	0.38	0.36
0.14	0.13	0.13	0.10	0.10
1.68	1.63	1.59	1.68	1.73
14.28	15.10	15.21	14.19	14.67
0.57	0.59	0.55	0.47	0.50
0.95	0.88	0.86	0.71	0.71
0.55	0.58	0.52	0.45	0.51
0.97	1.01	0.92	0.64	0.65
0.59	0.55	0.54	0.42	0.33
1.71	1.85	1.33	1.13	1.35
0.90	0.86	0.85	0.67	0.76
0.44	0.40	0.44	0.33	0.32
0.04	0.04	0.04	0.03	0.03
0.67	0.75	0.67	0.50	0.46
1.97	2.00	1.97	1.67	1.72
0.96	0.96	1.01	0.93	0.95
2.66	2.83	3.00	2.67	2.23
0.63	2.83	0.67	0.45	0.48
4.14	4.21	4.26	4.11	4.10
0.91	0.87	0.88	0.74	0.91
2.48	2.37	2.45	2.09	2.19
0.13	0.13	0.13	0.11	0.11
0.53	0.51	0.49	0.37	0.41
0.97	0.96	0.97	0.76	0.76
6.17	6.86	7.60	7.94	7.36
(13.74)	14.27	(14.65)	—	—
(3.97)	3.61	—	—	—
(10.66)	*11.24*	(*15.36*)	—	—
28.37	29.12	30.01	33.84	34.81
1.91	2.66	2.13	2.09	2.11
13.36	9.90	10.52	10.47	9.80
100.00	100.00	100.00	100.00	100.00
£103,829,950	£110,481,483	£118,297,222	£158,999,544	£175,818,447

Table 4.1: Middle-class Income Tax Assessed, 1806–1911/12 (cont.)
(percentages, by county)

	1875–6	Parliamentary Papers 1879–80*	1880–1	1885–6
Bedford.	0.19	0.20	0.18	0.20
Berkshire	0.43	0.45	0.42	0.45
Buckingham	0.25	0.19	0.21	0.21
Cambridge	0.33	0.33	0.30	0.29
Cheshire	1.26	1.15	0.99	1.09
Cornwall	0.43	0.31	0.29	0.32
Cumberland	0.81	0.61	0.58	0.55
Derby	2.19	2.03	1.91	1.88
Devon	1.20	0.85	0.79	0.77
Dorset	0.24	0.24	0.22	0.19
Durham	2.82	1.99	1.74	1.72
Essex	0.75	0.79	0.72	0.79
Gloucester.	0.93	1.60	0.80	0.77
Hereford.	0.13	0.12	0.11	0.11
Hertford.	0.33	0.31	0.28	0.28
Huntingdon.	0.09	0.09	0.08	0.07
Kent (extra-Metropolitan)**	1.22	1.42	1.18	1.19
Lancashire	16.26	13.95	12.93	13.51
Leicester	0.56	0.57	0.52	0.57
Lincoln.	0.76	0.72	0.66	0.67
Middlesex (extra-Metropolitan)**	—	—	—	0.68
Monmouth.	0.50	0.32	0.56	0.35
Norfolk	0.64	0.67	0.30	0.63
Northants.	0.39	0.42	0.39	0.41
Northumb.	1.64	1.27	1.15	1.20
Nottingham.	0.92	0.83	0.76	0.95
Oxford.	0.21	0.31	0.28	0.27
Rutland	0.03	0.03	0.03	0.02
Salop.	0.48	0.42	0.37	0.32
Somerset	1.66	0.66	1.34	1.28
Southants.	1.00	1.06	1.00	1.02
Stafford.	2.65	2.29	2.13	2.02
Suffolk	0.52	0.48	0.44	0.47
Surrey (extra-Metropolitan)**	0.77	1.19	0.74	0.83
Sussex	0.88	1.05	1.05	1.01
Warwick.	2.52	2.27	2.07	2.02
Westmorland	0.14	0.12	0.11	0.10
Wiltshire	0.18	0.35	0.34	0.33
Worcester	0.48	0.80	0.66	0.67
Yorkshire	5.26	7.89	7.25	7.61
Metropolis	33.18	37.55	41.28	38.83
Kent	—	—	(0.50)	(0.54)
Middlesex	—	—	(37.26)	(34.62)
Surrey	—	—	(3.52)	(3.67)
Wales	2.77	1.30	2.12	2.40
Scotland	11.43	10.81	10.10	10.92
GB	100.00	100.00	100.00	100.00
TOTALS	£253,808,883	£268,077,255	£276,612,837	£297,069,177

* Schedules D and E only—excludes business portions of Schedule A.
** Portions of Kent, Middlesex and Surrey within London Metropolitan area included with London figures (q.v.) from 1880–1.

1890–1	1895–6	1900–01	1905–6	1911–12
0.16	0.19	0.18	0.19	0.19
0.38	0.40	0.36	0.33	0.33
0.18	0.19	0.18	0.18	0.18
0.25	0.27	0.22	0.22	0.19
0.92	1.09	1.01	0.93	0.98
0.31	0.25	0.24	0.25	0.25
0.44	0.42	0.42	0.35	0.35
1.83	1.98	1.83	1.76	1.67
0.69	0.70	0.62	0.67	0.61
0.18	0.19	0.17	0.18	0.18
1.79	1.73	1.96	1.99	1.69
0.84	0.87	0.89	0.93	0.83
0.65	0.68	0.58	0.41	0.36
0.10	0.09	0.08	0.08	0.07
0.26	0.29	0.27	0.30	0.29
0.06	0.06	0.06	0.05	0.03
1.04	1.08	1.05	1.08	0.94
12.37	21.41	12.09	11.38	11.80
0.50	0.66	0.67	0.72	0.70
0.54	0.59	0.63	0.61	0.61
0.61	0.66	0.65	0.84	0.83
0.38	0.37	0.37	0.39	0.41
0.55	0.56	0.52	0.53	0.46
0.36	0.40	0.38	0.37	0.39
1.27	1.34	1.54	1.49	1.27
0.76	0.92	0.82	0.89	0.86
0.25	0.27	0.24	0.23	0.23
0.02	0.02	0.02	0.01	0.01
0.28	0.28	0.25	0.23	0.20
1.17	1.25	1.29	1.62	1.59
0.90	0.96	0.92	0.96	0.92
1.77	1.88	1.95	1.87	1.59
0.40	0.40	0.38	0.36	0.36
0.79	0.84	0.83	0.87	0.80
0.84	0.86	0.79	0.87	0.75
1.87	1.42	2.23	2.05	1.94
0.08	0.19	0.06	0.06	0.06
0.28	0.29	0.26	0.26	0.23
0.58	0.58	0.59	0.56	0.52
7.35	7.24	7.41	7.05	7.14
43.53	33.18	41.28	38.83	43.53
(0.43)	(38.19)	—	(38.94)	—
(39.73)	(0.43)	—	(0.50)	—
(3.36)	(3.41)	—	(3.03)	—
2.51	2.64	2.41	2.56	2.62
9.97	10.51	11.13	10.91	10.30
100.00	100.00	100.00	100.00	100.00
£369,403,026	£361,030,048	£460,516,749	£516,010,695	£611,486,743

Table 4.2: *Table 4.1 figures for Major Counties*

	1806	1812–13	1848–9	1851–2	1855–6	1857–8	1860–1	1865–6	1870–1	1875–6	1880–1	1885–6	1890–1	1895–6	1900–1	1905–6	1911–12
Cheshire	0.9.0	0.82	1.13	1.06	1.51	1.49	1.44	0.99	1.04	1.26	0.99	1.09	0.92	1.09	1.01	0.93	0.98
Durham	0.95	0.79	1.84	1.63	1.59	1.91	1.76	1.75	1.88	2.82	1.74	1.72	1.79	1.73	1.96	1.99	1.69
Lancashire	5.52	4.71	11.56	13.66	14.28	15.10	15.21	14.19	14.67	16.26	12.93	13.51	12.37	12.41	12.09	11.38	11.80
Northumberland	0.42	0.50	0.80	0.81	1.71	0.55	1.33	1.13	1.35	1.64	1.15	1.20	1.27	1.35	1.54	1.49	1.27
Stafford	1.38	1.58	2.37	2.58	2.66	2.83	3.00	2.67	2.23	2.65	2.13	2.02	1.77	1.88	1.95	1.87	1.59
Warwick.	1.68	1.83	2.44	2.42	2.48	2.37	2.45	2.09	2.19	2.52	2.07	2.02	1.87	1.42	2.23	2.05	1.94
Yorkshire	5.42	4.99	6.41	5.69	6.17	6.86	7.60	7.94	7.36	5.26	7.25	7.61	7.35	7.24	7.41	7.05	7.14
Metropolis	39.24	38.88	28.02	26.91	28.37	29.06	29.64	33.84	34.21	33.18	41.28	38.83	43.53	42.03	41.43	42.48	44.26
Hertford.	0.70	0.72	0.53	0.42	0.44	0.43	0.39	0.38	0.36	0.33	0.26	0.28	0.26	0.29	0.27	0.30	0.29
Kent	3.36	4.45	1.85	1.76	1.68	1.63	1.59	1.68	1.73	1.22	1.04	1.19	1.04	1.08	1.05	1.08	0.94
Surrey	4.59	4.50	3.75	4.13	4.14	4.21	4.26	4.11	4.10	0.77	0.74	0.83	0.76	0.84	0.83	0.87	0.80
Middlesex	—	—	—	—	—	—	—	—	—	—	—	0.68	0.61	0.66	).65	0.84	0.83

clearly understood that these percentages refer to the amount of middle-class income *liable* for taxation (*not* the amount of income tax paid) and *not* the *number* of individual taxpayers or taxation units. As repeatedly stressed, the true number of individual taxpayers is unknown, and while I.R.16 does often provide statistical breakdowns by income range, these do not refer to individual taxpayers but to taxation units, which include business units as well as individual persons, and under which an individual taxpayer might count several times if he was liable to income tax under more than one schedule.

It is clear on the face of it that two very broad trends may be seen from this data. The first, less germane to our purposes but significant nonetheless, is the ever-increasing concentration of middle-class incomes in the larger and more populous counties, and the concomitant decline in the significance of the smaller and more rural counties relative to the centres of urban life. The downward progression of the south-western counties like Cornwall and Devon, those in East Anglia, or in the extreme north like Westmorland—these three areas in particular being definite losers in the rearrangement of English wealth (and population)—was closely paralleled by the spectacular growth of the northern industrial counties. In other words, the standard deviation of middle-class incomes among the counties increased markedly with industrialization; this may serve as a reminder that in pre-industrial England the counties—with the obvious exception of London— were roughly equal in wealth, their county and market towns serving much the same role and enjoying a rough similarity of status. It was this rough equality which, among other things, urbanization and industrialization upset and greatly altered.

The second and more important general trend concerns the relative performance of London and the nearby Home Counties vis-à-vis the northern industrial ones, especially Lancashire.[18] The more conveniently grouped data in Table 4.2 includes most of the larger industrial counties—generally termed the 'Metropolis' in the I.R.16 manuscripts—as well as the non-metropolitan areas of Hertfordshire, Kent and Surrey. Most of the income assessed here, with the exception of that earned in the Kent coastal towns, would clearly come within the London ambit and much of it would represent the incomes of London commuters or former Londoners.

It will be seen that the performance of London, possibly as one might expect, resembles a very broadened 'U', with Greater

London's overall percentage accounting for nearly one-half of all middle-class incomes in the earliest period, 47.89 per cent in 1806, declining to about 33 or 34 per cent around 1850, and then rising from 1860 onwards, dramatically from 1880–3 so that by 1911–12 the overall percentage of the Greater London area was almost exactly the same (47.12 per cent) as it had been in 1806, when the industrial application of steam power was still in its relative infancy and twenty years before the railway age had even begun—in other words, almost as if the industrial revolution had not really occurred.

The other side of the coin is the performance of Lancashire and the other northern industrial counties. It is clear that Lancashire must have experienced a broad period of enormous relative growth and expansion for its middle classes between 1813 and 1848 (when there was no income tax and hence no data),[19] and it continued to see its middle-class incomes grow extremely rapidly relative to the rest of country until 1860. Lancashire actually 'peaks' in 1875–6, but the 1875–6 figures are quite anomalous and therefore suspect, and may well be the result of an error in the Inland Revenue's manuscript recording procedures or my transcriptions. By the 1860s, however, it seems clear that Lancashire is beginning relatively to decline. The word 'relative' should of course be stressed: Lancashire's decline was not, of course, an absolute one, given the ever-increasing national totals of middle-class incomes assessed. Lancashire's decline is relative to London's relative growth and the growth of other areas which rise faster than the national average.

The other major industrial counties present a more mixed picture. The statistics for Yorkshire—which here includes all the three Ridings—are remarkably constant in the 6.4–7.9 per cent range for nearly every year covered by the I.R.16 statistics here, representing a relative increase of 40 per cent or so from the early part of the century, much lower of course than the 200 per cent increase experienced by Lancashire. Staffordshire and Warwickshire, rather surprisingly, peak even earlier than Lancashire and decline thereafter. Presumably a rebound occurs in the inter-war period, with the rise of Birmingham and Coventry to pre-eminence in automobiles and as modern engineering centres, but there is no evidence of this down to 1914. Scotland, considered here from the available figures as a whole, rises rapidly to mid-century and then declines in the 1860s to the 10–11 per cent it continues to maintain until World War One; rather mysteriously there is no *relative* growth in the Scottish portion during the period of Glasgow's industrial zenith.

Although the rise and subsequent decline of Lancashire, and its mirror-image pattern in London, are clearly two phases of the same phenomenon, they are not, strictly speaking, halves of the same coin, since they did not occur at precisely the same time or, it seems clear, for similar reasons: Lancashire peaks around 1860 and declines fairly steadily from the 1860s, while London bottoms out, it would seem, around 1850 and then experiences a really remarkable spurt from around 1880. It is difficult to pinpoint a single all-embracing reason for the peaking of Lancashire around 1860 and its subsequent decline. Given the enormous relative growth in middle-class incomes which Lancashire did experience during the first half of the century, it would have been remarkable if such a rate of growth continued indefinitely: it was inherently most unlikely that such a growth rate, dependent as it obviously was upon the continuing growth of the cotton textile industry, could continue without a break. More specifically, there were in my view four factors which were influential in producing what might be termed— and has been termed, in another context—this 'climacteric of the 1860s'. The first was the very pronounced and probably underestimated effects of the cotton famine during the American Civil War which, needless to say, for several years increased the cost of raw materials enormously. Secondly there were the effects of high and rising wage costs in the cotton industry. Industrial wages in Lancashire were, of course, always higher than virtually anywhere in Britain, as E. H. Hunt has demonstrated very conclusively; this has long been a commonplace assumption of economic history.[20] Wages in the cotton industry rose quite substantially—arguably more than in any other industry—in just this period. According to A. L. Bowley and G. H. Wood's figures reprinted in Mitchell and Deane, normal weekly wages among cotton workers rose from 57–59 in 1855 (with 1891 = 100) to 67 in 1862 (when the series changes) to 85 by 1871, an increase seemingly higher than in any other industry for which figures exist.[21] Part of the reason for this rise lay in increased productivity, but a rise of this scale necessarily represented a decline in the potential profits of the cotton factory owners, which is exactly what is recorded in the income tax figures. Thirdly, foreign competition began to be felt even by the 1860s while, fourthly, there was the nature of the contemporary cotton textile industry, with its multiplicity of small and middle-sized rather than gigantic firms. As R. A. Church remarks, 'faced with rising prices of their raw materials, manufacturers invested in known innovations and new technologies, but this increased productive capacity and intensified competitive pressure'.[22]

Another related and possibly significant factor, difficult perhaps to prove conclusively, was the relative absence of a large white-collar administrative and 'middle management' class in typical Lancashire industries when compared with the commercial and financial business world of London—those men earning from just over £100 to £500 p.a. as superior clerks, bookkeepers, senior sales personnel, travellers, overseers, and the like, and who were apparently to be found in relatively greater and growing numbers in London than in the north. It would be difficult to prove this, given the imprecise nature of both the census and income tax data relevant to this question, but it does seem likely that the growth of this class was relatively faster in London than the north, especially after about 1870. According to C. H. Lee's *British Regional Employment Statistics 1841–1971*, male employment in industrial orders 23, 24 and 25 (covering the distributive trades, insurance, and banking, and professional and scientific services) and the 'not classified' category, which included merchants and commercial clerks (as well as many other occupations) increased in Lancashire from 1841 to 1911 by 125 per cent (from 88,929 to 200,103), but by 180 per cent in London (from 97,749 to 274,161).[23] This data is far from wholly satisfactory, and moreover tells us little or nothing about the incomes or liability to income tax of these men, but the trends are probably clear enough.

In toto, and so far as the middle classes of Lancashire are concerned, it seems fairly clear that the 1860s are more deserving of the description of a watershed than any later period. There is an older tradition among British economic historians of describing the 1860s rather than the 1870s as a 'climacteric', dating back to H. L. Beales' 1934 paper on 'The Great Depression in Trade and Industry'. This tradition has not become generally accepted for a variety of reasons: because the statistics of economic growth for the British economy as a whole continued normally and without reversal until after the 1860s, because of the strength of the long-held notion of the 'Great Depression' of the 1873–96 period, because of the force of 1870–1 and German unification as a historical landmark, and so on. Nevertheless, from the viewpoint of the middle classes and the highly important division between its commercial and manufacturing components, the years around 1860 do appear to be a major watershed: to appropriate Namier's phrase about the 1848 European revolutions, it was a turning-point at which history failed to turn, that is, when Britain and its middle classes failed forever to evolve into a class primarily industrial and northern in nature, although the relative growth rates among middle-class incomes from the beginnings of industrialization until that time suggested that such a transformation had been increasingly likely. It will be seen from Table 4.2 that the overall income percentages among the seven largely industrial counties detailed here was, in 1851–2, 27.85 per cent of the total, compared with Greater London's 33.22 per cent at the time. In 1806 the total percentage of these northern counties together was only 16.27 per cent compared with Greater London's 47.89, while in 1911–12 it was 26.41—slightly less than in 1851–2—while London's share had risen very considerably.

Although the reasons for Lancashire's relatively poor performance after 1860 are probably reasonably clear, we can be much less certain about London's really remarkable recovery from 1860 and especially from the 1880s. I must confess that no clear-cut and wholly satisfying explanation for London's resurgence in the later nineteenth century springs to mind. Further along we shall consider whether the increase in London's share might be an illusory artefact of the data, a chimera created by the nature of the collection and recording of the data. Suffice it to say that London's recovery, if indeed on the scale indicated by I.R.16, was due to two or three main causes. One, most obviously, was that the various broad developments and changes in both the British and world economies of the later nineteenth century strongly and genuinely 'favoured' the growth of London's middle class as opposed to the industrial north. The rise of intense and increasing foreign competition from Europe and American for British manufacturing did not mean or imply that British commerce and finance was threatened to the same extent, or indeed to any extent. Unless a vital centre of finance or commerce arose overseas—and none did—then the City's position as 'the Clearing-house of the World' was not only not threatened by the rise of Germany, America and other industrial powers, but might well have been enhanced, for London still financed a large share of this rival economic growth, insured its ships, acted as broker to much of the world's trade and investment, and so on. Similarly, the export of British capital in the later nineteenth century was largely or wholly channelled through London. The largest British individual incomes earned in a wide variety of fields, in finance and in London's other role as the centre of wealth, display, retailing, the professions, the press and service industries, especially the enormous incomes of the late Victorian and Edwardian plutocracy, were to be found disproportionately in London, as were, it would seem, the ever-growing lower middle class, a trend reflected in such matters as the considerably higher rents typically paid in London and the development of whole districts of expanding London along fairly rigid class lines, as well as its ever-increasing size.[24]

While all of these factors were doubtless true and important, it seems uncertain to me if, even taken together, they are sufficient to explain the sudden and dramatic relative rise in London's overall income percentage from 1880 onwards. A crucial point which must be considered here is whether the trends found here are an artefact of the data. Is there some reason or reasons for supposing that the great relative increase in the portion of London incomes is spurious? The first point which should be made concerning this is that although the format of the series I.R.16 allows us to answer this question to a certain extent, the surviving sources simply do not provide enough evidence or explicit written description of the data collection process to answer this question comprehensively. I.R.16 contains no explanations or instructions as to where individual income earners or businesses were geographically categorized or why; nor does any printed source, so far as I am aware.[25] It must be kept in mind that I.R.16 was a confidential and internal manuscript source seen only by employees of the Inland Revenue and was not made available to outside researchers until the 1970s. One must therefore assume *a priori* that it was 'accurate', as it is quite preposterous to suppose that the Inland Revenue would keep confidential and private records which were known to be inaccurate or misleading. If its confidential records classified an individal taxpayer or business concern as located in London or Lancashire or Cornwall one must surely accept that he or it was accurately classified, unless there is a good reason to the contrary.

There are, however, a number of quite plausible suggestions concerning whether the seeming growth in London's share may be an artefact of the data collection. First, it may reflect the movement of the head offices of mainly regionally-based companies and corporations to London in the later nineteenth century; secondly, it may reflect the movement of the provincial wealthy or their descendants to the West End or suburban London and their assessment there for taxation purposes; finally, it may reflect the deduction of dividends from fixed income securities—'coupon clipping'—at source (i.e., in London) rather than at the actual place of residence of the *rentier*; or some other similar systematic deduction—for instance of certain government pensions—in London rather than in the actual place of residence of the taxpayer.[26] Neither I nor anyone else can adequately answer these plausible suggestions, given the nature of the surviving evidence available to the researcher. I am personally prepared to admit that the seeming rise in London's share of middle-class incomes after 1880 may have been influenced and exaggerated by any or all of these factors. However, there are equally good reasons for believing that if such an exaggeration occurred it was counterbalanced by a number of factors to be considered shortly, on the opposite side, which suggest that these percentages may have been *understatements* of London's actual position in the structure of Britain's middle-class incomes.

Probably the most significant and plausible argument that the relative position of London is exaggerated is the contention that the head offices of provincially-based companies were increasingly located in London and assessed there, despite the fact that the bulk of the profits of such companies were earned outside London. However plausible, I know of no compelling evidence that this was true, but some good evidence that it was not. Briefly, the Schedule A business returns, even after they were transferred to Schedule D in the 1860s, were still separately kept and recorded in the I.R.16 manuscripts, and it is clear that the railways, ironworks, mines, and so on classified individually under these separate headings were certainly not included improperly as London-based concerns—nor was there any growing tendency to do this—but remained as recorded in the provincial county to which they properly belonged and where they did the bulk of their business. Nor do I actually know of many or indeed of any large-scale companies 'really' situated in the provinces whose head offices had by 1914 been transferred to London.[27] Perhaps the only exceptions to this known to me are the 'Big Five' clearing banks, which by 1914 had absorbed most, but by no means all of the provincial and country clearing banks. Each of the Five evolved in a fairly similar manner at roughly similar dates. Lloyd's Bank, to take one example, absorbed the

Birmingham Joint Stock Bank in 1889, the Bristol and West of England Bank in 1892, and in 1900 absorbed eight substantial provincial banks, including Williams, Brown & Co. of Leeds, Cunliffe Brooks & Co. of Manchester, and the Liverpool Union Bank. However, it was not until 1918 that it absorbed the Capital and Counties Bank, which at the time itself owned 473 branches, mainly in the West Country and East Anglia.[28] In 1919 Lloyds absorbed the West Yorkshire Bank, in 1921 Fox Fowler & Co. of Somerset, and in 1923 Cox & Co. of London.[29] Presumably the provincial banks named here would not have been recorded or assessed in London until their amalgamations but it seems likely that, once absorbed, all of the profits of the clearing banks would be recorded as assessed in London thereafter, even though they would have been earned up and down the country. Even here, however, some greater clarification is required. While the profits of the clearing banks may have been recorded in London, neither the salaries of their employees nor the interest accruing to their depositors would have been recorded as assessed in London unless they actually worked or lived there. Moreover, the head offices of the banks, their administrative headquarters, and a sizable percentage of their business *were* located in London or represented purely London business, and if an exaggeration of London's role is a product of the statistics here, it is in many respects an extremely plausible one. More clear-cut would be the case of a Manchester or Leeds manufacturing firm whose headquarters are transferred to London and whose entire profits are therefore assessed in London, but simply no evidence at all exists which implies that this may have occurred, and a look through such systematic business directories as *The Red Book of Commerce* of 1921 suggests that even after World War One the headquarters of such firms were rarely located in London unless they were genuinely London firms. It must also be reiterated that even if this did occur, we simply have no evidence that the Inland Revenue classified these as London firms in its internal records; the only direct evidence which exists, from the former business portions of Schedule A, strongly suggests that this was *not* done.

The question of wealthy businessmen and others being assessed in London where they may have lived rather than in the area in which their factory or enterprise was located is, even more than the previous consideration, a possible source of error. A great many prominent provincial businessmen rented a town house in London for part of the year, at least once they became highly successful and prominent. But in the main these were the very wealthiest and most successful ones; below a certain income it is improbable that many did. The sons and grandsons of these men often lived in the West End, occasionally severing completely their remaining ties with the provincial towns where their family firms were located. Conversely, of course, many London and provincial business leaders maintained country houses, and while the country houses of provincial business leaders were often near the town where their factory was located—in Cheshire, for instance, in the case of many Lancashire business leaders—it seems likely that the London wealthy were more widely spread. The whole issue may, indeed, be a red herring unless the I.R.16 series classified such men as 'belonging' to the county where their country home was located or as 'belonging' to the West End rather than to the ancestral workplace in the Black Country, Leeds or Liverpool. (There is, of course, a conceptual question about whether the Clubland and Guards grandson of a Leeds manufacturer, who may well never have set eyes upon Leeds, should indeed be counted with Leeds because his income is derived from shares in the family firm.) The evidence in I.R.16 itself does not permit any answer to this supposition or to any other of the same type. In 1860–1, 15.36 per cent of all middle-class income was assessed in Middlesex (i.e. London excluding the City of London and other areas) while in 1905–6 this total (from the manuscript sources) declined slightly to 13.89 per cent, indicating that the share of the West End and other strongly middle-class and upper-class areas of London was relatively less important compared with the profits of City companies and personal income assessed elsewhere in London. It does not seem from this as if there is compelling evidence for a *net* artificial drift to London in the late nineteenth century, although these figures are not inconsistent with some such drift occurring simultaneously with another drift out of London to the countryside and with the increasing importance of the business portion of the income tax assessed in the City of London, congruent with the ever-increasing relative role of the City in British business life. The figures do not provide more particular or specific information than this.[30]

The final point of possible error—counting the 'coupon clipping' of overseas and other fixed incomes, as well as other sources of government incomes systematically paid from a central location, in

London rather than where their possessors actually lived—is perhaps easier to deal with. As with the Schedule A business returns, we do have the geographical evidence about this in I.R.16, and it shows that such income was not invariably assessed in London. Furthermore, as noted, Schedule C—the schedule devoted exclusively to income arising from government securities or 'consols'—is not included in this study, even though very much of it must have accrued to London *rentiers* and owners of these securities.

On balance, it seems that while there may have been some progressive and systematic exaggeration of the role of London in these figures, its dimensions are probably not so significant as one might at first imagine. What is not, perhaps, satisfactorily explained is the sudden turning-point in London's fortunes from 1880 onwards; the reasons for this, assuming that the figures accurately reflect reality, probably lie in the very broad trends in the British and international economies which are, at least in their most general aspects, well known.

While London's importance may be exaggerated by the collection of the statistics in I.R.16 it must also be noted that London's role is certainly understated for a variety of reasons one can pinpoint with some precision. In the first place, strange as this may seem, the incomes of public office-holders, including the entire Civil Service, were *not* assessed as belonging to any particular geographical locale in the I.R.16 returns. Instead these were counted separately, although very detailed returns were compiled annually about the precise amount of taxable personal income in each particular government department. In 1806 the taxable assessment of these public offices amounted to £5,183,000 (of which taxable salaries in the army and navy accounted for £2,382,000). In 1860–1 this category had risen to £12,751,000 and in 1900–01 to £21,300,000—that is, respectively to 14.13, 10.78 and 4.63 per cent of the national total of middle-class incomes included in Table 4.1.[31] Although a good deal of these totals represented the incomes of military officers and colonial administrators overseas, the bulk of the domestic incomes assessed here was paid to Londoners and clearly should be counted with London, while virtually none of it at all represented the incomes of bona fide inhabitants of the industrial counties. This factor alone, even after discounting the overseas and military components of the public service, is probably sufficient to raise London's portion of the total by at least 2.5–5 per cent depending on the period.

Secondly, no part of the bona fide Schedule A, the assessment on rental incomes, is of course included here. Although much of this represented the landed incomes of the great landowners and squirearchy, a surprisingly large portion consisted of urban rents. Although much of this, especially in London, would have accrued to the large-scale urban magnates like the Dukes of Bedford and Westminster, or to corporate owners like the Anglican Church, a substantial amount would have been received by middle-class or even lower middle-class house owners who incidentally received a second income, or possibly a first one, from their rentals. Logically, this type of rental income should have been disproportionately higher in London, *ceteris paribus*, than in the provinces, since urban rentals were demonstrably so much higher in London than elsewhere. Thirdly, as we have noted, Schedule C is also excluded from the discussion in this chapter: that is, the income arising from government securities or 'consols'. This was a type of 'conservative', absolutely secure income, but one yielding a low rate of return, likely to be owned by those already in possession of some property or income, or who had inherited it, especially women and younger sons who received a fixed annuity as a legacy—that is, by the established owners of 'old money' rather than by self-made men building up incomes in new industries. It seems plausible that this was more likely to be owned by Londoners than by those in the industrial north, although there would probably have been a progressive evening-up in the later nineteenth century. The gross assessment of Schedule C was about £5 million in the early nineteenth century, £27,500,000 in 1861, and £49,600,000 in 1911.[32]

Two other points along the same lines are more speculative, but should be made. Wealth or property yielding no income—for instance, works of art, jewellery, houses and automobiles or, more significantly, freehold housing—are of course not included in any income tax schedule (although they would be valued for probate at the death of the owner, as privately-owned wealth) and again such property, representing *accumulated* income, was more likely to be held disproportionately by older established propertied persons and in London rather than the north. Finally there is the matter of tax evasion where, needless to say, we are entirely in the dark. There was, of course no PAYE in the nineteenth century, and income tax was not deducted in advance from one's salary as it is now; instead one paid income tax annually on the basis of self-assessment. There was a tax inspectorate with considerable powers, but it seems clear that the opportunities for evasion under such a system were wider than at present.[33] However, some forms of evasion were probably easier than others. In particular, it would seem much easier to hide and disguise one's income in the City of London rather than as a factory owner in an industrial town, since while factories are obvious and monumental artefacts of income-earning, the squalid and unimpressive offices in the City of London, as numerous as they were unprepossessing, often showed no relationship between the incomes earned there and their size or grandeur. The tiny office of an international merchant or broker, employing a meagre staff, may well have been far more profitable than a factory in Bradford or Bolton employing hundreds. If the proprietor of such an office was not a strictly honest man who conscientiously declared his income, he might well literally have been overlooked by the tax collector, while the factory owner could never be; moreover, the avoidance prospects of the financial entrepreneur were increased by the ease with which currency and specie could be moved about, nationally or internationally, or concealed. I do not know, and presumably no one knows, how much of this actually occurred, but it seems likely that in so far as any did this further resulted in an understatement of London's actual share of total income.[34]

That a number of important consequences for British economic and political history flow from the statistics highlighted here goes without saying. The first is the question of entrepreneurial performance and of Britain's long-term economic decline from 1870 onwards. Although this question is normally posed of Britain's economy as a whole, the picture found here reminds us that the British economy should perhaps be viewed as broken up into separate spheres which may have performed quite differently, and seeing the British economy in terms of comparative regional/occupational matrices seems a fruitful approach. The performances of the regions and, by extension, of the different spheres of commerce and finance which they represented, were clearly quite different, and it seems quite inaccurate to talk of London's post-1870 economic decline, whether relative or absolute, although the evidence presented here does seem to confirm the common view of a post-1870 economic decline in the manufacturing north of England, at least relatively and so far as the middle classes are concerned. *Why* did Britain's industrialists fail relatively if not absolutely? Can it really be that there was a collective failure, of many hundreds if not thousands of northern entrepreneurs, which affected only one type of business life but not another? Or was Britain's economic performance determined by very broad international trends? Or, again, can it be argued that British industrialism did indeed begin to fail within one lifetime after its beginnings, and that its flourishing was highly anomalous and uncharacteristic viewed in the long span of British history?

What seems certain, however, is that the trends we have observed in this chapter, if they are accurate, had profound political implications. It may well have struck some readers of this who are also concerned with modern British political history that the mainstream course of British politics in its middle-class aspects during the past century or so has followed the trends presented here logically and to a remarkable extent. In particular, it seems clear that the triumph of the Conservative party in the form it took—a party largely based on the Anglican, London, and suburban middle classes in contrast to the very different electoral bases of Liberalism—was in the long term as inevitable as anything in party political history can be. Similarly it seems clear that, from the 1860s or 1870s onwards, Liberalism was in an increasingly anomalous and untenable position, progressively losing its middle-class base in relative terms, and that it could compensate for this only via the registration and voting of democratic numbers—an effort which at most times in the late Victorian and Edwardian periods it made rather poorly. But once class became politically salient, only a working-class based party of the left could, in the long run, provide the opposition to London-based Toryism. If we accept that these economic trends were transferred to the political sphere at all and had political implications at all, World War One, it would seem, merely speeded up a break which was, if anything, overdue. Given that the economic trends of the post-1918 period, particularly the continuing and disastrous decline of Britain's old staple industries, must have still further accentuated the importance of London vis-à-vis the north for the middle classes, post-1918 Liberalism certainly looked untenable in any form and given any sort of leadership, so long as it relied on its traditional bases of support. It is in this overall context that such events as the Gold Standard decision of 1926 ought to be viewed.

More broadly, the evolution of British politics from the Pitt—Liverpool era onwards deeply bore the marks of the geographical trends discussed here. Although political reform primarily entailed the broadening of the political nation via the extension of the franchise it was also, and perhaps equally, an extension of political power to propertied segments of British society previously excluded; the Great Reform Bill was in part a recognition of the downslope of the 'U' discussed above, compared with the circumstances of pre-industrial Britain.

It might be worth considering what the course of British politics might have been like had the growth of the incomes and hence power of the northern middle classes continued to increase after 1860 at the same rate as in the decades before, or at least continued to grow until they became the predominant component of the middle classes. It is at least arguable, if not probable, that a thoroughgoing democratic radicalism of the Chamberlainite-Dilkeite variety, based upon middle-class nonconformity and manufacturing interests, would inevitably have come to power in a sweeping way at some point in the late nineteenth century, and that it would have attempted a thorough reform of the remaining seats of aristocratic power, especially the 'land monopoly', the privileges of the Church of England, and the traditional format of the House of Lords, with the aim of remoulding Britain into a society not dissimilar to the United States. The long years of Tory hegemony assured by the increasing unity of the aristocracy and the London-based middle classes would presumably not have occurred while, conceivably, the rise of a class-based Labour party might have been deterred or avoided, as it was in the United States, with the Liberal party evolving toward something like the American Democratic party. Of course the New Liberalism of Asquith and Lloyd George did have many affinities with the Democratic party of Woodrow Wilson and Franklin Roosevelt but its triumph was in many ways an unexpected *tour de force* of successful mid-passage steering between the still powerful and only partially reformed Conservative party and its interests, and the rising forces of Labour. By the Edwardian period the great bulk of the 'Establishment' was certainly Tory, a situation which seems to us natural and inevitable, but which had certainly not been the case even in the 1870s, when the City of London was strongly Liberal, as was half of the landed aristocracy.

One is perhaps on even firmer ground in asking if such a course of events might have produced a very different Britain from that which has evolved over the past century, reforming and 'modernizing' in a much more root-and-branch way much earlier, but without any ideological attachments to socialism; one might ask if some features of Britain's alleged long-term economic decline might have been avoided as a consequence. But, needless to say, this was a road not taken, London and the south resuming their rightful and time-honoured positions for the middle classes which had been temporarily interrupted by the short-lived and upstart commotion commonly termed the Industrial Revolution.

II

It remains to discuss several other significant findings, taken from the income tax statistics, which are not strictly comprehended in the previous analysis but which are too important for this chapter to omit.

It was noted earlier that both I.R.16 and the earlier printed returns of the first income tax in the Parliamentary Papers do present statistics for each schedule by range of income. It must be strongly stressed that these statistics are simply not what they purport to be, for both individuals and business units are included as 'individuals' in this data, while the income of a single individual might well have been assessed several times, under several schedules: indeed, the wealthier a taxpayer was the more probable it was that he had some smaller portion of his total income assessed under several schedules, and in a sense this data may demonstrate the very opposite of the real state of affairs. At best, the ranges of income suggested in these statistics are only roughly indicative of the range of individual incomes, while the information is in any case incomplete.[35] Nevertheless, in Table 4.3, the purported ranges of income for the larger counties at three dates—1806, 1860–1, and 1900–01—is given in terms of county percentages of the Great Britain total by income range.

The most striking finding here is, of course, the pronounced lead of London among very high income-earners and its surprisingly limited share of the lower middle-class income ranges—although it must be noted that the same effect is almost equally notable in Lancashire and Yorkshire in 1860–1 and 1900–01. This would strongly suggest that the lower ranges of middle-class incomes were much more widely and evenly distributed throughout the country, among the smaller and less industrialized counties, while the

highest ranges of middle-class incomes were very strongly
concentrated in a handful of areas, particularly in London. As this
table records both business units and individual income-earners,
and is subject to the other *caveats* discussed, probably nothing more
should be made of these findings. It would certainly not be
surprising to learn that the very wealthiest middle-class individuals
and the largest business units were to be found disproportionately
in London, Lancashire and Yorkshire, and less commonly

*Table 4.3: Percentage of Middle-class Income Assessed, by Range of
Income and Geography*

A: 1806*	£60–£500	£500–£3,000	£3,000+
Cheshire	1.12	0.69	0.60
Durham	0.88	0.60	1.09
Yorkshire	6.04	5.57	4.60
Lancashire	5.24	7.64	6.20
Northumberland	1.08	1.71	2.55
Warwickshire	2.14	1.33	1.24
London	27.63	49.45	64.63
Kent	5.08	2.06	0.48
Surrey	5.43	4.85	2.91
Scotland	6.12	5.51	2.50
GB	100.00	100.00	100.00

* Schedule D only.

B: 1860–1*	£100–1,000	£1–10,000	£10,000+
Cheshire	1.47	1.34	0.85
Durham	1.67	1.10	0.68
Yorkshire	3.41	7.71	6.79
Lancashire	10.00	20.04	23.60
Northumberland	1.17	1.32	0.85
Warwickshire	3.33	3.22	1.36
Staffordshire	3.46	1.65	1.02
London	18.81	34.04	44.82
Kent	3.41	1.56	0.68
Surrey	3.25	3.28	2.04
Scotland	14.96	10.19	6.28
GB	100.00	100.00	100.00

* NB: (1) Schedules D + E only—not business or portions of A.
    (2) Percentages of numbers of taxpayers by range, not of total income by
range.

Table 4.3: *Percentage of Middle-class Income Assessed, by Range of Income and Geography—cont.*

C: 1900–01*	Under £1,000	£1–10,000	£10,000+
Cheshire	1.41	0.75	—
Durham	1.86	1.54	1.84
Yorkshire	6.42	5.34	7.37
Lancashire	9.74	9.65	15.7
Northumberland	1.29	1.35	0.92
Warwickshire	2.11	2.32	0.46
Staffordshire	2.02	1.09	—
London	22.01	39.19	48.39
Kent	1.83	1.06	0.92
Middlesex (extra-Metropolitan)	1.19	0.82	0.46
Surrey	1.35	1.42	1.38
Scotland	10.18	7.57	4.61
GB	100.00	100.00	100.00

* (1) Excludes public offices.
  (2) Percentage of numbers of taxpayers by range, not their income.

elsewhere, though perhaps the complete or near-complete absence of *either* individuals or business firms with business incomes or profits of £10,000 or above in 1900–01 from counties like Cheshire, Staffordshire and Warwickshire is surprising. Similarly, the much more even spread at the lower levels is unsurprising: such occupations as clergyman, solicitor, and small- or middle-ranking merchant were to be found nearly everywhere, as were pensioner and *rentier*.

The final matter worth considering here is the light which the income tax sources can shed on the probable course of income distribution in Britain during the nineteenth century. Despite the fact that we do not know the size or range of incomes of individual taxpayers, we do know the amount assessed for income tax by taxpayers and moreover we have a number of presumably reliable estimates of total national income by contemporary economic historians; from a comparison of the two figures it is seemingly possible to ascertain the relative proportion of the total national income received by everyone with an income sufficient to pay income tax and those whose incomes fell below the minimum level for tax liability. The great majority of the latter were, of course, men and women of the working classes, and because the minimum level for income tax was, roughly, at the barrier between the incomes of

the working class and the lower part of the middle class, this seems
to be a neat and simple method of determining whether the shares of
the national cake going to the 'haves' and 'have-nots' were growing
or shrinking; it is strange that no one has attempted to do this
before.

There are—as always—several *caveats* to be made here. The
lower limit of liability for income tax changed throughout the
nineteenth century. In particular, it was £50 or £60 during the
period of the first income tax, while from 1853 to 1876 the limit for
liability was £100 rather than the normal £150 or £160. The figures
in Table 4.4 for 1850–1 onwards employ Stamp's estimates of

Table 4.4: Income-tax Payers, by Category

	Land	% of British income	Business profes- sionals	% of British income	British gross national income	Non-tax payers' income	%
1810							
£60	110.3	36.6	49.3	16.4	301.1	141.5	50.0
£150	90.4	30.0	36.4	12.1	301.1	174.3	57.9
1850–1	128.3	24.5	106.0	20.3	523.3	289.0	55.2
1860–1	145.1	21.7	152.9	22.9	668.0	370.0	55.4
1870–1	188.7	20.6	209.8	22.9	916.6	518.1	56.5
1880–1	225.6	21.5	301.2	28.7	1051.2	524.4	49.9
1890–1	232.3	18.0	410.9	31.9	1288.2	645.0	50.1
1900–1	265.6	16.2	555.4	33.8	1642.9	821.9	50.0

taxable income using a £150 lower limit of liability throughout,
together with the well-known calculations of British national
income prepared by Phyllis Deane and W. A. Cole.[36] A particular
snare here is that the national income figures may well be derived by
a constant or near-constant formula from the estimates of taxable
income according to total population growth, in which case the
percentage breakdowns reached here may be based upon circular
calculations of an especially insidious kind. This does not appear to
be the case,[37] but these calculations certainly have a margin of error
of several per cent, if not more.

The statistics in Table 4.4 reveal—as one would expect—a
continuing shift, among taxable income, from land to business and
the professions, although this trend is by no means as decisive as one
might imagine, probably because urban rents are included in the

landed figures. Concerning the distribution of income, there is remarkably little evidence of any increase in inequality—that is, of any sustained decrease in the share going to non-taxpayers—until the 1870s, when there is a sudden, sharp (6–7 per cent) decline in non-taxpayers' overall share of the income. This may well have been the result of continuing growth in both the numbers and pay of white-collar and poorer middle-class taxpayers, but after around 1870 there appears to be a marked increase in the size of top business incomes, with the beginnings of the late Victorian plutocracy. Certainly the impact of the new rich businessmen on the British consciousness rose significantly around this time.[38]

Both of these trends, however, seemingly run contrary to the most widely-accepted notions of the course of income distribution in industrial society. According to Kuznets' classical depiction, income distribution becomes markedly more unequal during the earlier stages of industrialization and then gradually becomes more egalitarian, in the manner of 'an inverted "U" '.[39] This was tentatively confirmed by Lee Soltow, in a well-known analysis of long-term trends in British income distribution.[40] The evidence found here, of virtually no change whatever in the class share of the national cake until the 1870s, when there is a marked increase in inequality, would seem to contradict this viewpoint, although the vagaries of the data and its interpretation should be kept very much in mind.

NOTES

1. See also my *Men of Property: The Very Wealthy in Britain Since the Industrial Revolution* (London, 1981), pp. 56–116.
2. So far as is known, the only named individual income-tax returns which survive in any number are those filed in Edinburgh around the period 1799–1816, currently held at the Scottish Record Office. On this material, see Hope-Jones, *Income Tax, op. cit.*, Appendix I, pp. 128–30.
3. Rubinstein, *Men of Property, op. cit.*, pp. 46–8.
4. Returns were also kept by parish and survive for every five-year period from the mid-nineteenth century at the PRO, Kew, classified at I.R.2.
5. As noted in Chapter 3, p. 76, note 20, there do exist at the PRO, Chancery Lane enormous—and quite unusable—unbound returns relating to the tax levied and paid in each administrative district. Hope-Jones has explored the changing assessments of some larger cities—

including London, Manchester and Birmingham in *Income Tax op. cit.*, pp. 71–110.

6. There are several anomalies in these printed returns, for instance the absence of some schedules for certain years. In practice 1806 is the earliest year for which complete information exists as to geography.

7. The lower limit of liability to the first income tax was £50 from 1798 to 1805, £60 in 1805–6 and £50 again from 1806 to 1815. For the second income tax, liability was £150 from 1842 to 1853, £100 from 1853 to 1876, £150 from 1876 to 1894, and £160 from 1894 until World War One.

8. Respectively *Property and Income Tax*, P.P. 1860 (546) XXXIX, Pt II and *Parliamentary Constituencies (Population)*, P.P. 1882 (149) LII.

9. Stamp, *British Incomes, op. cit.*, p. 15.

10. Defined as 'the profits of that section of the iron trade which is concerned with the smelting ore, whether such profits arise solely from smelting or from smelting carried on cojointly with other industries'. (*Ibid.*, p. 225).

11. *Ibid.*, pp. 222–6.

12. *Ibid.*, p. 81.

13. *Ibid.*, p. 163.

14. *Ibid.*, p. 170.

15. *Ibid.*, p. 263.

16. *Ibid.*, pp. 265–6. Measurement of the dimensions of this 'drain'—that is, of the growth of the corporate economy—would also be a valuable piece of research possible from I.R.16 although the combining of business and non-business corporations could be an impediment to far-reaching conclusions.

17. Although taxation information on the major industrial towns (as opposed to counties) is available in the 1882 return in the Parliamentary Paper (see note 8 above) it is *not* available in I.R.16 in a systematic way, as the boundaries of sub-county districts (termed, e.g. 'Manchester' or 'Liverpool') change without warning or definition, and are neither necessarily consistent nor coterminous with the town named. Conceivably a detailed study of I.R.2 could provide systematic information on incomes assessed in the major towns, and would be most welcome.

18. This paper might thus almost be entitled 'London *vs* Lancashire'.

19. Although I.R.16 does contain this information for every year from 1842, 1848–9 is the first year copied out by my research assistant in which full and complete county by county data is available for our purposes, because of some limitations in the presentation of Schedule E in the manuscripts.

20. E. H. Hunt, *Regional Wage Variations in Britain, 1850–1914* (Oxford, 1973), pp. 37–42.

21. Mitchell and Deane, *Abstract of British Historical Statistics, op. cit.*, pp. 348–50.

22. R. A. Church, *The Great Victorian Boom, 1850–1873* (London, 1975), pp. 142–3.

23. C. H. Lee, *British Regional Employment Statistics 1841–1971*

(Cambridge, 1979), pp. 16–18 and *passim*. (The pages of statistical tables are not numbered.)

24. Avner Offer, *Property and Politics 1870–1914* (Cambridge, 1981), esp. pp. 254–301.

25. Certainly the published statistics of income-tax assessment which appeared annually in the Parliamentary Papers are not merely unhelpful, but are quite misleading. Stamp (*British Incomes, op. cit.*, pp. 365–7) discussed the ways in which the *Irish* figures of income-tax assessment may be understated in the highly abbreviated annual printed national summaries of the income tax in the Parliamentary Papers. It is most unlikely that Stamp was permitted to see the I.R.16 manuscripts while writing *British Incomes and Property*. He makes no written reference to them, so far as I am aware. Similarly, it is even more unlikely that any other writer on this subject before the 1970s— Baxter (*National Income*, London, 1868) Chiozza Money (*Riches and Poverty, 1910*), etc.—had access to this series.

26. This was certainly the case in the assessment of Schedule C, not included in this discussion. See also Stamp's remarks on 'pensions paid from Indian revenues, *all* [assessed] in London, wherever the pensioner might be domiciled', in *British Incomes*, p. 367. Stamp here again refers to the printed returns in the Parliamentary Papers, not the manuscript returns, while such pensions might well have been classified as part of the incomes of 'public office holders' under Schedule E in the I.R.16 manuscripts. As we shall see, these were *not* assigned to a geographical locale in I.R.16.

27. Since no individual income-tax returns survive, it is, moreover, impossible to tell whether, if any such companies existed, they were assessed in London or a provincial county.

28. Luther A. Hart, *Branch Banking in England* (Philadelphia, 1929), pp. 70–2 and Appendix I.

29. *Ibid.*

30. For example, there are *no* figures in I.R.16 for specific London boroughs or neighbourhoods (e.g., St George, Hanover Square or Mayfair), only for the City of London and numbered (but not named or defined) districts in Middlesex. It should also be realized that the stocks and shares owned by the great landowners would be assessed under Schedule D if they properly belonged there rather than under Schedule A. An ever-increasing percentage of the income of the great landowners came from shares and business sources, at least among the great magnates lucky enough to own them, like the Dukes of Devonshire. Once again, it is not possible from the sources to ascertain where the Duke of Devonshire's personal income was assessed in the manuscript sources—in the West End, at Chatsworth, or somewhere else.

31. It may seem strange that the office-holders' percentage declines between 1860–1 and 1900–01, but this is simply because the middle class in the private sector grew relatively much more rapidly than did the public service.

32. Stamp, *British Incomes, op. cit.*, p. 516. Mitchell and Deane, *Abstract*,

op. cit., pp. 430–1. Only fragmentary figures exist for Schedule C in the first income tax. From 1872–3 to 1892–3 Schedule C also included the profits from Metropolitan Consolidated Stocks and Corporation Stocks. This sum rose from £205,000 in 1872–3 to £1,618,000 in 1892–3. (Stamp, *op. cit.*, p. 168).

33. Presumably some income-tax evasion did exist even among the singularly honest men of Britain. Since most estimates of British national income and British economic growth are derived in part from the annual tables of taxable income, they are all presumably underestimates, conceivably substantial ones. If, say, 20 per cent of taxable income was not declared, total British income would be underestimated by about 10 per cent.

34. It is also worth noting that the overall trend found here, especially London's 'U'-like percentage, is apparently paralleled by the numbers and business venues of top wealth-holders found in the probate records, where London's share declines in the fourth quarter of the nineteenth century before rising again. This would be the case if there is a time-lag of twenty-thirty years or so between maximum income accumulation and the death of a millionaire (as there most commonly is) and further indicates that the geographical distribution of the income tax found here is accurate.

35. In Table 4.3, the data for 1806 is for Schedule D only: no breakdowns by range are available for the business portion of Schedule A or for Schedule E. Similarly, the business portion of Schedule A is not available for 1860–1, while public offices are excluded from the 1900–01 data. The effect of this is probably to exaggerate London's lead among very high income-earners.

36. Stamp, *British Incomes*, *op. cit.*, pp. 518–19; Mitchell and Deane, *op. cit.*, pp. 430–1; Deane and Cole, *British Economic Growth*, *op. cit.*, pp. 166–7.

37. Deane and Cole, *British Economic Growth*, *op. cit.*, p. 165.

38. Rubinstein, *Men of Property*, p. 38.

39. Simon Kuznets, 'Economic Growth and Income Inequality', *American Economic Review*, XLV (1955).

40. Lee Soltow, 'Long-Run Changes in British Income Inequality', *Economic History Review*, 2nd ser. XXI (1968).

5

Entrepreneurial Effort and Entrepreneurial Success: Peak Wealth-holding in Three Societies, 1850–1939*

In this chapter it is hoped to draw some conclusions about the nature of entrepreneurial success from a comparison of the wealth structures of several countries, mainly Britain, the United States, and Australia, between about 1850 and 1939. The methodology and underlying assumptions follow those spelled out in my previous publications on the very wealthy in historical perspective,[1] although they ought perhaps to be outlined here. I initially undertook research on wealth-holding and the very wealthy in Britain following the Industrial Revolution, based largely on the probate records of individual wealth at death. My research subsequently turned to the international and comparative aspects of this question and I edited a volume of essays in which a number of historians have surveyed some of the other major Western nations through these sources or similar ones.[2] Although this field, especially in its comparative aspects, is still in its infancy, enough is now known about the nature of wealth-holding and its relation to entrepreneurship in these countries to make some fairly fruitful international comparisons possible, and this chapter is mainly concerned to draw a number of inferences about entrepreneurship from such comparisons. Perhaps the most significant failing of research in this field at the present time is the absence, as yet, of meaningful research on Germany, where the results would doubtless shed considerable light on the data available in other countries.[3]

The starting point of this discussion is the graph presented on

* This chapter first appeared in *Business History*, XXV, No. 1 (March 1983) published by Frank Cass & Company Ltd, London E11.

page 121, where the evolution of the peaks of wealth-holding—the scale of the largest individual fortunes—in Britain, the United States and the largest Australian state, New South Wales, has been traced between about 1850 and 1939.[4] The data for Britain and Australia differ from that for the United States. In the case of Britain and New South Wales, the graph plots the largest estates left in their respective countries in each five-year period (for example 1885–9, 1890–4, etc.), together with the tenth largest estates. This graph thus indicates the largest estates left *at death* in Britain and New South Wales. In the case of the United States, the graph presents figures for the largest personal fortunes accumulated since 1865 by America's richest men *during their lifetimes*. The names and wealth levels of these men were compiled from a wide variety of sources by Professor Frederic C. Jaher (University of Illinois), a historian who has studied this subject in great detail.[5] To figure in Jaher's study, an American must have possessed a peak fortune of at least $20 million at some time between 1865 and 1919, $30 million or more between 1920 and 1945, and $75 million since 1945; additionally, each multi-millionaire must have held his fortune long enough to be recorded in some source. Jaher's study includes 310 such American multi-millionaires whose wealth exceeded these minimal figures at some time between 1865 and about 1972. Two points about Jaher's data need to be made explicit. His data is plainly not strictly comparable to the British and Australian probate data because it includes not only wealth left at death, but peak levels of wealth as accumulated years before. The salient question is whether this significantly biases the conclusions indicated by the graph. Without going into this matter at length, it is my belief that this does not bias the results significantly. The main reason for this is that the gap between the peak level of wealth held during the lifetime of the British and Australians considered here, and their wealth at death indicated by the probate records, is almost certainly quite small in most cases, and certainly much smaller than the difference between peak wealth and wealth left at death among American multi-millionaires.[6] Stated another way, if peak wealth at death among British and Australian wealth-holders were taken as the basis of the graph, these wealth peaks would almost certainly be very similar, certainly, among the Englishmen, within one order of magnitude of the figures indicated in the graph.[7]

The second point which should be made about the wealth-levels indicated by the graph is that the identification of wealth-holders

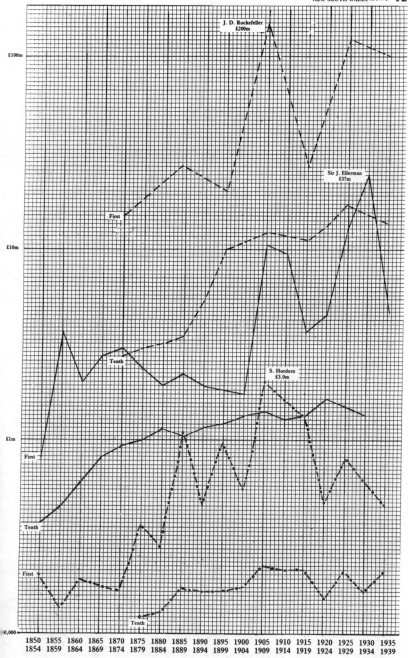

**Figure 5.1: Peak Fortunes, United States, Britain and New South Wales
1850-4 – 1935-9**

from the probate records, being comprehensive of *all* deceased persons, unquestionably records many more of the little known or unknown wealthy, as well as those among the 'idle rich' than does any study or listing of millionaires, like Jaher's, which is primarily based upon the fame or reputation of such men. Any such listing of millionaires is *not* comprehensive and exhaustive in the same sense as a study based upon the probate sources and is, in fact, only a sample of all millionaires, one almost certainly consisting of those who made the greatest impact upon contemporaries or enjoyed the most fame or notoriety. By thus omitting an unknown but possibly substantial proportion of America's wealth elite who would be found in more comprehensive data sources, the graph almost certainly understates the real wealth of America's wealth elite, since it excludes an unknown number of millionaires of little fame or renown. Throughout the study from which these figures derive, Jaher has in fact consistently understated rather than overstated the riches often attributed to America's richest men. For instance, it is commonly believed that, at their peaks, both Henry Ford (d. 1948) and Andrew Mellon, the steel magnate (d. 1937) were worth just in excess of $1 billion, but Jaher has given their peak fortunes as, respectively, 'only' about $600 million and $800 million, and there is similar evidence of caution among many of his other estimates of peak wealth. In compiling the graph, to make the American figures comparable to those for Britain and Australia, each American wealth-holder has been assigned to the decadal (not half-decadal) grouping he would be placed in at age 70, unless he died at an earlier age, when he is counted with the decade in which he died.

The first and most important conclusion to be drawn from this graph is evident at first glance: being very rich meant something entirely different in America, Britain and Australia. More particularly, there is a gap of between four and twenty times in the peak levels of wealth-holding between the United States and Britain, and again of between about three and ten times between Britain and New South Wales. These differences are apparent early in the history of each country and persist throughout the history of each; the exceptions—those who accumulated anomalously high levels of wealth, in the context of their national wealth structures— are few, and Britain's most striking such case will be discussed below. In the case of the United States, the wealthiest pre-Civil War fortunes, those of John Jacob Astor (d. 1848) and Cornelius Vanderbilt (d. 1877) were certainly already as large as or larger than the peak of British business fortunes of the day, despite Britain's predominant position in world trade and manufacturing: Astor was generally regarded as worth $25 million at his death, Vanderbilt as worth $100 million or more. The latter fortune was at least three and probably four times as large as that accumulated by any British businessman before the very end of the nineteenth century. By the early twentieth century, the largest American fortunes, those of men like Rockefeller, Ford, Mellon, Carnegie, Harriman, Frick, and Armour, were simply immeasurably larger than those of the richest British or Australian business millionaires, even tycoons like Overstone, Iveagh, the Willses or Coateses in Britain or their equivalents in Australia. In the period 1900–14, the two wealthiest Englishmen were almost certainly the Duke of Westminster, worth about £15 million, and from about 1905, Sir John Ellerman, who may have been worth over £20 million by 1914. The largest British estates probated in this period were those of Charles Morrison (d. 1909) who left £10.9 million and H. O. Wills (d. 1911) who left £5.2 million. The South Africans Sir Julius Werhner (d. 1912) and Alfred Beit (d. 1906) left, respectively, £10 million and £8 million in Britain. The largest Australian estate in this period totalled about £3 million. The most striking single fact to emerge from a comparative view of the wealth structures of these three countries then, is the immensely higher levels of wealth among America's richest men compared with those in Britain and Australia.

Although not enough is known as yet about the situation in other Western societies to generalize with confidence, it seems clear enough from what is known that by the late nineteenth century (if not before) America already held a similar long lead in her wealth peaks over those which probably were to be found in France and Germany, and that the levels of peak fortunes in these two countries closely resembled the levels found in Britain. In France the largest probate fortune identified by Professor Adeline Daumard among the sample of years she has investigated is one of about £10 million (250 million francs) in 1911, roughly the same as the largest fortune left in Britain at the time.[8] In Imperial Germany, it is known that the Prussian Census of Wealth and Income of 1911 recorded only four persons worth the equivalent of £5 million or more, 30 as worth between £1,500,000 and £5 million, and 88 as worth between £769,000 and £1,000,000. The average wealth owned by the four richest men in this census was over £10,600,000: in other words, almost certainly comparable to the wealth peaks found in Britain at the time, if these figures are accurate.[9] According to a contemporary German publication, *Jahrbuch der Millionäire* (1913), the three wealthiest Germans of the day were Bertha Krupp, worth 183 million marks (about £14,100,000), Prince Henckel von Donnersmark, worth 254 million marks (£12,700,000), and Baron von Goldschmidt-Rothschild, at 163 million marks (£8,100,000),[10] again very close to the British and French peak fortunes of the time.

One of the most curious features of these national wealth differentials is that they cannot readily be correlated with any of the obvious indices of economic development. *Per capita* income was probably somewhat higher in the United States than in Britain by the late nineteenth century, but it was also certainly higher in Australia than in Britain (and possibly higher in Australia than the United States).[11] National income or net national product, either in total or on a *per capita* basis, certainly did not demonstrate so marked a differential between Britain and America as these figures seem to indicate. America's resource base, its distances, and the scale of operations of its entrepreneurs were indeed vast and possibly without equal among advanced societies, but were they really more vast than the imperial and world-wide network of finance, trade and manufacturing centred in Britain?

Perhaps the most obvious way of explaining these differences is in terms of the differing size of firms in America, Britain, and elsewhere. As is well known from the research of Professor P. L. Payne and others, the largest industrial corporations in Edwardian Britain were much smaller than their counterparts in America, much less frequently found in heavy industry and manufacturing, and included many bizarre and marginal concerns (for instance, Maple's furniture shop and Bovril, the meat extract makers, were among the very largest corporations in Britain in 1905), while America's largest corporations of the time mainly consisted of genuine industrial super-giants like United States Steel and Standard Oil.[12] Any such differences in size of assets would, naturally, be reflected in the portfolios of their asset-owners. Yet, while differential size of firms is an important factor in explaining wealth differences, it is surely not the whole story. The differential in the size of fortunes between Britain and America was evident at least forty years before America's industrial flowering from 1870 onwards; it was already perceptible as early as the Jacksonian period, while Britain's centuries-long lead in economic development did not produce a group of wealth-holders richer than those in the United States. Not all, nor even many, of the wealthiest businessmen were associated with their nation's largest firms and industrial super-giants. Particularly in Britain, a disproportionate percentage of wealth-holders headed banks or commercial firms which remained private partnerships throughout the period under discussion and indeed, down to the present; others grew very rich via smaller companies and corporations. Much of the share portfolio in American enterprise was owned abroad, especially by Englishmen, and naturally the assets which comprised the portfolios of a nation's top wealth-holder would include more than shares or interest in one firm. Finally, the size of firm differentials themselves reflects more fundamental tendencies within each national economy which must themselves be identified.

It would seem, then, rather difficult to give an accurate and persuasive explanation for the national differences in wealth structures found here. Indeed, in surveying these differences, one is reminded of Daniel Defoe's remark about the prehistoric megaliths he found during his tour of England: 'All that can be learn'd of them is, that *there they are!*' While no doubt economists and cliometricians could devise appropriate mathematical models of British and American economic development which could reproduce the wealth differentials that actually occurred, it seems to this non-cliometrician that they would probably omit those essentially cultural and *sui generis* non-quantifiable differences which would be noticed by most historians of the subject.

This point might be added to by considering the figures of New South Wales here in more detail. In the entire period between 1817, when the Australian probate figures begin, and 1939, all of the Australian colonies, New South Wales included, produced fewer than twenty bona fide millionaires—some of whom left the bulk of their estates in Britain—and only one man (Samuel Hordern, a Sydney retail merchant who died in 1909) who left over £3 million.[13] Assuming that the structures of wealth-holding in France, Germany, and possibly other European nations are broadly similar to those found in Britain, Australia is plainly situated at the low end of the spectrum of Western nations in this characteristic, perhaps anomalously so. Naturally, with its relatively tiny population and limited resource base, its government-owned railway network, its barriers to internal trade, its ideology of equality and its general remoteness and marginality to the Western world's core of development—what Geoffrey Blainey has termed the 'tyranny of distance'[14]—it may indeed plausibly be supposed that the number and range of Australia's top of fortunes would indeed be low. Similarly, Australia was a 'new' nation in which nearly all wealth-holders were 'new' men in some sense; few wealthy dynasties had as yet emerged. On the other hand, a low ratio of population to resources might result in higher *per capita* takings for all, and it is often argued that, in essence, just such a low ratio of population to resources accounts for Australia's historically high *per capita* income, while its limited population and high transport costs might equally produce natural monopolistic or oligopolistic concentrations in many fields.[15] 'Self-made men' existed in America and Britain (though their number is commonly exaggerated), and genuinely self-made American entrepreneurs like Carnegie amassed fortunes in keeping with their national scales of wealth. Certainly too, Australia was not devoid of lucrative natural resources or exportable goods, and, since Dickens' Magwitch, has long possessed a reputation for sending its newly-rich men back to the old country to live like princes. A useful comparison might perhaps be drawn with the contemporaneous situation in California which, like New South Wales, also boomed following a gold rush and, like Australian colonies, contained a large-scale pastoral and single-port mercantile economy until World War One. Nevertheless, California certainly produced many more large fortunes than New South Wales or indeed, than any of the Australian colonies.[16] Yet, in terms of *per capita* income, New South Wales and the other Australian colonies were probably broadly comparable to the American states; in short, little can be inferred about the maximum range of individual fortunes from the obvious indices of economic development or indeed, from the fact of economic development itself.

Several of the other explanations which might readily come to the mind of an economist also seem, on historical reflexion, to lack compelling force. Although some of America's multi-millionaires (like Rockefeller) may have monopolized a scarce resource or commodity in demand, others (like say, Ford) became equally wealthy in markets which were highly competitive, while monopolization per se—as the German data seems to show—whereas it may indeed account for the creation of large fortunes, does not really explain the singular size of American wealth accumulation. Similarly, some economists might point to the greater profitability of risky areas of the economy, but were

America's fortunes made in these areas, and were they riskier, by the degree suggested by these wealthy differentials, than their British counterparts?

Some of the conclusions to which this discussion is pointing might become clearer if one considers the occupational distribution of the wealth elite in these three societies grouped by the major occupation sector—finance, commerce, manufacturing, landownership, and so on—in which the top wealth-holders were engaged. Although the British and New South Wales data derive from my own research, again the American data are derived from Professor Jaher's work and reflect his own classification schema and criteria. Although too, the British and American tables here contain *all* of the top wealth-holders in their respective studies, the New South Wales data comprise sample cohorts of the 50 top wealth-holders deceased by five-year periods at twenty-five year intervals (except for the final cohort, 1935–9).[17]

The main point to emerge from even a glance at Table 5.1 is, of course, that there are distinctive national typologies of the specific occupational fields in which each society's richest men were likely to earn their fortunes. These typologies persist over time, despite the fact that they often represent areas which the economic development of each country had appeared to pass by. Specifically, manufacturing and heavy industry were much more important as a breeding-ground of American multi-millionaires than was manufacturing in Britain, or still more, in New South Wales. Despite the industrialization of Britain and the high rate of urbanization characteristic of Australia, the importance of landownership in the British wealth structure and, perhaps more surprisingly, of pastoralism in New South Wales long after the Australian 'pastoral age' had passed are notable features of the occupational distribution indicated here.[18] Manufacturing was more important to the wealth structure of the more advanced and 'progressive' United States. In Britain—in contrast to the United States—the net effect of the Industrial Revolution was systematically to advantage the older and most conservative, rather than the newer and most radical sectors of the British wealth structure—above all, the great landowners and the bankers and merchants of the City of London, rather than the manufacturers and industrialists, a circumstance which had the most profound effects on the evolution of British society and its class system.[19] Is this surprising? Doubtless most observers would think not, as the

Table 5.1: Occupational Distribution of Top Wealth-holders in Three Counties

1. *United States—by Birth, Cohorts, Percentages*

Birth Dates	Finance	Commercial Commerce & Transport*	Real Estate	Mfg.	Others & mixed	Total
Pre-1830	18.5	33.3	14.8	29.6	3.7	27
		51.8				
1830–65	14.3	18.1	6.7	55.3	6.7	105
		32.4				
1866–99	9.7	12.4	1.8	68.5	8.0	113
		22.1				

* Includes railways.
Source: F. C. Jaher, 'The Gilded Elite', in W. D. Rubinstein (ed.), *Wealth and the Wealthy in the Modern World* (Croom Helm, 1980).

2. *Britain—by Death Cohorts, Numbers & Percentages (percentages apply to non landed only)*

A. *Millionaires*

	1809–58	1858–79	1880–99	1900–14
1. Manufacturers	5 = 55.5%	14 = 43.3%	22 = 37.7%	20 = 27.4%
Food, drink, tobacco	0	1 = 3.3%	14 = 23.7%	14 = 19.2%
2. Commerce & finance	3 = 33.3%	16 = 53.3%	23 = 39.0%	38 = 52.1%
3. Public admin., professionals, etc.	1 = 11.1%	—	—	1 = 1.4%
4. Land	181	117	38	27

B. *Half-Millionaires*

	1809–58	1858–79	1880–99	1900–14
1. Manufacturing	11 = 22.9%	32 = 31.7%	60 = 38.0%	59 = 32.6%
Food, drink, tobacco	1 = 2.0%	2 = 2.0%	23 = 14.6%	
2. Commerce & finance	28 = 58.3%	60 = 59.4%	66 = 41.8%	91 = 50.3%
3. Public admin., professional, etc.	8 = 16.7%	7 = 6.9%	9 = 5.7%	9 = 5.0%
4. Land	349	165	137	80

Source: W. D. Rubinstein, 'The Victorian Middle Classes: Wealth, Occupation and Geography', *Economic History Review* (1977).

3. *New South Wales (wealth-holders' three chief interests, by five-year periods, death cohorts; representative* cohorts only)*

	Field	% of known total
1850–4	1. Agriculture	35
	2. Commerce	31
	3. Services	14
1875–9	1. Agriculture	65
	2. Commerce	10
	3. (2 fields, each)	6
1900–04	1. Agriculture	51
	2. Commerce	24
	3. (3 fields, each)	4
1925–9	1. Agriculture	30
	2. Commerce	25
	3. Others	9
1935–9	1. Agriculture	49
	2. Commerce	29
	3. (2 fields, each)	6

* Every 25 years.
Source: Rubinstein: 'The Top Wealth-holders of New South Wales, 1817–1939', *Australian Economic History Review*, (1980).

secular decline of Britain after 1870 is very frequently blamed on the failure of its manufacturing industry to keep pace, especially during the so-called 'Second Industrial Revolution' of 1895–1914. But it is equally notable that bankers and financiers certainly did not dominate the American wealth structure. J. P. Morgan notwithstanding, and 'finance capital' notwithstanding, entrepreneurs like Andrew Carnegie, Henry Ford, and Andrew Mellon, whose base was in manufacturing and heavy industry, were not pre-empted by Wall Street and its financial oligarchs. The pattern elsewhere may well be different. In Germany, where the concept of 'finance capital' arose, it may well have been that banks were much more directly involved, and attained a much greater degree of control over manufacturing industries, than in the three English-speaking countries surveyed here, and this could be reflected in the structure of its wealthy elite as well as in other ways.

A number of important points concerning the nature of entrepreneurship and of entrepreneurial effort and success seem to follow from this comparative survey, and in the remainder of this chapter they and their implications will be considered. The first of these points, and the most obvious one, is simply that the notion of entrepreneurial success, and the rewards implied by that success, mean something markedly different from country to country, and these concepts must at all times be employed only with these national differences kept squarely in mind. It makes little sense, and certainly it is unwontedly imprecise, to talk of 'the very rich' in America, Britain and Australia, or any other countries in the abstract, given the order of magnitude differences which are demonstrated by societies culturally, politically, and even economically very similar.

Secondly, it follows from this that different types of entrepreneurial activities—that is, different occupational divisions in the economy—will meet with varying degrees of success in different countries. They will be more or less likely to flourish depending upon how that economy, as it were, 'favours' a particular occupation, and will meet with inherently different degrees or levels of reward. Plainly the entrepreneurial rewards gained by the most successful American businessmen were historically far larger than those of their British equivalents, and immeasurably larger than their Australian equivalents; manufacturers in heavy industry were far more likely to become exceedingly wealthy in America than in Britain or Australia.

This is perhaps the crux of the matter, for these differentials in reward were presumably gained despite the fact that the most successful businessmen in each of these countries possessed broadly the same levels of talent. One can argue, of course, that the reason American entrepreneurs were so rich was that they were better businessmen than their British counterparts, that they possessed, as a group, more of those qualities and abilities which make businessmen rich than did their British or Australian counterparts. Up to a point, few would dispute that there may well be an element of truth in such a contention. The ideology, legal system, and pervasive national spirit of nineteenth-century America probably favoured the development of the 'rational-capitalistic personality', with its gamut of conflicting but distinctive traits from thrift, foresight and innovativeness to low cunning, lack of conscience, and religious guilt. On the other hand, the restraints upon entrepreneurial ambition and scope—a matter discussed more fully below—were certainly less severe and inbuilt into the social fabric of society. These important cultural differences may indeed account for a portion of the difference. Successful nineteenth-century American entrepreneurs may in truth have been, say, twice as able as their British counterparts, always assuming such abilities may be objectively measured. I, for one, am prepared to believe this. But ten times as able? Frankly, I find this impossible to believe, and am certain that most historians of entrepreneurship would find this impossible to believe. Can it really be that Britain's greatest entrepreneurs, men like Arkwright, Peel, Overstone, Rothschild, Currie, Cassel, Leverhulme, or Northcliffe were only one-tenth as talented as Vanderbilt, Astor, Ford, Carnegie, or Morgan? The last two names in this series are instructive in the comparison, for Andrew Carnegie was born in Scotland, migrating to Pennsylvania at the age of thirteen, while J. P. Morgan, like his father Junius Spencer Morgan before him, lived for much of his life in London, where he had intimate and longstanding business links with the world of City finance. And can it really be that Australia's most successful entrepreneurs were only one one-hundredth as able as their American counterparts? Surely the suggestion is quite incredible. The similarities between Australia and America are obviously very great: both pioneer societies on immensely rich continents settled by migrants of virtually identical cultural and historical traditions and of identical ethnic and linguistic background. Even granting that Australia's population was only a fraction of America's, and that Australia's convict origins cast a long shadow over its historical evolution and national character, the absence of anyone at all who achieved a modicum of the financial rewards of America's greatest entrepreneurs argues strongly against the relevance of such a contention.

If the facts of these striking national differences are accepted, a number of significant conclusions flow from them. One of these—to put the matter in a provocative and doubtless extreme way—is that in terms of international comparisons, there would appear to be *little or no nexus between entrepreneurial ability and entrepreneurial success.* The second, which is to say much the same thing, is that *place (in a nation's economy and, more doubtfully in the world economic system) is more important than ability.* The third is that *both degrees of entrepreneurial success and the areas or fields in which entrepreneurial success are most likely to occur are virtually predetermined by the underlying structure of that society.* It is not a matter of who you are, or how talented an entrepreneur you may be. Beyond a certain minimum standard of entrepreneurial pluck and luck, possibly a rather minimal standard, success is virtually guaranteed, *if one is in the right place,* compared with other entrepreneurs of similar abilities who are in the 'wrong' place, or with the general run of businessmen. No one claims, of course, that if one had opened a steel mill in Pittsburgh in 1870 he would automatically accumulate a fortune of $200 million. Naturally, only the very luckiest, hardiest, and most able steel magnate in Pittsburgh could possibly build up a fortune of that magnitude or anything approaching it. But the Pittsburgh steel magnate would be far richer, in all likelihood, than his equivalent in Sheffield or Newcastle, New South Wales, even assuming, indeed, that the American steel magnate's entrepreneurial abilities were actually *inferior* to the equivalent overseas.

Such a conclusion—that place is more important than effort—is applicable to many areas of entrepreneurial activity beside those at the very top. It is obvious that no corner shopkeeper, regardless of how successful he is, will ever be as wealthy as even a moderately successful stockbroker. Yet in all likelihood the shopkeeper, possibly an excellent, sober Methodist, works literally five times harder than the mannered, epicene stockbroker, whose most vigorous activities probably occur not in the City but on the golf course or in training his prize basset hound for the next edition of Cruft's. Nor, surely, is it clear that the shopkeeper's work requires more intelligence or business acumen—however that might be defined or measured— than does the stockbroker. Yet, labour as he might, refine the business to shopkeeping as he might, no corner shopkeeper will ever make as much money, not by a long, long fraction, as even a good average stockbroker. He is simply situated in the wrong place. The parameters of affluence of the successful stockbroker are automatically higher than those of the successful shopkeeper. They are virtually predetermined, and one is unavoidably reminded in this case of the famous limerick which concludes, 'I continue to run in prearranged grooves/I'm not a bus, I'm a tram'.

It might perhaps be fruitful to examine a number of important concepts and theories in economic and social history from the perspective that place is more important than effort. One concept which would repay another look from this viewpoint is the Weber thesis, that there is a salient causal connection between the Protestant religion and entrepreneurial success. Weber originally postulated his thesis in relation to the Reformation, but in the recent past it has become a stock-in-trade of modern British social history, with Anglicans playing the role Weber assigned originally to Catholicism, and Protestant dissenters the role originally assigned to Reformation Calvinists.[20] From a study of Britain's top wealth-holders deceased between 1809 and 1914, it seems quite clear that the percentage of those wealth-holders originally nonconformist, or indeed, of nonconformist descent, is no higher than one would expect on a purely random basis.[21] While some dissenting sects, especially the Quakers, are indeed over-represented compared with their percentage in the general population, others like the Congregationalists are actually under-represented among Britain's richest businessmen. Anglicans outnumber dissenters in accordance with their numerical superiority in the whole population, while Jews and other migrant groups like the Greeks are phenomenally over-represented in Britain's Victorian and Edwardian wealth structure. Jews, for instance, account for more than 15 per cent of all non-landed millionaires deceased between 1900 and 1914, compared with their 0.5 per cent of the total population. While several plausible theories might be advanced to explain this degree of over-representation, perhaps the best explanation is that it was just these groups— migrant groups like the Jews and Greeks, together with Anglicans—who were disproportionately situated in the lucrative financial and commercial trades, especially those of the City of London and entrepôts like Liverpool (cities which were disproportionately Anglican), while successful dissenters were to be found for the most part in the northern manufacturing towns and industries seldom productive of immense fortunes. In the context of America's economic development, very nearly the opposite was the case: north-eastern Protestants predominated in the American wealth structure, in part because they dominated its most lucrative industries. In Australia, again in contrast, Anglicans and Scots Presbyterians made up the bulk of its wealth elite (in contrast to Protestant dissenters who were under-represented), again by virtue of being relatively more numerous among the leaders of its most lucrative trades.

While there was probably an affinity between particular groups and particular trades—the affinity of Jews with financial and commercial activities like those of the City of London is well documented—the ultimate success of any group was to a large extent determined by the nature and direction of the national economy in which they operated. In the Jewish case, for example (and despite what anti-semites have claimed on the matter) neither in the United States—where, after 1881, Jews were far more numerous than in Britain—nor in Australia, did Jews form so disproportionate a percentage of the wealth structure as in Britain. Indeed, even in America until World War One it is difficult to name more than a handful of the celebrated 'captains of industry' who were Jews. Can this really be because British Jews were, somehow, more dynamic entrepreneurs than their American co-religionists? And how can this be accounted for from abstract religious doctrine, or psychological traits alone? While the full explanation of this is plainly complex, in all likelihood the very affinity of Jewish entrepreneurs for commerce and finance in *both* Britain—where these fields were a disproportionate fraction of the total wealth structure—and America—where they were relatively less significant—played an important role in determining the differing success of the Jews, at this time, in either country.

This manner of looking at entrepreneurial success might usefully be extended to view the much-vexed question of whether Victorian England 'failed'. To be sure, the evidence presented here cannot address those larger questions of innovation and productivity, of comparative growth and investment rates, of the role of the government, the educational system, the Empire or of the class system in Britain's secular decline after 1870. But surely it can address the question of entrepreneurship, usually taken to be the heart of the matter, and here several propositions seem clear enough. Foremost and once again, Britain was not America, and the levels of wealth achieved by Britain's greatest entrepreneurs simply could not match those of America's greatest business leaders. This differential was inherent and persistent in the respective nature of British and American economic universes, and did not, in all likelihood, reflect any order of magnitude differences in the native abilities of their business leaders. Secondly, the pathway to wealth in Britain, as we have seen, was generally by way of finance and commerce, and especially by way of those areas of finance and commerce which led outside Britain into the wider world, like merchant banking and shipowning. Thirdly—and this is not so obvious from the data—British entrepreneurs were subject to a network of constraints inherent in the customary nature of the British firm, which probably was important in determining the maximum levels of success achievable in the context of British society. The overwhelming majority of successful British businessmen operated within the framework of a number of such constraints—those of religious, regional, class situation, communality, and aspiration, and more importantly, of the family-orientated organization of the firm—and were never truly disembodied entrepreneurial atoms of the kind postulated by Manchester liberalism. To be sure, these constraints were, at least initially, a help rather than a hindrance to entrepreneurial success. A Quaker or Unitarian could usually rely upon his co-religionists for venture capital, credit, market knowledge, business and marriage partners, and for rescue efforts in times of trouble, while spreading the risks among all partners. Yet conversely, this typical form of organization acted as a ceiling upon levels of success ultimately achievable by British entrepreneurs, most importantly by restricting the type, variety and methods of business undertaken by that family or group to the type always undertaken by that firm, and thus preventing the emergence of the true business tycoon on the American (or, perhaps, German) model who sought to control multiple key areas of the national economy. There were no Morgans or Rockefellers in Victorian Britain, not only in the sense that no one was as rich as Morgan or Rockefeller, but in the sense that no one achieved their degree of domination over the total economy.[22]

The family firm and late Victorian entrepreneurial effort in general have borne their share of the blame for Britain's decline for rather a long time, and it is certainly not the purpose of this chapter to exaggerate their role. Indeed, the issue is raised here in large part to highlight the career of the one, and perhaps only, British entrepreneur prior to 1939 who stands in sharp contrast both to the levels of entrepreneurial success achieved and the methods of entrepreneurship undertaken by the run of even very successful British businessmen. In considering whether these differing national levels of wealth were preordained and ineluctable, the British experience provides only one man whose career seems a partial exception to these relative differences. This man is Sir John Ellerman (1862–1933), whose career was so extraordinary and anomalous as to require a special discussion. Ellerman accumulated far and away the largest fortune in British history and left nearly £37 million at the nadir of the Depression. With the possible exception of Lord Nuffield,[23] Ellerman was certainly the most successful entrepreneur in modern British history, and the closest approach Britain produced in this period to a wealth-accumulator on the American scale. Ellerman's fortune was *three times* greater than the second largest British estate left prior to the 1970s, that of

Lord Iveagh, of Guinness breweries, who left a mere £13,500,000 not during the Depression but during the post-war boom in 1927. Ellerman was a self-made man—his father left £600—who was a shipping millionaire at thirty-five and later branched out into finance, newspapers, brewing and London property development. In 1916 he was quoted as saying that he was then worth £55 million which, if true, implies a rate of accumulation never otherwise seen in British history.[24] Ellerman the man and Ellerman the businessman have alike been surrounded by great mystery, and the secret of his success remains and doubtless will remain obscure.[25] Nevertheless, enough can be ascertained about his career and his methods to illuminate much of his success, and as well, to highlight the contrast between his fortune and those of other leading British entrepreneurs.

All contemporary sketches of Ellerman's life were agreed on his major interest in life. According to his obituary in the *Daily Mail*—and this was echoed in all the other accounts of his career—

> No legends have gathered round his name. He was the Silent Ford, the Invisible Rockefeller. He had no public life. He had hardly ever been photographed. He had only one interest in his life. That was his work. His work was his hobby and his hobby was his work. He enjoyed acquiring some enterprise and building it up into a success, just as a great doctor gets deep satisfaction from curing a difficult disease. He never spent as much as five per cent of his income in any year, investing the rest.[26]

His daughter, in her autobiography, provides us with some interesting insights as to his character.

> I was always more interested in money, I think, than my father. He was a mathematician and his interests were in abstractions. I have seldom known anyone more remote from the things of this world. The success or failure of an equation meant a great deal to him, its rewards to himself very little. He possessed the detachment that lifts finance to art, creates 'risk capital' and is one of the nation's most valuable assets. In antiquity, I suppose that he would have been an austere Pythagorean.[27]

Ellerman's 'detachment' is surely one of the keys to understanding his singular success. For Ellerman was an almost unique example of a successful British entrepreneur who was entirely free of those constraints which formed so notable a part of British business life. He was not the scion of a family firm nor, indeed, did he have a family for most of his career.[28] He was was a second-generation Englishman (his father had migrated from Germany) but had no links either to a foreign country or to an immigrant community. He grew up in Hull and later Birmingham but retained few links to either after establishing his businesses in London. Shipping was not in his blood: he had trained as an accountant. He was nominally an Anglican, but possessed no religious or communal attachments of any kind. He was, very definitely, a self-made man whose interests were, and continued to be until he died, in making money and continuing to make money in the strangely detached way—as an intellectual exercise or puzzle rather than for the sake of acquisitiveness—which his associates invariably mentioned. He never mixed in Society, never went beyond the baronetcy he had acquired in 1905 to the peerage he could unquestionably have attained, never held any office, public or honorary, of any kind. He lived, as it were, in abstemious luxury in a mansion in Mayfair, a seafront house in Eastbourne, and continental hotels.[29] He had few friends and was a lone wolf *par excellence*, his contemporaries all agree, but he simply cannot in fairness be compared to the malevolent and anti-social tradition of American multi-millionaires. Ellerman's business method in shipping consisted almost exclusively of buying and restoring to health old but essentially sound shipping firms which were at the point of entrepreneurial decline following the death or retirement of their founders.[30] His financial transactions were invariably the most sound and conservative he could choose, usually involving the purchase of debentures, and were, indeed, the opposite of financial speculation in the usual sense. Similarly, although during the 1920s he was probably among the four or five largest London property owners, he consistently purchased only high-quality sites for genuine rental purposes and did not employ any of the methods made familiar by the post-1945 property developers. Ellerman, then, was an entirely rational businessman, different in his social background, lifestyle, and methods from virtually any major British entrepreneur of his century, and more closely resembling a chess grandmaster tackling a difficult middle game than a Forsyte. No one would wish to infer too much from one example, but one cannot escape the conclusion that there was room in the British economy for many Ellermans, and that had these other Ellermans existed, the history of Victorian and Edwardian entrepreneurship might have been very different. For all of Ellerman's very successful contemporaries acquired only a fraction of Ellerman's wealth, and surely in the contrast between him and his contemporaries the lesson lies—though to determine the precise balance here among Ellerman's methods, his lifestyle, or his approach to entrepreneurship is more debatable. Ellerman's career was a genuine *tour de force* among those of Britain's leading entrepreneurs of his day; Ellerman was a unique figure who, by standing apart from them, indicates the nature of the consistent patterns among all of Britain's leading businessmen.

Finally something might perhaps be said about the cumulative effects of these national wealth differentials upon their respective societies. Perhaps most importantly, the fact of America's comparatively wealthier wealth-holders was highly significant, if not instrumental, in shifting the centre of the Western world's cultural and scientific base to the United States. Fortunes of such unprecedented size enabled wealthy Americans to endow universities, found scientific and cultural institutions of every kind, and endow research which, in less than a century, transformed the image of America in European eyes from that of a land of frontier barbarians to the centre of the Western world's intellectual and scientific life, exporting frames of reference, methodologies of knowledge, and concepts of normality to the old world.[31] While other factors in this process were obviously crucial—the self-destruction of Europe in 1914–18 and 1939–45, the rise of anti-modern totalitarian systems in central and eastern Europe, and the flight of many academics, scientists and intellectuals to the United States following 1917 and 1933—America's unique elites, uniquely wealthy and, with all the vigour and vulgarity of the novice, uniquely anxious to better the old world at its own game—provided the material and political incentives which made this transformation possible.[32]

NOTES

1. See the 'Introduction' to W. D. Rubinstein (ed.), *Wealth and the Wealthy in the Modern World* (London, 1980). On Britain, see my *Men of Property, op. cit.*, and for Australia, my 'Top Wealth-holders of New South Wales, 1817–1939, *Australian Economic History Review* (1980). Previous versions of this chapter were read at the Institute of Historical Research, London, at the University of Lancaster and at Deakin University. I am most grateful for the comments received on these occasions. I am also most grateful to Mr Ray Duplain (Deakin University) for drawing the graph.

2. Rubinstein (ed.), *Wealth and the Wealthy, op. cit.*, which surveyed the United States, France and Italy. Contributions on Australia, Germany and the Netherlands could not be published in this collection for reasons of space. I have also undertaken a detailed study of wealth-holding and the wealthy in the Australian states from 1817 to 1939.

3. Professor Hartmut Kaelble (Free University of Berlin) has begun to examine this question in several unpublished papers.

4. The sums given are all in sterling, taking $5 as £1.

5. They form the basis of the discussion in Jaher's essay on 'The Gilded Elite: The United States From 1865' in Rubinstein (ed.), *Wealth and the Wealthy, op. cit.* For reasons of space, a complete list of the names of these multi-millionaires, their level of wealth, and other salient information could not, as the author had hoped, be published in this volume, but is available from Professor Jaher.

6. The main reasons for this were the much greater degree of philanthropy among Americans, their greater employment of trusts and foundations aimed at tax avoidance, and the more speculative nature of the American economy generally and the fields most American multi-millionaires were engaged in.

7. With the possible exception of the case of Sir John Ellerman discussed below, I have seldom come across British press speculation, even the most lurid and unreliable, which estimated a British millionaire's wealth *substantially* above his wealth at death.

It ought to be pointed out that unsettled real property is excluded from the British probate figures until 1898, settled realty until 1926. Thus landed wealth (but not personal property—stocks, company shares, art works, etc.—of the great landowners) is excluded from the British data. Although this will make a difference (though not a crucial one) to this graph, it will not, of course, affect the conclusions about the differences in peak wealth among the *businessmen* and *entrepreneurs* in the three countries. Even if land is included, the relative British figures vis-à-vis America's are not much altered: according to John Bateman's *Great Landowners* (1884 edn), the largest landed income of any great landowner, as found in the *Return of Owners of Land* of 1873–6 was the £232,000 p.a. enjoyed by the Duke of Buccleuch, suggesting a landed capital value in his case of about £6,500,000. The income of the Duke of Westminster (mainly consisting of London real estate, excluded from the *Return of Owners of Land*) was probably at this time in the range of £290–325,000 p.a., suggesting a capital value of £10 million. (On this topic see Rubinstein, *Men of Property, op. cit.* pp. 193–213). The largest *personal* fortune left by a British landowner (that is, his investments and other non-landed property) between 1850 and 1914 was the £3,200,000 million left by Lord Allendale in 1907, a figure which almost certainly includes some unsettled land. It should finally not be forgotten that most agricultural land values declined sharply after 1879, and only those landowners with substantial urban or mineral properties were unscathed.

8. Adeline Daumard, 'Wealth and Affluence in France Since the Beginning of the Nineteenth Century', in Rubinstein (ed.), *Wealth and*

the Wealthy, op. cit., p. 105. It was left by a French Rothschild.
9. G. H. Knibbs, *The Private Wealth of Australia and Its Growth* (Melbourne, 1918), p. 62.
10. Cited in William Manchester, *The Arms of Krupp 1587–1968* (Boston, Mass., 1968), p. 263. (The reference is to the multi-volumned work by Rudolf Martin, *Jahrbuch des Bermögens und Einkommens der Millionäire* (Berlin, 1913).)
11. Lance Davis, 'The Capital Markets and Industrial Concentration: The US and UK, a Comparative Study', *Economic History Review*, 2nd ser. XX (1966), p. 259, note 2 states that British *per capita* income was 'about four-fifths of America's in 1890'. According to R. V. Jackson, 'The gold rushes left Australians as probably the richest people in the world. In 1860 real product and consumption per head were much higher than in Britain and probably higher than in the United States'. R. V. Jackson, *Australian Economic Development in the Nineteenth Century* (Canberra 1977), p. 11.
12. P. L. Payne, 'The Emergence of the Large-Scale Company in Great Britain, 1870–1914', *Economic History Review* 2nd ser. XX (1967), pp. 530–40. See also Lance Davis, *loc. cit.*, pp. 255–72, for an interesting and neglected comparison of capital markets in Britain and America, of much relevance to the discussion here. Davis suggests that, paradoxically, difficulties of entrepreneurs in acquiring external sources of finance in the United States, compared with Britain's 'adequate financial markets' (p. 272), 'provide an explanation of the basis of the fortunes of certain American entrepreneurs' *(ibid.)*. Davis discusses business ventures in steel, meat packing and petroleum, as well as comparing the careers of the American financier J. P. Morgan and the British company promoter H. Osborne O'Hagan (who was an early associate of Sir John Ellerman's). Stimulating as Davis's discussion is, the question remains, can access to finance alone explain the order of magnitude differences examined here? It is perhaps worth noting that O'Hagan noted—ingenuously or not—in his autobiography that 'Had I the feeling about money which was possessed by Sir John Ellerman and other of my friends, I should have become, like them, immensely wealthy, but I had no desire to look in the papers the day after my decease to find I had died a millionaire. I never attempted to stem the outgoing of money outside my City Life.' H. Osborne O'Hagan, *Leaves from My Life*, Vol. II (London, 1929), 217.
13. Since I have systematically gone through both the British probate records and those of the six Australian colonies, I have been able to identify all Australians who left substantial British estates and have included these with the appropriate Australian set of figures.
14. Hordern left £3,004,000. The largest estates left in the other Australian colonies and states up until 1939 were those of William Gibson (d. 1918) retail merchant of Melbourne, Victoria, who left £2,227,000; James Tyson (d. 1899) the pastoralist, who left £1,334,000 in Queensland (and over £1 million in other Australian colonies); and J. L. Bonython (d. 1939), pastoralist of South Australia,

£1,993,000. In Western Australia and Tasmania, the largest estates totalled only £600,000 and £429,000.

15. Geoffrey Blainey, *The Tyranny of Distance* (Melbourne, 1966). On the Australian economic development see R. V. Jackson, *Australian Economic Development, op. cit.*, and W. A. Sinclair, *The Process of Economic Development in Australia* (Melbourne, 1976).

16. For example the famous 'Big Four' of Californian railways:' Charles Crocker (d. 1888), Mark Hopkins (d. 1876), Collis P. Huntington (d. 1900), and Leland Stanford (d. 1893). Professor Jaher credits these men with peak fortunes of, respectively, $24 million, $20 million, $60 million, and $30–40 million. Huntington's fortune was larger than that of *any* British businessman of his lifetime.

17. I have not included *all* New South Wales cohorts in my study for space reasons. The pattern of occupational distribution among the remaining cohorts is *very* similar to those given here: see Rubinstein, 'Top wealth-holders of New South Wales', *loc. cit.*, pp. 147–9.

18. Pastoralism is an even more important factor in the wealth structures of the other Australian colonies, even in Victoria, where Melbourne's growth between 1835 and 1890 was more rapid than perhaps any city in the white Empire.

19. Arno J. Mayer, *The Persistence of the Old Regime: Europe to the Great War* (London, 1981), is a stimulating recent study which makes this point in a much broader European-wide context. Other recent works on British history implicitly written from this or a similar perspective include David Cannadine, *Lords and Landlords: The Aristocracy and the Towns, 1774–1967* (Leicester, 1980); Patrick Joyce, *Work, Society and Politics: The Culture of the Factory in Late Victorian England* (Hassocks, 1980); Raphael Samuel (ed.), *Miners, Quarrymen and Saltworkers* (London, 1977); Rubinstein, *Men of Property, op. cit.* and Martin J. Wiener, *English Culture and the Decline of the Industrial Spirit, 1850–1980* (Cambridge, 1981). It is wrong to link these authors together as a 'school': indeed it is the difference in the authors' ideological and historiographical perspectives, rather than their similarity, which is so striking.

20. On the Weber thesis, see Robert W. Green (ed.), *Protestantism, Capitalism and Social Science. The Weber Thesis Controversy* (Lexington, Mass., 1973); S. N. Eisenstadt, *The Protestant Ethic and Modernization. A Comparative View* (New York, 1968); and Kurt Samuelsson, *Religion and Economic Action* (New York, 1961).

21. The evidence is summarized in Rubinstein, *Men of Property, op. cit.*, pp. 145–63.

22. It is interesting to note that no heir to a great fortune in Victorian or Edwardian Britain ever used his inheritance to build up a vast, super-giant fortune on the American scale. The societal and economic constraints which worked against this variety of heroic accumulation were simply too great.

23. Nuffield died in 1963, leaving £3,500,000. He had given away over £30 million during his lifetime.

24. Quoted in *Morning Post*, 18 July 1933.

25. On Ellerman, see James Taylor, *Ellermans: A Wealth of Shipping* (London, 1976), pp. 9–94; 'Sir John Ellerman', *Dictionary of National Biography Supplement*; and my notice of his career in D. J. Jeremy (ed.), *The Dictionary of Business Biography*, (5 vols) Vol. II, pp. 248–61.

26. *Daily Mail*, 18 July 1933.

27. Bryher, *The Heart to Artemis* (London, 1963), p. 106. ('Bryher' has been the pseudonym employed throughout her life by the novelist and poet Annie Winifred Ellerman.)

28. Ellerman's father died when he was nine; his only son was not born until he was forty-seven, and at no time until shortly before his death (when his son came of age) did any relatives participate in any of his concerns.

29. He never deliberately purchased a single acre of agricultural land nor any country house. When in 1917 he was compelled to purchase Slains Castle and Loughaven House, in Aberdeenshire, from the Errol family as part of a financial transaction, he sold it two years later. According to the *Daily Mail* (*loc. cit.*), he 'never went there—he never even saw it'.

30. Thus Ellerman acquired such old-established shipping firms as the Leyland Lines, Papayanni & Co., Robert Alexander & Co., the Hall Line and Thomas Wilson & Co. of Hull, the largest private shipping concern in the world. See Taylor, *Ellermans, op. cit.*, pp. 177–256.

31. This important transformation—arguably the most important intellectual transformation of the past century, although it is largely overlooked by historians—has never been traced in the manner it deserves. See, however, Daniel J. Kelves, *The Physicists*. (New York, 1978); Donald Fleming and Bernard Bailyn, *The Intellectual Migration* (Cambridge, Mass., 1969); and Stanley Cohen, 'American Foundations as Patrons of Science: The Commitment to Individual Research', in Nathan Reingold (ed.), *The Sciences in the American Context: New Perspectives* (Washington, DC, 1979). On German (and European) perceptions of the inevitable rise of America to super-power status even before 1914, see Fritz Fisher, *The War of Illusions* (London, 1975) pp. 326–7 and Bradford Perkins, *The Great Rapprochement. England and the United States, 1895–1914* (London, 1969).

32. Consider, for example, the 'dollar princesses'—the wealthy American heiresses who married into the European aristocracy before 1914. Because they were so much wealthier than most European aristocrats, they could cross seemingly insurmountable barriers with disarming ease. For instance, George Nathaniel Curzon, regarded as the personification of Britain's landed aristocracy at its haughtiest, did not think it beneath him to marry Mary Leiter, the daughter of a self-made Chicago meat-packing king.

Elites

6

New Men of Wealth and the Purchase
of Land in Nineteenth-century Britain*

I

That at every time in British history since non-landed sources of
property first emerged, new men of wealth have quickly exchanged
their fortunes earned in business, the professions or government
service for the status and security of landed acres, is an accepted
commonplace of history. Most writers on nineteenth-century
economic and social history who have discussed this process have
assumed that it continued unabated in the century following the
Industrial Revolution. E. L. Jones, for instance, has noted that 'the
successful industrialist had every incentive to assimilate to the
existing status structure of buying a large block of land. He had
perhaps attained his wealthy eminence by novel means and
untraditional attitudes, but to fix his children in the social
firmament, as to the manner born, he would have to play by the
rules of established, landed society. Few families held out long
against its leisured, bucolic delights'.[1] Writing specifically of the
Leeds merchant community of the period 1700–1830, but more
generally of the entire mercantile world of the time, R. G. Wilson
pointed out: 'If the gentry provided occasional recruits to
merchanting, the merchants in return provided the greatest channel
of recruitment to the landed classes. . . . The same process,
whereby merchants became landowners through the profits of
trade, was taking place not only in Leeds, Bristol and Newcastle,

* World Copyright: The Past and Present Society, 175 Banbury Road, Oxford,
England. This chapter first appeared in *Past and Present: A Journal of Historical
Studies*, no. 92 (August 1981) pp. 125–47, and is here reprinted with the permission
of the Society.

but in every town that could boast a merchant, banker and attorney. In the eighteenth century it was a movement which broke down almost all social barriers between the gentry and merchant classes'.[2] And a recent historian of the Whitbread family, Dean Rapp, has cited 'the acquisition of a landed estate' as one of the normal 'scales of social hierarchy' in the upward rise of a mercantile family.[3]

Nevertheless, some demurrals from this general picture have always existed and have, moreover, tended to come from the foremost authorities on landed society in modern Britain. G. E. Mingay has asserted that eighteenth-century merchants were less likely to become landowners compared with their equivalents in previous centuries, because 'investment in the funds made stocks an acceptable alternative to land, both as a pure investment and as a means of settling an income on a wife and children'.[4] He has also argued that the influence and acceptability of new men was augmented more by marriages to the older aristocracy than by the actual purchase of land.[5] Writing of the nineteenth century, F. M. L. Thompson has noted that 'By no means all successful businessmen sought to set themselves up as landed gentlemen. But that a good many of the most able and forceful could do so was a great strength to the landed interest';[6] he found that sixteen of sixty gentry families in Oxfordshire in 1873 whose origins could be traced appeared to be new men,[7] but also wisely noted the difficulties inherent in becoming a landowner on a great scale in the nineteenth century and concluded that these 'might well induce some of the mercantile and industrial wealth to lower its sights and aim at the lesser properties of "yeoman" size'.[8] Recent quantitative evidence on the purchase of land by merchant groups long before industrialization has tended to contradict the image of near-universal purchase of land by businessmen. R. G. Lang's study of Jacobean London merchants, for instance, found that 44 of a group of 140 owned no land at a time when land was virtually synonymous with status and the only true safe investment.[9]

Nevertheless, it cannot be doubted that, overall, most historians both continue to regard the movement of new men of wealth into the land as natural and normal a feature of the nineteenth century as in any previous time in British history, and tacitly view the end of this process as a phenomenon of the late nineteenth and early twentieth centuries, when the collapse of land values and genuine acceptability of businessmen and top professionals into society and the peerage for the first time signalled a realignment of social values and of social allegiances: the relative landlessness of the business and professional peers created between 1886 and 1914, a genuine novelty in the history of British elites, has been documented by F. M. L. Thompson and others.[10]

It is the purpose of this essay to question whether the Industrial Revolution and its consequences engendered *any* large-scale movement of new men of wealth into the land. The evidence presented here suggests that the number of very wealthy entrepreneurs of the post-1780 period who purchased land on a large scale was very small indeed, either in terms of the total number of men of wealth or of the total landed acreage of Britain; fewer still transformed the bulk of their property into land. It is an inescapable corollary of this that the behaviour of new men of wealth in the nineteenth century was materially different from that of new men of wealth of any previous period of English history, and, consequently, that the cessation of land purchase by newly-created peers after 1886 post-dates this shift in status values by perhaps a century. This shift must, furthermore, be related to genuine and perhaps novel changes in the self-perception of both the business and landed elites.

As with so many questions in British economic history, our common image of the movement of businessmen into the land is for the most part derived from a handful of examples of large-scale land purchase by new men of wealth, tacitly extended far beyond the representativeness of these examples. For, unquestionably, there were wealthy and successful businessmen who purchased agricultural land on a grand scale, while there are as well celebrated industrialists who put virtually all of their resources into land purchase. These will be discussed in a more comprehensive way below. Samuel J. Lloyd, first Baron Overstone, the great banker who spent £1,700,000 on the purchase of land (and still managed to leave £2,100,000 in personalty), is perhaps the most clear-cut example of the former category. In 1883, the year both of his death and of the final edition of John Bateman's *Great Landowners*, the incomparable guide to late nineteenth century landed acreage and income, Overstone was, on my own reckoning, the twenty-first greatest landowner in Britain in terms of income *derived* from land.[11] His annual income from land totalled £93,000, a figure far in excess of that received by any new man who bought land.[12] Among industrialists in the latter class, perhaps the Arkwrights and Peels are the leading examples. The sons and grandsons of Richard

Arkwright (one of the first bona fide industrial millionaires in British history), who were set up in substantial landed estates, and often became rural Anglican vicars—as clear-cut an example of entrepreneurial decline as one could wish—illustrate this process in a particularly striking way.

Yet clear-cut examples are statistically misleading unless their representativeness can be shown. It is just this all-important element of representativeness which is missing from such accounts of the transformation of business into landed wealth after the Industrial Revolution, and the question which this chapter seeks most to discuss. It is one thing to assert that the purchase of land by the newly wealthy was common, another thing entirely to contend that it was universal or even the practice of the majority.

One of the most important virtues of the probate records is that they provide the historian with objective and comprehensive evidence on the entirety of the wealthy class in nineteenth-century Britain.[13] The value of this source is augmented, for the purposes of this chapter, by the fact that, until 1898, only personalty was included in the valuation figure.[14] Since the acreage and agricultural income of all significant owners of land is known for one point of time from Bateman's *Great Landowners*, all that is required to ascertain the penetration of Britain's wealthiest business and professional men into the landed elite is a comparison of the two sources. There is one qualification which needs to be made to this statement: non-landed wealth-holders[15] who purchased land sufficient to diminish their personal fortunes to a point where they would no longer be noticed among the personalty wealth-holders, would not be caught in such a study, and for this reason it is necessary to trace the social and economic origins of at least a sample of all substantial landowners. This has been done, and the matter discussed, further along.

My research has examined the lives and careers of everyone deceased in Great Britain between 1809 and 1939 who left £500,000 or more, and in addition two groups of 'lesser wealthy'—those leaving between £150,000 and £500,000 in the period 1809–29, and those leaving £250,000–£500,000 in the years 1850–69, and it is these groups of Britain's top wealth-holders whose landownership is to be traced.[16] In Table 6.1 the landed acreage held according to Bateman by all British non-landed wealth-holders deceased between 1840 and 1914 has been traced. Since the landed holdings detailed in Bateman are known at only one point in time,[17] it becomes increasingly less plausible to correlate the Bateman figures with wealth-holders deceased at dates very distant from 1883, although this can be done with all wealth-holders deceased between 1809 and 1939.

As Table 6.1 makes clear, there is no single cohort of non-landed wealth-holders, with the exception of the millionaire group deceased 1840–58, containing four members, in which a majority owned land of sufficient acreage to be included in Bateman—that is, 2,000 or more acres.[18] To be sure, among both the millionaire and half-millionaire groups the non-landed portion was steadily rising, until, among the groups deceased at about the time World War One seven-eighths were landless; but even in the mid-nineteenth century landless wealth-holders were in a majority, and the increase in the landless portion may have been the result of the fact that self-made men deceased in the years 1900–14 owned no land recorded in Bateman.

Most of the minority of non-landed wealth-holders who did buy estates, moreover, did not purchase immense amounts of land. Fewer than half of those wealth-holders recorded in Bateman owned estates of 10,000 acres or more; among the half-millionaires, the figure was less than one-third. These men by definition were still possessed of personal estates which made them among the wealthiest men in Britain on the basis of their non-landed assets, and in few if any cases can one point to a British business wealth-holder who invested more than half of his *total* fortune (or anything like it) in the purchase of land.

The greatest landowners among the business and professional wealth-holders deserve a more detailed examination. Only ten wealth-holders, including one in the 'lesser wealthy' class, owned 25,000 acres or more. (There are 12 *individuals* in Table 6.1 given as owning 25,000 acres or more, but two of these were members of the same families as earlier wealth-holders.) With no more than a handful of other families who are not included in this table because no member died sufficiently wealthy in the period 1840–1914 in terms of personalty to appear, this group represents the entirety of the post-1780 new men of wealth who purchased land on so vast a scale who were deceased up until World War One.[19] Inclusion of these other, omitted individuals brings the total number of post-Industrial Revolution great landowners to no more than about 15 at most, of a total of over 200 landowners listed by Bateman as owning 25,000 acres or more.[20] The greatest of these men were Lord

Table 6.1: Landed Acreage of Non-landed Wealth-holders*

Acreage (000 of acres)	Millionaires				Half-millionaires				Lesser Wealthy
	1840–58	1858–79	1880–99	1900–14	1840–58	1858–79	1880–99	1900–14	1850–69
+50	1	1	1		2		2		
25–50		1			2		1		
10–25	2	5	7	2	2	6	9	4	8
5–10	1	1	5	1	1	8	6	3	8
2–5		2	9	6	3	11	14	13	9
Unlisted		20	38	65	12	77	131	159	129
Total number	4	30	60	74	20	104	162	179	155
Percentage unlisted	0.0	66.7	63.3	87.8	56.0	74.0	80.1	88.8	83.2

* Sources: John Bateman, Great Landowners of Great Britain and Ireland, 4th edn (London, 1883; repr. Leicester, 1971); probate calenders at London, Principal Probate Registry, London, and Scottish Record Office, Edinburgh.

Overstone, the great banker, whose landed wealth has already been described; James Morrison (1789–1857), the warehouseman and merchant banker; Sir Josiah Guest, 1st Bt. (1785–1852), the ironmaster whose son was created Lord Wimborne; Sir Alexander Matheson, 1st Bt. (1805–86), the China merchant; the Baird family of Scottish ironmasters; and the Barings, the great merchant bankers.

Although Lord Overstone who, with his close relatives, owned about 54,000 acres yielding £93,000 p.a., was overall the greatest of these new landowners, the Morrisons, certainly less well known, were in some respects more remarkable. In 1883 they were credited with the ownership of some 106,900 acres yielding £53,900 p.a. These estates, which included the entire island of Islay in Argyllshire and the Fonthill estate in Wiltshire previously owned by William Beckford the famous eighteenth-century merchant, were mainly purchased by James Morrison, a self-made (he was the son of an innkeeper) multi-millionaire who was possibly the richest British commoner of the nineteenth century.[21] In 1883 they were owned by his five sons, whose personal fortunes amounted to nearly £15 million at their deaths. The bulk of the Morrison land—76,000 acres yielding £31,434 p.a.—was owned by Charles Morrison, the eldest son (1817–1909), a virtually unknown London financier, who habitually kept several million pounds in gold bullion, selling it judiciously whenever a general panic threatened the British economy.[22] The size of the Morrison landed estate may be put in its proper perspective if one realizes that in 1883 the Duke of Marlborough owned only 23,511 acres yielding an annual income of £36,557, while Lord Salisbury, the leader of the Conservative party, scion of a dynasty founded by Queen Elizabeth's greatest minister, and the very epitome of British landed society, owned 20,202 acres worth £33,413 p.a. Although one Morrison brother, Walter (1836–1921), did become a prominent back-bench MP, the family—which is still wealthy and influential, though not really prominent—did not achieve a title of any sort until 1965 when John Granville Morrison, formerly chairman of the Conservative 1922 Committee, was awarded one of the last hereditary peerages that has to this date been created in Britain, and became Lord Margadale.

In contrast, the Guest iron family of Dowlais in south Wales was given a baronetcy in 1838, a barony in 1880, and a viscountcy in 1918. The first baronet, Sir Josiah Guest, who left £500,000 in 1852, began the family's ascendancy into the old aristocracy by marrying (as his second wife) a daughter of the Earl of Lindsey; his son married a daughter of the Duke of Marlborough; his grandson a niece of the Duke of Westminster and also served as Lord Lieutenant of Ireland. In 1883 the first Lord Wimborne—as the head of the family had become—owned 83,500 acres worth £46,900 annually in Glamorgan, Dorset and Ross, in addition to the sizeable personalty still owned by the family.

The Bairds, the great Scottish ironmasters whose five Bateman-listed members held over 125,000 acres worth £59,000 p.a., were post-Industrial Revolution landowners throughout northern and central Scotland. In 1883 the Barings—with the Rothschilds the most celebrated of merchant banking dynasties—were credited with four members in Bateman (Lord and Lady Ashburton, Lord Northbrook, W. H. Baring) owning a total of 89,000 acres yielding about £71,000 p.a., although no single member owned more than about 37,000 acres. The last of these greatest of new landowners, perhaps not quite in the same category as the others, was Sir Alexander Matheson, 1st Bt., partner in the great trading firm in the Far East, Jardine Matheson, and director of the Bank of England, who left £644,000 in 1886. He owned no less than 220,663 acres which, situated in Ross- and Inverness-shire, yielded only £26,461 p.a.

Just below these were four other new families nearly in the same class. These were the Scotts, the London bankers, owners of 59,923 acres but worth £5,752 p.a.; the Baileys of Glanusk (later Lords Glanusk), ironmasters and relatives of the Crawshays, with 128,300 acres, yielding £25,600 p.a.; the Cunninghames of Craigends, ironmasters near Glasgow in the nineteenth century,[23] owners of 33,950 acres (£16,612 p.a.) plus £2,500 in mineral rents; and Lord Ardilaun, at the time head of the Guinness brewing family, with 31,300 acres worth £6,573 p.a. in three Irish counties. These men are the *only* examples of Britain's top wealth-holders to purchase land on so great a scale.

Below them were about 35 new wealthy families with landed holdings between 10,000 and 25,000 acres out of a total of well over 500 landowners throughout the United Kingdom in this class. Among the families at this level were the Arkwrights (cotton), Goldsmids (bullion brokerage), Brasseys (railway contracting), Rothschilds (merchant banking), Meuxes (brewing), Whitbreads (brewing), Ridleys (banking and colliery) and Cunliffe-Listers (silk plush). As a category it is not improbable that they exercised greater territorial influence than the very largest landowning businessmen. The most notable examples of such influence were provided by the Whitbreads, for generations among the leading families in Bedfordshire, and the Rothschilds, nearly as influential in Buckinghamshire politics and society as in the City of London. The class of landowners owning between 2,000 and 10,000 acres included many other business families—for instance, the Gurneys (banking), Watneys (brewing), Basses (brewing), Hardys (iron) and Armstrongs (engineering). Most of the many business peerages created between 1880 and 1914 were awarded to men in this category.[24] But the number of wealthy businessmen in this class must, once again, be balanced against the vast number of bona fide landowners—possibly 3,000 or more in all—who owned landed acreage of this size.[25]

There was seemingly very little difference among the different occupational categories of non-landed wealth-holders in their willingness to purchase land.[26] Among the non-landed millionaires who purchased land recorded in Bateman, 18 can be classified as primarily engaged in commerce or finance, 19 as industrialists, and 11 in other types of production (such as brewing). At first glance this is somewhat surprising, as one might have expected merchants and bankers, with their closer social distance to the landed aristocracy, to move more readily into the landed aristocracy. The reasons why this was not so are not straightforward, but among them, surely, are the facts that such men would probably have been more likely to purchase relatively small but very expensive estates in the Home Counties near London (although, as we shall see, this is open to much doubt), that the growth of the West End and later of suburban London might have served as a substitute for the old-style county neighbourhood, and that the very social distance between industrialists and gentility as commonly understood would have required them, in their search for status, to imitate their social superiors in a much more slavish manner than their London counterparts. Finally, it may simply have been that the only pleasant places for a rich man to live in the north of England were in the country.

The fact remains, however, that the majority of very wealthy businessmen in nineteenth-century Britain were either landless or owners of estates too small to be recorded in Bateman. This fact must be kept in mind when discussing either the structure of elites in British society during the nineteenth century or when attempting

to explain the decline of business dynasties. Such families as the
Crawshays of Cyfarthfa (iron), the Coatses (sewing thread),
Rylands (cotton), Bulloughs (engineering), Cunliffes (banking) or
Carr Glyns (finance) either owned no land in 1883 or too little to be
recorded in Bateman. By and large the very wealthiest of
nineteenth-century businessmen, like Lord Overstone, James
Morrison or the Rothschilds, also purchased the most land, while
run-of-the-mill millionaires owned the least, although there is no
hard-and-fast rule. Of the three wealthiest British industrialists
deceased before 1914, the sons of Thomas Brassey (d. 1870) owned
about 12,000 acres in 1883, Sir Charles Tennant (d. 1906) owned
3,616 acres, while John Rylands (d. 1887) apparently owned no land
at all. Men like the financier Herman, Baron de Stern (d. 1887), who
left £3,500,000, Hugh McCalmont (d. 1887),[27] the stockbroker and
foreign merchant who left £3,100,000, or John Gretton (d. 1899),
the great brewer who left nearly £2,900,000, owned no land at all
which is recorded in Bateman. The heirs of Richard Thornton (d.
1865), the insurance broker who left £2,800,000, are not to be found
in Bateman; the sons of Giles Loder (d. 1871), a Russia merchant
who left £2,900,000, owned a moderate estate of 10,241 acres
spread among four counties.

Yet if one reads obituaries or short notices of these wealthy men
in works like *Walford's County Families* or *Who Was Who*, one is
struck by the curious fact that most if not all seemed to own country
estates, in some cases several such estates. The 13 members of the
Crawshay iron family noticed in the 1895 edition of *Walford's
County Families* are credited with possessing 15 country houses,
including Cyfarthfa Castle, Glamorgan; Haughton Castle,
Simonburn, Hexham; Scole Lodge, Norfolk, and Brabourne Hall,
Sevenoaks.[28] Clearly, in such cases these country houses were either
rented, without the wealth-holder actually purchasing the freehold,
or stood on very small estates without any substantial surrounding
block of agricultural land. It is important for the historian not to
infer from such references the continuity of a genuine landed
aristocracy among former businessmen; at best, this represented
merely the respect that wealth paid to status, not an authentic
transfiguration of class placement.

The keen reader may have noticed a possible flaw in the
argument; it must be tested, and it shall be here. Given the
considerable expense of purchasing very substantial amounts of
land in nineteenth-century Britain—at £33 per acre, a 10,000-acre

estate would have cost £330,000, in addition to the price of buildings, agricultural equipment and livestock—it might well be argued that merely assessing the landed holdings of the owners of the great personal wealth at death might conceal the existence of substantial numbers of newly-rich business and professional men who, though possibly as wealthy *in toto* as those reviewed earlier, chose to spend their money on land, and hence failed to leave much personalty. This is a plausible argument and one amenable to empirical verification, although the process of verification entails a good deal of research. To test whether such men in fact existed in any number, it is necessary to investigate the family origins of a sizable sampler of *all* major landowners recorded in Bateman. This has been done, and the results are given in Table 6.2. Included in

*Table 6.2: Landowners Earning their Family Fortune Before and After 1780**

Acreage (in 000 of acres)	Before 1780	1780–1883	Unknown
+40	142 (89.3)	11 (6.9)	6 (3.8)
20–40	88 (88.0)	9 (9.0)	3 (3.0)
20–40	88 (88.0)	8 (8.0)	4 (4.0)
5–10	76 (76.0)	12 (12.0)	12 (12.0)

* *Note and sources*: Figures in brackets denote percentages. Bateman, *Great Landowners of Great Britain and Ireland; Burke's Peerage, Baronetage and Knightage* (1937, 1957, 1970 edns.); *Burke's Landed Gentry* (1895, 1913, 1937,.1954, 1965–70 edns.); Frederick Boase, *Modern English Biography*, 6 Vols. (London, 1892–1921; repr. London, 1965); *Dictionary of National Biography*.

this sample—and, given the number of large landowners in nineteenth-century Britain, this can only be a sample—are all landowners listed in Bateman as owning 40,000 or more acres in 1883, and the first 100 landowners (in alphabetical order) listed in each category as owning between 20,000 and 40,000 acres, between 10,000 and 20,000 acres, and between 5,000 and 10,000 acres in Bateman.[29] The family origins of each of these families have been traced in a wide variety of biographical and genealogical sources, with the aim of ascertaining what percentage in each category earned its family fortune between 1780 and 1883.[30]

It is plain from this table that no such hidden category of newly-rich landowners existed. Many of the men listed here as owning substantial landed holdings are men we have never met before as the top non-landed wealth-holders; among the 11 men at the very top of the landed stakes, men like John Baird, Charles Morrison and Lord Wimborne have already been encountered, while only seven new men and women of wealth did not leave very large personal fortunes. Even so, all of these men owned vast but largely worthless landed holdings in northern Scotland and Ireland which did not in fact cost very much to purchase. The first of these, for example, the London brewer Richard Berridge of Clifden Castle, Connemara, County Galway, was in 1883 the largest landowner in acreage in Ireland, owning 170,000 acres in Galway and Mayo, and 400 acres more in Middlesex and Kent. But these great holdings brought him only £9,503 in annual income, and certainly did not cost more than £300,000 to purchase (and as they were mainly in Ireland, probably far less).[31] Much the same is true, a fortiori, as one proceeds down the acreage scale. The bulk of the acreage of those men who did not figure among Britain's top personalty wealth-holders did not, in fact, own small but very expensive estates in the Home Counties, but vast and worthless estates in Scotland and Ireland, clearly bought, as it were, on the cheap to surprise and overwhelm by a fine excess.

The great majority of the landowners surveyed in Table 6.2 represent hereditary landed wealth created at every stage of British history from the Norman Conquest right through to mid-eighteenth century mercantile activities and 'Old Corruption', the world of government patronage and place. Many of these men were, of course, titled aristocrats, while the remainder constituted the untitled aristocracy and squirearchy, which still existed in considerable numbers in the late nineteenth century. The small percentage of landowners whose origins could not be traced in any source were, as with the newly-rich landowners mentioned above, very disproportionately situated in Ireland and Scotland; but there is absolutely nothing in any source available to me—including the probate records—to associate them with the new wealth created by the Industrial Revolution or with business life. Most, if not all, were almost certainly ancient untitled landowners of long lineage but slight renown.[32]

Considerably less than 10 per cent of all Britain's greater landowners in 1883, then, were the products of business and professional wealth created after 1780: if rental income rather than landed acreage is taken as the criterion, probably very much less. But this figure did not exist in an economic or historical vacuum, and we reach here perhaps the most salient point. For the number of potential business and professional men of wealth, and the wealth available to them for land purchase, did not remain static. Both grew phenomenally, as a result of Britain's industrialization, and at an incremental rate unparalleled in the world's history. Between 1801 and 1881 the total national income earned in Britain in manufacturing, trade and related business activities rose from £94 million to £638 million,[33] while the number of estates of £100,000 or more in personalty rose from an average of 16.5 per year in 1809–16 to 141.6 per year in 1880–4.[34] During the nineteenth century, then, for perhaps the first time in British history, the great majority of wealthy business and professional men voluntarily declined to transform their personal wealth into landed acreage; this occurred moreover, at a time when the number of wealthy business and professional men, and the level of their fortunes, was greater than at any previous time in British history. This was indeed a revolution in status values and class self-perception, and both the causes and the consequences of this change ought to be explored as well.

II

It is not easy to adduce a simple, clear-cut reason for the near cessation of land purchase on a sizable scale by new men of wealth in the nineteenth century. This task is especially difficult as the historian here seeks to explain, not some sequence of events, but a sequence of non-events, and there is necessarily little in the way of direct evidence which the historian can hope to find. It seems most judicious, however, to conclude that the diminution of substantial land purchase had its origins in a variety of factors, economic, social and psychological, which by turns defined and constrained the nineteenth-century middle classes as a whole. Doubtless the most compelling of these factors was the economic, and it is possible to suggest two primary elements which affected nineteenth-century British businessmen.

In the first place, despite all the wealth created by British industrialization and its attendent consequences, British business and professional men, even at the very peak of the wealth scale, were simply not rich enough to purchase land in quantities sufficient to make a real dent in the overwhelming domination of the pre-industrial landowners. A million pounds, spent entirely on land, would have purchased only about 33,000 acres in much of England, and the number of bona fide millionaires was very small in nineteenth-century Britain. For any British businessman of the nineteenth century, even a Rothschild or a Morrison, to have built up estates matching those of the greatest landed grandees—the 186,397 acres owned by the Duke of Northumberland, for example, or the 138,536 English acres held by the Duke of Devonshire—would have been quite impossible. Nineteenth-century Britain was not 'Gilded Age' America, and there were strict and surprisingly low limits on the size of fortune—about £5 million—which any British businessman ever acquired. One consequence of this, as we have seen, was that wealthy businessmen in search of vast acreage often acquired Potemkin fiefdoms in Ireland or northern Scotland.

That the British Industrial Revolution, despite the vast increase in wealth which it engendered, was incapable of producing any businessmen rich enough to transform themselves into really great English landowners—even if any had wanted to—is evidence of another important consideration, namely that the terms of the comparison between old and (potentially) new landowners is not, as it were, an equal one. For the old aristocracy, in many cases, did not acquire its holdings, as any new aristocracy was bound to do, by land purchase alone, but by every means—ancient tenure, royal or parliamentary gift, looting and rapine following a civil war or revolution, inheritance, fortune, marriage—except actual purchase; moreover, this was done over eight centuries, not one, even a revolutionary one. The new men of wealth who lived by the laws of property and capital had to abide by it as well.

But inability of any single businessman to become an English landowner on a truly ducal scale is not by itself a sufficient explanation for the fact that, as a class, new businessmen made so little impact on the structure of landed society, for, collectively if not individually, these new men were certainly wealthy enough to have had a considerably greater impact than they did. Another important economic factor was probably the typical form of British business life, the family firm or small private partnership, which predominated throughout all sectors of the economy, except railways, until the late nineteenth century or even later.[35] Partnership or the holding of shares in a small private firm, and particularly one dominated by a family or group of intimates, probably made selling up and investing the proceeds in something else, even land, exceedingly difficult; one's motives would necessarily be scrupulously examined by one's fellow partners; the proper market valuation of the shares to be sold was hard to ascertain; and the selling up by a firm's most prominent entrepreneur was certain to be misinterpreted in many quarters as a broad hint that the company was in grave difficulties. It was probably unrealistic, therefore, to expect any private partner in a nineteenth-century business firm, even the wealthiest among them, to contemplate the purchase of vast and costly amounts of land in a short period of time; this could be done, surely, only in piecemeal fashion, and a consequence of this was that all but the very richest businessmen were often unable to purchase very large estates, the typical form in which these came on the market.[36] Ironically, the coming of limited liability on a general basis—which did not occur until this century—may have facilitated the process of land purchase just at the time when this became less profitable (and certainly less socially necessary) than ever before.

It is also true that another formidable barrier existed to the sale to anyone of much British land during the nineteenth century: the strict settlement of the great estates. Yet this bar to land purchase should not be exaggerated: probably less than half of the land in England was subject to settlement;[37] even the greatest landowners generally held a portion of their estates outside of settlement;[38] and the factor of land settlement proved no hurdle to those new men like Lord Overstone who were truly bent on building up a great estate. The price of land during the nineteenth century never reached the historic highs of the Napoleonic period and for most of the century was much below them.[39]

There is, finally, the matter of land as an investment. It is well known that agricultural land yielded very little throughout most of the nineteenth century—about 2.5 to 3 per cent was the general rule of thumb, and even that yield required a troublesome amount and variety of investment in agricultural improvements of all types. Purely as a matter of rational economic self-interest for men of property who characteristically (one presumes) thought in this mode, land was a poor choice of investment. From a financial point of view, its greatest advantage was its permanence—unlike any business firm, no matter how firmly based, it could never go bankrupt—but the eighteenth and nineteenth centuries, as Mingay has pointed out, witnessed the emergence of government and colonial securities which were, for all practical purposes, just as safe, yielded a higher return, and could be acquired effortlessly.

If large-scale land purchase by new men made little sense on purely economic grounds, it was in the realm of status gains that better motives are perhaps to be sought. If the possession of large amounts of land, and a lifestyle indistinguishable from the older aristocracy, automatically brought with them acceptance as a member of the old aristocracy identical to any other, then probably far more wealthy businessmen would have transformed their personal wealth into land. But it did not. For the self-made man, there was an unbridgeable gap of behaviour, attitudes and accent (and often of more formal characteristics like religion) between the old aristocracy and the *nouveaux riches*, which no amount of land purchase would affect. We should, however, be clear on the limitations to this stricture. The really rich man, the Overstone or Rothschild, was invariably much more successful at integrating himself into the established elite structure than the 'average' rich man: but it was his wealth, rather than his land, which was probably the determinant factor. The Sassoons, for example, were Baghdadi Jews who did not wear Western dress, or even live in Britain, until the 1840s. By 1910 they were hereditary Tory MPs for Hythe, and baronets.[40] But the Sassoons were immensely wealthy, even by *fin de siècle* standards—estimates of their wealth in the Far East are often put at £20 million or more—on the basis of their oriental mercantile and textile empire. But the typical wealthy man was simply not rich enough to impress the English aristocracy, while the barriers to acceptability still remained. These barriers largely came down, of course, in the second, third and fourth generations, at the public schools and universities. But this had nothing to do with the acquisition of land.

As to the possible acquisition of a title, particularly a peerage, new men of wealth were in a 'no-win' situation throughout the nineteenth century. Land purchase in itself was insufficient to guarantee the acquisition of a peerage, even though (except for politicians and judges) until the 1800s the possession of land was a necessary pre-condition for a peerage. It is well known that the first former industrialist to acquire a peerage, Edward Strutt, Lord Belper, did not do so until 1856, and the peerages awarded to even the very wealthiest of the new men, like Overstone's or Wimborne's, were not given until the third quarter of the century.

Even so, most of the new men who purchased land on a great scale never received a peerage during the nineteenth century. The Arkwrights and Whitbreads, for instance, who had always been Anglicans and had held their land for generations, never received peerages. But when the flood of business peerages did come in the 1880s, the converse became true: land ownership was irrelevant or little relevant to the creation of new peerages. The 'acquisition of land', in F. M. L. Thompson's words, 'was no longer the obligatory step toward a peerage which it had once been': about two-thirds of peerage creations between 1886 and 1905 were completely landless.[41] By the inter-war period, although the purchase of land by wealthy new men certainly did not cease, there was a virtual end to the necessary connection between land and high status. Sir John Ellerman (1862–1933) for instance—the richest Englishman of the first half of this century, and a self-made shipping magnate and financier—had no country house at all, dividing his time between his South Audley Street mansion, his house at Eastbourne, and the Continent.[42]

These economic and status considerations were greatly influenced by another factor which continued to distinguish the middle classes from the older aristocracy. This was the continuing and apparently permanent propensity for business and professional men to divide their property equally, or nearly equally, among their children and other heirs at their death, rather than to leave virtually everthing to the eldest son, as was traditionally the case among landowners.[43] This had two important consequences, apart from the psychological distancing from the well-known habits of the old aristocracy which it effected. First, it assured that few sons or grandsons of even the richest millionaires were themselves individually rich enough to become landowners on a grand scale, unless—and this was done only rarely—they succeeded in building up their inherited portions into an estate vastly larger than that which they inherited. This habit played its important part in limiting the size of business fortunes and hence the possibility that wealthy men could purchase land on a grand scale, even if they had wished to.[44] Secondly, it meant that even those new men who did purchase large amounts of land normally divided it into separate landed estates among their sons, rather than concentrate it in the hands of the eldest. Bateman, for instance, lists two Arkwrights, one owning 10,600 and the other 5,100 acres; seven Peels each holding an estate of between 2,200 and 9,900 acres; and even five

Morrisons—although Charles held the bulk of the property his four brothers owned the hardly insignificant total of nearly 31,000 acres between them. It was Alfred Morrison, for instance, the second son, who owned Fonthill, not Charles. As F. M. L. Thompson has noted, citing several other examples of this tendency, the end result should have been a growth in the gentry class rather than an increase in the grandee class: yet he finds little convincing evidence even for this.[45]

These factors taken together were obviously of considerable significance. Yet even when added to one another they fail, I think, to provide a full explanation of this shift in attitudes. Certainly something more must be added, namely the voluntary, unconstrained decision of considerable numbers of very wealthy men not to purchase land. The world of the landowner, after all, is a very alien and not wholly pleasing one to men accustomed to urban life. Its adoption entails the absorption, not merely of new attitudes, but of new knowledge, knowledge of agricultural methods and procedures very alien to those of the business and professional men of the city. Country life is a milieu where procreation, birth, death, slaughtering, infection, defecation and mud cannot be hidden or disguised. If one accepts—as I think it should be accepted—that 'Victorianism' is essentially a process of the distancing of the middle classes (and, soon, the working classes) from life's unpleasantness— and not some nonsense about draping 'naked' table legs—then the world of the barnyard and the cattle shed was one by turns embarrassing, grotesque and macabre. There could hardly be many Victorian stockbrokers or cotton merchants, and fewer still among their wives and daughters, who would have preferred to come face to face with the everyday realities entailed in rural life. It is thus no coincidence, as E. L. Jones has perceptively pointed out, that most of the early industrialists—Arkwright, Peel and Strutt, for instance—operated in the countryside rather than in a town, and that, therefore, the great landowners were 'the ultimate social reference group' of such men.[46] It would seem to be true that men of this background were much more likely to have become landowners on a considerable scale than those of a purely urban background. And, as the factory system (and commercial life as well) became increasingly coextensive with the factory town or a purely urban setting, such an 'ultimate social reference group' became increasingly spectral.

This dissociation of business and landed society could not have failed to have had the most profound effect on the landowners themselves. Increasingly during the nineteenth century the landed aristocracy took on the appearance of a closed, caste-like group, hostile to new entries and jealous of any infringements on their status and esteem. This was a novel situation. In the Tory governments of Pitt and Liverpool, relatively or even entirely new men acquired land and were quickly accepted as genuine members of the aristocracy: for instance Lord Eldon, the son of the owner of a coal barge in Newcastle-upon-Tyne, who purchased some 26,000 acres of agricultural land in four counties, or of newly-risen members of the minor squirearchy like the family of Lord Liverpool himself. Such examples plainly decrease as the century proceeded. Under continuing attack on political and intellectual grounds during the nineteenth century, the survival and even increase in power, status and wealth of the old landed aristocracy was the more remarkable, and no theory of social fluidity can successfully account for it.[47]

Because of the increasing division between landowners and businessmen, it is possible to question another suggestion of E. L. Jones's that the 'check, in the rising rate of capital formation' following the Napoleonic Wars was possibly due to the transfer of the capital of industrialists into land purchase at the time, as was the case with the Arkwrights whom he has surveyed.[48] It would, however, surely be more sensible to consider what might have happened to the British economy and the structure of landed society if the nineteenth century's new businessmen of wealth had transferred their personalty into land. Between 1809 and 1880 alone about 3,430 individuals left £100,000 or more in personalty; probably about two-thirds of this number were businessmen or their close relatives. If the median businessman wealth-holder left £200,000, then not less than £457.4 million in personalty was left by British businessmen in this period, a figure which excludes the personalty of post-Industrial Revolution businessmen deceased between 1780 and 1809, those leaving under £100,000, or the diminution of their wealth at death by *inter vivos* gifts and philanthropy. Even if only half of this probated wealth had been spent on the purchase of land at its average price, the new business class would have owned among them 6,930,000 acres in England and Wales in addition to the land its members actually owned in 1883. This figure is considerably more than the 5,729,000 acres actually owned in England and Wales at the time by the entire peerage, and such a presence would have utterly transformed the structure of English landed society, effecting an impact greater than anything since the Reformation.[49] Conversely, since investment in land would have been a substitute for investment in industry and commerce, Britain would hardly have experienced economic development and growth to anything like the extent it did, and indeed the propensity of businessmen in other societies to purchase land, if markedly greater than in Britain, may have had a significant effect on business investment, and hence on economic development there.

Despite the withdrawal of new men of wealth from the world of the landed aristocrat, the notion existed, and continues to exist, that high society consisted of a 'network of country houses'. There is probably a good deal of truth in this. But such a characterization ignores the large number of wealthy men who owned no land and only rented a country house for the season, if they lived in one at all. This class was surprisingly large and, as a class, probably outnumbered those wealthy men who owned very small plots of land, too small to be recorded in Bateman's *Great Landowners*.[50] It was among this class of 'yeoman' landowners—Bateman's 'makeshift title for holders of between 100 and 1,000 acres'[51]—that a significant number of the nineteenth-century British Establishment was to be found: Bateman's 'yeomanry drill' naming 'Mr Goschen . . . Sir R. Cross . . . a popular Protestant Dean arguing a theological point with the Ex-President of the . . . [English Church Union], . . . the Poet Laureate and an eminent Hebrew financier' as typical of this class of very small landowners.[52] But, at the very best, and even if statistically representative of the wealthy and powerful, this was the shadow, rather than the substance, of land ownership: in no sense could such men be termed truly a part of landed society, and the money they laid out on the purchase of land was trivial besides their remaining personalty.

One should not, therefore, accept too uncritically the implications which seem to follow from the apparent universality of country-house building by the Victorian plutocracy.[53] It is far from clear just how universal country-house building really was: the Stones' very detailed study of Hertfordshire—which one might have expected to have been inundated by new City men—revealed, after an 'explosion of new construction in the late eighteenth century' what they describe as a 'puzzling slump in both numbers and new construction, a lull which has been noted by architectural historians, who have observed that the leading architects of the time devoted themselves to designing churches and commercial and public buildings rather than country houses in the period 1820–60'.[54] The number of Hertfordshire country houses in their study, which stood at 104 in 1799, declined to about 90 in the mid-nineteenth century and then rose only to 108 at its peak in 1879.[55] Girouard notes a perceptible rise in country-house building between 1860 and 1880, but most of this building was by 'old' rather than 'new' men.[56] Again Victorian country-house buildings should not be confused with the extensive purchase of land by these men. Nor do we really know just how common even this practice was; in the absence of detailed evidence its universality cannot be assumed.

Two very general analogous conclusions seem to follow from this study. First, if the period 1885–1914 should not be seen as a major break in the status and centrality accorded to land ownership by aspiring businessmen, neither should the twentieth century be viewed as a time when the purchase of land by new men entirely ceased. On a reduced scale, it continues to this day; indeed, the sharp decline in land prices between 1880 (and, especially, 1918) and the 1950s offered a golden opportunity to new men bent on acquiring sizable landed estates. Surveying the major private English landowners in 1976, Stephen Glover noted that virtually all of the great landowners found in Bateman had lost substantial portions of their nineteenth-century acreage: the Duke of Devonshire's English holdings, for example, declining from 133,000 to 56,000 acres, the Duke of Bedford's from 87,000 to 11,000, and so on. But Glover also found that among the major new landowners who owned no land at all recorded in Bateman were three great twentieth-century magnates—Lord Leverhulme, owner of 90,000 acres, Lord Iveagh of Guinness breweries (24,000 acres) and Lord Cowdray of the engineering and petroleum dynasty (20,000 acres).[57] Many other such examples can be found: F. M. L. Thompson pointed out that the Compton Verney seat of Lord Willoughby de Broke, one of the very oldest families in England, was sold in September 1921 to one Joseph Watson, a Liverpool soap millionaire, who was created Lord Manton of Compton Verney just three months later;[58] the millionaire Christopher Furness, first Baron Furness (d. 1912), West Hartlepool shipbuilder and shipowner (the seventh son of a grocer who had left £460) owned over 30,000 acres at the time of his death; a wealthy Grimsby trawler-owner named Sir George F. Sleight (d. 1921), who had started life as a cockle-gatherer, was probably the largest landowner in Lincolnshire at the time of his death, according to his obituary.[59] For some new men of wealth the old pattern persisted, although as a proportion of all wealth-holders, their numbers certainly decreased.

Finally, this increasing dichotomy between landed and business wealth should help us to situate the landed aristocracy in the schema of nineteenth-century society. The many mainstream economic historians who have treated the great nineteenth-century landowners as in some clear-cut sense separate from the business and professional world are undoubtedly correct in their approach; the Marxist historians and sociologists like Nicos Poulantzas, E. P. Thompson and Robert Gray who, following Marx, have tended to view them as a 'fraction of capital rather than a separate class'[60] are, in my opinion, less accurate and perspicuous. For capital is not anonymous, and this was never more true than in the individual- or family-oriented capitalism of nineteenth-century Britain, so marked by occupational and geographical diversity. The British landed aristocracy in the nineteenth century was a self-contained, largely self-demarcated group, a world where status considerations rose above profit, and stamped by a peculiar set of attitudes towards the rest of society, including its landed tenants and agricultural labourers. Moreover, their separateness became more rather than less marked in the course of the nineteenth century and did not fully 'merge' with the business worlds until after World War One.[61]

In the world of high politics and government, Britain became more dominated by genuine aristocrats in the half-century after 1832 compared with the half-century before; much of the nexus between the aristocracy and the older business and professional world which marked Old Corruption disappeared in the nineteenth century; the holdings of the largest landowners often became considerably greater in size.[62] Capitalism may provide the logic of the system and the rules of the game, but social classes and groupings are as variegated in number and type as the societies in which they exist, and no history of social structure which fails to recognize this fact is likely to be very successful.

NOTES

1. E. L. Jones, 'Industrial Capital and Landed Investment: The Arkwrights in Herefordshire, 1809–43', in E. L. Jones and G. E. Mingay (eds), *Land, Labour and Population in the Industrial Revolution* (London, 1967), p. 51.
2. R. G. Wilson, *Gentlemen Merchants: The Merchant Community in Leeds, 1700–1830* (Manchester, 1971), p. 220.
3. Dean Rapp, 'Social Mobility in the Eighteenth Century: The Whitbreads of Bedfordshire, 1720–1815', *Economic History Review*, 2nd ser. XXVII (1974), p. 380.
4. G. E. Mingay, *English Landed Society in the Eighteenth Century* (London, 1963), p. 47. This point has more recently been echoed by Nicholas Rogers, who has noted a 'shift towards suburban living and the purchase of smaller estates' among Hanoverian London aldermen: N. Rogers, 'Money, Land and Lineage: The Big Bourgeoisie of Hanoverian London', *Social History*, IV (1979), p. 450.
5. Mingay, *English Landed Society, op. cit.*, p. 73.
6. F. M. L. Thompson, *English Landed Society in the Nineteenth Century* (London, 1963), p. 119.
7. *Ibid.*
8. *Ibid.*, p. 122.
9. R. G. Lang, 'Social Origins and Social Aspirations of Jacobean London Merchants', *Economic History Review*, 2nd ser., XXVII (1974). These studies raise the important question of the extent of a consistent movement of new wealth into the land prior to the Industrial Revolution. Naturally no detailed analysis of this question can be attempted here. It seems fairly clear to me that many fewer really wealthy pre-industrial merchants failed to transform their riches into land than was the case after industrialization.
10. Thompson, *English Landed Society, op. cit.*, pp. 60–1, 292ff.; Ralph E. Pumphrey, 'The Introduction of Industrialists into the British Peerage: A Study in the Adaptation of a Social Institution', *American History Review*, LXV (1959).
11. John Bateman, *The Great Landowners of Great Britain and Ireland*, 4th edn (London, 1883; repr. Leicester, 1971). A ranked list of the 29 greatest landowners appears in my *Men of Property, op. cit.*, Ch. 7.
12. This figure includes the landed income listed in Bateman's *Great Landowners* as owned by Lewis Lloyd (Overstone's brother) and Sir Robert Lloyd-Lindsay (later Lord Wantage), his son-in-law.
13. On these sources and the top wealth-holders of nineteenth-century Britain, see Chapters 2 and 3, and my *Men of Property, op. cit.*
14. From 1898 until 1925 the figure consisted of personalty and unsettled realty; since 1926, settled realty has been included.
15. 'Non-landed wealth-holders' is the term employed throughout this chapter to denote wealthy business and professional men and their close relatives, even if they purchased land. Wealthy 'landowners' were those who had been bona fide great landowners from before about

1780. Few—for example, the great titled aristocrats—present any definitional problems.
16. For details of the probate records and the men included in this study, see my *Men of Property, op. cit.*, Ch. 1. I have also published a list of all British millionaires deceased between 1809 and 1949 (including landowners): 'British Millionaires, 1809–1949', *Bulletin of the Institute of Historical Research*, XLVIII (1974). It should be stressed that I have examined *all* of Britain's top wealth-leavers: sampling is not involved.
17. The parliamentary returns on which Bateman's *Great Landowners* is based appeared in 1874–6: *Return for 1872–3* . . . [of Every Owner of Land in England and Wales], Parliamentary Papers (hereafter P.P.), 1874, [c. 1097], LXXII Pts. 1–2; *Return for 1872–3* . . . *of Every Owner of Land* . . . [in Scotland], P.P., 1874 (c. 899], LXXII Pt. 3; *Return of Owners of Land* . . . *in Ireland*, P.P., 1876 [c. 1492], LXXX. Bateman revised and corrected the figures (largely through personal correspondence with the landowners) in the various editions of his work published between 1875 and 1883. He also rearranged the listings alphabetically by landowner rather than by county (as in the parliamentary returns). See the 'Introduction' by David Spring to the 1971 reprint of Bateman's *Great Landowners*, pp. 7–23, and Bateman's own preface, *ibid.*, pp. v–xxvi.
18. The parliamentary *Returns of Owners of Land* (and hence Bateman) did not survey land ownership in London. A number of recent sophisticated local studies which appear to give a different impression should be read with this evidence in mind. The impressive study of wealthy Tyneside families, *The Making of a Ruling Class: Two Centuries of Capital Development on Tyneside* (Final Report 6th ser., Newcastle-upon-Tyne, 1978), seems to show the effective merger of business and landed wealth in Newcastle during the nineteenth century. But the wealthiest Tyneside magnates—families like the Becketts, Ridleys and Fenwicks which emerged in the eighteenth century, and the Strakers, Joiceys and Armstrongs of the nineteenth— continued to hold vast amounts in personalty and to maintain close and direct business interests. Each of these families, for instance, produced several members who left £500,000 or more in personalty between 1809 and 1939—as, indeed, the evidence presented in *The Making of a Ruling Class* demonstrates. Tyneside, in any case, was *sui generis*, a manufacturing-based conurbation entirely dominated by an Anglican elite with pre-industrial roots and genuine ties to the gentry. Newcastle's *ambience* is particularly grim and fierce: it is no coincidence that Lord Eldon was a local product.
19. These would include such families as the Peels, owners of about 25,000 acres yielding approximately £50,000 p.a., and the family of Lord Eldon, the Tory Lord Chancellor, who owned 26,000 acres worth £28,500 p.a. Both of these families produced top wealth-holders, but they were deceased outside the period examined here (1840–1914). Other examples (for instance, the Gladstones) are discussed below.
20. See Bateman, *Great Landowners, op. cit.*, Appendix 1, Table 1, p. 495.
21. See Chapter 1, pp. 26, 30.

22. *The Times,* 27 May 1909.
23. The Cunninghames should probably be subtracted from this list as, strictly speaking, they were not new men. Their Craigends estate had been in the Cunninghame family since 1479. The half-millionaire ironmaster Alexander Cunninghame (1804–66) purchased this estate from his elder brother's son in 1858. *Burke's Landed Gentry,* 'Cunninghame of Craigends'. Most of these newly-landed families, it will be seen, were Scottish, Welsh or Irish: this perhaps indicates a major difference in status perceptions from the English pattern.
24. Thompson, *English Landed Society, op. cit.,* p. 298.
25. See Bateman, *Great Landowners, op. cit.,* Appendix 1, Table 1, p. 495. A total of 2,919 landowners owned between 2,000 and 10,000 acres; this figure excludes London landowners.
26. On occupational differences, especially between commerce and manufacturing, see Chapter 3, pp. 60–4.
27. In 1887, however, McCalmont purchased Bishops Wood on the Wye from the Partridge family: Thompson, *English Landed Society, op. cit.,* p. 319. This family is not recorded in Bateman.
28. *Walford's County Families of the United Kingdom* (London, 1895 edn). The Crawshays were millionaires by 1810 and would certainly have moved into land well before the compilation of the parliamentary *Returns of Owners of Land.*
29. These are not, strictly speaking, *random* samples, and the purist may object to using these particular alphabetical samples. But I can see no possible source of bias in these samples, and their results are so striking and so similar that they are probably very much the same as a purely random sample.
30. The year '1780' has been treated more as a convenient shorthand (for the Industrial Revolution and its associated manifestations) than as an absolute break, and it is in any case obviously very difficult to state precisely when a family first became wealthy.
31. The six other new men and women of wealth owning 40,000 or more acres in 1883 were: Sir Thomas Gladstone, Bt, brother of the Prime Minister (45,062 acres worth £9,174 p.a.); Sir John Fowler, civil engineer (47,200 acres worth £5,900 p.a.); James MacKenzie, foreign merchant (72,700 acres worth £4,535 p.a.); John Ramsay, merchant of Glasgow (54,000 acres worth £9,241 p.a.); Colonel George G. Walker, London merchant (78,400 acres worth £6,900 p.a.); Lady Matheson of Stornoway, widow of Sir James Matheson, foreign merchant (425,000 acres in Ross-shire and Sutherland worth £20,346 p.a.).
32. Some typical examples of the unknowns, those in the 20,000- to 40,000-acre category: William Arthur Bruce of Symbister, Zetland; Mrs Mary Cameron of Barcaldine, Argyllshire; Major Thomas Mouat Cameron of Garth, Zetland.
33. Mitchell and Deane, *Abstract of British Historical Statistics, op. cit.,* p. 366. These figures include, of course, working-class incomes. Mitchell and Deane present no figures (except Gregory King's for 1688) for the period prior to 1801.
34. See my *Men of Property, op. cit.,* Ch. 2. No figures are available prior to

1809. These figures include landowners leaving more than £100,000 in personalty.

35. See for example, P. L. Payne, 'The Emergence of the Large-Scale Company in Britain', *Economic History Review*, 2nd ser. XX (1967).

36. See Thompson, *English Landed Society*, *op. cit.* pp. 34–43, for examples of large estates bought by new men.

37. *Ibid.*, p. 68.

38. *Ibid.*, pp. 64–8.

39. See, for example, F. M. L. Thompson, 'The Land Market in the Nineteenth Century', *Oxford Economic Papers*, new ser. IX (1957).

40. On the Sassoons, see Chaim Bermant, *The Cousinhood* (London, 1971), Ch. 19. Many persons (including Hermann Goering, who once, extraordinarily, received Sir Philip Sassoon socially) believed the Sassoons were Parsees.

41. Thompson, *English Landed Society*, *op. cit.*, pp. 298–9.

42. Taylor, *Ellermans: A Wealth of Shipping*, *op. cit.*, p. 83.

43. For statistical evidence of this tendency among non-landed wealth-holders, see my 'Men of Property: Some Aspects of Occupation, Inheritance and Power among Top British Wealth-Holders', in Stanworth and Giddens (eds), *Elites and Power*, *op. cit.*, pp. 154–60.

44. For some remarks on this process, see Thompson, *English Landed Society*, *op. cit.*, pp. 120–1.

45. *Ibid.*, p. 120.

46. Jones, *loc. cit.*, p. 50.

47. Much of the purchase of land which was on the market in the nineteenth century was done by large landowners rather than new men: there is considerable evidence that the proportion of the English countryside owned by the great landowners increased during the period. See Thompson, *English Landed Society*, *op. cit.*, Ch. 2.

48. Jones, *loc cit.*, p. 68.

49. The peerage figure is from Bateman, *Great Landowners*, *op. cit.*, p. 515. Naturally these figures are highly artificial; for example, the price of land per acre would have risen with a demand of this kind.

50. Bateman lists all landowners owning 2,000 or more acres (apart from those exceptions noted previously). These comprised 3,820 individuals: Bateman, *Great Landowners*, *op. cit.*, Appendix 1, Table 1, p. 495. But the original parliamentary return found 972,836 owners of some freehold land in England and Wales outside London, of whom 43,000 owned 100 acres or more: David Spring, 'Introduction', to *ibid.*, p. 12.

51. Bateman, *Great Landowners*, *op. cit.*, p. 527.

52. *Ibid.* Goschen and Cross were Cabinet ministers of the period.

53. See Mark Girouard, *The Victorian Country House*, revised edn (New Haven and London, 1979), esp. pp. 4–13, and Girouard's other illuminating works.

54. Lawrence Stone and Jeanne C. Fawtier Stone, 'Country Houses and their Owners in Hertfordshire', in W. O. Aydelotte, A. C. Bogue and R. W. Fogel (eds), *The Dimensions of Quantitative Research in History* (London, 1972), pp. 108–9.

55. Girouard, *Victorian Country House, op. cit.*, p. 9.
56. *Ibid.*, p. 106.
57. Stephen Glover, 'The Old Rich: A Survey of the Landed Classes', *Spectator*, 1 Jan. 1977.
58. Thompson, *English Landed Society, op. cit.*, p. 333.
59. *The Times*, 11 Nov. 1912; *Grimsby Telegraph*, 20 March 1921.
60. Robert Gray, 'Bourgeois Hegemony in Victorian Britain', in Jon Bloomfield (ed.), *Class, Hegemony and Party: Lectures from the Communist University of London* (London, 1977), p. 75; Nicos Poulantzas, *Classes in Contemporary Capitalism* (London, 1975), p. 92; E. P. Thompson, 'The Peculiarities of the English', in *Socialist Register, 1965* (London, 1965), pp. 315ff. On Marx's approach on this question, see William H. Shaw, *Marx's Theory of History* (Stanford, 1978), esp. pp. 43–52.
61. See Chapter 3, pp. 69–72.
62. See Thompson, *English Landed Society, op. cit.*, Ch. 2.

7

Education and the Social Origins of British Elites, 1880–1970*

The aim of this chapter is to demonstrate that many of the so-called 'elite studies' of recruitment into British elite positions since the mid-nineteenth century are deficient in their conclusions. It will be contended that they are based upon insufficient historical evidence as almost invariably they take the secondary and tertiary educational qualifications of an elite position-holder as *prima facie* evidence of his childhood social position with education at a fee-paying school or a university normally taken as evidence of the high status and considerable family wealth of the elite position-holder. As a result they conceal the true extent of social mobility, based upon merit, into Britain's most prestigious and powerful positions, conceal the considerable degree of change, particularly in the economic status of the position-holders' families, and conceal the true nature, dimensions and degree of fluidity within Britain's so-called 'Establishment' during the past century. The view disputed here is, moreover, based upon a concealed circular argument which is not merely circular, but egregiously circular, in that the most comprehensive and salient evidence suggests that it is seriously deficient. Finally, some more general and, hopefully, useful observations on the evolution and nature of Britain's elites will be made, based upon the evidence set out in this chapter.[1]

I would like to begin by putting some examples, from previous studies of British elites and elite groups, of views which I believe to

* World Copyright: The Past and Present Society, 175 Banbury Road, Oxford, England. This chapter first appeared in *Past and Present: A Journal of Historical Studies*, no. 112 (August 1986), pp. 163–207, and is here reprinted with the permission of the Society.

be both relatively ubiquitous and incorrect. Anyone familiar with the by now extremely lengthy literature of this field will know that very similar statements can be found in literally dozens of other so-called elite studies.[2] The first set of quotes comes from an excellent and most valuable recent résumé of the literature of this field by John Scott, entitled *The Upper Classes: Property and Privilege in Britain* (London, 1982):

> A particularly important characteristic of the establishment was their public school and Oxbridge background. During the eighteenth century access to top social positions depended upon access to a particular individual patron. This system was increasingly replaced by the public schools and Oxbridge colleges, both of which were self-recruiting and self-perpetuating institutions *composed of men recruited from the establishment* (p. 107).

> The establishment, as a dominant status group which *brought together the most important members of the privileged classes, monopolized* both national and local political positions as well as recruitment to the military arm of the state and to *the important professions of the church and the law* (p. 108).

> The *'establishment' was a tightly knit group of intermarried families* which formed the political rulers and which *monopolized recruitment to all major social positions* (p. 110).

> The business class as a whole is characterized by *a high degree of social cohesion*, the main supports of this system being *its system of kinship and its educational experience*. The kinship system is marked by a high degree of homogamy (p. 158; my italics throughout).

I would like to suggest in this chapter that the italicized statements above are misleading and, however widely held, based upon quite insufficient evidence.

Similarly misleading is the following quote from a sociological study of 'Ecclesiastical Appointments, 1942–1961', by Paul A. Welby (*Prism*, VI, (No. 5), 1962). Writing of the appointment of Anglican diocesan bishops, Welby notes concerning the 'social and educational background' of Anglican bishops (p. 24) that 'whereas the social and educational background of the clergy has changed very considerably, that of the bishops has remained relatively static . . . [B]ishops come from a background which in no way reflects that of the immense majority of the people.' So far as I am aware, Welby does not present a shred of direct evidence concerning the 'social background' of these bishops, inferring his conclusions from the fact that many bishops attended a public school and Oxbridge. Below, we shall consider just how accurate this inference is.

Consider, thirdly, the table of 'social origins' of leading British company chairmen in an important and valuable study of this subject by Anthony Giddens and Philip Stanworth.[3] They confidently assert that 66 per cent of the 559 leading company chairmen between 1900 and 1970 emerged from an 'upper class' social background. Among those chairmen engaged in 'miscellaneous manufacture', by far the largest group in their study—and a group discussed in this present chapter—59 per cent were by origin 'upper class', 13 per cent 'middle class', and only 1 per cent 'working class'. According to a footnote (p. 234, n. 8), they define 'upper class' to include 'industrialists, land-owners, [and] others who possess substantial property or wealth'. So far as I am aware these researchers, astonishingly, did not study the 'property or wealth' of the families of their chairmen in any meaningful sense. Instead they apparently inferred that the families of their subjects did or did not possess 'substantial property or wealth' from the appearance of their families, and particularly the fathers of their chairmen, in such works as *Burke's Peerage* and *Who's Who* or from the attendance of the chairmen at a major public school.[4]

Finally, another good example of the view disputed here may be found in a 1964 Fabian pamphlet on 'The Public Schools' by H. Glennersten and R. Pryke,

> The argument 'that the advantage which public school men enjoy in obtaining top positions is due to their class background and family connections and not to their education' seems plausible at first sight, *because almost all public school boys come from fairly wealthy families* (my italics).

Obviously, no one expects to find profound scholarship in a tendentious political tract, but this discussion was reprinted in a widely-known university anthology on *Power In Britain* (London, 1973), edited by John Urry and John Wakefield. Once again, not an iota of evidence is provided for the sweeping statement italicized here. What these four and many other similar elite studies have in common in their methodology of ascertaining the social origins of elite position-holders is two things. The first is a near-exclusive reliance upon secondary and university education as an indicator of the social status of the elite position-holder, with attendance at a major public school, especially one of the so-called 'Clarendon

Schools',[5] and Oxbridge taken as evidence of considerable family wealth and high status.[6] The second and negative side of this facet of nearly all elite recruitment studies is an astonishing lack of *direct* evidence on the very matter they are purporting to investigate, namely the wealth and occupation of the father and family of the elite position-holder. In lieu of direct evidence, secondary and higher education has been accepted uncritically as identical with the information which only such direct evidence can supply. Obviously there is a large measure of truth to such an identification: plainly the fathers of Etonians were, as a rule, far wealthier than the families of boys whose education ceased at twelve. Nevertheless, as I should like to demonstrate, such an identification is also seriously deficient in many respects, the most important being the conflation of the scions of bona fide aristocrats and plutocrats with the sons of very ordinary and often virtually poor persons, certainly with no connection whatever to privilege, who attended the same sorts of school, into a spurious 'Establishment' hallmarked by an equally spurious homogeneity. So universal is this tacit association between the public schools and Oxbridge on one hand, and wealth and privilege on the other, that there is no apparent realization that its central premise remains untested and based upon a circular argument—that attendance at a public school and Oxbridge indicates considerable family wealth and high status, while the family wealth and high status of the man in question is proved by the fact that he attended a public school and Oxbridge.

It is just at this point that the historian can come to the assistance of the sociologist, for this crucial and hitherto missing direct evidence about the wealth and occupational status of the families of elite position-holders can indeed be provided from objective historical sources. Birth certificates and marriage licences[7] provide direct information about the occupation of the father of each elite position-holder (or anyone else), while probate records provide comprehensive and objective evidence about the wealth at death of the fathers and other relatives of elite position-holders (or anyone else).[8] Additionally, accurate historical evidence on occupation and socio-economic status may be found in such sources as local directories, census returns, the alumni directories of the public schools and universities, and obituaries in local newspapers. These basic tools of historical research are well known to all modern British historians, and this is one area where the historian should surely be exporting his tools and techniques to the sociologists, a transfer which can only be to the mutual profit of both.

The historical study on British elites which is here extended and modified was aimed at providing this missing information on the fathers and other relatives of the elite position-holders by a comprehensive use of birth certificates and marriage licences to provide accurate information on the occupations of the fathers of these elites, an equally comprehensive use of the probate records to provide information on the wealth of the fathers and families of the elites, and the use, wherever necessary, of other historical sources of the type mentioned above. To the best of my knowledge, no previous historical or sociological study made use of these sources nor, it is notable, has any sociological study of this type been undertaken since. The new information obtained was designed to supplement, rather than supplant, the traditional bases of elite studies, especially the educational background of the elite position-holder, and full information on education was collected on all of the 3,277 elite individuals in this study—or for as many of them as this data is available. By thus comparing the accurate and rather more comprehensive new information our study provided on the fathers' wealth and occupation with the traditional data on education, a clearer and, it will be suggested, quite different picture emerges of the social origins of Britain's main elite groups.

Mention was made above of the habit among many sociologists who have researched in this area to conflate into a single 'Establishment' individuals from immensely different social and class backgrounds. This point can be neatly made by a brief comparison of two such individuals. One is a gentleman by the name of Richard Walmsley Blair and the other is another gentleman named Spencer Compton Cavendish who was known for much of his life as the Marquess of Hartington and who in 1891 succeeded as the eighth Duke of Devonshire. Richard Walmsley Blair was born in 1857 and died in 1939. He was an archetypically prototypical member of the British middle classes in its Imperial phase, serving throughout his working life in the Indian administration, first as Assistant Sub-Deputy of Opium Agents, then as Sub-Deputy Opium Agent in various places in northern India. He retired in 1912 at the age of 55 and spent the rest of his life in London and the Home Counties. It is known that he was too poor to afford a live-in maid and relied upon a daily help. This Blair married late, and fathered a son, Eric, who was born in 1903. Eric Blair attended Eton as a colleger—that is, on a scholarship—and followed, at least at first, in his father's footsteps, joining the Burmese police force upon leaving Eton. Thereafter, it must be said, their paths diverged widely. Besides Burma, the younger Blair travelled to such places as London and Paris, Catalonia, and Wigan Pier, writing of his experiences under the pseudonym he adopted, George Orwell. Because of the man the younger Blair became, we know a good deal about Richard Walmsley Blair. We know, for instance, the precise value of the annual pension which Richard Blair received when he retired in 1912, and on which he lived for the remaining twenty-seven years of his life. It was £438.10.[9] We also know, with an equal degree of precision, the income enjoyed by Spencer Cavendish—or, more precisely, by his elderly father—in 1882-3. In that year (when the cost of living was less than half of what it would become after World War One) Spencer Cavendish's father, the seventh Duke of Devonshire, was in receipt of exactly £180,750 from the rentals of his landed estates and a further £112,541 from the dividend income on his stocks, securities and the like,[10] making a total annual income in 1882-3 of £293,291, or approximately 668 times as much as Richard Blair, even ignoring the factor of inflation.

The influence and power of the two differed as markedly as did their income. Richard Walmsley Blair had no influence and no power; it is absolutely safe to say that, except for the accident of fathering George Orwell, his name would not have been heard or mentioned outside his family circle since the day he died. Spencer Compton Cavendish's situation was rather different. As is well known, he served in Parliament as an MP and a peer for fifty-one years, holding six different Cabinet posts under both Liberal and Unionist governments over a period of thirty-four years. He was a Knight of the Garter and held local offices too numerous to mention. Despite the fact that even three-volume Victorian biographies were incapable of discerning the slightest intellectual distinction in him, he received honorary degrees from three different universities, including both Oxford and Cambridge, and served as Chancellor of the University of Cambridge for sixteen years. Most accounts of late Victorian political history record that he declined the Queen's offer of the Prime Ministership three times. In 1895, *Walford's County Families* recorded that he owned five stately homes—including Chatsworth, Hardwick Hall, and Chiswick House—as well as a town house at 78 Piccadilly.

Despite all this, in normal sociological terms Richard Blair and Spencer Cavendish are remarkably similar. Since in sociological

analysis the most salient division in society is between the working
class and the middle class, the relatively small (though large in
absolute terms)[11] percentage of persons above the line are often
telescoped into a single entity, despite the fact—to take one
measurement—that by the 1920s Richard Blair's pension was
considerably less than twice the average income of a skilled manual
worker. Indeed, and most bizarrely, on some sociological tests Eric
Blair would rank *above* Spencer Cavendish, as the younger Blair
attended Eton while Cavendish, educated at home by his father and
private tutors, attended no public school. Even in the more
sophisticated scale of father's social status which is employed in this
chapter, (see p. 190–3) although Cavendish obviously ranks as a
social grade 'I', Eric Blair—were he included in this study—would
rank as a 'II' (on a scale of seven), since—despite his rather meagre
income—Richard Blair held a responsible middle-senior ranking
post in the Indian administration.

George Orwell was, of course, acutely aware of what he
incorrectly termed the 'shabby genteel' class, the lower part of the
middle class whose status perceptions outstripped its income;
indeed his whole literary enterprise, in his fiction and in his essays,
up until the time he wrote *Animal Farm*, may be seen as an attempt
at class self-identification.[12] In his famous essay on his experiences
as a schoolboy at the expensive preparatory school St Cyprians,
'Such, Such were the Joys' Orwell records 'a conversation that must
have taken place about a year before I left St Cyprians' (i.e., about
1915).

> A Russian boy, large and fair-haired, a year older than myself, was
> questioning me.
> 'How much a year has your father got?'
> I told him what I thought it was, adding a few hundreds to make it
> sound better. The Russian boy, neat in his habits, produced a pencil and
> a small note-book and made a calculation.
> 'My father has over two hundred times as much money as yours', he
> announced with a sort of amused contempt.[13]

What were the essential differences between the circumstances of
a Richard Blair and a Spencer Cavendish? Blair, of course, lacked
capital, and one major hallmark of men of his social class was that
they lived primarily or wholly upon their income. Despite fathering
an Etonian, Blair left an estate of only £506 when he died in 1939.
(Devonshire left £1,165,000 in personalty alone.) Blair lacked social

prestige. He lacked connections or any access to patronage for himself or his progeny. But perhaps the most general point which may be made from this comparison of Richard Blair and Spencer Cavendish is, of course, that the bona fide British aristocracy and plutocracy was an almost incredibly small group during the nineteenth century and until the period—say, 1939—when the notion of an aristocracy-*cum*-plutocracy ceases to mean what it had previously. Quantifying actual numbers depends upon definition, and the area of high incomes remains largely one of guesswork, but in 1913–14 there were about 1,500 persons in Britain with hereditary titles (peers or baronets) and another 1,700 non-hereditary knights, while there were exactly 4,843 persons with an annual income in 1913–14 of £10,000 or more, of whom about 300 received £50,000 or more and 75 £100,000 or more.[14] Since the overlap between title-holders and high-income earners was obviously very great, the actual number of persons in both groups would have been about, say, 6,800 or so. During the nineteenth century their number would have been much lower, while even this figure of 6,800 includes many very obscure retired, titled generals, colonial officials, and the like who were unknown to anyone except the doormen of their clubs, as well as hundreds of backwoods baronets and peers of similar obscurity. It can be argued, indeed, that the bona fide British landed aristocracy should be confined only to the great landowners—especially the Whig oligarchs descended from 'the sacred circle of great-grand motherhood'—while the true British plutocracy, in either its London-based commercial element, or its northern manufacturing segment, should equally be confined to a very small group; even business millionaires for the most part lacked the permanence and absolute status of the great landowners perhaps into the twentieth century. Even if we accept the higher number suggested above—6,800 persons in 1913—add in another, say, 1,500 or 2,000 bishops, judges, notable barristers, surgeons, professors, members of Parliament, and so on to take into account other members of the bona fide British elite lacking a title or an income above £10,000, and finally agree that each such person was responsible for the welfare of five or even ten male relatives, it is evident that the British elite was still extraordinarily small, consisting in 1913 of not more than 85,000 adult males at the most generous possible estimate and probably far fewer. Beneath this elevated level, when one descends to sight the army of over 1.1 million adult males in the ordinary middle class, any association with the bona fide British elite becomes not only implausible but nonsensical, and this should be evident to anyone, regardless of his ideological or methodological presuppositions. The army of Richard Walmsley Blairs, Mr Pooters, commercial clerks, minor or even fairly major civil servants, small or even middling businessmen, respectable doctors or even Anglican vicars had no more even of an indirect, let alone a direct and salient connection with the bona fide British plutocracy or aristocracy, with the Duke of Devonshire and his peers, than with the King of Siam.

In his famous essay 'Storm Over the Gentry', J. H. Hexter criticizes Tawney's habit of counting 'manors' as equal units, although these are, in Hexter's words, 'incommensurate units of ownership.'[15] Hexter noted that in New York there were at the time also two properties or 'manors'—one, the lot 'in darkest Queens' (as he put it) on which stood his house, the other on the corner of 34th Street and Fifth Avenue, the Empire State Building.[16] One would suggest this useful analogy ought to be kept in mind when considering the graduates of public schools and universities and their proper place in the British social hierarchy.

With income and status, so very largely it is with education. Although a distinction is nearly always drawn by sociologists and historians alike between an education at a public school or a grammar school, the number of truly elite public schools in the sense implied by such a distinction is very small, certainly much smaller not merely than the number of public schools in the Headmasters' Conference[17] but smaller in number than the nine Clarendon schools. Indeed, if one asks what seems the most relevant question—to how many schools, since the early nineteenth century, would a member of the bona fide British elite send his sons—the answer must be very small indeed: Eton and Harrow, certainly; at differing times Westminster, Rugby and Winchester from the Clarendon schools, and Marlborough, Wellington, Stowe, and possibly one or two others from the rest of the Headmasters' Conference. Although very small numbers of aristocrats and second- or third-generation plutocrats might be found at possibly twenty other schools, the great majority of 'public schools' are purely and simply schools for the middle classes, and often the lower middle classes—the man with a few hundred a year before 1914—and *nothing more*. Indeed, even Winchester, generally ranked as the third or even second most distinguished public school, included in the great majority of cases the sons of men not classified as 'elite' figures according to the comprehensive study by T. J. H. Bishop and Rupert Wilkinson, the school's social historians. By their definition of 'elite'—which is much wider than the one suggested above—only 25.3 per cent of the 8,187 fathers of Wykehamists born between 1820 and 1922 belonged to the 'elite'.[18] During most of the nineteenth century the largest occupational contingent of Wykehamist fathers were clergymen, most, it would seem, ordinary vicars. Many others were professional men. Only 11 per cent of all the fathers in Bishop and Wilkinson's study were businessmen.[19]

Indeed, of all the British public schools, Eton alone is *predominantly* a school for sons of the bona fide elite—although, as we have seen, even the son of a Richard Walmsley Blair could occasionally attend if he were clever or lucky. The superiority of Eton as a school for the sons of the true British elite may be seen in a comparison of British peers at two different times: first, the secondary schooling of all peers listed in Bateman's *Great Landowners* of 1883—that is, peers who had an income of £3,000 or more from landed rentals—and, secondly, of two categories of peers listed in the 1950 edition of *Dod's Parliamentary Companion*, all those whose peerage creations date from 1880 or before, and all second or subsequent holders of peerages conferred upon businessmen.[20] In the first group, the secondary schooling of 308 peers was traced. Of this number, 208, or 67.7 per cent, attended Eton; 51, (16.6 per cent), attended Harrow, 13 (4.2 per cent) Westminster, 11 (3.6 per cent) Rugby, and just 5 (1.6 per cent) Winchester. Nine attended Roman Catholic schools and only 11 attended all other schools, including Charterhouse, Shrewsbury and Cheltenham. In the 1950 sample, the schooling of 482 peers was traced. Some 278 (57.7 per cent) attended Eton. Harrow had declined to 35 peers (7.3 per cent), while Winchester had risen to 22 (4.6 per cent). Only five other schools—Wellington (12), the Roman Catholic schools Downside (7) and Oratory (6), Charterhouse and Westminster (with 6 each) were attended by as many as five peers. Schools as famous and socially acceptable as Shrewsbury, Cheltenham, Haileybury and Clifton were attended by only one or two such hereditary peers each. Eton was, overwhelmingly, the secondary school not only of the old aristocracy but of the relatively new plutocracy, including, in 1950, the second or subsequent holders of such wealthy business peerages as Leverhulme, Melchett, Rothermere, Iveagh, Armstrong, Bearsted and

Devonport among many others. As everyone knows, when the old
Harrovian Stanley Baldwin became Prime Minister in 1923 he is
said to have wished to appoint a government 'of which Harrow
could be proud', and his Cabinet contained six old Harrovians. It is
certainly less well known that Baldwin was so proud of Harrow that
he sent both of his sons to Eton, just at the time (in the years
1914–22) when the personal fortune from his family iron foundries
had swollen to well over £500,000 and Baldwin was rising from
political obscurity to the Premiership.

What is true of public schools is true *a fortiori* of universities,
except that there is no real analogy to the position of Eton. A
number of Oxbridge colleges—certainly Trinity College,
Cambridge, Balliol and Christ Church, Oxford, possibly others like
Magdalen, Oxford, or King's, Cambridge—enjoyed considerable
social prestige, but none remotely rivalled Eton. Oxbridge as such
obviously enjoyed more prestige than the other British universities,
especially the newer ones. Nevertheless, to the true elite the
position of university education has always been basically dissimilar
to secondary education. Very many peers—those who went into the
army and navy, for instance—forwent university altogether, while a
surprisingly large percentage of the sons and even grandsons of
millionaire businessmen were taken into the family firm as soon as
possible, skipping university altogether. Universities have always
had many scholarships, which were awarded to genuinely
promising young men and, from the late nineteenth century (or
even before, as in the case of mathematics at Cambridge) they
included positivist areas of knowledge where talent was genuinely
cultivated and rewarded regardless of background. The whole
system of Oxbridge examinations, even in its most dismal period,
was based purely on merit, and a genuinely brilliant result at
Oxbridge was, in career terms, in many respects the equivalent of
discovering that one's father was somehow unsuspectedly in
Burke's Peerage.

The data on the social origins of the four elite groups presented
below may appear bewildering and impersonal, and before
considering them in detail it might be well to offer an epitome of
where this data will lead by considering in an explicit way the social
origins of one of the most establishmentarian of all elite groups, the
Archbishops of Canterbury. Between 1880 and 1970 eight men held
this most senior position in the Anglican Church, and it is proposed
to consider as well the backgrounds of the two other men, Coggan

and Runcie, who have served in this position since 1970.

By the usual educational tests of social origin, the Archbishops of Canterbury appear exceedingly, and increasingly, blue-blooded. Five—including four of the five most recent archbishops—attended a major public school (Davidson, Harrow; Temple, Rugby; Fisher, Marlborough; Ramsey, Repton; Coggan, Merchant Taylors) while four of the other five attended a middle-ranking public school (Tait, Edinburgh High School; Benson, King Edward's, Birmingham; Temple, Blundell's, Tiverton; Runcie, Merchant Taylors, Crosby). Only the Scotsman Cosmo Lang attended an institution not recognized as a public school, Park School, Glasgow. All attended Oxbridge (seven Oxford, three Cambridge), nearly every one making a distinguished career and taking a brilliant degree. A superficial view of these Archbishops of Canterbury would, then, necessarily agree that they were in origin typical products of 'the establishment . . . which brought together the most distinguished members of the privileged classes, monopolized . . . the church . . . and recruitment to all major social positions'.

As I should like to demonstrate, such a view, however superficially plausible, is as misleading as to confuse Spencer Cavendish with Richard Blair. This can be demonstrated very clearly by a brief consideration of the social background of each of the ten archbishops. Archibald Tait (1811–82; Archbishop 1868–82) was the son of a small landowner in Clackmannanshire who 'ruined himself by unremunerative agricultural experiments and had eventually to sell his estates.'[21] His father, who died in 1832, is unlisted in the probate returns—that is to say, he left nothing. Tait was not even an Anglican until he was first confirmed at the age of eighteen. Edward White Benson (1829–96; served 1883–96) was the grandson of a Yorkshire squire who 'squandered a handsome fortune.' His father, a ne'er-do-well Birmingham chemical manufacturer, was in 'reduced circumstances' for nearly the whole of his life after repeated business failures. Like Tait, Benson's father left nothing when he died. His son was then fourteen, and his widow, it is recorded, 'had much difficulty in surviving.' He was able to attend Cambridge only on a scholarship and through the unexpected gifts of friends and distant relatives.[22] Frederick Temple's (1821–1902; served 1896–1902) story is similar. His father, an army major, rose to be Governor of Sierra Leone, but died there when the son was thirteen. He left only £4,000 and his widow, who had fifteen children, was 'in narrow circumstances' after his death. Temple was able to attend Oxford only because he 'practised the strictest economy'.[23] Randall Davidson (1848–1930; served 1903–28) was the son of a small Edinburgh merchant who left £4,145. Like Tait, he was not originally an Anglican. Cosmo Gordon Lang (1864–1945; served 1928–42) was likewise a Scotsman who was originally a Presbyterian and the son of a Presbyterian minister who, though he served for a time as Principal of Aberdeen University, left only £3,866. As noted above, Lang was the only archbishop who did not attend a public school. The case of the next archbishop, William Temple, will be reserved until the last since it is the most interesting. Temple's successor, Geoffrey Fisher (1887–1972; served 1945–61) was the son of an obscure Anglican vicar in a place called Higham-on-the-Hill, Leicestershire. His sole distinction was that he left rather more than the other fathers, £16,023. Arthur Ramsay (b. 1904; served 1961–74) was the son of a Congregationalist mathematics don at Cambridge who left £12,861 in 1955.[24] Donald Coggan (b. 1909; served 1974–80) was the son of a 'company secretary' who lived in north St Pancras and left £4,399 in 1942. Finally, the current archbishop, Robert Runcie (b. 1921; served from 1980) is the son of a chief electrical engineer at a Tate and Lyle factory in Liverpool with its own electricity generator, who left only £744 in 1946.[25] Runcie's mother, according to his notice in the *Current Biography* series, 'worked as a hairdresser on Cunard liners' before her marriage. Like several of his predecessors, Runcie was born a Presbyterian and attended a Methodist Sunday School as a child.

Although all of these archbishops ostensibly came from middle-class backgrounds, not one was rich or even especially affluent and several apparently knew poverty or an immediate threat of poverty when young. Several attended secondary school and university only by sheer good luck or by winning a scholarship. Not one of them had the remotest connexion with privilege or with the bona fide British elite and five were not even originally Anglicans.

The only post-1880 archbishop who has emerged from a true elite background was William Temple (1881–1944; served 1942–4) who was the son of Archbishop Frederick Temple and his wife, a granddaughter of the Earl of Harewood. Temple, however, was not merely the bluest-blooded of modern archbishops, he was also certainly the reddest. Temple joined the Labour party in 1918—that is, when it was still a left-wing fringe party and four years before it became the recognized opposition party—and was a tireless publicist and broadcaster for Christian socialism. He was said to have been particularly disliked by Tories,[26] although his left-wing views did not prevent his becoming Bishop of Manchester two years after joining the Labour party or from being elevated to the see of York in 1929 and to Canterbury in 1942.

Except for Temple, then, the origins of all modern archbishops of Canterbury have been ordinary and even meagre; they rose through the imprimature of their secondary, and more saliently, their higher education and it is only because sociologists have not studied the actual and factual social background of this group that the notion of a privileged social background could possibly have taken hold. The pattern found here, one might suggest, is surprisingly widespread. Most elite figures in this study emerged from backgrounds very similar to those of Britain's archbishops. They came from the lower part of the middle class, from fathers with very moderate incomes and remarkably little capital. Only a small minority, even among bishops and industrialists, had any direct family connexion with the bona fide elite. Moreover, this pattern has become increasingly more prevalent in recent decades, with both the wealth and social class of the fathers of elite position-holders declining steadily and markedly. These patterns are very different from those which would be inferred from considering only the educational background of these elite figures.

Tables 7.3–7.18 present five sets of equivalent data for the four elite groups considered here. These four elite groups are:

1. All permanent under-secretaries in the British Civil Service holding their office between 1880 and 1970, with the exception of a number of wartime and short-term appointees of Civil Service rank, but outside the true Civil Service structure.[27] 312 top civil servants are included.
2. All Church of England bishops or archbishops holding a diocesan see in England between 1880 and 1970.[28] 213 bishops are included.
3. Vice-chancellors of English and Welsh universities holding office between 1880 and 1970.[29] 211 vice-chancellors are included.
4. Chairmen of the largest British industrial (mainly manufacturing) companies from the list prepared by Stanworth

and Giddens (*op. cit.*) and holding office between 1900 and 1970.[30] 226 chairmen are included.

For each elite position-holder, data is presented on the following indices of social origin:

1. The probate valuation of each elite figure's father in both current and constant terms.[31]
2. The father's social status, which is expressed in a seven-scale system (numbered I—the highest category—II, III, etc.) as follows:

   I. Top landowners (those with 3,000 or more acres); top businessmen, including all businessmen leaving £50,000 or more; top professionals (judges, bishops, professors); other 'top people'; all titled persons.

   Additionally, for each cohort a number is given of elite position-holders who sprang from what is termed the 'elite'. This includes all persons who had a titled parent or grandparent, a parent or grandparent who left £500,000 or more, or a father or grandfather who served in either House of Parliament.

   II. Smaller landowners (1–3,000 acres or mentioned in *Burke's Landed Gentry*); businessmen leaving £10,–50,000 or holding an equivalent position; middle-ranking professionals, public servants, etc.

   III. Farmers: small businessmen leaving up to £10,000; lower professionals, civil servants.

   IV. The lower-middle class: clerks, small shopkeepers, ordinary teachers in state schools, etc.

   V. Skilled manual and manual supervisory workers.

   VI. Semi-skilled manual workers.

   VII. Unskilled manual workers.

In every case the social status was derived by obtaining the actual occupation of the father from such sources as birth and marriage licences, local directories and obituaries, and these are supplemented, wherever necessary, by the probate data. These social rankings, moreover, represent the *peak* status obtained by the father.

3. The final secondary school attended by the elite position-holder.
4. The university attended by the elite position-holder.
5. The geographical venue in which the elite figure spent the

greater portion of his childhood, in so far as this can be ascertained.

A point which should also be made is that each elite is arranged by twenty-year cohort groups, which include only those figures entering the elite in that period. For this reason, there is a cohort 'Before 1880'. (The industrialist group includes only four cohorts, beginning with 1900–19.) Table 7.1 which examines the median value of the estate left for probate by the father of each elite figure, begins this examination of these elite position-holders.

Table 7.1: Median Value of the Estate of Fathers of Elite Position-holder (£s)

Cohorts:	Before 1880	1880–99	1900–19	1920–39	1940–59	1960–70
A. Constant Figures						
Bishops	3,526	18,333	7,856	5,278	1,254	610
Civil servants	15,363	14,800	5,341	1,368	1,286	1,067
Vice-chancellors	227	6,640	11,330	3,195	1,793	524
Industrialists	—	—	49,091	28,954	7,101	1,778
B. Current Figures						
Bishops	4,000	20,500	7,203	6,801	1,994	1,744
Civil servants	18,000	18,000	7,683	2,155	2,614	3,229
Vice-chancellors	280	7,035	10,592	4,709	5,949	880
Industrialists	—	—	39,543	43,470	5,967	5,316

The figures here are given twice, in constant and current figures. In constant figures—that is, taking price changes into account—the median figure for bishops' fathers' estates was £3,526 for those (serving in 1880) appointed before 1880; £18,333—an anomalously high figure—in 1880–99, then (for each respective cohort) £7,856, £5,278, £1,254, and then, for those bishops first appointed in 1960–70, only £610, thereby proving that whether or not the bishops did so, their fathers seemed to live in the manner of the early Christians. Except for the 1880–99 figure—which is itself certainly not princely—all of these median values are extremely meagre by any standards, and closely resemble those likely to be left by fathers predominantly from the lower part of the middle class or even the lower-middle class. To put these average figures in a specific context, Margaret Thatcher's father, the Grantham grocer

Alfred Roberts, left £8,320 when he died in 1970. The median values, moreover, decline steadily. With this overall decline has gone an equally steady and continuing decline in the number of very wealthy fathers. This is made clear in Table 7.2, which details the number of fathers' estates (for each of the four elite groups, and by cohorts) of £100,000 or more and of £50–100,000 in current and constant figures.

Rich fathers of bishops were always surprisingly few in number, and decline to vanishing point in recent decades. The median figures for the fathers of civil-servants are strikingly similar to those for bishops' fathers and follow a remarkably similar pattern in the decline of wealthy estates. Vice-chancellors' fathers were (with the exception of one cohort) midway between the meagre bishops' fathers and the more meagre civil-servants' fathers, differing in that only a small handful of vice-chancellor fathers were rich. Industrialist fathers were obviously far richer and include substantially more very wealthy men, including many millionaires. Yet even here by no means every father was wealthy. The reasons for this will be discussed in due course, but the earlier cohorts include many self-made men, while the latter ones include, besides their own self-made men, many managerial promotees from the same starting point in the lower portion of the middle class as among other meritocratic groups.

This section of the discussion might profit from a few more specific examples. Six typical cases may serve as examples: the three most median (in terms of fathers' probate valuations and in constant figures) bishops and top civil servants deceased in the three most recent cohorts (1920–39, 1940–59 and 1960–70).[32] Among the three civil-servant cohorts, the earliest was Edmond G. A. Holmes, the father of Sir Maurice Holmes (1885–1964; Permanent Under-Secretary for Education, 1937–45), under whom the Education Act of 1944 was formulated. The elder Holmes was the Chief Inspector of Elementary Schools, a significant position, but left only £1,781 in 1936.[33] The median estate among the 1940–59 cohort fathers was left by Joseph G. Lee, an ordinary schoolmaster in Brentwood, Essex, who left £2,125 in 1928 and fathered Sir Frank G. Lee (1903–71), Permanent Under-Secretary of Food, at the Board of Trade (1949–62) and, jointly, at the Treasury. Frank Lee was educated at a board school in Brentwood and won a scholarship to Cambridge. Finally, George Haddow, the father of Sir Douglas Haddow (b. 1913), Permanent Under-Secretary for Scotland from

Table 7.2: Number of Very High Probate Values of Fathers

	Before 1880	1880–99	1900–19	1920–39	1940–59	1960–70
A. Constant Figures						
Bishops						
Above £100,000	1	5	2	2	2	0
£50–100,000	2	4	4	3	3	0
TOTAL	20	27	30	45	50	26
Civil servants						
Above £100,000	2	8	6	2	4	1
£50–100,000	1	4	5	4	1	1
TOTAL	15	40	61	52	81	40
Vice-chancellors						
Above £100,000	1	1	3	2	0	0
£50–100,000	0	1	3	0	1	3
TOTAL	3	22	39	48	36	40
Industrialists						
Above £100,000	—	—	21	24	7	7
£50–100,000	—	—	4	3	9	2
TOTAL	—	—	54	64	53	38
B. Current Figures						
Bishops						
Above £100,000	1	6	2	2	1	0
£50–100,000	1	3	5	3	1	0
TOTAL	20	27	30	45	50	26
Civil servants						
Above £100,000	2	7	8	2	1	0
£50–100,000	0	2	4	1	1	0
TOTAL	15	40	61	52	81	40
Vice-chancellors						
Above £100,000	1	1	4	2	0	0
£50–100,000	0	0	4	1	0	0
TOTAL	3	22	39	48	36	40
Industrialists						
Above £100,000	—	—	21	23	5	6
£50–100,000	—	—	5	7	6	1
TOTAL	—	—	54	64	53	38

1965, was similarly an obscure schoolmaster in Crawford, Lanarkshire who, dying in 1919 when the son was seven, left £2,375.

Among bishops the earliest of our three fathers was Henry

Mosley, a draper in Newcastle-under-Lyme, who fathered Henry Mosley (1868–1948, bishop of Southwell 1928–41). The elder Mosley left £5,176 in 1910. His son attended Newcastle High School. The father of John Moorman (b. 1905; bishop of Ripon, 1959–75) is described as a professor in Leeds. He left £2,825 in 1919 when his son was twelve. Lastly, Rev. Hector Reindorp, the father of George Reindorp (b. 1911; bishop of Guildford and of Salisbury, 1961–81), was an ordinary Anglican vicar in Ruislip, Middlesex, who left £2,840 in 1963. Although two of these six fathers held senior positions, the school inspector and (more cautiously) the professor, the remainder sprang unequivocally from the very ordinary middle class, and in three cases (on some definitions) from the lower middle class. Not one had the remotest connexion with privilege or (with the possible exception of Holmes) with power or the 'Establishment' in any real sense. Finally, in considering these *median* examples it must be clearly kept in mind that exactly *half the fathers were poorer*.[34]

Turning from wealth to social status, Tables 7.3–7.6 detail the social status of the father. Among the civil servants' fathers, 43 per

Table 7.3: Social Class of Civil Servants' Fathers

	Before 1880	1880–99	1900–19	1920–39	1940–59	1960–70
I.	4 = 24%	16 = 36%	11 = 18%	12 = 21%	13 = 16%	7 = 16%
II.	4 = 24%	17 = 39%	15 = 24%	10 = 17%	16 = 20%	8 = 19%
III.	9 = 53%	9 = 21%	32 = 52%	29 = 50%	42 = 52%	9 = 21%
IV.	—	1 = 2%	2 = 3%	5 = 9%	8 = 10%	9 = 21%
V.	—	—	1 = 2%	1 = 2%	6 = 7%	0 = 0%
VI.	—	—	—	—	—	5 = 12%
VII.	—	—	—	—	—	4 = 9%
Total known	17	44	62	58	81	43
Others unknown	0	1	1	1	2	2
Average	2.29	1.88	2.46	2.53	2.74	3.43
Elite	10 = 59%	22 = 50%	16 = 26%	10 = 17%	7 = 9%	5 = 12%

Grand Totals: I: 63 = 21%; II: 70 = 23%; III: 130 = 43%; IV: 25 = 8%; V: 8 = 3%; VI: 5 = 2%; VII: 4 = 1%.
(Total known = 305); Elite = 30 = 14%.

cent came from the lower part of the middle class, 8 per cent from the lower-middle class, and 5 per cent from the working classes. 21 per cent emerged from the upper class—our Class I—and 23 per cent had elite connexions. These percentages are roughly similar to the social class origins of the bishops' fathers, although among the bishops there are even fewer upper-class or elite fathers. Vicechancellors' fathers—despite the importance of Oxbridge in the earlier cohorts—are even less likely to be drawn from the upper classes. Industrialists, though clearly the 'poshest' of the four groups (mainly because of the wealth of these fathers, not their aristocratic lineages), are certainly not overwhelmingly upper-class and over a third were drawn from below the upper-middle class.

In all of these groups, and especially the meritocratic ones, there is a steady opening-up of class origins, entailing a steady decline (except in the case of industrialists) in the number of upper-class fathers, a steady decline in those with 'elite' connexions and a concomitant increase in those from lower-middle class and working-class backgrounds—although these are still, of course, very few in number. This process may be traced by the 'average'

Table 7.4: Social Class of Bishops' Fathers

	Before 1880	1880–99	1900–19	1920–39	1940–59	1960–70
I.	6 = 23%	10 = 36%	8 = 23%	9 = 20%	8 = 16%	0
II.	4 = 15%	8 = 29%	6 = 17%	14 = 30%	10 = 20%	5 = 22%
III.	14 = 54%	10 = 36%	19 = 54%	19 = 41%	21 = 41%	9 = 39%
IV.	2 = 8%	—	2 = 5%	4 = 9%	8 = 16%	4 = 17%
V.	—	—	—	—	0	3 = 13%
VI.	—	—	—	—	3 = 6%	1 = 4%
VII.	—	—	—	—	—	1 = 4%
Total known	27	28	35	46	51	23
Others unknown	1	0	0	1	0	3
Average	2.46	2.00	2.43	2.39	2.82	3.52
Elite	4 = 15%	10 = 36%	7 = 20%	6 = 13%	3 = 6%	0

Grand Totals: I: 41 = 20%; II: 47 = 23%; III: 92 = 44%; IV: 20 = 10%; V: 3 = 1%; VI: 4 = 2%; VII: 1 = 0.5%.
(Total known = 208); Elite = 30 = 14%.

Table 7.5: Social Class of Vice-Chancellors' Fathers

	Before 1880	1880–99	1900–19	1920–39	1940–59	1960–70
I.	1 = 50%	6 = 25%	6 = 15%	4 = 8%	3 = 8%	2 = 4%
II.	—	5 = 2%	11 = 28%	8 = 15%	12 = 32%	6 = 13%
III.	1 = 50%	11 = 46%	20 = 50%	32 = 61%	13 = 34%	18 = 39%
IV.	—	1 = 4%	3 = 8%	8 = 15%	4 = 11%	8 = 17%
V.	—	0	—	1 = 2%	4 = 11%	6 = 13%
VI.	—	1 = 4%	—	2 = 4%	2 = 5%	3 = 7%
VII.	—	—	—	—	—	3 = 7%
Total known	2	24	40	53	38	46
Others unknown	1	2	1	0	1	1
Average	2.00	2.46	2.50	3.00	3.00	3.67
Elite	1 = 50%	4 = 17%	3 = 8%	0	1 = 3%	0

Grand Totals: I: 22 = 11%; II: 42 = 20%; III: 95 = 46%; IV: 24 = 12%; V: 11 = 5%; VI: 8 = 4%; VII: 3 = 1%.
(Total known = 205); Elite = 9 = 4%.

Table 7.6: Social Class of Industrialists' Fathers

	1900–19	1920–39	1940–59	1960–70
I.	26 = 46%	26 = 40%	18 = 33%	15 = 37%
II.	9 = 16%	22 = 34%	11 = 20%	10 = 24%
III.	13 = 23%	8 = 12%	16 = 30%	3 = 7%
IV.	5 = 9%	8 = 12%	7 = 13%	8 = 20%
V.	1 = 2%	0	1 = 2%	5 = 12%
VI.	0	1 = 2%	1 = 2%	0
VII.	3 = 5%	0	0	0
Total known	57	65	54	41
Others unknown	8	5	3	1
Average	2.26	2.03	2.35	2.46
Elite	14 = 25%	18 = 28%	9 = 17%	9 = 22%

Grand Totals: I: 85 = 39%; II: 52 = 24%; III: 40 = 18%; IV: 28 = 13%; V: 7 = 3%; VI: 2 = 1%; VII: 3 = 1%.
(Total known = 217); Elite = 50 = 23%.

figure given for each cohort, which, for most groups, steadily declines—the lower the figures, the less exclusive the group—with this figure indicating the cohort average on the scale adopted here.[35] Among the fathers of civil-servants and bishops the average figure fell below the middle class (i.e., below social class III) for the 1960–70 cohort.

From what social class then, are these elites likely to be drawn? As has been suggested throughout, they emerged disproportionately from the lower part of the middle class, those without capital or connexions, who must rise, if at all, by sheer talent. This has been pointed out before. In 1941 an extremely perceptive, clear-headed and well-informed civil servant, H. E. Dale, wrote a highly informative but long-neglected account of *The Higher Civil Service of Great Britain.* Dale made this point very perceptively:

> [W]hat kind of young man enters the Home Civil Service? He is nearly sure to possess both ability and industry above the average of his contemporaries at school and the University. Secondly, many of the entrants are poor and without family influence—the sons of country parsons or small tradesmen, or widows living on tiny incomes who for years have made sacrifices in order that their clever boys may not be robbed of a university career and the chances that it offers. A young man of this origin must earn his own living from the moment he leaves the University; sometimes his family are looking for help from him . . . as soon as he has finished his education. In any case they can do nothing more for him and he knows it.[36]

Dale suggests that such young men go into the Civil Service or teaching because they are secure and reasonably well-paid from the start. He concludes that such fields as business or the Law require too much capital and that the Church is 'usually out of the question, for well-known reasons'.[37] One may question whether any of these fields is in fact ruled out; certainly the Church and corporations with a managerial structure based on merit include many men of just this background—in the case of the Church, the majority. By weight of number, ability and ambition, such men are likely to swamp any opposition in their rise to the top, given a reasonably open promotion structure.

The long existence and the key importance of the meritocracy and the pervasiveness of a meritocratic basis of promotion throughout even the highest ranges of the British elite structure would possibly have been more fully appreciated long before except for the preoccupation by sociologists and social historians with education as the test of social origin and family background. We must now address the question of the educational background of these elites in the light of what we have found. Tables 7.7–7.10 and 7.11–7.14 list, respectively, the secondary and higher educations of each cohort. The tables concerning secondary education specify the numbers attending Eton, Harrow, the other Clarendon schools collectively, twenty-two other major public schools, both boarding and day,[38] and other public schools (including direct grant schools were known). Tables 7.11–7.14 specify much the same sort of information about higher education, with numbers attending four of the posher Oxbridge colleges specified, as well as the total number of different Oxbridge colleges attended in each cohort. For a substantial number of elite figures, an Oxbridge BA degree followed a BA degree at a provincial or foreign university. Such cases are not indicated here but will be commented on below.

Perhaps the most striking point about these two sets of tables is that by no means as high a proportion of elite figures attended a public school, especially a first-rate one, as one might have imagined if one gave uncritical credence to the normal view of the public schools in British elite recruitment. Nevertheless, over half of the civil servants and bishops did attend a public school—in the case of the bishops, over two-thirds among two of the cohorts. The case of the industrialists is especially interesting. What is one to

Table 7.7: Secondary Education of Civil Servants

Cohorts	Before 1880	1880–99	1900–19	1920–39	1940–59	1960–70
Eton	7	12	8	5	3	3
Harrow	0	2	2	2	1	1
Other Clarendon	1	10	10	14	17	4
22 other Top P.S.*	0	2	13	7	16	6
Other P.S.	1	0	2	0	1	4
	9	25	35	28	38	18
Total in cohort	17	45	63	59	83	45
% at P.S.	53	56	56	47	46	40

* Includes direct grant where known.
P.S. denotes public schools.

make of a group of people whose fathers were predominantly drawn from the upper- and upper-middle classes—many among the wealthiest men in the country—yet among whom only 21 out of 234 attended Eton or Harrow? Why was this? The reason seems to be that until surprisingly late many wealthy industrialists—

Table 7.8: Secondary Education of Bishops

Cohorts	Before 1880	1880–99	1900–19	1920–39	1940–59	1960–70
Eton	4	4	4	4	2	0
Harrow	0	3	1	3	0	0
Other Clarendon	6	8	8	11	14	3
22 other Top P.S.*	0	1	8	13	11	7
Other P.S.	2	1	2	3	1	0
	12	17	23	34	28	10
Total in cohort	27	28	34	47	52	25
% at P.S.	44	61	68	72	55	40

* Includes direct grant where known.
P.S. denotes public schools.

Table 7.9: Secondary Education of Vice-Chancellors

Cohorts	Before 1880	1880–99	1900–19	1920–39	1940–59	1960–70
Eton	1	3	5	1	1	0
Harrow	—	2	1	1	0	0
Other Clarendon	—	2	4	4	14	4
22 other Top P.S.*	—	6	12	9	6	7
Other P.S.	—	6	7	14	6	11
	1	19	29	29	17	22
Total in cohort	3	26	41	53	39	47
% at P.S.	33	73	71	55	44	47

* Includes direct grant where known.
P.S. denotes public schools.

Table 7.10: Secondary Education of Industrialists

Cohorts	1900–19	1920–39	1940–59	1960–70
Eton	3	2	4	2
Harrow	4	3	1	2
Other Clarendon	1	4	2	5
22 other Top P.S.*	3	16	12	3
Other P.S.	10	8	12	12
	21	33	31	24
Total in cohort	65	70	57	42
% at P.S.	32	47	54	47

* Includes direct grant where known.
P.S. denotes public schools.

industrialists as opposed to bankers or merchants—had no time for social climbing of this type and preferred to take their sons into their companies as early as possible. This is further evident from the strikingly low percentage, until very recently, of leading industrialists with a university background—only 35 per cent of industrialists in the 1940–59 cohort attended any British university, for example. Furthermore, many industrialists went to Protestant denominational rather than mainstream Anglican public schools—for example the Quaker Cadburys attended Leighton Park or Bootham, the Quaker public schools, until well into this century.

One must now make what may seem the most paradoxical point in this survey. Comparing the four elite groups, one can hardly come to any conclusion other than that the *poorer* the family background of each elite group the *more likely* the elite figure was to attend a public school.* Not often Eton or Harrow, but regularly a recognized and respectable public school. I would like to suggest that such a conclusion is not as paradoxical as it might seem at first glance, and there are two reasons for this. First, the true elite was, as we have observed, exceedingly small, and substantial numbers of

* I am *not* arguing that the poorer the individual's father the more likely he was to attend a public school. Obviously working-class or lower-middle-class fathers were less likely to send their sons to a public school than those from the solid upper-middle-class, although occasionally some did. What is asserted here is that groups with relatively low median probate values were very likely to send their sons to a public school.

Table 7.11: Higher Education of Civil Servants

	Before 1880	1880–99	1900–19	1920–39	1940–59	1960–70
OXFORD	7	15	24	28	35	14
Balliol	2	5	4	7	1	1
Christ Church	2	5	1	3	2	2
Total Oxford colleges with one or more	(5)	(6)	(11)	(12)	(15)	(9)
CAMBRIDGE	1	5	12	11	16	18
Trinity College	1	3	10	3	1	5
King's	0	0	0	1	2	1
Total Cambridge colleges with one or more	(1)	(3)	(3)	(6)	(10)	(12)
London Univ.	0	0	4	3	5	3
Redbricks	0	0	0	0	1	2
Scottish	2	3	0	6	11	2
Other UK	0	1	2	0	3	1
Other tertiary*	0	2	4	2	0	0
	10	26	46	50	71	40
Foreign univ.	0	0	0	0	1	0
Total in cohort	17	45	63	59	83	45
% at UK univ.	59	58	73	85	86	89

* Military colleges, technical colleges, etc.

the plutocracy did not educate its sons at such schools until the inter-war period or even later. Most boys who were sent to a public school must, therefore, have come from the lower part of the middle class rather than the upper and wealthier part. As we have seen, this is borne out by what is known by quantitative historians even of so elite a school as Winchester, with vicars and other professional men comprising the bulk of fathers.

Secondly, these tables are not, it must be remembered, any sort of a random sample. They are instead a complete sample of an infinitesimally small group of persons who climbed to the very top of their fields or professions.[39] As such, it may well be imagined that in a reasonably open promotion structure where merit (or, in the

Table 7.12: Higher Education of Bishops

	Before 1880	1880–99	1900–19	1920–39	1940–59	1960–70
OXFORD	12	20	16	29	25	8
Balliol	3	2	1	3	1	0
Christ Church	2	3	4	3	0	2
Total Oxford colleges with one or more	(8)	(12)	(11)	(13)	(11)	(6)
CAMBRIDGE	14	7	16	17	22	11
Trinity College	5	2	6	6	1	3
King's	0	0	2	2	2	0
Total Cambridge colleges with one or more	(8)	(5)	(9)	(9)	(14)	(8)
London Univ.	0	0	0	1	1	3
Redbricks	0	0	0	0	0	0
Scottish	0	0	0	0	0	0
Other UK	1	1	0	0	3	1
Other tertiary	0	0	0	0	0	0
	27	28	32	47	51	25
Foreign univ.	0	0	1	0	0	0
Total in cohort	27	28	34	47	52	25
% at UK univ.	100	100	94	100	98	100

case of the industrialists, business acumen) plays even a partial role in advancement, the combination of ability, ambition and self-reliance evidently found in the characters of such men proved a successful one.

Turning to the university statistics (Tables 7.11–7.14), it will be seen that for the civil servants, bishops and vice-chancellors, overwhelmingly and increasingly, university education has been a *sine qua non* for advancement (and, indeed, for entry to the profession) although, even among vice-chancellors, there were always some with *no* university education.[40] Among civil servants, many of this sort rose through the ranks, occasionally rising to the administrative class from a lesser beginning.[41] Among leading industrialists—paradoxically the wealthiest of the four groups—until the 1960s two-thirds or more did *not* attend a university.

Table 7.13: Higher Education of Vice-Chancellors

	Before 1880	1880–99	1900–19	1920–39	1940–59	1960–70
OXFORD	1	10	16	21	17	14
Balliol	0	3	4	5	2	1
Christ Church	0	0	1	1	2	2
Total Oxford colleges with one or more	(1)	(6)	(8)	(14)	(11)	(8)
CAMBRIDGE	1	11	18	16	14	15
Trinity College	0	3	3	3	5	3
King's	0	1	2	3	1	0
Total Cambridge colleges with one or more	(1)	(9)	(10)	(8)	(9)	(9)
London Univ.	0	5	5	5	3	2
Redbricks	0	0	0	3	4	5
Scottish	0	0	0	1	0	4
Other UK	0	0	0	7	1	3
Other tertiary	0	0	1	0	0	1
	2	26	40	52	39	43
Foreign univ.	0	0	0	1	0	1
Total in cohort	3	26	41	53	39	47
% at UK univ.	67	100	98	98	100	91

Among universities, Oxbridge clearly produced far more than any other universities, even though its percentage of all British university graduates was much lower. Its proportion in these figures is artificially inflated since all those who took a second BA at Oxbridge have been counted as among its graduates. Very many—around 20 per cent of all Oxbridge graduates here—of these persons, especially many from Scotland and Wales, took a first BA at a provincial university and then a second one at Oxbridge—both, one imagines, for its social and employment advantage and for its educational value. Additionally, among the older cohorts (and possibly the newer ones) one may see at work what might be termed the 'Lichfield effect'—'Lichfield' with reference to Samuel Johnson—the arrival at Oxbridge of students from older, smaller provincial towns via a closed local scholarship or the beneficence of

Table 7.14: Higher Education of Industrialists

	1900–19	1920–39	1940–59	1960–70
OXFORD	6	5	4	8
Balliol	0	1	0	1
Christ Church	1	0	1	1
Total Oxford colleges with one or more	(6)	(4)	(4)	(6)
CAMBRIDGE	0	10	8	11
Trinity College	0	3	5	1
King's	0	2	0	3
Total Cambridge colleges with one or more	(0)	(5)	(5)	(6)
London Univ.	2	0	1	2
Redbricks	1	1	1	3
Scottish	3	0	4	0
Other UK	0	1	1	1
Other tertiary	0	1	1	2
	12	18	20	27
Foreign univ.	2	0	1	0
Total in cohort	65	70	57	42
% at UK univ.	15	26	35	64

local friends or relatives. Many if not most university men of this background attended the local grammar school and virtually none had any salient connexion with the national elite.

Among the Oxbridge colleges, the number of different colleges which produced one or more elite figure, and the number produced by four of the most prestigious, have been indicated. Although Balliol and Trinity College (Cambridge) did account for a disproportionate number of elite figures, many colleges—up to fifteen in a single cohort—did produce at least one elite figure and it is not really plausible to speak of, say, a 'Balliol mafia' or its equivalent. Again, the promotion net, once the dimensions of the system are realized, appears to be genuinely wide. A far higher percentage of elite figures attended a university than a public school, especially a 'great' one. As we have seen, among several elite cohorts virtually every single elite figure attended a university. This is highly consistent with a promotion system based upon merit rather than connexion or patronage, as the universities drew their students, via scholarships, from a wider social background even than the minor public schools. What, then, was the role of the public schools and the universities in the recruitment of British elites? If the smallness of the bona fide elite is again realized, as well as the limited wealth and meagre social backgrounds of surprising numbers of elite families, the only fair inference which can in my view be made must be that the public schools and, more definitely, the universities immensely expanded the universe from which Britain's elites were recruited, to virtually the entire middle class and, beyond it, to the particularly lucky or able from the lower-middle class and, occasionally, the working classes. Moreover, once the meritocratic system had largely replaced the eighteenth- and early nineteenth-century system of patronage and connexion around the middle-late nineteenth century, each successive generation (since those born in the 1880s at least) has been drawn from a wider and wider net, as the fathers' probate and social class data demonstrates.

Whenever the subject of British elite recruitment and its base in the public school system is mentioned, several elites not surveyed in this chapter are almost invariably mentioned as examples of groups drawn overwhelmingly from an exclusive and privileged background, and these have done much to formulate our image of the British elite. Perhaps the elite groups most often mentioned in this connexion are the large landowners, bankers and City of London merchant bankers, and Tory politicians and Cabinet ministers. The received image of the continuing role of the public schools in elite recruitment is almost certainly formed to a disproportionate extent by an image—however truthful—of these three groups. Something will be said below of landowners and bankers; as to Conservative politicians, many observers regard 'Tory Cabinet minister', 'privilege', and 'the old school tie' as virtually interchangeable terms, often inferring from this as much about the alleged nature of the contemporary British Establishment as from any other single source. I should like to suggest that, so far as the evolution of Tory Cabinets and indeed the class origins of all Conservative MPs is concerned, exactly the same transformation has taken place over the past seventy years as among the other elites studied here—indeed, the actual change has been much more dramatic, since Conservative MPs and Cabinet ministers (unlike, say, civil servants) were, prior to 1911, unpaid, and hence drawn overwhelmingly from the very wealthy with the centuries-old tradition behind them of political families, nomination boroughs and aristocratic patronage.[42] There can be no doubt whatever of the decline in the number of wealthy Tory MPs or the movement as early as 1910 if not before from a party whose members had a predominantly landed-aristocratic background to one based on industry and the professions.[43] Since 1945 this has increasingly changed, too, as the typical Tory MP has become neither a landowner nor an industrialist but a professional full-time political advocate, drawn disproportionately from the Law and those businesses concerned with public relations. Such persons are mainly (but not necessarily) middle-class in origin, but only infrequently have the remotest personal connexion with the aristocracy or the plutocracy. There have, of course, been disproportionate numbers of Tory MPs drawn from the aristocracy and the plutocracy and, in particular, related to the old ruling landed aristocracy. Additionally, there have been disproportionate numbers of Tory MPs who attended a public school and Oxbridge. But there is no doubt that each generation, without exception and without a break, has since 1906 at the latest seen a diminution in the number of genuinely aristocratic Tory MPs. As John Ramsden, the most astute historian of this matter, has noted:

> [Between 1914 and 1939] a change had really taken place, albeit a slow and gradual one. Critics of the party like Simon Haxey, who concentrated on how many MPs were related to the Duke of Buccleuch, missed the point that the proportion would probably have been higher in any previous generation; the same numbers game was played with equally misleading effect by Anthony Sampson twenty years later. In a conservative party, the element of social change can only be usefully measured against an expectation of continuity, and in this context quite a substantial difference had emerged by 1939. The party in parliament was accommodating itself gradually to the social groups that supported it in the country.[44]

As for using public school and university attendance as an indication of the social background of Tory MPs and ministers, precisely the same strictures may be made against it as in the case of bishops and civil servants: such a test entails the inference, without further evidence, that public school attendance necessarily indicates considerable family wealth and status; additionally it conceals both the real nature of the class backgrounds of the elites and the real changes which have occurred in elite recruitment across the decades. To the best of my knowledge, no searching and thorough study of the social origins of the contemporary Tory party has been made, although in Perkin's project the 1970–4 Tory Cabinet was surveyed in the same manner as other elite groups. The findings of this group were strikingly similar to those for other recent elites—a rapid decline in the number of persons saliently connected with the aristocracy or plutocracy and a rise in the number of leading Tory politicians from the lower part of the middle class (or below), a shift disguised by a continuing high level of public school and university attendance. The successful camouflaging of this shift in the social origins of Tory politicians produced misperceptions of the sort (to cite one such example) turned out in the *New Statesman* just after the 1979 General Election:

> But there is no room in the Cabinet for Fat Stan Flashman [a 'self-made man']. And if he wished to stand for Parliament one can be sure that the Tories would give him a hopeless seat to fight: despite their oft-professed fondness for the 'self-made man', the Tories persist in giving their safest seats to Old Etonians and other members of the aristocracy ... [Mrs Thatcher] does not wish in any way to change those institutions (one of which is a Conservative government); rather, she seeks to alter *herself* in order to make herself acceptable to them. Aristocrats have always liked to keep a healthy distance between themselves and their womenfolk.[45]

In fact the Tory Cabinet which took office in 1979 contained only a relatively small percentage who belonged to the bona fide aristocracy or plutocracy—Lord Carrington and possibly Sir Ian Gilmour to the aristocracy, William Whitelaw, Lord Soames, Sir Keith Joseph and George Younger to the plutocracy. At least as typical of the original Thatcher Cabinet, however, were Peter Walker—the son of a grocer who left £4,742; James Prior—the son of a solicitor in Norwich who left £12,281 in 1964; Patrick Jenkin—the son of a chemist; Norman Tebbit—the son of a salesman; John Biffen—the son of a tenant farmer in Somerset—or Mrs Thatcher herself. Political events within the party since 1979 have acted to broaden the social origins of its inner elite still further. At the mid-point in 1983, only two very senior Tory Cabinet ministers are either peers or old Etonians, certainly the lowest total in either category since the Tory party's foundation.[46] Although Edward Heath was frequently depicted as heading a government of self-made men, the surviving Heath-style centrist 'wets' who have been systematically squeezed out of Mrs Thatcher's inner counsels since 1979 have been replaced, by and large, by products of lower social origin.

The final dimension of social classification considered here is that of geographical origins. Tables 7.15–7.19 detail the main geographical locale of the childhood of each elite figure, as ascertained by the best available biographical evidence. The tables are arranged by fifteen distinctive geographical regions in the United Kingdom.[47] The figures in brackets indicate those elite figures who grew up in a main industrial city or region (including Liverpool). The information here records where each elite figure spent the bulk of his childhood. An examination of geographical origin is relevant if it suggests that the divide between suburban south and industrial north in modern Britain is reflected in

Table 7.15: Chief Childhood Venues of Civil Servants*

	Before 1880	1880–99	1900–19	1920–39	1940–59	1960–70
1. London	6	12	10	10	21	12
2. Home Counties	—	4	10	12	11	7
3. S. England	1	2	4	3	3	—
4. S.W. England	1	5	6	6	4	3
5. East Anglia	1	1	3	0	4	—
6. E. Midlands	1	3	1	0	1	1 [1]
7. W. Midlands	2 [1]	—	—	4 [3]	4 [2]	1
8. Lancs. & Cheshire	—	—	7 [6]	5 [5]	6 [6]	6 [4]
9. West Riding	—	—	—	0	3 [3]	2 [2]
10. Other Yorks.	—	—	2	—	2	—
11. North East	1	—	1	1 [1]	1	—
12. North West	—	—	2	—	—	—
13. Scotland	2 [1]	6 [1]	7	8 [1]	11	4 [1]
14. Wales	—	—	—	2	1	2 [1]
15. Ireland	1	2	5	2	2	1
16. Abroad	—	4	2	4	8	3
Unknown	1	4	1	1	4	1
Total known	16 [2]	39 [1]	60 [6]	57 [10]	82 [11]	41 [9]

* Numbers in brackets indicate numbers in chief industrial area towns and areas: Manchester, Liverpool, Birmingham, Newcastle, Glasgow, etc., with their outlying areas.

promotion within the major hierarchical structures of the 'Establishment', with London and the south presumably over-represented—possibly because of accent, possibly because of the mutually reinforcing effect of wealth, schooling and life values typically found in London and the south vis-à-vis the north.

Table 7.16: Chief Childhood Venues of Bishops

	Before 1880	1880–99	1900–19	1920–39	1940–59	1960–70
1. London	3	1	8	11	11	6
2. Home Counties	3	2	8	5	5	2
3. S. England	2	4	1	2	3	1
4. S.W. England	1	—	3	5	4	7
5. East Anglia	3	1	1	—	—	1
6. E. Midlands	3	2	3 [1]	2 [1]	2	—
7. W. Midlands	1 [1]	2	2 [1]	4 [3]	4 [1]	3 [1]
8. Lancs. & Cheshire	2 [2]	3 [3]	4 [4]	3 [2]	7 [6]	1 [1]
9. West Riding	1 [1]	3 [3]	—	3 [3]	2 [2]	—
10. Other Yorks.	—	—	—	1	1	1
11. N.E. England	—	2 [2]	—	2 [1]	1 [1]	—
12. N.W. England	1	1	2	—	—	—
13. Scotland	—	2 [1]	—	1	1	2 [1]
14. Wales	—	1	—	1	1	—
15. Ireland	1	—	1	1	2	—
16. Abroad	—	—	1	—	—	—
Unknown	1	—	—	3	5	2
Total known	21 [4]	23 [9]	34 [6]	41 [10]	44 [10]	24 [3]

Indeed, at first glance the London, Home Counties, and south-of-England bias demonstrated by these tables is fairly obvious. However, this bias is, perhaps, less pronounced when two bases of comparison are taken into account. Table 7.19 details very broadly and by overall percentages, the geographical distribution of taxable (i.e. above £160 p.a.) business and professional incomes in 1848–9 and 1911–12 according to the manuscript income-tax summaries (I.R. 16) in the Public Record Office.[48] In Table 7.20, the total populations of these regions in 1851 and 1911 are listed, by percentages. The lead of London and south-eastern England in middle-class (i.e. income taxable) income, when compared to the

Table 7.17: Chief Childhood Venues of Vice-Chancellors

	Before 1880	1880–99	1900–19	1920–39	1940–59	1960–70
1. London	1	10	7	11	8	3
2. Home Counties	—	1	5	5	3	2
3. S. England	—	2	1	2	2	2
4. S.W. England	—	1	8	6	1	6
5. East Anglia	1	1	3	2	1	—
6. E. Midlands	—	1	3	2	1	3 [1]
7. W. Midlands	—	2 [1]	5 [3]	2 [2]	2 [2]	4 [1]
8. Lancs. & Cheshire	—	2 [2]	2 [2]	5 [4]	6 [4]	9 [9]
9. West Riding	—	—	2 [2]	1 [1]	4 [4]	3 [3]
10. Other Yorks.	—	—	1	1	—	1 [1]
11. N.E. England	—	—	1	—	—	1 [1]
12. N.W. England	—	—	—	—	1	—
13. Scotland	—	—	2	7 [2]	4 [2]	7 [1]
14. Wales	1	1	1	5 [2]	—	—
15. Ireland	—	2	—	2	—	—
16. Abroad	—	—	—	3	2	4
Unknown	—	2	1	2	—	—
Total known	3	23 [3]	40 [7]	54 [11]	39 [12]	48 [18]

population distribution, is, of course, perhaps the most remarkable feature of these tables.[49] The British middle classes—from whom most elite group members were drawn—were disproportionately resident in London and the south-east. It is therefore not surprising that disproportionate numbers of elite group members should have been drawn from this part of Britain, especially when the barriers to the entry of practising dissenters into the public schools and universities is recalled. Broadly, then, the geographical origins of the meritocratic elites closely resembles the distribution of the British middle classes as a whole. But, for a number of reasons, the northern industrial areas were never by any means excluded from entry into elite positions. The 'Lichfield effect' certainly took in (where relevant) Anglican, centrist-oriented, upwardly mobile northerners of talent. In recent times the spread of the redbrick and new universities, as well as the openings for science-oriented and numerate civil servants, have worked to increase the advancement of men of this background. Yet the drift of population and wealth to

Table 7.18: Chief Childhood Venues of Industrialists

	1900–19	1920–39	1940–50	1960–70
1. London	9	18	10	16
2. Home Counties	2	2	3	—
3. S. England	1	—	—	1
4. S.W. England	4	4	3	3
5. East Anglia	—	2	—	—
6. E. Midlands	—	2	3	—
7. W. Midlands	1 [1]	3 [3]	8 [8]	4 [4]
8. Lancs. & Cheshire	21 [20]	10 [9]	8 [8]	5 [4]
9. West Riding	7 [7]	5 [5]	3 [2]	2 [2]
10. Other Yorks.	3	3	4	—
11. N.E. England	1 [1]	1 [1]	1 [1]	—
12. N.W. England	—	—	—	—
13. Scotland	11 [7]	8 [6]	8 [6]	3 [1]
14. Wales	—	5 [3]	—	—
15. Ireland	4	2	2	—
16. Abroad	1	4	4	3
Unknown	3	1	1	2
Total Known	65 [35]	69 [27]	57 [25]	37 [11]

the south has counteracted these trends to a certain extent, as is evident from the recent cohort results in these tables. (Not evident from these figures, but true nonetheless, is the fact that many ostensible northerners were educated at southern public schools.)

This is perhaps most clear in the statistics of the original venue of leading industrialists. Among them a majority were, in the earliest cohort, from the major industrial towns. The percentage of such persons has steadily declined; by the 1960s, though not low, it was certainly not anomalously higher than among other elites. Concomitantly, the number of Londoners has clearly risen. This rise has been due to two factors: the relocation of industrial headquarters in the London area—managerial recruitment is often from among local boys—and the growth of a recognizable managerial structure in most individual corporations in place of family firms or firms founded by an old-style tycoon (although these still exist). The social backgrounds, including the venue, of these managers closely resemble those of the other meritocratic elites, with a middle-class or lower-middle class base, and one disproportionately in the south of England. The position of the

Table 7.19: Percentage of British Middle-class Income, by Region 1848–9
and 1911–12

		1848–9	1911–12
1.	London*	28.65	43.94
2.	Home Counties	8.89	4.64
3.	S. England	2.06	2.09
4.	S.W. England	6.57	3.51
5.	East Anglia	2.23	1.18
6.	E. Midlands	3.76	5.05
7.	W. Midlands	7.02	3.99
8.	Lancs. & Cheshire	12.98	11.17
9/10.	Yorkshire**	6.56	7.29
11.	N.E. England	3.13	3.04
12.	N.W. England	0.56	0.44
13.	Scotland	15.27	10.43
14.	Wales	2.33	3.21
15.	Ireland	(N.A.)	(Ireland = 3.36 of GB) total)

* This region, termed the 'Metropolis' in 1911–12, included substantial areas in Kent, Surrey and Essex in 1848–9.
** Separate West Riding figures not available.

Table 7.20: Percentage of British Population, by Region 1851 and 1911

		1851 (000)	1911 (000s)
1.	London	2,504 = 12.03	5,648 = 13.83
2.	Home Counties	1,847 = 8.87	4,439 = 10.87
3.	S. England	742 = 3.56	1,616 = 3.96
4.	S.W. England	2,264 = 10.88	2.507 = 6.14
5.	East Anglia	965 = 4.64	1,091 = 2.67
6.	E. Midlands	1,686 = 8.10	3,129 = 7.66
7.	W. Midlands	1,428 = 6.86	2.896 = 7.09
8.	Lancs. & Cheshire	2,487 = 11.95	5,724 = 14.02
9.	West Riding	1,366 = 6.56	3,131 = 7.67
10.	Yorkshire	432 = 2.08	852 = 2.09
11.	N.E. England	695 = 3.34	2,067 = 5.06
12.	N.W. England	253 = 1.22	330 = 0.81
13.	Scotland	2,889 = 13.88	4,761 = 11.66
14.	Wales	1,006 = 4.83	2,027 = 4.96
15.	Ireland	6,552 = 31.47% of GB population)	(4,290 = 10.75% of GB population)
	Great Britain	20,817	40,831

north of England in the British elite structure has indeed become progressively less fortunate. Whereas in the nineteenth century it could offer, as it were, an alternative set of elites based upon values alternative to those of the conservative south—most notably, of course, in manufacturing industry—the drift of population and wealth in this century to the south, and the general encroachments of the values of the 'Establishment' upon this alternative set of elites, has made their position increasingly precarious and untenable. This is a process which increasingly appears irreversible; indeed the developments of the past decade or two—the 'deindustrialization of Britain', the rise of a computer-based service sector, Britain's entry into the EEC—have greatly accelerated these trends, despite deliberate rescue efforts by successive governments well aware of the problem.

As has been seen repeatedly, then, there is not much correlation between family wealth and public school attendance and less between family wealth and university attendance. Little, however, has yet been said about the value-system of these institutions and the attitudes they supposedly engendered. According to nearly all accounts of the English educational system, the public schools engendered a value-system which emphasized conformity, rote learning, the cult of the 'gentleman' and of athleticism, and a thinly-disguised, pervasive sado-masochism and repressed homosexuality. Originality or eccentricity in any form were, according to this critique, assiduously extracted from students in a system which prevailed from the 1850s until the 1960s, peaking between 1885 and 1939.[50] There is no way of knowing how 'correct' this familiar critique might be; certainly its constant reiteration argues that very many people believe it. England's 'national character', especially the behaviour of its elites, plainly became less rowdy and more gentlemanly and conformist between, broadly, say 1820 and 1920. To the argument that the public schools diminished true originality and high talent some direct evidence might be adduced: of the 46 winners of a Nobel Prize in science between 1901 and 1970 who were educated in Britain, only 25 were educated at a public school, including all minor ones and direct grant schools. Only eight were educated at a major public school, none at all at Eton or Harrow, and only one (Richard Synge, Chemistry Nobel prize winner in 1952) at Winchester. Considering the resources and opportunities available to the major English public schools, this is probably a performance below expectation, although it should not be forgotten that, despite its scientific emphasis, the Soviet Union has produced only four Nobel laureates in science since 1917.[51]

If it be accepted that some or even most of the traditional critique of the public schools is true, the clear implication is that much of D. C. Coleman's well-known thesis on British industrialists—that the 'cult of the gentleman' in the second and third generations opened the way to new men—must also be true of the effect of the public schools upon elite structures, with two important provisos: that entry into these elite structures was not limited exclusively to public school products, and that the consequences of the poor public school product's need to obtain a secure job from the first opportunity, as in Dale's description, be noted. With regard to the first of these points, as we have seen by no means all elite position-holders attended a public school, especially an exclusive one, even among groups where this might have been expected. Even if public school products stood a very distinct advantage in securing entry on to the elite ladder, there is simply no convincing evidence that they enjoyed a monopoly or that entry was closed to others; there is even less evidence that one had to be rich or well-connected. It necessarily follows that Britain's elites in the past century have been considerably more open than many historians and sociologists have believed, with the entire middle class—up to a quarter of the population—serving as the 'candidate group' for elite recruitment, and with the occasional elite figure from below the middle class. If true, this must put paid to the notion that one's childhood origins stamped one for life in a variety of personal and irredeemable ways—no doubt, for instance, a would-be Anglican bishop had to look and sound like a bishop and not like a Methodist field preacher, but evidently such characteristics were easier to acquire than many would believe. Furthermore, the apparent ubiquity of the pattern found here—the relative similarity of opportunities in quite diverse elites—argues that it is inherent in contemporary bureaucratic structures throughout wide areas of British society if not across all elites. It might be argued, for example, that Church of England bishoprics are now more open to outsiders because, as the influence and popularity of Anglicanism has waned, the Church must seek its leaders from men of talent regardless of their origins; but the fact that a nearly identical pattern of leadership selection is evident among heads of the Civil Service, an elite which has manifestly grown enormously in influence and power during this century, suggests that this shift is a function of more underlying forces.

It might be objected to this examination of elite social mobility that meritocratic groups have been considered to the exclusion of those where wealth and family connexion remain crucial to senior promotion. Are there significant areas of power in British society where this is still true? Probably the two best candidates are large landowning and the City of London financial sector, especially the merchant banks but also the clearing banks and other key financial institutions. As noted above, with the leadership of the Conservative party it is these groupings which are probably most responsible for the continuing popular notion of a closed, quasi-hereditary 'Establishment' in the full-blown sense. The notion that Britain's landed elite is hereditary and virtually closed is certainly true, as of course one might expect given the nature of British landownership, its titled aristocracy, and primogeniture.[52] But if Britain's landed elite is and remains the most tightly-knit and caste-like of major elite groups, it is also the elite which has unquestionably experienced the most thorough and complete loss of power and influence during the past century (with the arguable exception of the Anglican bishops). A century ago, a majority of all Cabinets consisted of great landowners and their close relatives; today, the presence of a single bona fide landed aristocrat, even in a Tory Cabinet, is a considerable and noteworthy oddity. Similarly, the wealth of all but the very greatest landowners diminished steadily between the 1870s and the 1950s, although the colossal rise in land values during the past quarter-century has revived the fortunes of Britain's landowners very considerably,[53] a revival in economic fortune wholly unaccompanied by a revival in political fortune, it should be noted.

The case of the City is different and, it would seem, a clear exception to the patterns found in this chapter. Compared with industry, where a managerial executive structure has long been the rule, much of the older sectors of the City remain apparent islands of hereditary succession—though without apparently affecting the profitability or entrepreneurial skills of the firms in question. In 1983 several of the best known merchant banks still had scions of the founding families as chairmen, including Baring Brothers, Rothschilds, and Hambros, while the chairmen of several others sprang from illustrious and long-established City families.[54] At the same time Barclays Bank in 1982 appointed as chairman Timothy Bevan 'the direct descendant of Silvanus Bevan who joined the original Barclays in 1767'.[55] Nevertheless, however much the City

elite may genuinely differ from the pattern found in other
hierarchies, several points should be kept in mind: firstly, many of
the City's most eminent and important institutions, in particular
the merchant banks, were founded and expanded by low-status
immigrants entirely outside the British status structure, especially
continental Jews as well as Germans and Greeks. It is the scions of
these families who have proven especially adept at hereditary
entrepreneurship. Many of the British-origin continuing financial
dynasties, moreover, were non-conformists or Scotsmen.
Secondly, there has been a relative secular shift of power within
Britain's financial sector during this century away from the
traditional merchant banks to newer institutions like building
societies and the large insurance companies with a more modern
and meritocratic promotional structure and fewer pretensions to
aristocracy. And finally, although the data in this study may indeed
ignore landowners and the City, equally it has failed to mention
those trade union and labour elites whose thrust into the British
ruling structure between 1910 and 1930 have shaped the
dimensions of British history in this century.[56] Plainly the
leadership element among the labour/trade union elite has
necessarily been overwhelmingly working-class, the significant
minority of middle-class Labour Cabinet ministers
notwithstanding.

If, however, most meritocratic elites in this century have been
drawn predominantly from the lower part of the middle class, one
may ask what the consequences have been for the governance of
Britain. This chapter has assiduously avoided drawing any
inferences about political stance from social background alone, and
it seems doubtful to me whether, in the absence of compelling
evidence, this is a fruitful subject to pursue. However, some very
general conclusions probably can safely be drawn from the facts of
elite recruitment. Perhaps the most important is that most
meritocratic elite members drawn from outside the privileged
classes had no vested interest in the maintenance of capitalism, since
they were not personally wealthy and, for most of their adult lives,
lacked substantial sums of capital.[57] To suggest that such men were
likely to be socialists is, of course, highly unwarranted, but the
Toryism of such men—if the widespread notion of a right-wing
Anglican Church and an anti-socialist Civil Service is at all
accurate—must have derived from the patriotic and traditional
strands within Conservatism, not from a self-interested defence of

free enterprise. Such a stance is, of course, not inconsistent with Fabianism and a preference for central and rational planning and efficiency, and the Fabian Society apparently drew its main strength from this milieu.[58] Given the educational processes through which most meritocratic elites were educated, it must be assumed that they reflected the rationalism and cogency associated with the British examination system, and were consistently literate (if not numerate) and intelligent—indeed, among the most literate and intelligent men of their day. This applied even to the bishops, and a résumé of their careers in *Who's Who* and similar works reveals a spectacular record of academic success, with many if not most of the bishops taking double firsts and carrying off famous university prizes.[59] There was nothing dim or mediocre about this elite, which is indeed a fair sample of England's best and brightest. They entered their chosen field by open competition or as a result of outstanding academic performance and largely rose on their merits. The seeming paradox, which will doubtless have occurred to many readers, is that Britain's modern decline has taken place simultaneously with the rise of the meritocracy and, indeed, began at the very time when competition for entry into the Civil Service replaced patronage. Whether there is a connexion between the two is, of course, both highly arguable and unprovable. Merit and rationality may be relevant to Britain's long-term performance, or the factors which produced it may be quite irrelevant to the ability of Britain's elites. The cynical verdict, that outstanding men have consistently made deplorable choices and decisions, may or may not be true, but the coincidence is so striking as surely to require examination.

Turning to the present and future course of elite recruitment patterns in Britain, one must certainly expect the avenues of recruitment to widen still further. This study ends in 1970 and takes virtually no account of the effects of the 1944 Education Act, of the vast growth in the tertiary sector since World War Two, or of recent developments such as the growth of the comprehensive system. There is no reason to suppose that an accurate and searching examination of the social origins of today's and tomorrow's elites would not find the median fathers' social class declining still further, until the father of very solid middle-class background—a surgeon or barrister—becomes as rare as an aristocratic father is now.[60] On the other hand, the radical improvement in the

educational quality of England's public schools since the 1950s, and
the continuing middle-class demand for them in the face of the
effective end of the grammar school system, may give the products
of public schools a renewed lease on life in elite recruitment.[61] On
balance, however, it seems most unlikely that the broadening in the
social bases of elite recruitment in this century will not continue.

NOTES

1. Something ought first to be said about the natural history of this
   chapter, as it is most relevant to understanding what is trying to be
   achieved. In 1974 and 1975, I was Research Associate to Harold
   Perkin, then Professor of Social History at the University of Lancaster
   and engaged in researching a historical project on the 'Social Origins of
   British Elites, 1880–1970'. This project (funded by the Social Science
   Research Council) studied 26 elite groups or elite position-holders
   between 1880 and 1970. Three of the four groups discussed in detail
   here—top civil servants, leading industrialists, and university vice-
   chancellors—were included in Perkin's study, but the fourth group,
   Church of England bishops and archbishops, were not included and
   my discussion of them represents fresh research. Perkin gave several
   lengthy conference papers based upon his research, but in only one or
   two published articles of his taken from this project does he in part
   touch upon the points I will make here, with a different stress and
   emphasis. Surprisingly, neither Perkin nor myself have hitherto
   returned to this important subject, which is too significant a topic to be
   left to the dust and silence of the upper shelf. I should note that, of
   course, the views expressed here are my own and in no way represent
   those of Professor Perkin. Perkin's articles on this subject are entitled
   'The Recruitment of Elites in British Society Since 1800', which
   appeared in *The Journal of Social History*, XII, No. 2 (Winter 1978)
   and 'Who Runs Britain? Elites in British Society Since 1880', in his
   book of essays *The Structured Crowd: Essays in English Social History*
   (Brighton, 1981).
   Although they have similar titles, the first of these is longer and more
   detailed, and makes a number of points close to those made in this
   paper, without its particular emphasis or viewpoint. Perkin also
   presented a longer, unpublished, paper based upon this research to the
   inaugural Social History Society Conference in 1976 and at the
   Conference of Anglo-American Historians of that year.
   The information in this paper differs from that provided by Perkin
   in his published and unpublished essays in the following respects: (a)
   Church of England bishops and archbishops, not included in the
   original study, are discussed here; (b) the cohort groups (e.g. those
   holding elite positions in 1880–99, 1900–19, etc.) contain only

individuals who were first appointed to these positions in that period, rather than (as in his original study) those who either were first appointed at the time or continued to hold office in a later cohort period. This will serve to highlight change and also makes necessary an additional cohort period, 'Appointed before 1880' not in the original study; (c) my study also includes comprehensive data on the geographical origins (by county or major town) of the four elite groups surveyed here. This information was not included in the original study; (d) little or no information is provided here about the wealth of the elite position-holders, only information about their social origins; (e) a limited amount of additional information on the occupations and probate valuations of the elite fathers, not available in 1974–5, has been added to the data.

Much of the probate data for the bishops' fathers was collected for me by Mrs Rachel Britton (University of Essex), while I have to thank the School of Social Sciences, Deakin University, for a grant to purchase the bishops' birth certificates/marriage licences. An earlier version of this paper was read at the seminar of the School of Social Sciences, Deakin University and at the Conference of Anglo-American Historians, University of London, in July 1983. I am most grateful for the comments received on both occasions.

2. The best recent study, though from a sociological perspective, is Scott's book. It contains a very full bibliography (pp. 191–207) of works in this field. Another good bibliography was compiled by Philip Stanworth in Ivor Crewe (ed.), *Elites in Western Democracy* (London, 1974), pp. 337–50. Both of these, it should be stressed, were compiled by academic sociologists and miss many historical works (including theses) which are relevant to the field.

3. Philip Stanworth and Anthony Giddens, 'An Economic Elite: Company Chairmen', in Stanworth and Giddens (eds), *Elites and Power*, *op. cit.*, pp. 81–101.

4. See their footnotes 4 and 8. Despite these reservations, I regard the Stanworth/Giddens study as exceedingly valuable, and found their work particularly useful both in this project and in my research on wealth-holding (see my *Men of Property*, *op. cit.*, pp. 178–92).

5. The 'Clarendon schools' are Eton, Harrow, Winchester, Rugby, St Pauls, Merchant Taylors, Charterhouse and Shrewsbury. They are so-called from being the subject of a famous parliamentary investigation by Lord Clarendon's Commission in 1861.

6. Additionally, such sources as *Burke's Peerage* and *Burke's Landed Gentry* are usually taken as evidence of considerable wealth and high status of those included, without—this being the key point—any additional evidence about the actual wealth or occupation of the father or family of the elite position-holder.

7. That is, marriage licences of the elite position-holder provide the occupation of his father. Scottish (but not English) death certificates also provide the occupation of the father of the deceased.

8. On the probate records, see my *Men of Property*, especially Ch. 1.

9. Bernard Crick, *George Orwell. A Life* (Boston, 1980) p. 11. Crick adds

that 'He retired on his pension with no family inheritance beyond some monogrammed silver and a few pieces of furniture' (p. 6).

10. [David Spring (ed.)] John Bateman, *The Great Landowners of Great Britain and Ireland* (1883; repr. Leicester, 1971), p. 130; Cannadine, *Lords and Landlords, op. cit.*, p. 294. The total figure quoted here differs from that given by Dr Cannadine.

11. Because of the peculiarities of the British income-tax system, there is no definite way to ascertain the distribution of income in Britain until the inter-war period. L. G. Chiozza Money claimed that in 1908, of 44,500,000 persons in Britain, 1,400,000 (3.1%)—having an income of £700 or more—were themselves rich or belonged to rich families, 4,100,000 (9.2%) were 'comfortable'—incomes between £160 and £700—and 39 million (87.6%) were 'poor'. (Chiozza Money, *Riches and Poverty 1910, op. cit.*, pp. 33, 44–9). Chiozza Money also estimated that there were 1,100,000 individual persons (not members of households) in receipt of an income of £160 or more, the minimum level of liability for income tax. Josiah Stamp—whose discussion of this topic remains unsurpassed—also put the number of incomes over £160 at 1,050,000—1,100,000 in 1909–10 (Stamp, *British Incomes and Property, op. cit.*, p. 448. He claimed (*ibid.*) that there were roughly 268 (280,000) such incomes in 1860–1 and 604 (632,000) in 1881–2. Note that these are estimates of income, not of status or occupation. Some white-collar groups like junior clerks, as well as aspiring or retired white-collar workers, would have had incomes below £160.

12. As well as defining a unique political position which may broadly be defined as that of a 'radical patriot'.

13. Orwell and Angus (eds), *Collected Essays, Journalism and Letters of George Orwell, op. cit.*, Vol. IV, p. 418. Orwell believed his position to be highly anomalous. As an Etonian he was probably correct, but merely as a graduate of a public school he was, on the contrary, absolutely typical.

14. *Annual Report of the Inland Revenue, 1914–15*; *Burke's Peerage*; Scott, *The Upper Classes, op. cit.*, p. 110.

15. J. H. Hexter, 'Storm Over the Gentry', in *Reappraisals in History* (London, 1961), p. 128.

16. *Ibid.*

17. The 'Headmasters' Conference' was formed in 1869 and includes most recognized public schools. It had 71 member schools in 1873 and has about 140 today.

18. Bishop and Wilkinson, *Winchester and the Public School Elite, op. cit.*, pp. 98–101. Some recent research of mine on a random sample of Harrow students entering in 1840, 1870, and 1895–1900 suggests that no more than 15–20 per cent even of these emerged from the smaller elite as defined in this paper.

19. *Ibid.*, pp. 104–8, 112.

20. All businessmen who were themselves ennobled are thus excluded from the 1950 sample, as are all other peers—e.g. ennobled politicians, military men, judges, etc. Additionally, Scottish and Irish peers without seats in the Lords were excluded, as were minors.

21. *Dictionary of National Biography (DNB).*
22. *Ibid.*; see also E. F. Benson, *As We Were* (London, 1930), esp. pp. 30–63.
23. *DNB.*
24. Arthur Ramsay was also the brother of Frank Ramsay, the brilliant mathematical philosopher who wrote a celebrated review of Wittgenstein's *Tractatus* before dying at the age of twenty-nine.
25. Margaret Duggan, *Runcie: The Making of an Archbishop* (London, 1983), p. 46.
26. *DNB.*
27. Lists were taken from *British Political Facts, 1900–75*, *British Historical Facts 1830–1900*, and *Whitaker's Almanac, passim.* An example of a wartime permanent under-secretary excluded is Arnold Bennett, the novelist, who in 1918–19 held the office of Director of Propaganda in the Ministry of Information.
28. Welsh and other non-English bishops have been excluded, as have suffragan bishops. Lists were taken from the *Handbook of British Chronology* and *Whitaker's Almanac.*
29. Scottish and Irish universities have been excluded. Oxford and Cambridge changed vice-chancellors every year or two until the 1930s, ensuring a sufficient sample size.
30. Other types of businessmen—shipowners, merchant bankers and bankers, iron and steel manufacturers—as defined by Stanworth and Giddens (who included the chairmen of such concerns in their study), are excluded from this chapter's discussion, although they were included in Perkin's original project. No lists of major British companies by size are available for the nineteenth century.
31. Constant figures have been calculated by using the Rousseaux index in B. R. Mitchell and Phyllis Deane, *Abstract of British Historial Statistics* (Cambridge, 1971), pp. 471–3, and, for the period since 1913, from the table of retail prices in *British Political Facts, 1900–75*. On the Rousseaux index, an average of prices in 1865 and 1885 equals 100 and is the base line for other years.
32. Among some cohorts the median value is half-way between two probate valuations. In such cases I have taken the higher of the two.
33. That is, in current, not constant terms.
34. Actually, *more than half*, since these are the median examples only among fathers whose probate valuations are *known*. The unknown are almost certainly poorer than the median since they were too obscure to be traced by any means.
35. It is arrived at, for each cohort, by multiplying the number (i.e., I, II, etc.) of each social class by the number of fathers in each and dividing by the total number of fathers.
36. Dale, *Higher Civil Service, op. cit.*, p. 69.
37. *Ibid.*, p. 70.
38. These are Marlborough, Wellington, Repton, Rossall, Malvern, Tonbridge, Clifton, Cheltenham, Christ's Hospital, Sherborne, Haileybury, Uppingham, Fettes, University College School, King's College School, City of London School, Bedford, Brighton, Dulwich

(including Alleyn's College, Dulwich), Felsted, Radley, and Oundle. This list is not 'definitive' in any sense and no doubt—like the Lord High Executioner—everyone 'has his little list'. (On this point, see the interesting discussion of J. R. De S. Honey, *Tom Brown's Universe*, London, 1977, Ch. 4, esp. pp. 238–82.) Note that major direct grant schools in the large provincial cities, like Manchester Grammar School, are not included. Honey (pp. 274–82) makes the important point that some public schools are included among sociologists' lists of elite public schools because of their alleged current clientele, while in the nineteenth century they were considerably less prestigious. If any of the schools in my list (Honey, p. 277, suggests that Oundle 'had [no] claims to anything like the status of a leading public school') in truth are anachronistically counted as 'elite' institutions, I am quite ready to concede the point.

39. Strangely enough, of the four elites surveyed here, the elite least likely to represent the most talented among their peers are the vice-chancellors. Until recently very few truly outstanding or nationally known scholars apparently became vice-chancellors, although nearly all vice-chancellors were senior and obviously competent academics drawn from a wide variety of academic fields. It is significant, for instance, that of 50 Britons who won a Nobel Prize in science between 1901 and 1970 only one (Lord Adrian of Cambridge) ever became a vice-chancellor. Since 1945, however, a greater number of figures with wide academic reputations have become vice-chancellors than before, for instance Asa Briggs and Sir Ivor Jennings.

40. Among vice-chancellors, such persons were mainly educated at technical or other non-university tertiary institutions, or were barristers.

41. On such cases, see R. K. Kelsall, *Higher Civil Servants in Britain* (London, 1955), pp. 20–58 and 106–17.

42. There is, of course, normally a 35-40-year time lag between the education of an elite figure and his promotion to the highest ranks of the elite. An Oxford graduate of 1930 would not normally reach the top until the 1960s, and the 1960–70 cohort will bear the stamp of social mobility patterns of a previous generation.

43. On the wealth of MPs see my 'Men of Property: Some Aspects of Occupation, Inheritance, and Power Among Top British Wealthholders', in Stanworth and Giddens (eds), *Elites and Power, op. cit.*, esp. pp. 166–9. On the occupational backgrounds of Tory MPs see Thomas, *The House of Commons, 1832–1910, op. cit.*, and *The House of Commons, 1906–10* (Cardiff, 1958). See also John Ramsden's illuminating *The Age of Balfour and Baldwin 1902–1940* (London, 1978), pp. 97–9.

44. Ramsden, *Age of Balfour, op. cit.*, p. 362. Simon Haxey was the author of *Tory M.P.*, a 1939 critique of the Conservative party published by the Left Book Club. Sampson is, of course, the author of the invaluable *Anatomy of Britain* and its revisions published since 1962.

45. Francis Wheen, 'Return of the Jolly Good Chaps', *New Statesmen*, 11 May 1979. The last sentences of this passage make particularly rich

reading at this distance.
46. It is of interest to note that at the beginning of 1985 no fewer than four Cabinet ministers—Leon Brittain, Nigel Lawson, Sir Keith Joseph and Lord Young—were Jewish, in a Cabinet headed by a woman. Cecil Parkinson—until his dismissal, the most rising Tory figure of the day—was the son of a railway worker, a product of Lancaster Grammar School who was trained as an accountant. At the same time the cabinet contained only three Old Etonians (Lord Hailsham, Douglas Hurd and Nicholas Ridley), a historically low figure.
47. 'London' includes Middlesex. The 'Home Counties' are Bedfordshire, Berkshire, Buckinghamshire, Essex, Hertfordshire, Kent, Oxfordshire and Surrey. 'South England' includes Hampshire and Sussex. The 'South-west' comprises Cornwall, Devonshire, Dorset, Gloucestershire, Somerset and Wiltshire. Cambridgeshire, Norfolk and Suffolk are 'East Anglia'. The 'East Midlands' includes Derbyshire, Huntingdonshire, Leicestershire, Lincolnshire, Northamptonshire, Nottinghamshire, Rutland and Worcester. The 'West Midlands' includes Herefordshire, Shropshire, Staffordshire and Warwickshire. 'North-east England' comprises Durham and Northumberland. 'North-west England' includes Cumberland and Westmorland. Channel Islands figures have been included with 'South-west England', Manxmen with the 'North-west'.
48. As is well known, one cannot ascertain the number of individual *persons* who paid income tax (which was levied from 1799–1815 and from 1842) prior to 1911 at the earliest (and then only in the case of very high income-earners). Table 7.19 includes the county returns of the business portions of Schedule A (moved to Schedule D in 1869), Schedule D, and Schedule E in 1848–9 and 1911–12. Four caveats should be made about these figures: very high plutocratic/aristocratic business incomes (including the non-landed incomes of landowners) are included here; no geographical breakdowns exist for Schedule C, levied on government securities; Schedule B, the tax on farmers, is entirely excluded here; no geographical assessments exist for £24 million of the 1911–12 figures representing the incomes from public offices (about 4 per cent of the national total). The first of these factors probably, though not certainly, exaggerates the importance of London, while the second and fourth understate London's role. Finally, these figures take no account of wealth yielding no income (like freehold housing or art treasures). This whole subject is extremely complex. See Stamp, *British Income, op. cit.*, and Rubinstein, *Men of Property*, Ch. 1.
49. Broadly, London's proportion of the total taxable income resembles a 'U' and, after declining relative to Britain's industrial areas in the mid-nineteenth century, rises sharply again after the 1870s.
50. On the public schools see—among many others—Jonathan Gathorne-Hardy, *The Old School Tie* (London, 1977), and Honey, *Tom Brown's Universe, op. cit.*, perhaps the two best general accounts; George MacDonald Fraser (ed.), *The World of the Public School* (London, 1977), Brian Gardner, *The Public Schools* (London, 1973)—an

excellent guide to the different schools and their histories—and Bishop
and Wilkinson, *op. cit.*

51. See Gardner, *The Public Schools*, *op. cit.*, p. 237. Many British
laureates, especially the early ones, appear to be low-born northern
dissenters who rose through sheer ability. English public schools were
capable of producing originality in totally unexpected ways. For
instance Dulwich College, of all places, produced the unlikely trio of
P. G. Wodehouse, Raymond Chandler—who despite his authorship of
the tough LA private eye Philip Marlowe, was the product of an
English public school—and Ray Noble, the great band-leader who
wrote 'The Very Thought of You' and many other hits. All, it should
be noted, found fame and fortune in America.

52. But several of Britain's largest contemporary landowners are 'new'
men, representing twentieth-century fortunes, including Lords
Leverhulme, Iveagh, and Cowdray. (Rubinstein, *Men of Property*, *op.
cit.*, p. 244.)

53. *Ibid.*, pp. 205–9, 243–4.

54. Anthony Sampson, *The Changing Anatomy of Britain*, (London,
1983), p. 315.

55. *Ibid.*, p. 307. Sampson notes that 'Bevan presides over a board which
still includes a Pease, a Tritton, and a Goodenough' *(ibid.)*. None of the
other three main clearing banks, it should be noted, appear to have
much connexion with their founding families *(ibid.*, pp. 307–8.)

56. On their effect, and attempts by the 'Establishment' to co-opt their
leaders and demands see the controversial and stimulating works of
Keith Middlemas, *Politics in Industrial Society* (London, 1979) and
Maurice Cowling, *The Impact of Labour*, *1920–1924* (Cambridge,
1971) written from opposite ideological perspectives.

57. The managerial business chairmen did, of course, have a vested
interest in both the overall profitability of their firm and the business
success of whatever unit within the firm within which they were
initially situated, but even they were compensated for success by an
increased salary and promotion rather than through ownership of the
assets of their firm or receipt of its profits.

58. E. J. Hobsbawm, 'The Fabians Reconsidered', in *Labouring Men*
(New York, 1967), pp. 295–320, and A. M. McBrair, *Fabian Socialism
and English Politics*, *1884–1918* (Cambridge, 1966), pp. 163–9, 183–6.

59. Examples might be given from among the archbishops: Tait was Snell
Exhibitioner and took a first at Balliol; Benson was placed eighth in the
classical tripos and was a senior optime in mathematicals at Trinity
College, Cambridge, and additionally won the senior chancellor's
medal; Frederick Temple took a double first in classics and
mathematics at Balliol and was *proxime accessit* for the Ireland
scholarship; Lang, who had matriculated at Glasgow University at the
age of fourteen, gained a first in modern history at Balliol and was
President of the Union, etc. As to the public schools, it is perhaps
relevant to recall the autobiographical remarks of the Wykehamist
Nicholas Montsarrat, the novelist, that 'with the exception of a few
eccentrics [Winchester] produced a breed of almost compulsive

conformists: brilliant yet safe men . . .' (cited in Honey, *op. cit.*, p. 224). Similarly, it is a striking fact that the *sort* of public school one might have thought most appealing to the more intelligent members of the middle classes for their sons—emphasizing 'modern' rather than classical learning, making learning interesting and a matter of discussion rather than rote memory and the cane, seeing sport as an enjoyable diversion rather than an obsessive, all-consuming fetish—simply did not emerge in Britain until the twentieth century. To the abler products of the public schools, the transition from school to the rational and purely intellectual realms of the university must often have seemed a passage to Eden.

60. In 1983, among the civil servants heading the 20 largest government departments, two attended Eton, one Westminster, four smaller public schools (Bedford, Taunton, Wimbledon College), but all the others grammar schools or direct grant schools. (Sampson, *op. cit.*, pp. 201–2).

61. See John Rae, *The Public School Revolution—Britain's Independent Schools 1964–1979* (London, 1981) and Sampson, *Changing Anatomy, op. cit.*, pp. 129–46.

8

The Evolution of the British Honours System Since the Mid-Nineteenth Century

It would seem true by definition that the awarding of titles in the British honours system—and especially the creation of peerages, the highest honours of all—automatically confers upon its recipients high status, and such titles are awarded exclusively to persons deemed to be worthy of high status. Title and rank, and especially a rank within the peerage, would seem by definition to denote high status. Moreover, as in any society in which the private ownership of considerable amounts of property in whatever form confers upon its holders considerable privileges, as well as considerable power, it is not unreasonable to expect that in modern Britain the private ownership of considerable property would also very often confer high status as well: in other words, that private wealth, held in sufficient quantity, is a regular and necessary (although possibly not sufficient) pre-condition for the official conferment of high status via the acquisition of a title. But is it? Surprisingly, so far as I know, this proposition has never been tested nor, in its broadest historical context, ever addressed, except in the research project on 'British Elites 1880–1970' which Professor Harold Perkin undertook in 1974–5. Indeed, remarkably little is known about the evolution of peerages and other honours in modern Britain: there is R. A. Pumphrey's classic article on the introduction of industrialists into the peerage in the late nineteenth century (now twenty-seven years old), and F. M. L. Thompson's account of the evolution of landowning as a criterion for peerage creations in the same period, again now well over twenty years old, but apart from this there is really remarkably little, reflecting, very broadly, the general neglect of elites in modern British historiography and possibly also the absence of research into so small and recent a social grouping.[1] Below the level of peerage creations, among baronetcies and knighthoods, there is absolutely nothing whatever on any broad scale, and this remains one of the unexplored corners of modern British social historiography. One certain result of this neglect is that, needless to say, myth flourishes: the myth of the Lloyd George peerages is one good example which will be addressed here.

The thesis of this chapter is that the creation of new peerages and, to a lesser extent, other honours, has evolved from a system mirroring almost precisely the *ownership* of landed wealth and property to one mirroring much less closely but still recognizably business wealth, to one in which, since World War Two, the ownership of property or the effective control of large business units has become increasingly and demonstrably irrelevant to the creation of peerages and other titles. The main reasons for this, it will be argued, are the abrogation of the previously-existing nexus between wealth, status and power, and the rise of notions of merit and achievement to which the ownership of wealth and property are irrelevant, as well, thirdly, as the constraints imposed in the case of peerage creations by the fact that the House of Lords is a legislative body whose members are legislators. These changes, it will be argued, are genuine, and are not disguised or modernized forms of the old pattern. In so far as the formal system of titles in Britain is a genuine guide to status there has, in other words, been a clear and undeniable change in the status system which is *not* mirrored in changes in property ownership, or property relations.

Before proceeding, it should be noted that most, but not all of the statistical data used in this paper was collected in 1974–5 by myself, for Professor Perkin's project on elites. Harold Perkin made some use of it in his essay on elites in *The Structured Crowd*, as I did in *Men of Property*, but neither of us has treated in detail or previously addressed the question of honours and peerage creations at any real length.[2]

As noted above, the evolution of the modern peerage, and to a lesser extent the other titled ranks of the honours system, over the past century may be divided into three phases. The most clear-cut and easiest to understand, in terms of its relationship to wealth, status and power, was unquestionably the first phase, that which existed throughout the eighteenth century and through the nineteenth century until about 1880, a surprisingly late date indeed, given the evolution of British society and its electoral bases which occurred during the nineteenth century. This earliest phase of the modern aristocracy was hallmarked in my view by a number of main features and characteristics which set it apart from subsequent status systems and the subsequent evolution of the British aristocracy. Firstly, place in the titled honours system was largely congruent with, and determined by, the amount of landed wealth owned, with rank in the aristocracy bearing a remarkably close relationship to this.

This titled status system was nearly universal among substantial landowners. After many centuries of its evolution—one might say perfection—the great majority of substantial landowners had achieved a titled position equivalent to their landed wealth, and only a small minority remained untitled.

Thirdly, other forms of wealth which had not been transmuted into landed property were not, with rare exceptions, recognized as worthy of official titled recognition. Although there were 'short cuts' to a title or rank in the peerage—the Lord Chancellorship, of course, as well as other judges and successful military commanders—many of these had acquired, and were naturally expected to acquire, substantial amounts of landed wealth, and few if any could achieve real status beyond the first generation without it.

Following from this, there was a clear-cut nexus between landed wealth, status and power such that any of these elements in elite stratification was, in the medium term, transmutable into any other. Moreover each sought, as it were, its own equivalent level, with landed wealth, status and power transmissible in the longer term into a degree in the other element of stratification equivalent to the initial one. In my view this was the most salient and notable feature of the old status system in Britain, and was nothing less than the underlying *raison d'être* of nearly all high politics in Britain from 1688, if not earlier, through to the mid-nineteenth century—the aim of personal political power in Britain, under the old status system, was the achievement of status and wealth. The aim of acquiring landed wealth was to achieve status and power. The aim of obtaining high status, apart from being an end in itself, was, for those who wanted it, the acquisition of power and further wealth. The congruence and transmutability of wealth, status and power which demarcated this phase of the evolution of the aristocracy also delimited it from the second and third phase, in which this transmissibility of elements was either much more difficult, or impossible, or not desired by the successful actors in the system. A notable feature contributing to the success of this system was the fact that new men of great influence, power or esteem who did not themselves possess the other elements in elite stratification, could 'short-circuit', in particular, the process of the acquisition of land and landed wealth, either obtaining it for free or below the market price or by transmitting political power into the vast amounts of money necessary to acquire really substantial amounts of land. One important aspect of the system which facilitated this has come to be termed 'Old Corruption', and its passing, in the 1830s and 1840s, essentially changed the nature of the system, closing it to many outsiders. So long as this element in the status system worked, however, while many notable leaders of British high politics up until 1840 or so began life as members of the minor gentry or even the poor in some cases, most finished life as substantial owners of landed wealth, with a rank in the aristocracy and, by definition, a previous enjoyment of power equivalent to this. The obvious effect of this was literally to buy off potential trouble-makers and upstarts willing to work within the accepted status system, thus ensuring a remarkable degree of social peace at the elite level during the period in which these aspects of the elite status system existed.

Next, the old status system was both remarkably resistant to attacks upon it—whose nature we shall discuss shortly—and to an equal degree remarkably 'functional' in the sociological sense, to a degree which is probably not appreciated even by its historical admirers. In the formal titular sense, after all, the Honours system has not merely outlived its socio-economic base by over 150 years, but in its present greatly modified and transmuted version has outlived all of the trenchant criticism made of it, from Cobbett and Spence to Michael Foot, and I would not be surprised if it still existed in the formal and titular sense a hundred years hence.

Finally, it should be noted that under the old 'honours' system, the term 'honour' was meant in the old-fashioned sense of he whom the Sovereign delighted to honour for reasons best known to himself. Only tangentially and rarely was it meant in the modern sense of honour implying a reward for merit as, for instance, in the universities' honours system—the notion of personal merit or achievement rather than the acquisition in notable measure of landed wealth, status or power.

The unique *Return of Owners of Land*, compiled by Parliament in

1872–4, documented the landed acreage and gross annual rentals of all substantial landowners in Britain—apart from those owning London land—at the very climax of this process of land accumulation before it had in any way broken down. Thanks to John Bateman's remarkable compilation, the famous *Great Landowners of Great Britain and Ireland*, whose best and final revised edition appeared in 1884, we can see just how accurate and comprehensive, among title-holders, was the nexus between titled rank and landed property ownership. As will be seen from Table 8.1, the 'match' between rank in the aristocracy and landed acreage or income was consistently an accurate one, extending to the six ranks of the titled hereditary aristocracy and, I am quite certain, to ordinary knights and non-titled landowners as well. Dukes by and large held more landed property than anyone; marquesses were next wealthiest, although with much variation between them; then earls; and so on. When there was a 'poor' duke or an even 'poorer' earl, there was normally a good reason. The 'poorest' duke, the Duke of St Albans was, of course, in the first instance a royal bastard of Charles II whose successors had never, for whatever reason, married, inherited, or accumulated enough wealth or property to receive more than £10,955 p.a.—a most niggardly sum for a duke— in landed rental income in 1884.

Because of the clear nexus which existed between the acquisition of status, power and landed wealth, as noted, even successful actors in the game of high politics who flourished long after the zenith of heroic accumulation during the eighteenth century almost necessarily enriched themselves to a degree very often in keeping with the rank they acquired. Such leaders of the Liverpool government as Liverpool himself, F. J. Robinson (who became Viscount Goderich and Earl of Ripon), Lord Eldon the Lord Chancellor, whose case will be discussed shortly, and Henry Addington, Viscount Sidmouth, are all examples of political leaders who climbed up the ladder of wealth, status and power in nearly equivalent steps. Addington, for example, was the son of a successful doctor and minor landowner. Addington's descendant, the third Viscount Sidmouth, in 1884 owned 5,909 acres yielding £8,220 p.a., highly appropriate for one of his rank and status, although the family would appear to have inherited little or nothing from its marriages, so far as can be determined. For those bent upon quickly acquiring a landed estate in keeping with their status or power, the process was regularly and often, but not invariably,

Table 8.1: Acreage and Gross Annual Landed Income of Peers and Baronets, 1884 (excluding London)

I. Acreage

Acres	Dukes	%	Marquesses	%	Earls	%	Viscounts	%	Barons	%	Baronets*	%
200,000+	4	14	0	0	3	2	0	0	0	0	0	0
1–200,000	7	25	5	15	6	3	0	0	4	2	0	0
75–100,000	2	7	2	6	4	2	1	2	3	1	0	0
50– 75,000	4	14	5	15	16	8	0	0	3	1	0	0
25– 50,000	6	21	9	27	53	27	6	11	25	11	3	3
10– 25,000	4	14	9	27	73	37	16	29	71	32	13	13
2– 10,000	1	4	3	9	39	20	24	43	77	35	26	26
500– 2,000	0		0		3	2	6	11	17	8	3	3
under 500	0		0		2	1	3	5	21	10	55	55
Total	**28**		**33**		**199**		**56**		**221**		**100**	

II. Income

	Dukes	%	Marquesses	%	Earls	%	Viscounts	%	Barons	%	Baronets*	%
£200,000	1	4	0	0	0	0	0	0	0	—0	0	0
£1–200,000	4	14	3	9	3	2	0	0	1	0	0	0
†75–100,000	5	18	1	3	4	2	1	2	1	0	0	0
£50– 75,000	7	25	4	12	17	9	0	0	6	3	0	0
£25– 50,000	7	25	9	27	55	28	7	13	24	11	2	2
£10– 25,000	4	14	12	36	76	38	16	29	89	40	13	13
£2– 10,000			4	12	39	20	23	41	61	28	31	31
under £2,000				5	3	9	16	38	17	54	54	54
Total	**28**		**33**		**199**		**56**		**221**		**100**	

* Baronets: First 100 alphabetically, as listed in *Walford's County Families 1895* and in existence in 1884.

possible largely because of the super-profits of office-holders under
Old Corruption. The heirs to the four Lords Chancellor holding
office between 1766 and 1827 with living, titled descendants at the
time of Bateman's compilation in 1884 are examples of this type of
acquisition of land fully consistent with the acquisition of power
and status by a Lord Chancellor. In 1884, the Lord Thurlow of the
day owned nearly 14,000 acres worth £6,847 p.a., Lord Camden
owned 17,400 acres worth £16,400, the Earl of Rosslyn 3,310 acres
worth over £9,100, while Lord Eldon owned not less than 25,761
acres worth nearly £28,500 p.a. As I have pointed out before, the
first Lord Eldon, the son of a coal barge owner in Newcastle-upon-
Tyne, in the course of twenty-seven years as Lord Chancellor
accumulated over £700,000 plus the landed acreage and income
noted above. Eldon was among the last great beneficiaries of Old
Corruption, earning on average £18,000 p.a. throughout his long
reign as Lord Chancellor, mainly from fees and perquisites of the
office, and mainly over and above his official salary. During the
eighteenth century, before the partial reforms to this sort of
corruption brought about by Burke, Pitt and Liverpool began to
have an effect, the scale of expected accumulation was legendary
and vast. The chief aim of this accumulation, as well as being an end
in itself, was to achieve a sufficient degree of wealth to buy a landed
estate fully in keeping with one's rank and title. Land was always
among the most expensive of commodities to buy in any amount,
and was certainly so in the acreage requisite for equivalence to a
high rank in the peerage. There was, I would suggest, a national and
notional concept of what was proper and normal for any particular
rank in the aristocracy. Plainly the situation of a poor duke was
scandalous. Equally, a national hero—as the term was defined at the
time—who was raised to the peerage was frequently given a vast
sum of money explicitly intended for the purchase of a landed estate
or estates. Wellington, the classic example, was given £600,000 by
Parliament and another £400,000 by grateful foreign governments
to purchase an estate equal to his dukedom and his rank in the
national pantheon. In 1884 the Duke of Wellington owned over
19,000 acres yielding £22,000 p.a.—not, perhaps, a truly princely
estate for a duke, but far more than Wellington, the younger son of a
remote Irish earl who was placed in the army precisely because he
would inherit so little, could conceivably have inherited or earned
by any other means. Similarly, Lord Nelson's immediate heir was
granted not merely an earldom but £100,000 by Parliament

following Trafalgar; in 1884 his successor owned 7,196 acres yielding £5,800 p.a.—again, not truly princely perhaps, but vastly more than the family would otherwise have owned.

In addition to these special and admittedly remarkable instances of peerage advancement equalled by landed accumulation, if and when a landowner acquired enough land, or his land through urbanization grew mightily in value, an equivalent rank quite often followed in its wake. The specific nexus here is harder to trace precisely during the middle and later nineteenth century than before, when naked and undisguised accumulation continued apace. Plainly, the fact that so many landowners, their heirs and relatives, remained leading parliamentarians and ministers for so long was a factor in securing an equivalent rise in status. The first Duke of Westminster, for instance, was an MP before 1847 and succeeded to his father's marquessate in 1869. He served in the honorary position of Master of the Horse in Gladstone's second ministry and it was easy enough to give him the final advancement to the peerage in 1874. The rise of the Grosvenor family, from only a baronetcy in 1760 to a barony in 1761, an earldom in 1784, a marquessate in 1831 and, finally, a dukedom in 1874, is a quintessential example of this process attaching to the very wealthiest of all British aristocrats, the owners of most of Mayfair, Belgravia and Chelsea in addition to agricultural land in Cheshire and elsewhere. But often the same sort of advancement came to those who apparently had less access to the Prime Minister and other leading ministers who determined the recipients of honours, seemingly because of their increased wealth alone. Mr Edward Berkeley Portman was already a most substantial agricultural landowner in the 1830s, and a title might well have been expected in any case. He served as backbench MP for only four years when in 1837 he was created Baron Portman and, much later, in 1873, Viscount Portman. Portman's main source of wealth, however, was his vastly lucrative urban estates in Marylebone—Portman Square is evidence of this—and it was this newly-risen landed wealth, evidently, which was instrumental in his viscountcy. Similarly, in another vein, the mergers of two already vastly wealthy landed families by intermarriage and inheritance into one still vaster unit, was sometimes the occasion for an appropriate advancement. The most important instances of this were the creation of the phenomenally wealthy dukedom of Sutherland following the marriage of the Marquess of Stafford and the Countess (in her own right) of Sutherland in 1833, and as late as in 1892, the creation of the Earldom of Ancaster following the marriage of Lord Aveland and Baroness Willoughby de Eresby. The resultant peerage, or rather super-peerage, owned 163,500 acres yielding £121,000 p.a., one of the dozen or fifteen wealthiest of peerages.

After so many generations of successful operation, the nexus between landed wealth, status and power produced a situation where, by the late nineteenth century, the great majority of substantial landowners in Britain held a title of some sort. In 1884, of 221 persons who owned 25,000 landed acres or more, 168 (76 per cent) were peers, 21 baronets, one—Sir Robert Lloyd-Lindsay, son-in-law of Lord Overstone, the millionaire banker, and later created a peer in his own right as Lord Wantage—was a knight, while only 41 (18.6 per cent) remained completely untitled or just plain 'Mr' or, very occasionally, 'Miss' or 'Mrs'. Of these 41, five themselves received peerages during the next forty or fifty years, the best-known being Henry Chaplin, the Tory politician, who became Viscount Chaplin in 1916. Others were collateral descendants of former peerages where the title, but not the property, had died out. Several, like the Weld-Blundells, were Catholics; at least ten appear to have owned Lancashire urban property and minerals whose annual rental rose during the nineteenth century far in excess of their acreage, while one, and only one such man out of the 41, Charles Morrison (1817–1909) the merchant banker and warehouseman, represented landed wealth acquired wholly since the Industrial Revolution began. The remainder appear just to be the inevitable residue of landowners who, through ill-luck or lack of ambition, failed to acquire a title. The point is that over 80 per cent of all really substantial landowners benefited from the system down the generations sufficiently to acquire a title, or employed their status and power to acquire more land.

This overlap between landed wealth, status and power continued largely unabated until the 1880s or even later, despite political reform and despite three separate and important ideological attacks upon the system of honours and titles as it then existed. The first such ideological attack, which triumphed in large measure from 1880 to 1945, criticized the exclusive rewards granted to landed wealth as opposed to any other forms of property, and in particular the lack of high rewards, especially peerages, granted to businessmen who prospered as a result of industrialization. As is well known and will be discussed shortly, virtually no businessmen, and certainly none who were not thoroughly entrenched in landed society, received peerages prior to 1880, while surprisingly few received even lesser titles before then. The second such ideological attack, which is sometimes viewed as largely identical with the first but is actually rather different, held that honours should have much more to do with personal merit and reward for achievement than with the ownership of property as such. A great scientist, a notable disease-curing physician, a moving poet or artist who has enriched mankind, according to this critique was far more deserving of reward than any property-owner as such. Apart from the occasional national hero like Wellington, virtually no one received a peerage for service of this sort alone prior to the late nineteenth century, the authors Macaulay and Bulwer-Lytton being possibly the only exceptions and both of these were of course public figures of significance. Rather more knighthoods and baronetcies came to men of this stamp, but the overwhelming majority of Britain's eminent men (and women) of letters and of the sciences and arts went to their graves unrewarded and their names unadorned, a meagre state pension (as in the case of Dr Johnson) or burial in Westminster Abbey being the highest token of the nation's gratitude. This notion of reward, too, was closely bound up with the very narrow definition of what constituted national service— military heroes and (orthodox) religious divines were often honoured; writers, scientists, or unorthodox thinkers seldom.

The third critique is, of course, the democratic one which, following Paine, Spence and other radicals, viewed all honours as they existed, especially hereditary ones, as unjust, corrupt and unnecessary. They pointed to the United States, Switzerland and republican France as examples of flourishing societies without a titled aristocracy, and with little or nothing in the way of a formal system of honours, but which had consistently produced as many, if not more, genuinely eminent and distinguished men of achievement as Britain.

The formal system of British titles and honours was remarkably resilient to all of these critiques. During the entire century between the beginnings of industrialization and 1880, only a handful of businessmen or men connected with business life received peerages, and only one industrialist, Edward Strutt the cotton manufacturer, who was created Baron Belper in 1856. Only a handful even of bankers, socially closer to the aristocracy than industrialists, received peerages, chiefly several members of the

Baring family like Lord Ashburton in 1835 and Lord Northbrook in
1866. More businessmen received baronetcies—Peel the Prime
Minister's father, a millionaire cotton spinner, being the best
known—and many, including many lord mayors of London,
received knighthoods, but the numbers of these and, still more, the
density of their coverage of all significant businessmen was very
meagre, as, for example, Anthony Howe has recently shown for
important Lancashire cotton-spinners.[3] As noted, too, personal
merit played virtually no role in the creation of peerages, while even
among knighthoods most meritorious men were unrewarded;
merit, where it was rewarded, was defined mainly to include
generals, admirals, colonial governors and ambassadors
plenipotentiary rather than scientists or artists. The democratic
critique, it need not be said, was held in contempt, and certainly no
Whig or Whig-Liberal government until 1880 created peerages or
other titles on the basis of merit alone. It is important to note,
however, that the part of this critique, if it may be so called, which
was universally accepted after Reform was the agreement that
political place and office should not bring with it vast financial
rewards in the manner of Old Corruption, while some element of
rationality should enter into the ordering of income derived from
the holding of office, especially the disparity between the princely
incomes formerly enjoyed by bishops, judges and top sinecure-
holders, and the meagre incomes of the lower clergy, middle-
ranking office-holders and the like. By eliminating this element of
Old Corruption, Reform made it much more difficult for an
individual office-holder or placeman to acquire wealth sufficient to
become a landowner on a vast scale in a brief period of time and thus
in the long term made it inevitable that among 'new men' only
successful businessmen would hitherto enjoy an income or acquire
wealth sufficient to match that of the old aristocracy.

Why was there so much resistance to change? Briefly, we can
point to four main reasons. A business, no matter how successful,
was always suspect because, unlike the land, it was not permanent
and might go bankrupt at any moment, as even Baring Brothers did
in 1890. The House of Lords might be stuck at any time with a
bankrupt peerage. Secondly, at least some landownership was
regarded as a requisite for ennoblement except, possibly, in the case
of judges, until the 1880s. It would seem that comparatively few
businessmen owned land on any really significant scale.[4] This was
the case even for the very wealthiest ones; most businessmen were

simply too poor to buy land on any scale at all. Thirdly, one chief criterion for title was service in Parliament. Until the 1860s or 1870s most MPs were landowners or relatives of landowners. Comparatively few, and virtually no leading ones, were businessmen. As James Cornford has pointed out, even during the Cecil ascendancy in the late Victorian Tory Party, most business MPs entered Parliament late in life, were poor speakers or political operators, and were culturally far removed from the Party's grandees.[5] Finally, there is the matter of snobbery and any feeling of superiority which the landed aristocracy might have felt over businessmen. This is a complex question, but in general the lack of business peerage creations for a century after industrialization was in many respects a curious exception to a general pattern of widespread acceptance of the new rich by the old.

However, change eventually did come, and Tables 8.2–8.6 reveal something of the magnitude of the change which came over the creation of peerages after 1880 when, as is well-known, increasingly businessmen were granted peerages in numbers, while dozens and dozens were granted baronetcies and knighthoods. The change, it is agreed, came around 1880 but was far from dramatic, Lord Wimborne, previously Sir Josiah Guest the ironmaster, being the first post-1880 business peer. He was followed within a few years by Lord Rothschild, the great merchant banker and the first Jewish peer, another Baring in the person of Lord Revelstoke, and three brewers—Arthur Guinness, Lord Ardilaun; Henry Allsopp, Lord Hindlip; and Michael Bass, Lord Burton; who collectively gave their name, inevitably, to the 'beerage', which, like most facets of the modern aristocracy, has been greatly exaggerated. Before exploring the nexus between property and title which existed between 1880 and 1945, it is well worth examining the numerical dimensions of business penetration of the aristocracy in this period. The central question here is the extent to which this second period in the evolution of the aristocracy—when businessmen were a major element among the ennobled and newly titled—paralleled the previous era when landowners virtually alone received peerages.

As is noted in Table 8.4, business peerages as a percentage of all peerages rose steadily from one-quarter in the 1880s to over one-half of those created in the inter-war period. They then sharply declined after World War Two, especially in the very recent past. This is paralleled for all titles among major company chairman (those holding office in 1900–70 in Stanworth and Giddens' well-

Table 8.2: *Probate Valuation (Including Land) of Newly-created Peers, 1880–1970, in Current Terms, by Decade of Creation**

Lower limit of class	1880–89	1890–99	1900–09	1910–19	1920–29	1930–39	1940–49	1950–59	1960–69
£2 m	2	20	3	8	6	4	2	1	2
£1 m	4	3	5	6	7	3	0	1	5
£500,000	6	11	5	9	3	10	2	2	3
£300,000	4	8	6	8	12	10	8	5	9
£200,000	7	6	7	11	11	10	4	7	9
£100,000	23	17	14	19	17	16	17	19	23
£50,000	10	10	8	20	15	10	25	18	15
£25,000	25	3	7	14	12	14	25	22	19
£10,000	10	1	8	14	5	13	13	13	13
£5,000	0	2	2	1	5	4	10	6	4
£1,000	1	2	1	4	1	7	9	3	2
Total	93	65	66	117	95	101	115	97	104
Still alive							4	18	123

(includes a small number of peers, whose estates were probated in Scotland or Northern Ireland since 1975 and who could not be traced because of changes in the Scottish and Northern Irish probate indexes).

Median

1880–89	£129,567
1890–99	£158,376
1900–09	£153,746
1910–19	£123,228
1920–29	£144,605
1930–39	£87,226
1940–49	£47,800
1950–59	£54,594
1960–69	£92,636

* Includes all life peers; excludes peerages awarded to members of the Royal Family, to foreigners, peerage promotions, and titles called out of abeyance.

... *Valuation (including Land) of Newly-created Peers, 1880–1970, in Constant Terms, by Decade of Creation**

Lower limit of class	1880–89	1890–99	1900–09	1910–19	1920–29	1930–39	1940–49	1950–59	1960–69
£2m	2	3	5	4	3	0	0	0	0
£1m	5	4	0	3	3	1	0	0	0
£500,000	5	8	5	10	5	3	1	1	0
£300,000	6	8	3	6	5	7	0	1	2
£200,000	6	5	8	4	6	4	1	0	0
£100,000	16	18	17	15	18	14	6	1	2
£50,000	8	12	8	21	19	17	10	6	5
£25,000	5	3	9	15	13	9	6	8	14
£10,000	5	1	3	21	13	18	49	26	19
£5,000	1	0	5	11	5	13	20	21	22
£1,000	0	3	2	3	5	14	25	30	33
0	1	0	1	4	1	7	10	3	16
Total	60	65	66	117	96	107	128	97	113

Median

1880–89	£136,031
1890–99	£167,757
1900–09	£116,666
1910–19	£56,657
1920–29	£71,362
1930–39	£29,124
1940–49	£10,084
1950–59	£9,956
1960–70	£5,882

* Same peers as in Table 8.2. Retail price index: Rousseaux index as in B. Mitchell and P. Deane, *Abstract of British Historical Statistics, op. cit.*, in which an average of 1865 and 1885 = 100, supplemented by David Butler and Gareth Butler, *British Political Facts 1900–1985* (London, Macmillan, 1986), pp. 380–2.

*Table 8.4: Percentage of Business Peerage Creations, by Decade,
1880–1970**

	Total Creations	Businessmen/ families	Percentage
1880–89	60	15	25.0
1890–99	65	22	33.8
1900–09	66	27	40.9
1910–19	117	45	38.5
1920–29	94	47	50.0
1930–39	107	55	51.4
1940–49	125	34	27.2
1950–59	119	36	30.3
1960–70	236	56	23.7

* Includes those from business families not themselves active in trade, so far as can be traced. About 10–15 per cent of 'businessmen/families' were apparently not active in trade.

known study) in much the same way.[6] Only a minority were titled before World War One; less than 40 per cent *un*titled in the 1930s and 1940s, while by the 1980s only 40 per cent are titled. Among company chairmen, peerage creations peak at only a small minority in the 1940s. The point here is that, unlike the ubiquity and near unanimity of peerage creations among large landowners, only a minority of leading businessmen ever received a peerage, even when the business-peerage nexus was at its zenith, while at most only a small majority of new peers were businessmen. This is also paralleled among the richest top wealth-holders (Tables 8.5 and 8.6) where a majority of male millionaires and, still more, half-millionaires, were always untitled. Once again, the nexus peaks in the inter-war period and declines precipitously by the 1970s and 1980s.

The exact mechanisms of the nexus whereby prominent businessmen received (or did not receive) peerages is a much more complex matter to examine precisely than in the case of landowners. The first point which must be made is that there was no real way, except by common repute, to determine which businessmen were 'naturally' entitled to a peerage by virtue of heading a business of sufficient size or importance. There really was no clear-cut way to ascertain the relative importance of, say, a merchant bank and a steel factory or, except by repute, the relative success or wealth of its

Table 8.5: Percentage of Top Company Chairmen by Highest Rank, by Decade of Becoming Chairmen, 1900–69, plus Rank of Top Company Chairmen, 1983

	Total	Created peer (& %)	Created baronet	Created knight	Inherited peer	Inherited baronet	No Title (& %)
1900–09	119	13 (10.9)	23	5	8	1	69 (58.0)
1910–19	49	7 (14.3)	12	3	3	0	24 (49.9)
1920–29	99	20 (20.2)	13	14	6	4	42 (42.4)
1930–39	63	10 (15.9)	6	17	5	1	24 (38.1)
1940–49	67	14 (20.9)	5	17	4	2	25 (37.3)
1950–59	59	7 (11.9)	0	16	5	2	29 (49.2)
1960–69	113	19 (16.8)	1	37	4	3	49 (43.4)
1984	80	6 (7.5)	23	4	4	—	47 (58.8)

Sources: Company chairmen 1900–70 from P. Stanworth and A. Giddens' study of major company chairmen; 1984 chairmen from Anthony Sampson, The Changing Anatomy of Britain (1983), Parts 3 and 4.

Table 8.6: Male British Millionaires, Deceased 1880–1984, by Title at Death

	Total	New Peers %	New Baronets %	New Knights %	Overall Total, New Titles %	Inherited Peerages	Inherited Baronetcies	Untitled
1880–89	26	1 = 3.8	4 = 15.4	0 = 0.0	5 = 19.2	2 = 7.7	1 = 3.8	18 = 69.2
1890–99	43	1 = 2.3	5 = 11.6	1 = 2.3	7 = 16.3	3 = 7.0	2 = 4.7	31 = 72.1
1900–09	54	4 = 7.4	6 = 11.1	1 = 1.9	11 = 20.3	7 = 13.0	0 = 0	36 = 66.7
1910–19	67	9 = 13.4	14 = 20.9	1 = 1.5	24 = 35.8	10 = 14.9	1 = 1.5	32 = 47.8
1920–29	98	10 = 10.2	11 = 11.2	6 = 6.1	27 = 27.6	18 = 18.4	3 = 3.1	50 = 51.0
1930–39	79	11 = 13.9	9 = 11.4	6 = 13.2	26 = 32.9	5 = 6.3	3 = 2.6	45 = 57.0
1940–49	76	7 = 9.2	10 = 13.2	1 = 1.3	18 = 23.7	17 = 22.4	2 = 2.6	39 = 51.3
1950–59	47	4 = 8.5	4 = 8.5	2 = 4.3	10 = 21.3	10 = 21.3	0 = 0	27 = 57.4
1960–69	71	7 = 9.9	3 = 4.2	5 = 7.0	15 = 21.1	7 = 9.9	3 = 4.2	46 = 64.8
1970–79	143	4 = 2.8	1 = 0.7	6 = 4.2	11 = 7.7	19 = 13.3	12 = 8.4	101 = 70.6
1980–84	276	5 = 1.8	0 = 0.0	16 = 5.8	21 = 7.6	19 = 6.9	8 = 1.3	228 = 82.6

heads. Many key businesses were unfashionable or unnoticed. In particular, only rarely were the most successful businessmen given peerages unless they had some national political or, especially, parliamentary service. At least a few years in the House of Commons became the major form of 'service' by which a business peerage could be described as a reward for merit. To be sure, a number of very major businessmen did receive peerages without any parliamentary service or other 'public service' of an obvious kind. These included such celebrated businessmen as Alfred Harmsworth, Lord Northcliffe—who, although he might claim to make and unmake Houses of Commons in his newspapers, never sat in one—Marcus Samuel, Lord Bearsted, founder of Shell Transport and Trading, who had once been Lord Mayor of London but was never an MP, and William Morris, Lord Nuffield, the great automobile builder and philanthropist. However, and especially during the pre-World War Two period, surprisingly few businessmen ever received peerages *because* they were talented entrepreneurs, and for no other reason, and many remarkably successful businessmen never received one. Sir John Ellerman, Britain's all-time richest man and probably the greatest business entrepreneur in British history, had to settle for a mere baronetcy, possibly because of his notorious publicity-shyness.[7] Such families as that of Arkwright's among early industrialists never received a title of any sort, despite being Anglicans, landowners and immensely rich, and among businessmen there is, as noted, only the most cursory attempt at creating a 'hall of fame' of business peers to parallel that created down the ages for landowners. (All business peerages created between 1880 and 1945 are listed in the Appendix to this chapter).

Apart from the very rare cases in which sheer business ability and its national recognition apparently determined the reward (and even in the cases I have cited, this was far from clear), there were four major aspects to the nexus whereby businessmen were created peers in the period 1880–1945. These were, in descending order of obviousness: political and public service, especially service for a time in the House of Commons; notable charitable or philanthropic activity; lavish contribution, in an open way, to political party funds; and the open purchase of a title, for cash down.

Plainly the most significant simple pathway to ennoblement (in particular) and to many baronetcies and knighthoods as well, was service in the House of Commons. Of course this was nothing new;

Table 8.7: Male British Half-Millionaires, Deceased 1880–1968, by Title at Death

	Total	New peers	New baronets	New knights	Total new titles	Inherited peerages	Inherited baronetcies	Untitled
1880–89*	77	3 = 3.9%	4 = 5.2%	0 = 0.0%	7 = 9.1%	2 = 2.6%	1 = 1.3%	67 = 87.0%
1890–99	102	2 = 2.0%	6 = 5.95%	0 = 0.0%	8 = 7.8%	3 = 2.9%	2 = 2.0%	89 = 87.3%
1900–09	131	7 = 5.3%	11 = 8.4%	3 = 2.3%	21 = 16.0%	6 = 4.6%	3 = 2.3%	101 = 77.1%
1910–19	166	4 = 2.4%	17 = 10.2%	3 = 1.8%	24 = 14.5%	10 = 6.0%	2 = 1.2%	130 = 78.3%
1920–29	193	5 = 2.6%	19 = 9.8%	8 = 4.1%	32 = 16.6%	19 = 9.8%	5 = 2.6%	147 = 76.2%
1930–39	194	7 = 3.6%	19 = 9.8%	10 = 5.2%	36 = 18.7%	9 = 4.7%	4 = 2.1%	144 = 74.6%
1940–49	169	7 = 4.1%	11 = 6.5%	5 = 3.0%	23 = 13.6%	15 = 8.9%	13 = 7.7%	118 = 69.8%
1950–59	103	6 = 5.8%	6 = 5.8%	10 = 9.7%	22 = 21.4%	9 = 8.7%	5 = 4.9%	67 = 65.0%
1960–68	151	2 = 1.3%	3 = 2.0%	3 = 2.0%	8 = 5.3%	12 = 7.9%	10 = 6.6%	121 = 80.1%

* Two of these three were landowners created before 1880 (Lords Robartes and Penrhyn). Only Lord Hindlip was a post 1880 businessman.

previously, when land was king, the nexus between power and status meant that most politicians of note eventually secured peerages. Increasingly in the nineteenth century many MPs, especially those for the large industrial cities and other urban areas, were businessmen, and often the very largest employers of labour in the manufacturing towns. After a decade or two of parliamentary service, even without any front-bench experience, such men frequently appeared as good candidates for a peerage, and certainly for a baronetcy or knighthood—in particular if they proved generous to the range of local charities and to their party machinery. Sidney James Stern, (1844–1912) was a very successful merchant banker who left £1,600,000 at his death. It was reputed that he had given over £1 million to charities and orphanages, and it was widely suggested that he was just as generous to the Liberal party machine. After he had served only four years as Liberal MP for Stowmarket, Suffolk, *Truth* magazine noted that 'he knew what he wanted—it was a peerage', and in Rosebery's Dissolution honours of 1895 he was created Baron Wandsworth. The other businessman-peer created by Rosebery at the same time was a man of just the same stamp, James Williamson, MP for Lancaster from 1886–95. Williamson was the 'linoleum king' of Victorian England, amassing a fortune of no less than £10,000,000 from floor coverings and marrying his only child to Viscount Peel, the Prime Minister's grandson. Williamson was created Baron Ashton in 1895, and, apart from serving as Constable of Lancaster Castle, played virtually no part in public life. It has been noted that parliamentary service, combined with philanthropy and legitimate generosity to the party machinery, was at this stage what put one on the flight path to a title. But the two party machines were not equal. The Tories, generally speaking, had all the peers they needed and, increasingly, all the money they needed. It was the Liberals who needed both money and more representation in the Lords, and it was they who granted peerages far more lavishly than the Tories. Salisbury and Balfour created 62 peerages in their ten years of power (1895–1905) while Campbell-Bannerman and Asquith created 105, advancing 40 others in rank, in the ten years 1905-1915. A great many of these were businessmen, especially industrialists and manufacturers who were more likely to be Liberals than Tories. For this reason, and despite their greater social distance from the old aristocracy, dissenters or former dissenters, captains of industry from northern England and the Celtic fringe, were ennobled in considerable numbers in late Victorian and Edwardian Britain. Very few of these were self-made men in the sense of starting life poor. So far as I am aware, the first businessman-peer who was 'self-made', in the sense of starting in poverty, was George Stephen, the son of a carpenter in Dufftown, Banffshire, who served three years behind the counter at a drapery business in London, migrated to Canada with his cousin Donald Smith, became President of the Bank of Montreal and then founder of the Canadian Pacific Railway, moved back to England and was created (without parliamentary service) Baron Mount-Stephen in 1891. He left £1,400,000. His cousin and fellow migrant-entrepreneur in Canada, Donald Smith, son of a 'tradesman' who left £694, himself became Baron Strathcona in 1897. Most business peerages, however, went to the heads of either well-established firms or entrepreneurs who built up established, moderate-sized family firms into the leading firms in the field.

The most controversial and most notorious way for a businessman to obtain a peerage during this period was, in effect, by open bribery, that is by paying a very large sum of money, usually said to be £50,000 or even £100,000, to either the Prime Minister, *sub rosa* to the party machine or, briefly, to a tout with connexions with the Prime Minister. Of course during the latter part of the Lloyd George period this erupted into one of the greatest and most famous scandals of the century, certainly the most notorious involving honours. Several important points need to be made about the Lloyd George honours scandals. First, it is certainly far from clear what the essential difference is between £10,000 given to the Liberal or Tory party machines at five consecutive general elections, being rewarded with a baronetcy as a result, and paying Maundy Gregory £50,000 in one lump sum for the same thing. Every government of modern times, including Labour governments, has rewarded its wealthy backers with peerages and titles. This is neither improper nor illegal, and also occurs in one form or another in all democratic countries—in the USA ambassadorships and the like commonly take the place of knighthoods and titles. Secondly, it is far from clear how this was more reprehensible than the nexus which existed in the past, wherein title begot wealth; with Lloyd George (and everyone else) wealth begat title. Which, morally, is worse? Moreover, a close inspection of Lloyd George's peerage creations reveals that the scandalous reports are exaggerations, just as one might expect. Lloyd George created 91 new peers and advanced 25 in rank, a total which indeed was the highest for any Prime Minister of the century until Harold Wilson. In the same period—seven years—of his term of office (1908–15) Asquith, for instance, created 68 new peers and advanced 13 in rank. *This* is the differential order of magnitude between Lloyd George's government and those of his contemporaries. But there are numerous mitigating factors. First, there was a World War, and Lloyd George created perhaps 30 or 40 new peers directly concerned with the war effort, including not merely numerous generals and admirals, but prominent advisers, civilian leaders of importance, Empire figures including one Indian, Lord Sinha, behind-the-scenes men and grey eminences. The figure of 91 new peers also comprises royal title-holders, including the German princelings who renounced their German nationality during the war and received British titles in exchange, like Lords Carisbroke and Milford Haven. Then, too, by 1918 Parliament had continued for seven years without an election; there were an unusual number of worthy retirees deserving of reward. As well, Lloyd George was the head of a two-party coalition, both of which clamoured for their deserts. Of Lloyd George's 91 peers, around 40, it would appear, were businessmen, including all former MPs with business backgrounds. This was a high figure, but certainly not grossly out of line. Most peerages, moreover, were unremarkable, and the fact that no legends attach to their creation is evidence of this.

The trouble, and the historical legend, really centred around Lloyd George's very last group of peers, in 1922, and in particular upon a group of four or five who were probably rather below par. This group included Samuel J. Waring, the head of Waring & Gillow, the Oxford Street furniture retailers, who became Lord Waring; Archibald Williamson, an overseas merchant and financier who became Lord Forres; William Vestey, the shipowner and frozen-meat import king, who became Lord Vestey; Robert H. Borwick, the custard-powder tycoon who became Lord Borwick and, most notoriously, Sir Joseph Robinson, the South African gold and diamond 'Randlord' who, as a result of what transpired, has the unusual distinction of being perhaps the only man in history who ever had to return a peerage. Of the four, only Williamson had any previous parliamentary experience; this was a major part of the problem. When his peerage was announced, and despite his electoral service, Williamson was accused in the House of Lords of having traded with the enemy. None of these five was really a man of any distinction apart from his business career, and all were widely believed to have purchased their peerages for cash down.

The straw which broke the camel's back, however, was clearly the case of Robinson, whose early business ethics will, admittedly, not bear too close an examination. Nevertheless, it seems crystal-clear that right-wing Tories in the House of Lords seized upon this last, rather unfortunate group of peers to down the lot, in the context of the frenzied political situation of the day.[8] This, believe it or not, constitutes the entirety of the Lord George peerage scandal, and it is obvious that the legend of the appalling Lloyd George peers is just that—a legend with very little factual substance. Lloyd George's peers seem to have differed very little from Asquith's before or Baldwin's later. In so far as one can generalize, they appear, if anything, to be rather 'progressive', if the term has any meaning in the context of peerage creations. Titles were given in number to Empire leaders like Lord Forrest of Australia, Lord Morris of Newfoundland and, as noted, the first non-white peer for many decades, Lord Sinha, as well as to unusual figures like Lord Askwith the industrial conciliator and Lord Ashfield, the talented head of London's Underground system. If this period marked any sort of a change in the relationship of wealth and property to the peerage, it was, if anything, a decrease in the importance of the former, not the reverse. The most important and lasting result of the honours 'scandals' was the initiation of the Political Honours Scrutiny Committee, which effectively outlawed naked bribery of the type which was widely alleged to prevail, thus in all likelihood eliminating one effective way in which the rich could acquire a title and probably making the peerage less comprehensive than it would otherwise have been.

Although the whole period 1880–1945 may be seen as the zenith of the business peerage, a majority of creations were not given to businessmen, while describing many as 'businessmen' needs a good deal of qualification. In fact, there were at least five ways in which a view of peerage creations during this period as marking the hegemony of business honours might be challenged; two of these refer to business peers themselves. Many peerages and other titles went to politicians who were only incidentally businessmen and who were honoured for their political career rather than their business acumen. A good many of these were, in fact, only small or medium-sized businessmen who were simply not in the same class in terms of economic status as the Leverhulmes and Rothschilds.

Some, indeed, were certainly not wealthy and, indeed, were virtually poor. It was one thing to ennoble a multi-millionaire with a significant impact on the British economy; few traditionalists, by the Edwardian period, could object to this. To ennoble a man who was virtually a small tradesman, who incidentally had served in the Cabinet as Postmaster-General or Secretary for the Dominions, was quite a different matter: it lowered the tone and you were stuck, in those days of all-hereditary peerages (except for Law lords), not merely with the man but with his male progeny forever. As will be seen from the tables of probate valuations, there were more and more peers of this type.

Secondly, the nature of modern business life was changing. In particular, as is well-known, capitalist enterprises were, increasingly, headed not by tycoons who owned the assets of their companies and who were often very wealthy men, but by managers who at most received a high income for only a part of their careers, were often not wealthy and certainly did not own the company they managed. Many of these had specialized professional or technological training and were, for instance, accountants or industrial chemists who worked their way up the corporate ladder, or were brought in from outside, eventually to become chairmen of quite major concerns. This was especially common in heavy industry, chemicals, car manufacturing, electronics, and the like. So long as such men remained chairmen, they were certainly major figures on the British business landscape, but their influence entirely ceased with their retirement, and they possessed few of the other usual requisites for ennoblement. Again, given the all-hereditary nature of peerages until 1958, the question forcefully arose whether men of this type should be honoured in the same way as a Northcliffe or Cowdray—as well, more importantly, as whether the House of Lords should be lumbered with their progeny forever? Until World War One, so far as I am aware (with possibly two exceptions, e.g. Lord Aberconway in 1911), no manager was given a peerage, but by the 1930s their ennoblements had become fairly common. The first three manager-peers in the strict sense were Albert Stanley, managing director of the London Underground Companies (then privately owned), who was created Lord Ashfield in 1920; James Stevenson, who entered Johnny Walker, the distillers, as a commercial traveller, rose to become managing director, and was created Lord Stevenson in 1924; and George Ernest May, the chairman of Prudential Insurance, and of the

famous May Committee, who became Lord May in 1935. By the
end of the decade such notable manager-industrialists as Lord
McGowan of ICI and Lord Perry of Ford received peerages, and
this type became even more common after World War Two, as
more notable enterprises were headed by managers.

Throughout the whole modern period, possibly most peerages,
certainly a plurality, were granted to professional men, especially
lawyer-politicians and High Court judges. The number and
significance of peerages increased during this period, particularly
during the inter-war period, as they were granted more frequently
to politicians of middle-class professional background, and as the
number of major judgeships increased. So, after 1914, did military
peers. Increasingly, notable professionals of importance in other
fields also received peerages, reflecting the critique of honours and
peerages that insisted that they should be merited, and be given to
persons who benefited humanity in some sense. Rather
surprisingly, some recognition of this critique came to the honours
system in the 1880s, at the same time as businessmen began to
receive peerages in number. Within a few years of one another in the
1880s and 1890s four notable cultural figures were given peerages,
despite their obvious lack of political experience, great wealth or
substantial landowning, and for no other reason than their personal
distinction—Lord Tennyson the poet, Lord Leighton the artist and
President of the Royal Academy, the great scientist Lord Kelvin,
and the discoverer of antiseptics, Lord Lister. (The honour was too
much for Lord Leighton, who promptly died six days after his
peerage was announced. I am informed that when Lister was
introduced to the Lords, one peer was overheard to make a loud
remark critical of 'damned sawbones' entering the chamber; Lister
noted in his diary that he had made a 'manual examination' of that
particular peer's rectum the week before!)

There were actually not many more very distinguished British
cultural figures so honoured for many decades thereafter. Lord
Rutherford, the great physicist, received a peerage, but no other
pre-1939 scientist, and no notable writer, not even, say, Rudyard
Kipling, nor any artist received one, although many were rewarded
by knighthoods or by non-titled honours like the Order of Merit.
After 1945 this was to change radically. The other somewhat
unexpected group whose leaders began to receive peerages around
1880, and who have continued to receive them without a break ever
since, are senior civil servants. The first of these, it would appear,

was Lord Lingen in 1885; Lingen began as a master at Rugby, and then served as Chief Secretary to the Education Committee of the Privy Council and Permanent Under-Secretary to the Treasury from 1870–85. He was followed over the next few years by such figures as Lord Sandford, ennobled in 1891, the first Permanent Under-Secretary for Scotland, Lord Farrer, Permanent Under-Secretary of the Board of Trade in 1893, and Lord Welby, another Permanent Under-Secretary of the Treasury, in 1894. Ever since, to this day, virtually all permanent under-secretaries of the Treasury, the Foreign Office, and the Secretary to the Cabinet from the first, Lord Hankey, onwards, have received peerages, as have many other top civil servants. Virtually all, automatically, have received knighthoods. Perhaps more than even with the scientists, this was a truly radical departure. Civil servants were pre-eminently middle-class men and nothing more; most came from archetypal middle-class backgrounds and could acquire no wealth apart from their salaries and whatever they inherited. Moreover they were, at least nominally, public *servants* (even if they ran the country) who at least in theory took their orders from largely aristocratic Cabinet ministers in the same manner as a butler. And, again, the question was raised in a stark form: whatever their personal merits, should the genuine aristocracy be saddled with their offspring? Strangely enough, in most continental aristocracies top civil servants also automatically became aristocrats, despite the 'backward', pre-modern nature of the regimes, although none, of course, became a hereditary legislator. Perhaps the ultimate answer to this conundrum lies in the fact that if the Civil Service does run the country it is not surprising that civil servants appear on honours lists.

The final new type of non-business peer to emerge toward the end of this long period was even more novel still; indeed, even twenty years before the creation of the first, it would have seemed utterly impossible that even one should exist: the Labour peer. A number of pre-existing peers, like Russell, Ponsonby, Parmoor and Haldane, did join the Labour party in 1922–4 when it first rose to opposition and government—a surprising number, in fact, given the party's novelty and its theoretical commitment to doctrinaire socialism of a sweeping kind. When Labour took power for the first time in 1924, Ramsay MacDonald had to create the first deliberately ennobled Labour peerages. It must be appreciated that members of the House of Lords were not paid a salary of any kind until 1957 (apart from those who were government ministers) and, necessarily, every peer had to possess an independent income. Most of the early Labour peers were thus middle-class men of some means. The first three Labour peerages awarded by MacDonald in 1924 went to Lord Olivier, the distinguished civil servant who helped to found the Fabian Society in 1884; to a Manchester stockbroker named Lord Arnold who had become a convinced socialist; and to that peculiar military officer Lord Thomson, who crashed with the R101 dirigible in 1930. Sidney Webb, the archetypal middle-class socialist, was created Lord Passfield at the outset of MacDonald's second government, in 1929. The first genuinely poor working-class socialist peer appears to have been one Henry Snell, Chairman of the British Ethical Union and of the Secular Society, who was created Lord Snell in 1931, serving as Leader of the Opposition in the Lords from 1935 to 1940. Snell was illegitimate, began life as a farm-hand and indoor servant, experienced only 'casual, seasonal attendance at a village school', possessed what he described as 'a considerable experience of unemployment' and in occupation never rose higher than secretary to Sidney Webb as Director of the London School of Economics. He left nothing when he died in 1944, and his autobiography is entitled *From Farm Hand to House of Lords*. Although it is safe to say that his name is totally unknown to more than one person in 10,000, Snell was in some respects as much an absolute pioneer as Lady Astor; moreover, as Chairman of the British Ethical Union he appears to have been the first agnostic peer as well. Only a handful of working-class socialist peers were created up until World War Two but, when the Attlee government took office in 1945 the flood began, and Attlee granted about 17 newly-created peerages to working-class and trade union figures. Probably the best known of these went to Lord Citrine, but many other such peers are virtually unknown and it is extremely difficult for the historian of this subject to trace their careers. Many lived in council houses and left no estate or virtually no estate at death. F. E. Smith, Lord Birkenhead, wrote to Lord Irwin in the 1920s asking: 'Are we then to have a dozen more hereditary peers, very unsuitable in every way for hereditary rank, and so on *ad infinitum* with the creation of each new Socialist Government? If so . . . I think that the H of L will perish very rapidly amid public contempt.' Time seems to have proven F. E. wrong and unduly alarmist in this as in much else. In 1922, it will be recalled, two of the leaders of the so-called 'Red Clydesiders', David Kirkwood and (strange to relate) Emanuel

Shinwell vowed not to return to Glasgow until the red flag flew over Glasgow Town Hall. One may debate whether or not Glasgow has ever been red; what is certain is that at the end of their careers Kirkwood and Shinwell returned as Lord Kirkwood and Lord Shinwell, as have so many other Labour men. Additionally, Attlee created many middle-class Labour peers, and made the upper house much more representative.

The entire post-war period has seen these trends in the creation of peerages become the rule. As will be obvious from Tables 8.4 and 8.5, there has been a rapid and dramatic decline in the number of new peerages awarded to the wealthy, to major businessmen, or to businessmen—politicians. Additionally there has been a sharp decline, especially in real terms, in the wealth at death of newly-created peers, really a quite dramatic shrinkage. Some of this decline, without doubt, is due to large-scale estate duty avoidance by the wealthy, while much of the shrinkage in constant terms in recent years has been due to the hyper-inflation of the 1970s. Nevertheless, it is impossible to doubt that a real change has occurred during the past thirty or forty years. In particular, the major criterion for the granting of peerages at the present time appears to be merit, as defined by those who create peerages, which in practice means the elevation of 'the great and the good', those tiresomely worthy and public-spirited academics, publicly-notable scientists and writers, local government officials of note and, especially, chairmen of public committees and royal commissions. Every commission, it seems, has its peer and its peerage. Fulton, Redcliffe-Maud, Diamond, Wolfenden, Kilbrandon—the list is endless. Perhaps the most notable feature of 'the great and the good' is that in general they are left-liberals who invariably combine 'tender-mindedness' on social issues with moderate 'tough-mindedness' on economic ones; in other words, their prejudices are in direct contradiction, in all likelihood, to those of the great majority of the British population. The 'great and the good' are overwhelmingly middle-class and university-educated, but are certainly not wealthy, although they may perhaps be temporarily powerful.

As the tables make clear, as a percentage of all new peers, businessmen have markedly and precipitously declined. Fewer and fewer, in the 1960s and beyond, have been drawn from among the old type of tycoon, although of course some existed, like Marks & Spencer's Lord Sieff, Lord Pilkington of the glass company, the showbusiness magnates Lords Bernstein and Delfont, and Lord Matthews of the Beaverbrook Press. Some indeed, continue to emerge from landed backgrounds, like George Howard, Lord Howard of Henderskelfe, the late owner of Castle Howard and briefly Chairman of the BBC. But even among businessmen-peers, tycoons may well be outnumbered by manager-peers like Lord Stokes and Lord Kearton who are not asset-owners in the old sense. If Mrs Thatcher has reversed this trend at all, it has only been in a very marginal way.

Apart from the very substantial number of business peers, there have been dozens of creations from among former politicians, including local politicians, often appointed because their vote was needed in the upper house, and trade union officials and Labour figures. There have been many signs of a vast broadening, especially since about 1960, in the *type* of person normally granted a peerage. Many have gone to heads of professional societies—architects, solicitors and surgeons—who would previously have settled for knighthoods; to cultural notables, including fairly controversial ones, like C. P. Snow (Lord Snow), Benjamin Britten (Lord Britten), and Kenneth Clark (Lord Clark of Saltwood; he was, incidentally, one of the very wealthiest of recent peers, inheriting a fortune from Coats and Clarks sewing thread, the family firm, and building up an immensely valuable private art collection; he left over £5 million at his death); to scientists like Lord Adrian and Lord Blackett; while two have been granted to leaders of Britain's non-white communities. Many divorced men and women, previously barred in most cases, have been ennobled, as have some quite extreme left-wing politicians who evidently saw no inconsistency in accepting a peerage. For instance, Harold Wilson granted a peerage to Fenner Brockway, the tireless left-wing campaigner and, in 1970, to Harold Davies (Lord Davies of Leek), well known in the 1960s as the leader of missions to Hanoi during the Vietnam war, and regarded as an 'ultra-leftist' within the Labour party. At least two recent peerages, both since 1970, have gone to men who were well known to be overt homosexuals, and whose homosexuality must certainly have been known to the Prime Minister and his advisers; one of these was, in addition, a former communist. Apart perhaps from convicted IRA terrorists, it is difficult to think of any class of persons now automatically debarred from receiving peerages.

Besides these changes, two other quite major alterations have taken place in the peerage over the last thirty years. Since 1958 women have been eligible to sit in the House of Lords. Although some women were given peerages in their own right in the course of the century before, only since 1958 have they, and newly-created peeresses and life peeresses, been eligible to sit. In 1984, there were 291 living life peers and 46 life peeresses, with probably a disproportionate number of regular women attenders at Lords' sittings. None of these, so far as I know, was a prominent businesswoman, and most are either former politicians or drawn from 'the great and the good' of academics, local notables and the like.

Secondly, the creation of life peerages from 1958 onwards and, in particular, the virtual ending of hereditary peerages—none was created between 1965 and 1983, and even Mrs Thatcher has created only four—has altered, at a basic level, the whole nature of the honours system. Similarly, no baronetcies have been created since 1965. There are no more peerage dynasties, with the rarest of exceptions, and all titles cease with the death of their holder.

Are these changes illusory, a clever way of disguising, in a democratic and credulous age, the continuing authority of old structures of wealth and power? I think it is quite implausible to maintain that they are, and we must, I think, accept that since 1945 a fundamental change has come over the nature of the honours system and hence of high status in England. The nexus between wealth and high honours simply no longer exists in the old sense; nor, indeed, does the nexus between economic power, more broadly defined, and high honours. For the first time in British history, other definitions of status, strikingly different from those which existed in the past, have taken its place. To be sure wealth and economic power are considered worthy of merit, but not more meritorious *per se* than any other sort of achievement, whether in the field of public service, the professions, learning or the trade unions. I fail to see, given the objective nature of the evidence on this question, how this viewpoint can be refuted or denied.

It must follow, therefore, that the evolution of the relationship between property and wealth on one hand, and the British honours system on the other in the post-war period, cannot be explained by, and is inconsistent with, any system of sociological explanation which emphasizes the continuing intrinsic importance of capitalist wealth and property ownership in the old sense. It is, however, fully consistent with systems of explanation that emphasize the rise of newer and 'rational' determinants of status and recognize the pluralism of the dimensions of stratification determinants, especially the independence of wealth, status and power, and possibly other facets of stratification as well. Finally, it seems clear that sheer historical accident has often played an important role in determining the individual recipients of high honour; it is likely that this element has greatly increased in importance, given the pluralism of the contemporary honours system and the seeming difficulty of fitting its determinant structure into any clear-cut mould, as it may have been possible to do in the past, when land and business seemed to form the backbone of the system.

NOTES

1. R. A. Pumphrey, 'The Introduction of Industrialists into the British Peerage: A Study in the Adaptation of a Social Institution', *American Historical Review*, LXV (1959–60). F. M. L. Thompson, *English Landed Society*, *op. cit.*, esp. pp. 60–1, 292ff.
2. Harold Perkin, 'Who Runs Britain? Elites in British Society Since 1880', in *The Structured Crowd*, *op. cit.*, pp. 151–67; Rubinstein, *Men of Property*, *op. cit.*, pp. 169–72.
3. Anthony Howe, *The Cotton Masters 1830–1860* (Oxford, 1984), pp. 29–32.
4. See Chapter 6.
5. James P. Cornford, 'The Parliamentary Foundations of the Hotel Cecil', in R. Robson (ed.), *Ideas and Institutions of Victorian Britain* (London, 1967).
6. Philip Stanworth and Anthony Giddens, 'An Economic Elite: A Demographic Profile of Company Chairmen', in Stanworth and Giddens (eds), *Elites and Power*, *op. cit.*, pp. 81–101.
7. On Ellerman's career and life, see my biographical notice in Jeremy (ed.), *The Dictionary of Business Biography*, *op. cit.*, Vol. II, pp. 248–61.
8. Kenneth Rose, *King George V* (New York, 1984), pp. 245–59.

APPENDIX

Names, Occupations and Probate Valuations of Businessmen (or Members of Business Families) Given Peerages, 1880–1945 (Including Sons and Grandsons of Businessmen, not in Trade), by Decade of Creation

1880–89

1. Wimborne (Guest)*	Ironmastery	(d.1914)	£718,856**
2. Ardilaun (Guinness)	Brewing	(d.1915)	£795,000**
3. Tweedmouth (Marjoribanks)	Banking	(d.1894)	£925,074**
4. Rothschild	Merchant banking	(d.1915)	£2,780,100**
5. Revelstoke (Baring)	Merchant banking	(d.1897)	£36,897
6. Hillingdon (Mills)	Banking	(d.1898)	£1,540,180**
7. Hindlip (Allsopp)	Brewing	(d.1887)	£557,577
8. Grimthorpe (Denison-Beckett)	Banking; Law	(d.1905)	£2,202,170**
9. Stalbridge (Grosvenor)	Railways	(d.1912)	£105,303
10. Burton (Bass)	Brewing	(d.1909)	£1,173,170**
11. Brassey (*N*)	Railway building	(d.1918)	£178,976
12. Armstrong	Engineering	(d.1900)	£1,467,060
13. Cheylesmore (Eaton)	Silk brokerage	(d.1891)	£117,514
14. Addington (Hubbard)	Russia Merchant	(d.1889)	£209,725
15. Cross	Banking	(d.1914)	£86,431

1890–99

16. Iveagh (Guinness)	Brewing	(d.1927)	£13,486,000
17. Mount Stephen (Stephen)	Railway finance (in Canada)	(d. 1921)	£1,414,319
18. Masham (Cunliffe-Lister)	Worsted manuf.	(d.1906)	£648,558
19. Hambleden, Viscountess	Retail newsagency (estate of husband W. H. Smith)	(d.1913)	£1,982,700

20.	Cromer (Baring)	Merchant banking	(d.1917)	£117,609
21.	Battersea (Flower)	Australia merchant	(d.1907)	£186,747
22.	Dunleath (Mulholland)	Flax-spinning	(d.1895)	£971,747
23.	Crawshaw (Brooks)	Banking	(d.1908)	£325,977
24.	Ashcombe (Cubitt)	Building	(d.1917)	£127,258
25.	Overtoun (White)	Chemicals	(d.1908)	£689,023
26.	Swansea (Vivian)	Copper-smelting	(d.1894)	£215,033
27.	Rendel	Engin.	(d.1913)	£652,329
28.	Wandsworth (Stern)	Merchant banking	(d.1912)	£1,555,985
29.	Peel (N)	Cotton manuf.	(d.1912)	£158,376
30.	Ashton (Williamson)	Linoleum	(d.1930)	£10,501,595
31.	Pirbright (DeWorms)	Banking	(d.1903)	£368,906
32.	Glenesk (Borthwick)	Newspapers	(d.1908)	£400,052
33.	Aldenham (Gibbs)	Merchant banking	(d.1907)	£762,591
34.	Inverclyde (Burns)	Shipowning	(d.1901)	£886,546**
35.	Strathcona (Smith)	Railway finance (in Canada)	(d. 1914)	£418,553
36.	Farquhar	Banking	(d.1923)	£313,705
37.	Glanusk (Bailey)	Ironmastery	(d.1906)	£360,143
38.	Currie (N)	Banking	(d.1906)	£152,281

1900–09

39.	Avebury (Lubbock)	Banking	(d.1913)	£315,137
40.	Allerton (Jackson)	Leather tanning	(d.1917)	£291,014
41.	Burnham (Levy-Lawson)	Newspapers	(d.1916)	£302,891
42.	Biddulph	Banking	(d.1923)	£211,321
43.	Armstrong	Engin.	(d.1941)	£216,846
44.	Leith of Fyvie	Steel (in US)	(d.1925)	£393,490
45.	Northcliffe (Harmsworth)	Newspapers	(d.1922)	£5,249,000
46.	Michelham (Stern)	Merchant banking	(d.1919)	£2,000,000
47.	Faber	Banking/ newspapers	(d.1920)	£647,698

48. Desborough (Grenfell)	Banking/copper smelting	(d.1945)	£134,883
49. Joicey	Coal	(d.1936)	£1,520,000
50. Nunburnholme (Wilson)	Shipping	(d.1907)	£834,978
51. Winterstoke (Wills)	Cigarettes	(d.1911)	£2,548,000
52. Pirrie	Shipbuilding	(d.1924)	£707,786
53. Glantawe (Jenkins)	Tinplate manuf.	(d.1915)	£66,367
54. Armitstead	Foreign merchant	(d.1915)	£185,266
55. Airedale (Kitson)	Locomotive build.	(d.1911)	£1,126,000
56. Swaythling (Montagu)	Merchant banking	(d.1911)	£1,146,000
57. Blyth	Distilling	(d.1955)	£211,666
58. Peckover	Distilling	(d.1925)	£901,602
59. Merchamley (Whiteley)	Cotton manuf.; brewing	(d.1925)	£287,375
60. Holden	Woollen manuf.	(d.1912)	£470,744
61. St Davids (Phillips)	Finance	(d.1938)	£123,736
62. Goschen	Merchant banking	(d.1907)	£141,560
63. Ritchee of Dundee	Jute merchant	(d.1906)	£116,245
64. Grenfell (N)	Copper smelting	(d.1925)	£46,779
65. Knaresborough (Meysey-Thompson)	Railway chairman; land	(d. 1929)	£197,620

1910–19

66. Devonport (Kearley)	Retail grocery	(d.1934)	£1,898,000
67. Cowdray (Pearson)	Engin.; petroleum	(d.1927)	£4,000,000
68. Rotherham (Holland)	Cotton manuf.	(d.1927)	£25 [*sic*]
69. Furness	Shipowning	(d.1912)	£1,844,000
70. Glenconner (Tennant)	Chemicals	(d.1920)	£852,173
71. Aberconway (McLaren)	Colliery, engineering (manager)	(d. 1934)	£15,043
72. Merthyr (Thomas)	Colliery	(d.1914)	£615,552
73. Inchcape (Mackay)	Shipowning	(d.1932)	£2,214,707

74.	Rowallan (Corbett)	Australia merchant	(d.1933)	Unlisted
75.	Ashton of Hyde	Cotton manuf.	(d.1933)	£208,926
76.	Emmott	Cotton manuf.	(d.1926)	£91,757
77.	Pontypridd (Thomas)	Limeworks	(d.1927)	£37,022
78.	Hollenden (Morley)	Hosiery manuf.	(d.1929)	£1,541,000
79.	Whitburgh (Borthwick)	Meat importing	(d.1967)	£2,134,065
80.	Rochdale (Kemp)	Flannel manuf.	(d.1945)	£454,395
81.	Rothermere (Harmsworth)	Newspapers	(d.1940)	£335,308
82.	Ranksborough (Brocklehurst)	Silk manuf.	(d.1921)	£63,421
83.	Cunliffe	Banking	(d.1920)	£905,192
84.	Faringdon (Henderson)	Stockbroking	(d.1934)	£1,117,000
85.	Astor	Real estate (in USA)	(d.1919)	£478,713
86.	Rhondda (Thomas)	Colliery	(d.1918)	£1,169,000
87.	Somerlyton (Crossley)	Carpet manuf.	(d.1935)	£192,679
88.	Glentanar (Coats)	Sewing thread	(d.1918)	£4,324,000
89.	Stuart of Wortley	Miscellaneous (manager); law	(d.1926)	£33,716
90.	Beaverbrook (Aitken)	Newspapers; Finance (in Canada)	(d. 1964)	£379,530
91.	Gainford (Pease)	Distilling	(d.1943)	£26,878
92.	Forteviot (Dewar)	Distilling	(d.1929)	£4,405,000
93.	Roe	Timber merchant	(d.1923)	£11,320
94.	Doverdale (Partington)	Paper manuf.	(d.1925)	£250,000
95.	Leverhulme (Lever)	Soap; chemicals	(d.1925)	£1,625,000
96.	Colwyn (Smith)	India-rubber	(d.1946)	£305,919
97.	Cawley**	Chemicals	(d.1937)	£901,138
98.	Queenborough (Paget)	Railways (in USA)	(d.1949)	£255,275
99.	Weir***	Engin.	(d.1959)	£3,304,000
100.	Glanely (Tatem)	Shipowning	(d.1942)	£2,068,000
101.	Wittenham (Faber)	Banking	(d.1931)	£867,424
102.	Inverforth (Weir)	Shipowning	(d.1955)	£548,214
103.	Wyfold (Herman-Hodge) (N)	Cotton manuf.	(d.1937)	£155,362

104. Clwyd (Roberts)	Timber merchant	(d.1955)	£94,995
105. Dewar	Distilling	(d.1930)	£5,016,000
106. Wavertree (Walker)	Brewing	(d.1933)	£876,735
107. Southwark (Causton)	Stationery	(d.1929)	£21,283
108. Gladstone*** (N)	Foreign merchant	(d.1930)	£64,212
109. Buxton*** (N)	Brewing	(d.1934)	£158,894
110. Armaghdale (Lonsdale)	Export merchant	(d.1924)	£306,821
111. Glenarthur (Arthur)	Cotton export merchantry	(d. 1928)	£50,181

1920–29

112. Ashfield (Stanley)	Underground railways (manager)	(d. 1948)	£59,971
113. Riddell	Newspapers	(d.1934)	£2,208,000
114. Cullen of Ashbourne (Cokayne)	Banking	(d.1932)	£34,980
115. Marshall of Chipstead	Newspaper agency	(d.1936)	£182,151
116. Invernairn (Beardmore)	Shipbuilding	(d.1936)	£858,092
117. Cable	East India merchant	(d.1927)	£218,616
118. Illingworth	Cotton & woollen manuf.	(d.1942)	£297,329
119. Bearsted (Samuel)	Petroleum	(d.1927)	£4,000,000
120. Dalziel of Kirkcaldy	Newspapers	(d.1935)	£435,490
121. Glendyne (Nivison)	Stockbroking	(d.1930)	£175,111
122. Woolavington (Buchanan)	Distilling	(d.1935)	£7,150,000
123. Manton (Watson)	Soap manuf.	(d.1922)	£1,000,000
124. Waring	Furniture retail	(d.1940)	£138,626
125. Forres (Williamson)	Foreign merchant	(d.1931)	£184,590
126. Vestey	Meat shipping	(d.1940)	£261,515
127. Borwick	Baking and custard powder	(d.1936)	£377,030
128. Mildmay of Flete	Merchant banking	(d.1947)	£546,031
129. Barnby (Willey)	Woollen merchant	(d.1929)	£100,000
130. Maclay	Shipowning	(d.1951)	£1,179,555

131. Wargrave (Goulding)	Finance	(d.1936)	£265,626
132. Bethell	Finance; property development	(d.1945)	£456,618
133. Daryington (Pease) (*N*)	Colliery	(d.1949)	£24,134
134. Kylsant (Phillips)	Shipowning	(d.1937)	£62,567
135. Younger of Leckie	Brewing	(d.1929)	£327,643
136. Lawrence of Kingsgate	Railway chairman	(d.1927)	£449,536
137. Hunsdon (Gibbs)	Merchant banking; merchant	(d.1935)	£116,286
138. Banbury of Southam	Stockbroking	(d.1936)	£290,209
139. Arnold	Stockbroking	(d.1945)	£26,543
140. Stevenson	Distilling (manager)	(d.1926)	£313,706
141. Lloyd	Banking; steel	(d.1941)	£56,967
142. Buckland (Berry)	Colliery; steel	(d.1928)	£1,116,000
143. Greenway	India merchants, petroleum (manager)	(d.1934)	£298,954
144. Craigavon (Craig)	Distilling	(d.1940)	£27,366
145. Hayter (Chubb)	Locks & safes	(d.1946)	£82,366
146. Daresbury (Greenall)	Brewing	(d.1938)	£1,436,000
147. Dalziel of Wooler	Newsagency; pullman cars	(d.1928)	£2,274,000
148. Wraxall (Gibbs) (*N*)	Merchant banking	(d.1931)	£368,027
149. Strickland	Cotton planting; newspapers	(d.1940)	£15,517
150. Melchett*** (Mond)	Chemicals	(d.1930)	£1,044,000
151. Ebbisham (Blades)	Printing	(d.1953)	£151,733
152. Trent (Boot)	Retail pharmacy	(d.1931)	£222,317
153. Fairhaven (Broughton)	Finance (in USA)	(d.1966)	£2,485,191
154. Brotherton	Chemicals	(d.1930)	£1,780,000
155. Camrose (Berry)	Newspapers	(d.1954)	£1,481,000
156. Dulverton (Wills)	Cigarettes	(d.1956)	£4,268,000
157. Luke (Lawson-Johnson)	Meat products	(d.1943)	£411,607
158. Alvingham (Yerburgh) (*N*)	Brewing	(d.1955)	£214,072

1930–9

159. Wakefield of Hythe	Lubricating oil	(d.1941)	£776,221
160. Kirkley (Noble)	Shipowning	(d.1930)	£168,097
161. Noel-Buxton*** (N)	Brewing	(d.1948)	£232,848
162. Hyndley (Hindley)	Coal merchant	(d.1963)	£241,321
163. Rochester (Lamb)	Carrying	(d.1955)	£15,598
164. Selsden*** (Mitchell-Thomson)	West India merchant	(d. 1938)	£37,148
165. Moyne*** (Guinness)	Brewing	(d.1944)	£2,000,000
166. Woodbridge (Churchman)	Cigarettes	(d.1949)	£1,361,000
167. Essendon (Lewis)	Shipowning	(d.1944)	£48,163
168. Davies	Colliery	(d.1944)	£506,445
169. Gladstone of Howarden	India merchant	(d.1935)	£473,274
170. Runciman	Shipowning	(d.1937)	£2,896,000
171. Brocket (Nall-Cain)	Distilling	(d.1934)	£442,062
172. Duveen	Art dealing	(d.1939)	£2,814
173. Mottisone*** (Seely)	Colliery	(d.1947)	£14,712
174. Iliffe	Newspapers	(d.1960)	£510,367
175. Palmer	Biscuit manuf.	(d.1948)	£1,015,000
176. Nuffield (Morris)	Autos	(d.1963)	£3,253,000
177. Hirst	Electrical manuf.	(d.1943)	£498,651
178. Wakehurst (Loder)	Railway (chairman); merchant	(d. 1936)	£159,707
179. Portal	Paper manuf.	(d.1949)	£2,122,000
180. Blackford (Mason)	Printing; finance	(d.1947)	£307,489
181. Riverdale (Balfour)	Steel manuf.	(d.1957)	£87,226
182. May	Insurance (manager)	(d.1946)	£195,903
183. St Just (Grenfell)	Merchant banking	(d.1941)	£880,331
184. Swinton (Cunliffe-Lister)*** (N)	Worsted manuf.	(d.1972)	£454,430
185. Glenravel (Benn)	Timber merchant	(d.1937)	£47,181
186. Kemsley (Berry)	Newspapers	(d.1968)	£310,866
187. Catto	Banking	(d.1959)	£501,805

188.	Austin	Autos	(d.1941)	£509,712
189.	Wardington (Pease)	Banking	(d.1950)	£83,264
190.	Windlesham (Hennessey)	Brandy merchant	(d.1953)	£5,286
191.	Mancroft (Samuel)	Shoe manuf.	(d.1942)	£136,011
192.	McGowan	Chemicals (manager)	(d.1961)	£207,453
193.	Rea	Merchant banking	(d.1948)	£311,432
194.	Cadman	Colliery; petroleum (manager)	(d.1941)	£234,746
195.	Marchwood (Penny)	Exchange broking	(d.1955)	£126,072
196.	Kenilworth (Siddeley)	Aeroplanes; engin.	(d.1953)	£354,597
197.	Southwood (Elias)	Newspapers	(d.1946)	£165,063
198.	Pender	Telegraphs	(d.1949)	£49,065
199.	Brassey of Apethorpe (N)	Railway building	(d.1958)	£308,209
200.	Belsted (Ganzoni) (N)	Sugar broking	(d.1958)	£716,468
201.	Perry	Autos (manager)	(d.1956)	£77,699
202.	Stamp	Railway chairman	(d.1941)	£163,549
203.	Bicester (Smith)	Merchant banking	(d.1956)	£212,277
204.	Ennisdale (Lyons)	Insurance	(d.1963)	£1,920,000
205.	Harmsworth	Newspapers	(d.1948)	£524,679
206.	Glentoran (Dixon)	Shipowning	(d.1950)	£162,283
207.	Rotherwick (Cayzer)	Shipowning	(d.1958)	£636,924
208.	Woolton (Marquis)	Retailing	(d.1964)	£407,790
209.	Baldwin of Bewdley***	Ironmaster	(d.1947)	£208,971
210.	Milford (Phillips)	Shipowning	(d.1962)	£281,167
211.	Horne***	Finance	(d.1940)	£64,923
212.	Samuel*** (N)	Merchant banking	(d.1963)	£28,919

1940–5

213.	Abertay (Barrie)	Shipowning	(d.1940)	£296,518
214.	Croft	Maltsting	(d.1947)	£101,756
215.	Teviot (Kerr)	Banking	(d.1968)	£3,835

216. Sherwood (Seely)	Colliery	(d.1970)	£124,488
217. Kindersley	Merchant banking	(d.1954)	£388,886
218. Leathers***	Coal shipping	(d.1965)	£151,515
219. Stansgate*** (Benn) (N)	Publishing	(d.1961)	£5,623
220. Margesson***	Banking	(d.1950)	£84,279
221. Wedgwood	Pottery manuf.	(d.1943)	£56,234
222. Brabazon of Tara***	Engin.; finance	(d.1964)	£46,650
223. Courtauld-Thomson	Finance	(d.1954)	£499,669
224. Norman	Banking	(d.1950)	£253,316
225. Royden	Shipowning	(d.1950)	£746,393
226. Chattisham (Brass) (N)	Building; property	(d.1945)	£137,964
227. Cope	Colliery	(d.1946)	£162,061
228. Courthorpe	Brewing, chartered surveying, miscellaneous	(d.1955)	£209,925
229. Quibell	Building	(d.1962)	£43,821
230. Ramsden	Cloth merchant; engin.	(d.1955)	£209,253
231. Hacking	Insurance	(d.1955)	£209,253
232. Sandford (Edmondson)	Building	(d.1959)	£26,550
233. Lyle of Westbourne	Sugar	(d.1954)	£664,910
234. Broadbridge	Tin mining	(d.1952)	£91,847
235. Templewood*** (Hoare)	Banking	(d.1959)	£186,884
236. Gretton	Brewing	(d.1947)	£2,303,000

Notes

* Surname where different from title.
** Includes estimated valuation of land.
*** Cabinet minister.
N From business family, but no active participation in trade.

Survivals

9

The End of 'Old Corruption' in Britain, 1780–1860*

The common or narrow meaning of 'Old Corruption' is fairly plain. It is the widespread use of pensions, sinecures and gratuitous emoluments granted to persons whom the British government, between the earlier eighteenth century and the Age of Reform, wished to bribe, reward or buy. It was an all-pervasive feature of British politics in this period—indeed, among the elements which most distinguished eighteenth-century British politics from that of the nineteenth—although many historians have seen its essential passing, in the wake of Burke's 'economical reform' of the 1780s, as predating the Age of Reform by fifty years.

My aim in this chapter is to draw attention to the much wider and far more extensive ramifications for the evolution and transformation of British society which Old Corruption and its passing seem to have had, not merely for British high politics but in areas at first glance far removed from the narrower sphere of bribery and corruption usually taken as comprising the realm of Old Corruption and which, I believe, have received little or no systematic treatment from the historian. Putting a concise but

* Previous versions of this paper were read at Professor F. M. L. Thompson's seminar at the Institute of Historical Research, London, and at the 1981 Modern British History Conference in Melbourne. I am most grateful for the comments received there. I am also most grateful to Professors Ian Christie, F. B. Smith, F. M. L. Thompson and Martin J. Wiener, and to Drs J. R. Dinwiddy and I. Prothero for their helpful comments and suggestions. My wife, Dr Hilary L. Rubinstein, assisted by a Deakin University grant, undertook much of the source research for this study, for which I am especially grateful. World Copyright: The Past and Present Society, 175 Banbury Road, Oxford, England. This chapter first appeared in *Past and Present: A Journal of Historical Studies*, no. 101 (November 1983) pp. 55–86, and is here reprinted with the permission of the Society.

cogent definition of this wider meaning of Old Corruption that is initially compelling is somewhat difficult, and perhaps the most fruitful way in which this can be done is to relate briefly how the subject attracted me and something of what has gone through my mind in the course of my research. In the course of my work on Britain's top wealth-holders I found, much to my surprise, that a sizable proportion of those who flourished during the early nineteenth century were neither landowners in the strict sense, nor manufacturers nor merchants, but were engaged in activities which would now be classified as in the professional, public administrative and defence occupational categories, including expecially Anglican clerics, soldiers, lawyers and judges, government bureaucrats and placemen. Nearly 10 per cent of all British half-millionaires[1] deceased in the early nineteenth century, and as many as 23 per cent of those leaving more than £150,000 but less than £500,000 during the years 1809–29 were engaged in such activities. Their numbers, moreover, decreased strikingly between the early and middle nineteenth century. For example, the number of lawyers and judges who left fortunes of between £150,000 and £500,000 declined from 15 to four between 1809–29 and 1850–69, and this decline is paralleled in other related occupational fields. The routes by which such men acquired their fortunes appeared to be strikingly and in some cases grotesquely pre-modern or early modern in nature and ambience, and glaringly at variance with the historian's common perceptions of wealth-making in Britain during the period of industrialization. To cite some examples of this, Sir William Wynne (d. 1816), Official Principal of the Court of Arches and Master of the Prerogative Court of Canterbury, left £180,000; Samuel Richard Fydell (d. 1868), Receiver-General for Lincolnshire between 1794 and 1834, left £250,000; Charles, Lord Arden (d. 1840), brother of Spencer Perceval and Registrar of the Court of Admiralty for fifty years, left £700,000; Hon. William Stuart, Archbishop of Armagh (d. 1832), left £250,000; George Pretyman-Tomline (d. 1827), Pitt's tutor and Bishop of Winchester, left £200,000. An obscure Archbishop of Canterbury, John Moore (d. 1805), was said by one recent historian to have left £1 million at his death.[2] More celebrated, and very much in the same mould, were such men as Lord Eldon (d. 1838), the symbol of Tory reaction, Lord Chancellor for twenty-seven years, whose father is described in the son's franker biographies as the owner of a coal barge at Newcastle-upon-Tyne, and who accumulated a fortune of £707,000 in personalty and great quantities of land; or, indeed, the Duke of Wellington himself, the younger son of a none-too-wealthy Irish earl, whose personal fortune of £600,000 and ducal estates were the product of the munificent parliamentary and foreign grants which came to him in the wake of his military victories. Such men—and there were many others of a similar stamp—were among the very wealthiest of their time in Britain, far richer than most successful manufacturers. Yet Wellington's death in 1852 marked the virtual cessation of this type of top wealth-holder in the British elite structure.

In considering these men and their milieu, several things must strike the historian as requiring a fresh—or, indeed, a preliminary—examination, especially that there was a major fraction of the British elite structure in the later Georgian period which remains little explored in any serious history of the age, and that this world vanished almost completely between about 1830 and about 1860, a fact which must have had a profound effect upon the structure of Britain's elites. The existence of this world and its subsequent disappearance is also surely significant in coming to terms with several important elements of Britain's historical development in the nineteenth century, as well as important to understanding a number of areas at first glance apparently far removed from the subject of political corruption as such, and to which this chapter will shortly return. For want of a better descriptive phrase, I will continue to employ the term Old Corruption, as radicals of the day like William Cobbett and John Wade often referred to it, to specify this wider general milieu as well as political corruption in the narrow sense, and indeed it is this wider meaning of Old Corruption, the nature of its milieu in British society and the manner of its ending, rather than the details of corrupt political practice as such, which the historian ought most usefully to research.

The term Old Corruption was used by radicals to mean not one, but a rather wide variety of practices which they held to be at the heart of much of what was wrong with Britain's unreformed government. Briefly, one might usefully distinguish between the 'political influence of the crown'—the patronage which the government continued to have at its disposal to bribe or reward members of parliament, voters, municipal corporations and the like—and the pre-existing varieties of corruption, or the fruits of previous corruption which, though gradually reformed, continued to exist and continued to be a charge on the public purse. Among the latter—and from the most to the least objectionable, according to the radical critics of the English *ancien régime*—one may distinguish between existing sinecures (rewards or lucrative office without any duties), sinecures for those who had performed services in the past and which continued to be paid, reversions (expectation or promise of a future sinecure) and the pluralist holding of office by leading government officials with or without real duties to such an extent as to be the source of real wealth to these officials.

It seems clear that while the 'political influence of the crown' had by 1830 been reformed to a very considerable extent,[3] and while much, but certainly not all (and less than many historians have credited) of the other varieties of corruption were mitigated between 1783 and 1832, much still remained, while other aspects of Old Corruption, invariably viewed by radicals as part of the system, had hardly been touched. These included the highly unequal emoluments paid in respect of similar services (as with the varying salaries paid to Church of England clergymen, especially bishops), the enormous fees earned by many office-holders, especially those in the legal world, the near-universality of nepotism and patronage among aristocratic families, particularly those with links to the Tory party, and the nexus which had been built up between the Tory government and the older sections of the middle class. Additionally, such features of the pre-Reform landscape as the closed municipal corporations and the East India Company awaited genuine reform. Each of these was consistently included under the heading of Old Corruption by radicals of the period, and the remaining sources of such corruption were, it is contended here, lucrative to a degree largely unappreciated by subsequent historians, and indeed one of the major hinges upon which the English *ancien régime* turned.

Whether the term be employed in a narrow or wider sense, several facets of the nature and ending of Old Corruption seem to suggest that this is a somewhat unusual historical problem. In the first place Old Corruption remains to a large extent a historical blank. To be sure, there are innumerable studies of borough-mongering and high politics in this period, as there are very many studies of radical and reform movements, but there is seemingly little which focuses specifically upon this world, its anatomy and ambience, the level of its top rewards and their implications of Britain's elite structure and its manner of passing. One of the best general accounts of the manner in which successive governments prior to 1832 attempted to modify the network of crown influence still remains Archibald S. Foord's article, 'The Waning of the "Influence of the Crown" ', which appeared as long ago as 1947.[4] This is surely rather strange, as one has only to open a radical journal or newspaper dating from the period between 1810 and 1835 to find, with almost unvarying regularity, an exposé of the extent of patronage and perquisite and an attack upon their existence.

Secondly and, it might be suggested, of more fundamental importance, the world of Old Corruption is, as it were, not 'right'. Much of it appears, as has been suggested, to be a relic of the early modern period or of distinctly pre-modern modes of thought which somehow linger on into the age of the Stockton-Darlington railway and the cotton factory. If historical research into modern British history is to advance beyond those frames of reference which normally mark its conceptualization, it is surely just to these bizarre and anomalous—and hence, ignored or camouflaged—trends and tendencies to which the historian ought to turn, and it is one of the aims of this chapter to draw attention of this element in Old Corruption.

The question of why so few have ever studied the world of Old Corruption in detail remains obscure, and one cannot really point to any compelling reasons for it. There was, of course, no dramatic and specific reform movement similar to that which effected the Great Reform Bill or the New Poor Law to sweep away Old Corruption at a stroke; there is no Old Corruption reform movement to study. Reform of Old Corruption was piecemeal, while reformers and radicals of the period were never centrally concerned with Old Corruption, although they were certainly well aware of its existence. There is as well a continuing impression that Old Corruption was largely synonymous with the political influence of the crown, and that the type of patronage it represented diminished substantially with Burke's 'economical reform' in the 1780s and with the long Pitt ministry, and was almost wholly gone before 1832. In Archibald Foord's words: 'The destruction of the influence of the crown occurred, not in the 1780s nor in 1832, but in the period in between'.[5] In *The Reign of George III* John Steven Watson has noted, concerning Burke's economical reforms, that 'the real curbing of patronage lay in the day-to-day scrutiny of the working of the public offices, conducted by Pitt in ensuing years,

and not in Burke's over-simplified plan [of 1782]', and that
'economic reform, the cutting away of sinecures and influence, had
not been a Foxite speciality since Burke had left them. It had rather
been Pitt's quiet achievement'.[6] While no one would deny that both
Burke and Pitt did much to reform the type of direct venality in
government so common during the eighteenth century, and while
several historians, including J. Mordaunt Crook and M. H. Port in
their study of the King's Works, have drawn attention to specific
reforms of corrupt government administration undertaken long
before 1832, it is surely mistaken, given the wide variety of practices
which came under the heading Old Corruption, to view it, except in
its narrowest sense, as a phenomenon which had vanished by 1832.
Certainly no British radical of the period believed that it had, and
time and again they presented detailed evidence of the continuing
volume of patronage and sinecure of the old sort. The celebrated
Black Book and *Red Book*, first published in 1816, detailed the
names and takings of literally thousands of placemen and
pensioners in many editions; even the 1832 edition of the *Black
Book*, consisting of 683 dense pages, contained a detailed 83-page
list of government placemen.[7] But more important, to focus
narrowly upon the political influence of the crown is to miss the
wide and extensive ramifications of Old Corruption, virtually
coextensive with the pre-1832 British Establishment itself, which
Cobbett and Wade plainly had in mind in their indictment of Old
Corruption, and which, as has been suggested, persisted until the
Age of Reform. It is thus crucial in considering Old Corruption not
to conflate the waning of the crown's direct electoral influence via
bribes and patronage with the much wider and more fundamental
notion of Old Corruption which is arguably of much greater
historical importance. It was certainly true for instance that thanks
to Burke's reform of the 1780s, government contractors could no
longer sit in Parliament, but it nonetheless also remained true that
in 1820 Lord Eldon received not merely £18,000 p.a. from his
formal salary as Lord Chancellor but additionally had in his gift
other legal offices and perquisites estimated in the *Black Book* as
worth £42,000 p.a., while Eldon's brother Sir William Scott earned
£6,740 p.a. from his post as judge of the Admiralty Court and other
offices, and while Eldon's eldest son was to receive nearly £7,000
p.a. from two offices coming to him in reversion. It was still true in
1832, according to the *Black Book*, that Lord Bathurst received no
less than £32,700 p.a. as clerk of the Crown Court of Chancery,

Secretary at War, Commissionary of the Affairs of India, Teller of
the Exchequer—a post which, claimed the *Black Book*, paid him
£23,117 p.a.—and as holder of an office entitled Clerk of
Dispensations and Faculties, which provided him with £4,313 p.a.,
while two of his close relatives received £6,400 p.a. from the three
offices which they held. Even in the 1820s such offices and salaries
could be multiplied many hundredfold, if the radical journalists of
the period were even approximately accurate.[8] Shortly before, in
1809, the *Supplementary Report* of the Committee of Public
Expenditure showed that the net value of the principal sinecure
offices alone, including those of the English law courts, was
£356,555 p.a.[9] The same report also claimed that 76 members of
parliament at that time received £164,003 in salaries and
pensions.[10] Whatever retrenchment had occurred in the
intervening years, by 1820 Wade found 1,109 persons in receipt of
£642,621 p.a. in pensions and grants alone, including £51,589 p.a.
paid to 47 retired ambassadors.[11] In the same year, Wade's *Black
Book* identified 40 persons who received £10,000 or more annually
from the public revenues. Wade included in his list royal dukes and
Cabinet ministers, but among the wealthy placemen still in receipt
of such enormous incomes in 1820 were Lord Arden, who is
credited with a gross income of £38,574 and a net income of
£12,562 as Registrar of the Court of Admiralty, Rt Hon. W. W.
Pole (Wellington's brother) who received £12,450 as Master of the
Mint and Joint Remembrancer of the Court of Exchequer in
Ireland, and Lords Henry and Robert Seymour, jointly in receipt of
£14,043 p.a. from three obscure Irish legal offices.[12] Wade also
found 54 such offices with a salary of between £5,000 and £10,000
and 413 worth between £1,000 and £5,000. Although praising the
Whig government of 1830–2 for some reduction in the salaries of
offices, Wade found even in 1832 that the number of offices, places
and pensions worth £1,000 or more had actually risen to 956.[13]
However many of these positions were legitimate offices of
government, some remained sinecures and reversions of the old
type, and many office-holders continued to be paid salaries and fees
grossly in excess of their rational deserts.

It is this world, this way of conducting British government,
which ought to be studied as an integral part of Old Corruption.
And, equally importantly, the radicals of the period viewed as
integral to Old Corruption not merely the direct sinecures and
offices, or even the fringe emoluments received by the major office-

holders and their relatives, but the close involvement of many middle-class businesses and professions which, they claimed, also benefited directly or indirectly from both the general policies pursued by Pitt and Liverpool, and, as well, from the ethos which produced the wealth of Eldon and Bathurst. This is an important and interesting point, for it suggests that a fundamental nexus existed between the aristocratic government of the British *ancien régime* and the *older* commercial and professional middle classes. For example, in *The Black Book* (1820 edn) Wade discusses the Bank of England and one of its directors, John Whitmore, and it is worth citing him at some length:

> It hardly appears possible that any disinterested individual should be the advocate of the present system of pillage and injustice; and, therefore, we generally find those who come forward in its defence, are connected with it either in state, law, divinity, or some other way. As soon as we saw the name of John Whitmore affixed to a Declaration of London merchants, bankers, traders, and others, in defence of property and social order, we felt quite sure that John Whitmore would turn out to have some great stake in the sort of social order that Declaration was intended to support. Accordingly, we found, after a little inquiry, that this gentleman was the governor of the Bank of England, at the time of the famous Bullion Report in 1810, and that the same person is now a Bank director.
>
> This circumstance alone will sufficiently explain Mr Whitmore's meaning, when he declares his abhorrence of 'seditious and blasphemous publications', and his 'full reliance on the efficacy of the laws, the purity of their administration, and the wisdom of the Legislature'. This language is now well understood; and no one is so little informed as not to comprehend its meaning when proceeding from the mouths of sinecurists, placemen, judges, bishops, and Bank directors.
>
> There is no establishment which has such a powerful interest in the continuance of the present system as the Bank of England. The policy of the last twenty-five years has been the source of all its wealth and influence. It is to the war against liberty and knowledge, the Bank owes all its greatness and inordinate gains. . . . It is to the war, too, the Bank is indebted for the increase in the amount of public deposits. . . . It is not merely the Bank of England, but nearly the whole banking-system of the country that is indebted for its origins and prosperity to the war . . . [W]e should suppose that there are at least 2,000 individuals in the metropolis; who, from dependence on the Bank, as well as their own supposed interests, would be ready at any time to sign any Declaration to which John Whitmore might affix his signature.
>
> The whole of these classes owe their origin to the Pitt System, or, to ascend a generation higher, to the Borough System . . . [which] begat the whole race of bankers, loan-contractors, and speculators; . . .[14]

Wade and other radicals of the day similarly linked such middle-class institutions as the East India Company, professional groups such as lawyers and the Anglican clergy and, of course, the unreformed parliamentary system together as forming, in some salient sense, parts of a whole. One does not have to go the entire way with this radical critique to recognize the considerable element of truth in their perceptions and, once again, the limitations inherent in viewing 'economical reform' as having effectively ended this world and the nexus implied in Wade's critique. Indeed Wade and his colleagues argued that the French wars and the 'Pitt System' materially increased the scale and dimensions of Old Corruption and their arguments surely deserve a serious analysis.

Finally, in considering the neglect of this topic, it should not be forgotten that subsequent historians, rightly concerned with restoring a balance to the radicals' perception of the ills of Georgian England as mainly due to the influence of blood-sucking placemen and parasites, have themselves overlooked the actual importance of the wider and extremely lucrative features of Old Corruption for maintaining the unreformed system. In their indulgence towards the enlightened and defensible features of the British aristocracy, they have failed to quantify and often neglected the rapacity which underpinned the whole system.

These considerations in turn raise another fundamental question, namely what it was about Old Corruption that was corrupt. Joel Hurstfield in his essay on 'Political Corruption in Modern England: The Historian's Problem' explicitly links eighteenth-century corruption as a continuous piece with the time-honoured British tradition of the chief ministers of the state enriching themselves as, say, Thomas Cromwell and Francis Bacon did in the sixteenth century.[15] Foord notes that the 'chief resources employed' by the crown in the mid-eighteenth century 'may be grouped under four headings'[16]—government money, used to subsidize the ministerial press, to provide pensions, and carry on election campaigns; patronage, to provide jobs for voters, placemen, relatives and minions; honours; and 'imperceptible influence', the distribution of contracts, loan issues, the lease of crown lands, and the like, which, he suggests, played an important part in securing the support of both mercantile and landed classes.[17] It is thus significant that Foord does not seem to include under any of these headings two of the facets of Old Corruption which, it might be argued, were at least as typical and lucrative: what may be termed the secondary and fringe rewards of office and place—the fees and payments which came to, say, a judge or bishop as unofficial but expected perquisites of office, and simply the grossly non-egalitarian features of the system itself, which largely vanished during the Age of Reform. According to Norman Sykes, while the income of the see of Canterbury averaged £19,182 in 1829–31, that of York £12,629, of London £13,292, and of Durham £19,066, the income of the poorest bishopric, Llandaff, averaged only £924, with Rochester at £1,459 and St Davids at £1,897.[18] With the most lucrative rewards—real wealth in most cases—went the ceaseless search for lucrative place and office which marked the entire Georgian period: bishops and prebends and, *a fortiori*, secular placemen, shamelessly seeking preferment by any and every means, and offices openly acknowledged as a legitimate form of property, often hereditary property. Everyone knows of this as a commonplace of Georgian history; yet a narrow focus upon the strictly political forms of influence exercised by the crown and ministry has, perhaps, led many historians to ignore the structure of the system itself and the multiplicity of its wider ramifications throughout English society which the system continued to engender until the 1830s.

Yet perhaps the major reason for the void in the historical literature concerning Old Corruption is that it wears, as it were, two faces. To employ an overworked word, there is a dialectical (or, if you will, contrapuntal) appearance to the subject and its meaning for English history which must, in my view, be kept in mind by historians. The bizarre, pre-modern nature of Old Corruption was mentioned above, and this aspect must be enlarged upon, for it forms one side of the dialectic in our understanding of the subject, in both the narrow and the extended senses of Old Corruption we have tried to distinguish. This side of the dichotomy is extraordinarily intriguing and suggestive in its implications for English history and is perhaps the most significant wider insight which a study of this subject provides. Many of the patronage offices and places—and, more widely, the system itself—were, I should like to contend, pre-modern and non-rational in the Weberian sense of failing to obey the rational criteria of all modern bureaucracies which Weber and other sociologists have distinguished as crucial to, and inherent in, the process of modernization.[19] Rewards did not accord with effort or duty; promotion did not occur according to merit or seniority even in a nominal sense; the highest and most lucrative places had the fewest duties and, often, the least *raison d'être*. Indeed, the most lucrative and impressive offices frequently had no duties at all, and their holders no objective qualifications for holding them. Succession to responsible office was often determined by hereditary succession to that office or by open sale, criteria which even the Victorian period would find unacceptable. It may seem at first as if all governmental bureaucracies and, indeed, structured organizations of all sorts exhibit some or all of these characteristics, but this in fact is not so: all *modern* bureaucracies and structured organizations, as sociologists have pointed out, obey certain rational criteria of appointment, promotion and hierarchy. Promotion is determined, at least in part, by merit, and offices bear some resemblance to the needs and duties they are supposed to discharge, with the most senior and best rewarded offices in any organization responsible, at least nominally, for taking the most fundamental decisions.[20] The rationalization and modernization of Britain's Civil Service and much else of its governmental structure of course form one of the central themes of the Age of Reform, and certainly by the time of the Northcote-Trevelyan reforms and Gladstonian retrenchment they had become aims almost universally approved by intelligent opinion and by the political nation. Only a generation before, however, this was far from being the case. One could here cite literally dozens if not hundreds of examples, ludicrous and bizarre, of what appear to be pre-modern, non-Weberian offices and hierarchies in the world of Old Corruption—examples abound in the *Black Book* on nearly every page and in many radical journals in nearly every issue. The *Black Book*, for instance, noted the case of Lord Auckland, who received £1,400 p.a. as Vendue-Master at Demarara, 'where he had never been', and £1,900 p.a. as 'Auditor at Greenwich Hospital', in its words 'for doing nothing', as he certainly never audited. Similarly, Hon. Charles Wyndham had received a salary of £4,000 p.a. since 1763 as Secretary and Clerk of Emoluments in Jamaica, while his brother, Hon. Percy Wyndham, had likewise received £7,000 p.a. as Registrar in Jamaica. Cobbett noted in 1822 that 'they have received £649,000 principal money from these places without, I believe, ever having seen poor Jamaica'. Cobbett remarked that Percy Wyndham also held the office of Secretary and Clerk of the Courts in Barbados and concluded that its salary 'would, perhaps, go far towards marking up the round million'. There is the case of Lord Henry Seymour, who in 1830 received compensation of £1,251 for loss of his office of Craner and Wharfinger of the Port of Dublin. The Duke of St Albans, who was Hereditary Grand Falconer and Hereditary Registrar of the Court of Chancery, in the words of the radical journal *Medusa*, 'without catching or keeping a single hawk or registering a single dudgeon entangled in the meshes of the law, pockets £2,000 per annum of the public money . . . wrung from the wants of sickening misery'. Hon. Patrick Plunkett received £500 p.a. as Purse-Bearer to the Chancellor of Ireland, who happened to be his brother, Lord Plunkett. Hon. Thomas Kenyon held the position of Filazer, Exigenter, and Clerk of Outlawries in the Court of King's Bench, which brought him some £1,254 p.a. in fees. When this vital office was abolished in 1826, Kenyon received compensation of £5,463. In 1832 Wade took note of an annual hereditary pension of £4,000 still paid out of post office revenue to the 'heir of the duke of Schomberg' and found 'there is no peerage of the name, and to whom the pension is paid, or for what, we are unable to ascertain'. The Band of State Pensioners, created by Henry VIII in 1509, had the duty:

> to attend the King's person with their pole-axes, to and from chapel royal, receive him in the Presence Chamber on his coming out of his privy lodgings. They likewise attend at all great and solemn occasions. . . . On the Coronation Day and at St George's Feast, they have the honour to carry up the King's dinner.

As the *True Sun*, another radical journal, put it, 'the annual cost of the pole-axing brotherhood to the country (omitting the salaries of the secretary, paymaster, harbinger axekeeper, and messenger, which we have not at present ascertained) was a sum equal to the salary of the President of the United States'. Its captain, Lord Hereford, received £1,000 p.a., its Standard-Bearer £510, while its 40 ordinary members received £100 each. The journal also stated that they are 'to call a general meeting of its members to consider the propriety of petitioning the King for an increase in salary'! A similar logic of those seen in these examples perhaps prevailed in 1805 when at the death of Lord Nelson, a grateful nation bestowed an earldom, £100,000, and a perpetual annuity of £5,000 p.a. upon Nelson's closest living male relative, his brother, who happened to be, not a sailor, but a Norfolk clergyman who had never been to sea in his life. Wade commented that he 'could have had as little claim to the rewards of the hero of the Nile as any other chance person picked up in St Paul's Church-yard'.[21] Similar, too, was the case of Arthur Onslow, Speaker of the House for thirty-three years, who retired with a pension of £3,000 p.a. payable for his own life and that of his son. As *The Poor Man's Guardian* put it in 1832, 'the fortunate youth, the younger Onslow, must have received £130,000 for performing no service whatever, but simply for being born the son of a public officer', and contrasted this case with that of the Speaker of the American House of Representatives, who 'receives for similar labour $3,000 or £660 p.a., and this only while he holds office, without a shilling of pension after he leaves it'. In the endless search for preferment and financial reward the accepted norms of status and apparent occupational description often seemingly disappeared. Wade pointed out that as late as 1832:

> From the large emolument of Sinecures, and the granting them in reversion, have originated some ludicrous incongruities. Many noble lords and their sons, right honourable and honourable gentlemen, fill the offices of clerks, tide-waiters, harbour-masters, searchers, gaugers, packers, craners, wharfingers, prothonotaries, and other degrading situations. Some of these offices are filled by women and some by children . . . the *duchess dowager* of Manchester [receives] £2,928 a-year, as late collector of the customs outwards! Not long since a right honourable lady, a baroness, was *sweeper* of the Mall in the Park; another lady was *chief usher* in the Court of Exchequer. . . . Then of noble Lords; the Beresfords hold the appropriate offices of *wine-tasters, storekeepers, packers, and craners,* in Ireland: the Duke of Grafton, and Lords Ellenborough and Kenyon, with deputies to help, are clerks, sealers, and keepers of writs . . . and Lord Wm Bentinck, now located in India as governor-general of Bengal, is clerk of the pipe, part of whose office it is to attend or assist the man who holds up Lord Chancellor Brougham's train![22]

In other spheres, even those not merely far removed from politics, but ostensibly dependent upon a pervasive and omnipresent rationality, one can often catch a glimpse of the same thing. Witness, for example, the mooted appointments in political economy at Oxford:

> [W]hen Nassau Senior resigned from the Oxford Chair of Political Economy in 1829, Richard Whateley was elected; he had no obvious professional qualifications, but was persuaded that as a prominent Christian he might be able to rescue economics 'permanently from disrepute'. On Whateley's elevation to [the archbishopric of] Dublin, Frederick Denison Maurice let himself be proposed (unsuccessfully) on the grounds that no one else was ready to come forward and argue that

'political economy is not the foundation of morals and politics, but must have them for its foundation or be worth nothing' . . . Maurice had even fewer qualifications than Whateley: 'I shall of course endeavour to master the details of the subject—with its principles, alas! I am not acquainted' [he wrote] . . . He was turned down by the Puseyites, not because of his unfitness for the job but because of his views on baptismal regeneration.[23]

Similarly, in Brougham's famous six-hour speech of 1828 on the abuses of the judiciary, he noted that although the privy council acted as the ultimate court of appeals for the whole British empire:

it had neither a regular Bench nor a regular Bar. Of the lawyers only the Master of the Rolls attended, assisted by an ex-ambassador or 'now and then a junior Lord of the Admiralty who was neither ambassador nor lawyer, but would be exceedingly fit for both functions only that he happened to be educated for neither'.[24]

What does the existence of these offices without duties, whose rewards were either grotesquely higher than their deserts or palpably misdirected, signify? I would suggest—and I reiterate that this is but one side of the dichotomy of explanation—that they and their analogous phenomena are genuinely indicative of a pre-modern, non-Weberian conceptual mode, which lacked at least an element of the modern notions of merit, individual responsibility, and organizational rationale and which, furthermore, must be taken at least partly at face value. In a word, the world of Old Corruption was *irrational* (in Weber's sense of rationality); there is a dreamlike or nightmarish quality which pervaded the system and which, I think, must be appreciated by its historians. It is perhaps just this conceptual gap between Old Corruption and modernity which may account most fundamentally for its disregard by later historians.[25]

Closely akin to this is the survival of the old in Britain for anomalously long periods of time. A number of historians have recently drawn attention to the subject of what might be termed ready-made customs—the investiture ceremony of the Prince of Wales, invented in 1911 to seem a time-honoured survival, is the best-known of these—but the reverse of this, the survival of the old, and the mentality and rationality which attended it, must be equally striking to nineteenth-century historians, who encounter it in the unlikeliest places,[26] and as well, I think, to the many social and economic historians who have increasingly recognized how misleading it is to view Britain as an urban industrial society prior to the late nineteenth century. Something of the irrational, pre-modern ambience of Old Corruption may be seen in many other spheres of British life at the time—for instance, in much of the penal system, with its incredibly savage punishments[27] founded in a rationale alien even in the early nineteenth century, or in the rights enjoyed by the Church of England in non-ecclesiastical spheres, for instance the monopoly it enjoyed until 1858 in the probating of wills. Perhaps the most important pre-modern and non-rational survival was the unreformed House of Commons itself, not so much because its forms and constituent elements had their origins in medieval England—as Michael Brock has noted, any long-lived political system necessarily consists of survivals[28]—but because it advantaged and disadvantaged sections of the community and even social classes on an entirely haphazard basis. 'This was not a system based on property', Brock astutely notes, 'but a caricature of one'.[29] All of these old frames of reference were, needless to say, utterly antithetical to whatever we mean by the Victorian consciousness, which identified individual reward strictly with individual merit and voluntary agreement—from status to contract—according to rational and 'modern' criteria of merit.

Yet as late as the mid-nineteenth century or even after in some cases, Britain contained wide areas of custom and authority surviving from a previous epoch. These were not destroyed by industrialization or by the revolutions in government down the centuries. When in the early part of this century the Webbs magisterially surveyed the history of English local government, with an erudition and indeed a perception that has not been surpassed, they were genuinely surprised at the extent of pre-Reform ordinances, institutions and customs surviving at every hand, and their thick volumes on the history of local government are virtually an extended description of these survivals. Manorial courts—which even well-informed modern historians might be excused for believing had not outlived Piers Plowman—continued to function, though much decayed in power, until the mid-nineteenth century or in some cases later still:

> At the outset of our inquiries we shared the common opinion that these Manorial jurisdictions had, so far at any rate as Local Government functions were concerned, come silently to an end before our period [i.e., before 1688]. But as we extended our researches from County to County this impression wore off. We are even inclined to suggest that, in 1689, the holding of a Manorial Court for the suppression of nuisances,

the management of the common pasture, and, less frequently, of the commonfield agriculture and the appointment of Constables and other officers for the district, was, in the thousands of Manors that must still have existed, the rule rather than the exception.[30]

The Webbs give numerous examples of such ancient local customs and institutions surviving till the nineteenth century or later.[31] Another striking mid-nineteenth-century example of this may be found in a description of the surviving rights of the Lords of the Manor of Hampstead, as depicted in James Thorne's *Handbook to the Environs of London* (1876):

> It was on the slope behind the Castle that the corpse of the unhappy John Sadleir, M.P. for Sligo, was found on the morning of Sunday, Feb. 17, 1856 . . . Hampstead is an awkward place for a suicide to select. The lord of the manor possesses very extensive rights, among them being that of deodand, and is therefore, in the case of a person who commits suicide within the manor, entitled as heir to 'the whole of the goods and chattels of the deceased, of every kind, with the exception of his estate of inheritance, in the event of a jury returning a verdict of *felo de se*' [that is, lord of the manor was entitled to all personalty belonging to an intestate suicide]. Sadleir's goods and chattels were already lost or forfeit; but the cream-jug was claimed and received by the lord as an acknowledgment of his right, and then returned.[32]

All this is but one side of the coin. The other side, the other way to look at Old Corruption is that it was quite plainly a system of achieving wealth and status, the system *par excellence* of outdoor relief for the aristocracy and its minions. Such an interpretation would dismiss what has been said of Old Corruption as misleading. Most if not all historians of modern Britain, whatever their ideological moorings, would unite in agreeing that Britain was unique among European nations in the degree to which it had, long before, rid itself of pre-modern modes of thought and consciousness and adopted (perhaps via Puritanism, if not earlier still) a national mentality of rationality in Weber's sense and an all-pervasive cash nexus which dissolved all pre-existing bonds.[33] Since the high middle ages if not before, Britain had never possessed a peasantry; its landed aristocracy, differing from those of the Continent in a dozen ways, was virtually a bourgeoisie under another name and had, seemingly, swept away any neo-feudal remainders by the mid-seventeenth century. So runs the familiar interpretation, and no historian of Old Corruption would deny that it can be seen in this light. Rewards did possess a rationale, albeit one largely unacceptable to a later age: its rewards were, plainly, the fruits of political patronage or bribery. The hereditary aspects of Old Corruption, so strange to subsequent generations, were simply another example of the desire by all successful Englishmen, then or now, to create a dynasty, a desire as much alive among the industrial magnates who bought their titles from Lloyd George as it had been a century before. The system was both functionally and rationally successful—in the words of one well-known historian, Britain possessed 'an open aristocracy based on property and patronage', for, as another great historian has so elegantly put it, 'no one bribes when he can bully', while the grosser and more unacceptable features of Old Corruption were indeed modified voluntarily from Burke onwards.

This view of Old Corruption is of course highly plausible and no doubt 'correct', but it may be said to beg or leave unanswered a number of important questions about the system and its dimensions. How, for example, did it come about that a country uniquely 'modern' in most if not all essential respects by the seventeenth century, and perhaps by the thirteenth century, could take, as it were, such a giant step backwards? The answer which is perhaps likely to occur to most historians is that which might be termed, *pace* Wordsworth on Milton, the 'fen of stagnant water' view of Georgian England, and especially of its elite structure, half-transformed, half-preserved by the events of the seventeenth century. Locked into a political and constitutional structure which had become virtually unalterable in most important respects despite the economic and social changes of the eighteenth century, Britain's elite structure, as it were, ballooned in grotesque ways, feasting and bloating itself upon the economic enormities which Old Corruption made possible; under little or no necessity to tailor public office or official reward to public need or public opinion, it simply grew fatter and fatter. The necessity for the leading politicians and placemen to become fat and bloated as quickly and voraciously as possible was greatly increased by the fact that status was crucially dependent upon land and a title, and land, especially the broad acreage and its upkeep required to enter the aristocracy, was even then among the most expensive commodities one could buy. It was perhaps for this reason above all that the sheer size of the rewards which the British Establishment paid to itself were so large. No subsequent ruling group in Britain has possessed a modicum of the sheer greed of these men; compared with them, the Victorians were ascetics.[34] As late as 1830, according to Cobbett's *Political Register*, 113 members of the aristocracy were in receipt of £650,000 p.a. of public money. According to *Carpenter's Political Letters* of November 1830, two families, the Grenvilles and the Dundases had 'during the last forty years taken more money in sinecures alone than it had cost during the same time to maintain the whole of the civil government of the United States'. 'A Peep at the Peers', the continuing column in the *Black Dwarf* of 1820 described as follows the many emoluments of Lord Liverpool, who is normally viewed by historians as a Tory reformer and under whose government much reform of corruption undoubtedly took place:

> He is first set down as First Lord of the Treasury, at £6,000 a year! Now one as simple as myself would think that there was business enough in the treasury for the *first lord*, at any rate (or the others ought to be dismissed) and the £6,000 a year was as much as *Lord* Liverpool was worth to the state. But, God help our poor optics which cannot distinguish the value and abilities of these lordly things! After discharging all the business of the treasury, as first lord, and pocketing the £6,000 a year I find him with enough time on his hands *to be a commissioner of affairs in India*, with room enough in his pocket for £1,500 more every year! I have scarcely recovered my astonishment at this, when I am also informed that he has also time to discharge the duty of a *Warden of the Cinque Ports* which consists, I am told, of putting £4,100 a year more in his bottomless purse! But even this is not all—he has leisure enough, by working *over hours*, I suppose, to be *Clerk of the Rolls in Ireland*, for which he pockets £3,500 a year more! Talk of the business talents of his Satanic Majesty! Can he do more than manage the affairs of the Treasury, India, Ireland and the Cinque Ports at one and the same time! There are people who say, that these pretended places, are only so many *excuses* for giving the fellow the *salaries*! They whisper, that he neither keeps the Rolls of Ireland, nor attends to the affairs of India, nor knows anything about the Cinque Ports; and that a deputy does all his work at the Treasury for a few hundred a year which is also paid by the *country*! . . . These things are incomprehensible to me.

Even in 1832, the *Poor Man's Guardian* noted that Lord Grey and nineteen of his relatives had received among them £171,892 p.a. from all the government offices and posts which they held. The remarks of the *Black Book* on Lord Eldon's £18,000 p.a. ('This is a huge monster! The noble lord is the Atlas of the borough system . . .') or upon Lord Arden's £38,000 p.a. ('This is, indeed, a voracious pauper . . .') seems very just.

If this consideration of the remarkable size of the top rewards possible under Old Corruption is accurate, it in turn raises a number of other important considerations: what, for instance, was the effect of the 1832 Reform Bill and the other major reform landmarks of the period upon Old Corruption? How was it that aristocratic governments, Tory and Whig, changed and reformed Old Corruption so profoundly? And what, if anything, took its place as a source of revenues for the aristocracy and its minions?

Granting that Old Corruption in its broad sense persisted until after 1830, it seems to me to be undeniable that the 1832 Reform Bill and the consequent period of Whig reform during the Age of Reform were the key mechanisms in ending it, despite all the reforming work which had been going on since Burke. Important remnants too, still survived of sinecures and reversions in the old sense until 1832. In both the 1820 and 1832 editions of the *Black Book*, Wade notes that 'A considerable number of offices to which no duties whatever are attached, and of which the holders, without either employment or responsibility, have only to receive the salaries and emoluments' still existed, mentioning such offices as the Chief-Justiceship in Eyre, north of the Trent, and the position of Lord Justice-General in Scotland 'held for many years by persons not brought up even to the profession of law'.[35] Wade also presented a list of the 'numerous class' of offices whose 'salaries are vastly disproportionate to their employment, and of which the duties are discharged wholly by a deputy'.[36] Strictures against numerous existing reversions, pensions and grants follow.[37] Offices in the colonies—described by Wade as 'the chief *nidus* of sinecures'—especially the West Indies, where 'The duties of nearly all offices . . . are discharged by [a] *deputy*, while the principal resides in England'[38] were still a rich source of sinecures, as were 'governors, lieutenant-governors, town-adjutants, town-majors, constables, gunners, wardens, lord-wardens, and God knows what beside' of local government.[39] 'But the Courts of Justice', according to Wade, still in 1832, 'present the most rank and unweeded garden of lucrative offices without employment, or of which the employment is executed by a deputy'.[40] These are a few of the examples noted by Wade and his colleagues of surviving sinecures in the old sense, and do not include any of the other varieties of corruption—often very similar in nature—which remained. For example, Wade examined the 'profuse grant of pensions and compensations to the members of the [former] Irish parliament' to whom 'more than £75,000' was still paid annually in 1832.[41] On the other hand it is unquestionably true that much reform of Old

Corruption, especially in its narrow sense, had occurred before
1830, while the 1820s in particular saw a degree of reform of Old
Corruption in its broader sense.[42] The reform of Parliament itself
was seen by nearly all radicals as a necessary preliminary measure
for the systemtatic ending of Old Corruption, and whatever the
reforming work of the previous Tory governments it is difficult to
disagree with this assessment. If one studies the long-term effects of
the Great Reform Bill upon Britain's elite structure, I think one sees
just how fundamental a reforming measure it really was, and why
one should not underestimate its importance or interpret it merely
as a clever holding action by the old elite. To find the mechanisms
whereby post-1832 governments essentially ended Old Corruption
in its wider sense one ought to look to those reforms which have
received relatively less attention than the great instruments of
reform of this period like the New Poor Law. Most of these were
piecemeal in the sense of remedying one separate facet of
corruption, but cumulatively they effectively and quietly ended the
pre-existent system. For example, the Ecclesiastical Commission,
established by Sir Robert Peel's short-lived Tory government in
1835, together with the subsequent Whig government's
Established Church Bill of 1836, quite effectively ended the
possibility of ecclesiastical wealth accumulation on the old heroic
scale, as well as many other churchly abuses, so prevalent until
1832. Bishops could no longer acquire fortunes of a quarter of a
million pounds or more by venality and pluralism—the probate
records, so far as I am aware, record no instance after about 1860—
and, I think it is fair to conclude, the face of the Church of England
was genuinely revolutionized in this period. Similarly, the closed
municipal corporations which had governed England's cities and
towns prior to 1835, and which radicals invariably perceived as
another rich source of corruption, venality and nepotism, were of
course swept away in 1835. But it was not until then that such root-
and-branch reform was politically possible.

Apart from self-interest and the limits of the political agenda
possible before Reform, there were other salient reasons why
patronage and corruption were not rooted out before the mid-
Victorian period. Up until 1780 at least, in Sir Norman Chester's
words, 'it was well accepted that an office constituted a form of
property, particularly the longer and more certain its tenure and the
more pronounced the rights and pecuniary benefits attached to it'.[43]
Even Burke recognized that office could be property, a type of

property which, he proclaimed in 1780, when respected by law, was 'sacred to me'.[44] Something of this spirit unquestionably lingered throughout the period of Tory rule, although, equally certainly, the modern notion of office as a legally responsible post, to be filled for a specified period of time, became generally accepted. Buying and selling of office was prohibited in 1809, as was the promise of granting an office to procure a seat in Parliament;[45] other reforms made at this time have also been documented by Chester.[46] Secondly, many extreme Tories, like their radical counterparts, paradoxically considered the unreformed system a whole which could not be reformed in a piecemeal fashion without destroying the system: 'touch one atom and the whole is lost' was Eldon's famous warning.

Yet Old Corruption was reformed by both Tory and Whig aristocratic governments, and this inevitably raises the second question posed above, how was it that an essentially aristocratic government changed the old system so fundamentally? This is obviously a complex matter which no historian could answer without a profound study of the surviving papers of Grey and his ministers. One can, however, draw a few broad strokes which very detailed evidence is likely to support. First, the Whig government and the Whig aristocracy in general represented both that portion of the aristocracy which had shared relatively less thoroughly in the largesse of Old Corruption, and which in any case was generally wealthier than the Tory aristocracy and wealthy enough to live as grandees through the possession of 'legitimate' property like agricultural land and mineral deposits.[47] Given that the great Whig families had indeed been excluded from the fruits of office for so long, it was in fact largely true that they did not benefit from place and sinecure in the same sense as the Tories. In contrast, the radicals of the period trumpeted over and over again just how essential to the Pitt-Liverpool Tories was Old Corruption and its bounty, and how opposition to parliamentary reform was founded, as much as anything else, in economic self-interest. (Croker estimated just before Reform that the 'Tory aristocracy' controlled 203 nomination seats, the Whigs only 73.)[48] The 'Black List!', a widely distributed poster, compiled by W. P. Chubb following the defeat of the Reform Bill by the House of Lords in October 1831, detailed the 'annual amount of pickings of the peers' who had voted against Reform. According to Chubb's list these 200 Tory peers and bishops received 'upwards of £2 million' from sinecures, official

places, military and civilian salaries and offices, and, in the case of
the bishops, livings and prebends. (Agricultural rental incomes and
other personal wealth of these men, it must be emphasized, are
excluded from Chubb's list.) Nine living peers (including those in
retirement like Eldon) and two bishops received £40,000 or more
from official sources.[49] Not merely the Eldons and Wellingtons
appear as massive placemen and beneficiaries on Chubb's 'Black
List!', but very junior and virtually unknown peers as well.[50] Even if
Chubb and his colleagues were systematically exaggerating the
extent to which the Tory aristocracy was finally benefitting from
Old Corruption, not merely by attaching inflated values to their
takings, but by counting the incomes of aristocratic relatives and
from non-political appointments, the sum suggested by Chubb in
1831 (not 1780) may well have been equal to, or even exceeded, the
entire agricultural income which the Tory aristocracy derived from
its rent-rolls at the time. Surely, at the very least, a connexion exists,
and this aspect of the British *ancien régime* demands a searching
examination. It is for this reason that, though doubtless true, it is
perhaps disingenuous to claim that many different reasons existed
for the use of patronage besides the sinister and corrupt—for
instance, to supplement the inadequate salary of another office, to
assist the dependents of those who died prematurely in service, or to
provide retirement pensions for public officials. To focus upon
these aspects of pension and sinecure without a more searching look
at their role as central prop for the old regime is to miss its single
most significant feature.

Secondly, and conversley, the genuine nexus which had been
built up between the Pitt-Liverpool Tories and the older, more
conservative segments of the middle classes like the East India
Company and the legal profession largely ceased to exist after 1832,
while the allegiances which the Whig aristocracy was forming were
increasingly with the newer segments of the middle class, like the
northern manufacturers and the dissenters, who had not fully
shared the old consensus. Yet, paradoxically, the price which the
Tories had to pay for their consensual government and its many
alliances with the middle class was that, increasingly, the irrational
and pre-modern bases of Old Corruption could no longer be taken
as a salient or persuasive framework of state policy even by those
who benefitted from them. For this reason, among others, the
Tories themselves frequently took the lead in apparent reform—
under Pitt and Liverpool, and after 1832 with Peel and Church

reform, for instance, although they never touched the central props
of the system as was done from 1832 onwards. One more than half
suspects that the irrational features of Old Corruption were
becoming increasingly intolerable and unacceptable to the Tories
themselves—certainly the gap between, say, Eldon and Peel (who
was the extremely wealthy scion of a cotton millionaire) was
immense. There can be no doubt that, for whatever reason, by the
1830s the 'spirit of the times' simply could not rationally justify, in
the light of day, the abuses of the old system. This may be seen as
the third of the reasons why Old Corruption came to an end,
because it was increasingly intolerable and unacceptable, for
fundamental ideological and cultural reasons, to the elite which
benefitted from it. Modernity was by stages arriving in England,
although whether this should be seen as representing the 'triumph
of the entrepreneurial ideal', the middle classes imposing its frames
of reference upon the rest of society, as Harold Perkin has argued,[51]
is perhaps more debatable, for as we have seen it was the aristocracy
which carried through these reforms to the detriment, perhaps, of
much of the middle class.[52] Indeed at the end of the day much about
the ending of Old Corruption is obscure and rather mysterious, for
the end of Old Corruption is surely among the few examples in
history of an elite reforming itself in some quite basic respects,
which cost it very considerable amounts of money and altered many
of the recognized patterns of mobility and status attainment.[53]

This naturally leads to the third of the questions posed above:
what took the place of Old Corruption for those aristocrats and
placemen who had benefitted from it? Given that the aristocracy
and its minions no longer had at their disposal the vastly lucrative
offices without duties, appointments without merit or
responsibilities, how did they get on? Again, this is a complex and
ill-explored area, which awaits its historian. The short answer is
that those aristocrats who flourished during the nineteenth century
were the wealthiest magnates with vast rent-rolls and urban and
mineral properties as well.[54] Disproportionately they were Whig-
liberals rather than Tories.[55] The smaller (but still very wealthy)
variety of landowner who was apt to have been a Tory before and
after 1832 either adapted to the changed conditions, supporting
himself from his landed property alone, or underwent a secular
decline; in any case by the late nineteenth century, the gap between
this type and the great magnates was very pronounced. One must
conclude that for such men, as well as the erstwhile non-landed

minions of the pre-1832 elite, nothing took the place of Old Corruption, and a lucrative and invaluable source of revenue had disappeared. To be sure, there remained colonial administration, the army and navy, even the Church, and eventually business directorships, but one must conclude that had the period between 1837 and 1879 not fortuitously been one of agricultural prosperity, much of the decline of the lesser aristocracy and gentry, so notable after 1879, would have occurred long before. Similarly, although the military and the Empire doubtless absorbed many an aristocratic relative after 1832, its rewards could simply not be compared with those possible in the past; for many minor aristocrats one cannot help feeling that the Reform Bill marked the end of a way of life and the beginning of an era of diminished opportunities.

The dichotomy concerning the nature of Old Corruption was left unresolved; possibly, at least given our present historical knowledge of the subject, it is unresolvable. Nevertheless, whether Old Corruption ought best to be viewed as a rational facet of a rational and modern society, or an irrational facet of an irrational and pre-modern one, might become more clear if the impact of Old Corruption and its ending upon other spheres of British life is examined and discussed. Some of these are, at first glance, seemingly far removed indeed from the matter at hand. No sensible historian would wish to exaggerate the contribution of Old Corruption to any such area, yet equally the lack of attention paid by historians to Old Corruption implies that the limits of its influence ought to be explored.

The effect of the ending of Old Corruption upon the British middle classes has been touched upon before but needs to be made more explicit. It is a common view of nineteenth-century British history that the middle classes 'rose' to pre-eminence in the wake of 1832. In many respects this view is surely misconceived. There seems clearly to have been a nexus between the Pitt-Liverpool Tory governments and the older middle classes. The Napoleonic Wars and their economic consequences were perceived by radicals as benefitting the City of London financial aristocracy; the older professions, the Church, the bar and bench, the East India Company were certainly as much a part and parcel of Britain's elite structure and unreformed constitution as the House of Lords itself. The effective ending of this nexus in 1832 had several important consequences for these bonded elements of the Establishment. One was a *decrease* in the level of top rewards which practitioners of these old businesses and professions could expect. The nineteenth century witnessed a *decline* in the levels of peak incomes and fortunes which the most successful of these older middle-class institutions could accumulate. It is quite certain, for example, that the spectacle of quarter-millionaire bishops had no parallel by the time of Wilberforce; similarly, the three-quarter millionaire judges like Eldon no longer existed. In many respects the Age of Reform witnessed the passing of an old middle class whose nature and orientations remain ill-explored, but which plainly differed from our common view of the nature and aspirations of the Victorian middle classes which succeeded them. Similarly it might not be entirely fanciful to suggest that, as well as the peak rewards, the power and influence of the middle classes diminished from after 1832 until the Second Reform Bill and possibly until the Third, as the old nexus between government and old non-landed wealth broke up. The Whig grandees and peers who dominated British politics for over fifty years after the Great Reform Bill were much more of a closed, caste-like group than the Pitt-Liverpool Tories had ever been.[56]

The importance of Old Corruption for the development of political ideology in nineteenth-century Britain is also considerable and has been underestimated and neglected; here I should like to discuss its effect upon British radicalism, utilitarianism and conservatism. The attack upon Old Corruption forms one of the most important, popular, and reiterated themes in the British radical press of the period between 1800 and 1830s, especially during the 1820s. One has only to open a radical journal or newspaper of this era to find attacks upon it in abundance, and, as many of the quotations in this paper indicate, our knowledge of the extent of Old Corruption derives to a considerable extent from this radical indictment.[57] The attack upon the unreformed constitution to which it was closely allied was one which could unite working-class radicals with much of the newer middle classes who failed to share in its bounty (and were taxed to pay for it) and found its irrationality incomprehensible and even repellent. The radical attack upon irrationality in all spheres of public life predated the radicals' specific attack upon Old Corruption, stemming from Thomas Paine if not from French leaders of the Enlightenment.[58] Then as now, straightforward cases of public money scandals—as much of Old Corruption would be classed—are supremely salient and largely indefensible to outraged public opinion. Nor did Old Corruption cease to be a stock-in-trade of British radicalism even after its passing: it was still present, in much the same format as twenty years earlier, in Chartist periodicals like Feargus O'Connor's *Northern Star*, and it remained a staple of the popular Sunday newspapers of the middle and even later nineteenth century.[59] What one recent historian has termed 'an outdated view of society with an emphasis on the monarchy, aristocracy, landownership, places, pensions, and the church' formed a major component of mass circulation newspapers like *Reynold's* and *Lloyd's* until the 1880s. 'There is no doubt of the popularity of such a stance'.[60] Perhaps only in the later nineteenth century, long after the passing of its grosser abuses, and with the elevation of the British monarchy to semi-divine status, the emergence of right-wing press lords dominant over the popular press, and the shift of the left to a general and 'scientific' critique of capitalism, did the final echoes of the radical attack upon Old Corruption die away; even then it is quite probable that there remained, and possibly remains, a latent popular chord ready to be struck again.

Even more than the British radical tradition, utilitarianism cannot be fully understood, in my view, without situating its development against the background of the pre-1832 constitution and especially, in this case, the irrational features of Old Corruption. While no one would wish to exaggerate the importance of Old Corruption in the thinking of a Bentham, Chadwick, or *Westminster* reviewer, what might be termed the peculiar ultra-rationality of English utilitarianism (and, via utilitarianism, of Fabian socialism) may surely be seen as a reaction, above all, to the irrational elements of the English *ancien régime*. Bentham frequently attacked sinecures, and is the author of a lengthy unpublished work (written in 1810) opposing them;[61] of course much of his career was taken up with a concerted attack upon the irrational features of the unreformed legal system and with plans for a model, rational government apparatus. This is well understood by all historians. The 'massive detail' of Bentham's *Constitutional Code*, according to David Roberts, 'was exactingly subordinated to universally valid, rational, and efficient principles. . . . Nothing differed more from that blueprint than England's public administration in 1833. It was not orderly, it was not planned, it was not centralized, it was not efficient . . .'.[62]

Yet Bentham's concern for *rationality*, and for the attributes of a rational society which, it could be argued, is possibly crucial to understanding his whole endeavour, have long been camouflaged in the continuing debate over the attitude of utilitarianism towards the role of the government, and in the paradox that it seemingly advocated both much greater *laissez-faire* and much greater government intervention at one and the same time. Much of the mystery surrounding Benthamism would evaporate, I should like to suggest, if rationality, and the goal of increasing the rational organization of society, are seen as central to its view of the just society, and the amount or degree of government intervention a dependent variable which could and should justly be altered to achieve these goals.[63] It should also be understood that Benthamism's advocacy of rational and theoretical general principles of societal organization, including those in the economic sphere, was the product of thinkers who, literally, had little direct knowledge or experience of industrial Britain or the conditions which industrialism brought about in the industrial north of England.[64] Given the revolution in sensibility in the direction of greater rationality in British government and society which occurred in the time of the Philosophical Radicals, it is probably most judicious, in the debate over Bentham's influence, to view him as an important and central advocate for ideas whose time had come, but no more.[65]

Finally there is the case of British conservatism. Via Burke, Coleridge and Disraeli, conservatism in England enunciated a set of distinctive principles, of which four may be said to stand out in any brief résumé: the commonality of interests shared by the landed aristocracy and working classes against atomistic Manchester liberalism and the ideology of the middle class, the superiority of rural England and its values to urban England, the justification by age of old traditions, and, closely allied to it, the organic genuineness of age-old institutions like the British aristocracy. None of these principles, I would suggest, had much to do with the British elite which existed in the Georgian period, and the ideology of British conservatism seems to no small extent to have been a ready-made utopia devised to meet the radical and democratic attack. Quite paradoxically, the governing classes, especially the aristocracy in Britain, may well have grown much more like the Burkean depiction after 1832 than before, as the nexus between the aristocracy and the old middle classes came apart, and as a wealthy, self-reliant and high-minded landed aristocracy, animated by *gravitas* and Whig liberalism, superseded the Tory alliance. Burkean conservatism fails as well to understand that the *locus* of Old Corruption, and of the elite it benefited, was urban as much as rural, and was centred upon London, with its nexus of Parliament, government offices and older professions and in the legal, clerical, and mercantile worlds. The more familiar and indulgent view of eighteenth-century life, of the squire at peace with his tenants and labourers, was true—if it was true of anyone—for those not at the centre of power and influence. If this is true, then English conservatism cannot claim to enunciate a continuing tradition in any real sense, and must in fact wear the same label which Burke branded upon liberalism, that its doctrines were devised by 'sophistors, calculators and economists', although ironically Burke's continued depictions may have presented a more appealing vision than the squalid facts of the matter.

Old Corruption is also relevant to aesthetics—not at first glance the likeliest of topics, but one where a connexion exists. Although one might discuss at some length the most evident and brilliant use of the Old Corruption theme by artists, its depiction in the great satirical cartoons of the day from Hogarth through to Cruikshank, rather I should like here to draw attention to the importance of this world and its ambience for Charles Dickens, and beyond him for a little-recognized tradition of writers who perceived what might be termed the *urban non-dynamic* world of London in the nineteenth and early twentieth centuries, with its quaint survivals and inherent and pervasive irrationality so different from the industrial north. In the words of the French literary historian Louis Cazamian:

In childhood Dickens had known and loved the old-fashioned provincial life of Rochester and Chatham. In London he had lived in a lower-middle-class setting, and it had not been the terrors of industrialism that he suffered. In the unique metropolitan situation, where the oldest customs survived cheek-by-jowl with the most up-to-date, chance and temperament had cast Dickens on the side of the former. It was not the factories in working-class districts that he came to know but the small industries housed in old buildings, and the wretched businesses from which small shopkeepers and street-traders scraped a living. He saw the relics of the old economic order, with corporations and apprentices and outdated officials. He loved the monuments to the past which survived in picturesque corners of the City and the Strand . . . he appreciated the drowsy charm of the Temple . . . [and] explored the dusty corridors where legal tradition slumbered . . . [I]ndustrial expansion, the first railways . . . the flight to the towns . . . none of these attracted the young Dickens's attention.[66]

I would suggest that in works like *Bleak House* Dickens emerged as the greatest artistic delineator of Old Corruption, precisely catching its irrationality and the Kafkaesque terror of uncertainty this produced, and that his works ought largely to be read as a critique of this world, above all of its pre-modern and irrational character, rather than as a critique of industrial capitalism.[67] Nor is it really paradoxical that Dickens should have been so much of two minds about this world, hating its delay, abuses and injustice, yet loving its irrationality and eccentricity.

It remains to consider whether Old Corruption still exists. Some radical critics of contemporary English society, like E. P. Thompson, have viewed today's Establishment, with its 'old school tie' and 'military-industrial complex' as in some sense an extension in modern dress of 'the Thing' as attacked by Cobbett and Wade, although noting its distinctive differences. Thompson, in his unusually perceptive commentaries on this period and its implications for the present notes that 'if Old Corruption still presides over Oxford and Cambridge, yet London, the Civil Universities, the technical colleges etc., have long developed upon a different pattern'.[68] Although Thompson seems explicitly to reject a direct continuation between Old Corruption and any contemporary political formation,[69] yet he and others have perceived a similarity if not a direct connexion. Others would perhaps go further, stressing the lack of radical discontinuities in modern British history and the relative unimportance of industrialization in transforming Britain in the nineteenth century.[70] Although I am personally sympathetic to this view, and although the consensual nature of today's Establishment—battered as this consensus has been in the past decade—has been compellingly argued, the essential differences seem as clear as the similarities. In particular I believe that nothing whatever now remains of the pre-modern non-Weberian elements which formed so striking a part of Old Corruption, despite whatever superficial appearances there may be.[71] Despite their seeming resemblances, later systems of accumulation which may seem like Old Corruption took as their justification different sets of value and frames of reference. In this regard the radical, revolutionary nature of Victorian liberalism and reform becomes more apparent, as do the real bases of 'Victorianism': not sexual prudery or an apology for capitalist exploitation, but the imposition of rationality and 'modernity' upon the irrational and pre-modern—a gain for the ordinary man, not a loss—as well as individuality, the coincidence of merit and reward, and the extension of responsibility and of privacy.[72] The revision of sensibility which began in the Georgian period continues essentially unchanged to the present time, and is marked by frames of reference so different that it is indeed difficult, without effort, to place oneself amidst those which existed before.[73]

NOTES

1. That is to say, persons leaving between £500,000 and £1 million in personalty after 1809, when the probate valuations from which my research is derived begin in a usable form. This is discussed in my *Men of Property, op. cit.*, pp. 71–2.

2. R. A. Soloway, *Prelates and People: Ecclesiastical Social Thought in England, 1783–1852* (London, 1969), p. 72 n. 3.

3. It has been pointed out to me that, for instance, when Wellington said in 1830 that he commanded, as Prime Minister, virtually no patronage, his statement was not refuted; crown influence was widely regarded as—in the words of one 'Old Whig' in 1831—having been 'completely destroyed' since the eighteenth century. Brougham's attempted revival of Dunning's motion (in June 1822) similarly fell flat. Michael Brock, *The Great Reform Act* (London, 1973), p. 45 n. 78.

4. Archibald S. Foord, 'The Waning of the "Influence of the Crown" ' *English Historical Review*, LXII (1947). On this and related topics, see also J. R. Breiham, 'Economical Reform, 1785–1810' (Univ. of Cambridge Ph.D. thesis, 1977); J. E. D. Binney, *British Public Finance and Administration, 1774–1792* (Oxford, 1958); John Brooke, 'Placemen and Pensioners', in Sir Lewis Namier and John Brooke, *The House of Commons, 1754–1790* (Oxford, 1968), pp. 174–85; I. R. Christie, 'Economical Reform and "The Influence of the Crown, 1780" ', *Cambridge History Journal*, XII (1956); Emmeline Waley Cohen, *The Growth of the British Civil Service, 1780–1939* (London, 1941); J. Mordaunt Crook, 'The Office of Works and Economic Reform, 1780–82', and M. H. Port, 'Parliamentary Scrutiny and Treasury Stringency, 1828–1831', and 'Retrenchment and Reform: The Office of Woods and Works', in H. M. Colvin (ed.), *The History of the King's Works*, 6 Vols. (London, 1963–73), Vol. VI, *1782–1851*; D. L. Keir, 'Economical Reform, 1779–1787', *Law Quarterly Review*, I (1934); Betty Kemp, *King and Commons, 1660–1832* (London, 1957); E. A. Reitan, 'The Civil List in Eighteenth-Century British Politics: Parliamentary Supremacy versus the Independence of the Crown', *Historical Journal*, IX (1966); Gillian Sutherland (ed.), *Studies in the Growth of Nineteenth-Century Government* (London, 1972). The great classics by Halevy and Namier still remain extremely valuable, as does

Simon Maccoby, *English Radicalism, 1786–1832: From Paine to Cobbett* (London, 1955), pp. 81–7.

The most important recent study of this topic is Sir Norman Chester, *The English Administrative System, 1780–1870* (Oxford, 1981), esp. pp. 12–30, 58–66, 123–68. Its outline of the various steps by which sinecure posts were abolished (pp. 123–40) is especially valuable and impressive. Nevertheless I do not believe that this work—written from the perspective of an authority on public administration—takes sufficient note of the extent of the monetary rewards still possible under Old Corruption, especially in its extended definition. Significantly, none of the radical critics of Old Corruption like Wade and Cobbett appear to be mentioned, or their critique discussed. Nor is there any discussion of the great individual beneficiaries of Old Corruption, like Eldon, or of the size of their fortunes.

5. Foord, *loc. cit.*, p. 506.
6. John Steven Watson, *The Reign of George III, 1760–1815* (Oxford, 1960), pp. 249, 439.
7. Apart from the *Black Book*, systematic attacks upon Old Corruption emerge from the writings of radical commentators like Cobbett—whose works might be read as a very extended dissertation on this subject in all its aspects—and Francis Place. At least as systematic in their continuing descriptions and denunciations of Old Corruption between *c.* 1810 and 1835 were the radical journals of the period, especially *The Black Dwarf*, *The Independent Whig*, *The Poor Man's Conservative* and *The Poor Man's Guardian*. The various *Black Books* and *Red Books* offered extended analyses of corruption in all its manifestations. The most complete and interesting were edited by John Wade (1788–1875)—leader-writer to the *Spectator* and middle-class radical—*The Black Book: or, Corruption Unmasked* (London, 1820), and *The Extraordinary Black Book* (London, 1831; repr. New York, 1970). Parliamentary inquiries into sinecure offices were held in 1807, 1810 and 1831.
8. Were they? The answer seems to be that indeed they were: their figures were derived from official Civil List reports. In the only case in which I have been able to compare closely the claims made by the radicals with the *admitted* earnings of a large-scale government placeman or office-holder, Lord Eldon, the two are in surprisingly close accordance. In Wade's *Black Book, op. cit.*, pp. 36–7, it is claimed that Eldon's 'fixed income as speaker [i.e., of the House of Lords] and Lord Chancellor' was £18,000 p.a. In Horace Twiss's official and defensive *Public and Private Life of Lord Chancellor Eldon*, 3 Vols. (London, 1844), Vol. III, p. 315, it is stated that the 'total of what [Eldon] received from his court and from the speakership of the House of Lords, was an average of £17,556 per annum in [1801–6] and £16,118 in [1807–27]'. Wade also notes that Eldon had in his gift offices with an annual salary of £42,600 p.a., much of which went to his relatives, but does not include this with his income. Twiss is silent on this point. There is also the undeniable fact, referred to above, that many of the leading placemen left enormous personal estates at death although they often

inherited little and, not occasionally, began in rather meagre circumstances. As noted above, Eldon left £707,000 in personalty, in addition to land which had cost at least another £500,000 to purchase. Eldon's brother Lord Stowell, another senior judge, left £200,000. Wade notes in the *Black Book* (p. 37) that by 1820 Eldon had received 'more than £600,000 principal money' from his official salary alone.

9. Cited in Wade, *Black Book*, p. 7.

10. *Ibid.*, p. 6.

11. *Ibid.*, p. 8. Wade notes that since the previous official accounts, 'there has been a very considerable addition to the Pension-List. In the Ordnance department alone we have already noticed an addition of more than £6,000 per annum': *ibid.*, n.

12. *Ibid.*, pp. 11, 75–6. Namely Prothonotary in the Court of King's Bench, Ireland, Crown Officer, and Keeper of Declarations.

13. Wade, *Extraordinary Black Book*, p. 499.

14. Wade, *Black Book*, pp. 238–41.

15. Joel Hurstfield, 'Political Corruption in Modern England: The Historian's Problem', in Joel Hurstfield, *Freedom, Corruption and Government in Elizabethan England* (London, 1973), pp. 137–62. On this subject, see also Linda L. Peck, 'Corruption and Political Development in the Early Modern State: The Case of Britain', in Abraham S. Eisenstadt (ed.), *Before Watergate: Problems of Corruption in American Society* (Brooklyn, N.Y., 1979).

16. Foord, *loc. cit.*, p. 488.

17. *Ibid.*, pp. 494–7.

18. Norman Sykes, *Church and State in England in the 18th Century* (Cambridge, 1934), p. 409, citing a report of the Ecclesiastical Commissioners in 1835. The see of Llandaff, it should be noted, was usually held with another preferment.

19. Max Weber's theories of bureaucracy, modernization and rationality may be found in C. Wright Mills and H. H. Gerth (eds), *From Max Weber: Essays in Sociology* (Oxford, 1947), pp. 196–244; Max Weber, *The Theory of Social and Economic Organization* (Oxford, 1947), pp. 329–41; Max Weber, *Economy and Society* (Berkeley, 1978), pp. 956–1005. By far the most coherent explication of Weber's views in this area is Reinhard Bendix, *Max Weber: An Intellectual Portrait* (London, 1960), pp. 423–30. Bendix cogently notes that Weber 'was preoccupied throughout his career with the development of rationalism in Western civilization' (p. 33), and his works ought to be read with this clearly in mind.

20. Bendix has usefully summarized Weber's theories of bureaucratic organization: see *Max Weber, op. cit.*, p. 419. Among those relevant to the argument here: 'a bureaucratic organization . . . is conducted in accordance with the stipulated rules in an administrative agency characterized by three interrelated attributes: (a) the duty of each official to do certain types of work is delimited in terms of impersonal criteria; (b) the official is given the authority necessary to carry out his assigned functions; (c) the means of compulsion at his disposal are strictly limited, and the conditions under which their employment is

legitimate are clearly defined; . . . Every official's responsibilities and authority are part of a hierarchy of authority. Higher offices are assigned the duty of supervision, lower offices, the right of appeal. . . . Officials . . . do not own the resources necessary for the performance of their assigned functions but they are accountable for their use of these resources. Official business and private affairs, official revenue and private income are strictly separated. . . . Offices cannot be appropriated by their incumbents in the sense of private property that can be sold and inherited'.

Bendix also summarizes Weber as believing that 'the bureaucratic official's position is characterized by the following attributes: (1) He is personally free and appointed to his position on the basis of contract. (2) He exercises the authority delegated to him in accordance with impersonal rules, and his loyalty is enlisted on behalf of the faithful execution of his official duties. (3) his appointment and job placement are dependent upon his technical qualifications. (4) His administrative work is his full-time occupation. (5) His work is rewarded by a regular salary and by prospects of regular advancement in a lifetime career' (*ibid.*, p. 421).

Weber contrasted the modern-rational bureaucratic structure with what he termed 'patrimonalism', where government is organized as a direct extension of the royal household. This was characteristic, for instance, of early China, but must itself be contrasted with feudalism, which is organized, according to Weber, on the basis of fealty between ruler and vassal (*ibid.*, p. 119 n. 7). Thus it would seem that British Old Corruption, according to Weber's criteria, is more akin to 'Oriental despotism', as in the Ottoman empire, than a continuation of feudalism. This might usefully be kept in mind in trying to account for its emergence in Georgian England.

21. The Nelson dynasty's perpetual annuity continued to be paid until 1947, when the Attlee government ceased being grateful to the hero of Trafalgar. While large cash grants to victorious military commanders continued in Britain until 1919, the point is that they were given to the officer himself, not to his non-combatant relatives.

22. Wade, *Extraordinary Black Book, op. cit.*, pp. 488–9.

23. Boyd Hilton, *Corn, Cash, Commerce: The Economic Policies of the Tory Governments, 1815–1830* (Oxford 1977), p. 308 and n. 12.

24. Cited in E. S. Turner, *May It Please Your Lordship* (London, 1971), p. 192.

25. It is perhaps not far-fetched to identify other striking examples of the irrational in government or society in non-Western societies; their amusing benightedness offered much pleasure to Victorians whose view of Old Corruption was probably similar. For instance, J. R. McCulloch, the Benthamite Whig liberal economist, noted a good many in his monumental gazetteer-with-commentary, *A Dictionary, Geographical, Statistical and Historical of the Various Countries,* 2 Vols. (London,1844). Of Japanese jurisprudence, McCulloch states: 'It frequently happens, also, that the courts visit with punishment not only the delinquents themselves, but their relatives and dependents,

and even strangers who have accidentally been spectators of their crimes;': *ibid.*, Vol. II, p. 74. Of the Ottoman Empire—naturally a treasure house of corruption and irrationality in all its aspects— McCulloch notes that 'no previous study or preparation, nothing, in short, but the favour of the prince . . . is required to elevate individuals from the very lowest to the very highest stations! . . . When Marshal Marmont visited Constantinople, towards the close of the late sultan's reign, . . . a black eunuch was a general of brigade; and Achmet Pacha, who was then a general of cavalry, had been bred a shoemaker, and practised at a more recent period as a waterman in the harbour! And a short while subsequent to this the same Achmet Pacha was made *capitan pacha*, or high admiral of the fleet, of the duties of which station, it is hardly necessary to add, he knew no more than he did of the Principia of Newton': *ibid.*, p. 826.

It is perhaps not too far-fetched to note here that 'Irish humour', emphasizing the ludicrous illogicality and self-contradictions of Irishmen, especially Irish peasants, is possibly unique in Europe: elsewhere the peasantry is renowned for its shrewdness and hard bargaining abilities, especially towards outsiders.

Much has been written in social anthropology about the concept of rationality which is useful here. See especially Bryan R. Wilson (ed.), *Rationality* (Oxford, 1974), and the works of Lévy-Bruhl on the thought of 'primitive' people as 'pre-logical'.

26. I am not here necessarily referring to such survivals as brass-rubbings, cathedrals and castles, colourful fishing villages, or any of the other quaint 'olde world' stops on the tourist circuit. Their existence is too obvious to need pointing out and, rather often, not genuine. The locus of what I have in mind—whose ambience must perhaps be intuited or felt as much as described—is as often urban as rural, and exists in London at least as strongly as anywhere else. A brilliant recent synthesis which argues that all of Europe remained pre-modern and pre-industrial in its essential features until 1914 is Mayer, *The Persistence of the Old Regime, op. cit.*

27. See, for example, Leon Radzinowicz, *A History of English Criminal Law and its Administration from 1750*, 4 Vols. (London, 1948–68), Vol. I, *The Movement for Reform*, esp. Pt I and pp. 206–30.

28. Brock, *Great Reform Act, op. cit.*, p. 18.

29. *Ibid.*, p. 26, and see also pp. 17–36 for an excellent description of these haphazard and illogical features.

30. Sidney and Beatrice Webb, *English Local Government from the Revolution to the Municipal Corporations Act,* 9 Vols. (London, 1906–29), Vol. I, *The Manor and the Borough*, p. 116. As late as 1688 there occurred the trial for parricide of Philip Stanfield, 'the last person convicted in [Scotland] upon the ancient ordeal of *Bahr-rechtt* or Law of the Bier—the bleeding of the slain corpse at the murderer's touch', according to the famous criminal writer William Roughead, 'The Ordeal of Philip Stanfield', in his *Mainly Murder* (London, 1937).

31. The Salford Hundred Court Leet, for instance, combined the medieval and industrial in a remarkable fashion on 9 April 1828: 'The

jurors of our Lord the King upon their oaths present that at Ancoats Bridge within Ardwick . . . is a manufactory for making sal ammoniac next to the King's common highway . . . which emits great quantities of noisome and noxious fumes and vapours to the great nuisance of all the King's subjects passing and travelling there, by the default of Ebenezer Breillatt . . . Therefore he is in mercy . . . And they amerce him in five shillings . . .': Webb, *English Local Government*, *Vol. I*, p. 55 n. 1.

32. James Thorne, *Handbook to the Environs of London*, 2 Vols. (London, 1876; repr. Bath, 1970), Vol. I, p. 284.

33. The most provocative and uncompromising exposition of this view is Alan Macfarlane, *The Origins of English Individualism: The Family, Property and Social Transition* (Oxford, 1978). See also Karl Marx, *Capital*, 3 Vols. (London, 1867), Vol. I, pp. 717–24; Friedrich Engels, introduction to his *Socialism, Utopian and Scientific*, trans. E. Aveling (London, 1892), repr. in *Dynamics of Social Change: A Reader in Marxist Social Science*, ed. H. Selsam, D. Goldway and H. Martel (New York, 1970), pp. 241–5, 254–8; Perkin, *Origins of Modern English Society*, *op. cit.*, Chs. 1–3.

34. See Chapter 6, which details the virtual cessation of large-scale land purchase by post-1780 business magnates, might be read with this in mind.

35. Wade, *Black Book, op. cit.*, p. 6. A similar passage is retained in Wade, *Extraordinary Black Book*, p. 485.

36. Wade, *Black Book*, p. 6.

37. *Ibid.*, pp. 7–9.

38. Wade, *Extraordinary Black Book*, p. 487.

39. *Ibid.*

40. *Ibid.*, p. 485.

41. *Ibid.*, p. 495.

42. 'By the 1820s the "economical reform" movement had reduced the volume of patronage even in Scotland', where old-style government control had survived longer than in England: Brock, *Great Reform Act, op. cit.*, p. 32.

43. Chester, *English Administrative System, op. cit.*, p. 18. See also Brock, *Great Reform Act, op. cit.*, p. 36.

44. Chester, *op. cit.*, p. 20, citing Cobbett's *Parliamentary History of England*, Vol. xxi (11 Feb. 1780), col. 48.

45. *Ibid.*, p. 132. There were several exceptions to the prohibition on the buying and selling of offices, for example the sale of army commissions.

46. *Ibid.*, pp. 131–40.

47. As D. C. Moore has pointed out, the Whig reformers also contrasted 'legitimate' with 'illegitimate' electoral influence, and, as much as anything, 1832 was about the elimination of such 'illegitimate' influence, strongly associated with Tory borough-mongering: D. C. Moore, *The Politics of Deference: A Study of the Mid-Nineteenth Century Political System* (Hassocks, 1976). See also Chapter 3, p. 67–8.

One possible result of the ending of the period of Tory hegemony was the ending of the type of social mobility into the old ruling class, often startling and dramatic, which had previously been possible. In 1805, for instance, Lord Eldon told Henry Legge that both he and Admiral Cuthbert Collingwood, ennobled after Trafalgar, 'were class-fellows at Newcastle. We were placed in that school, *because neither his father nor mine could afford to place us elsewhere . . .*': Twiss, *Public and Private Life, op. cit.*, Vol. II, p. 118, cited in John Derry, 'Governing Temperament under Pitt and Liverpool', in John Cannon (ed.), *The Whig Ascendancy: Colloquies on Hanoverian England* (London, 1981), p. 145.

48. Cited in Brock, *Great Reform Act, op. cit.*, p. 36.
49. The royal Dukes of Gloucester and Cumberland, the Dukes of Wellington and Dorset, Lords Bute, Talbot, Eldon, Westmorland and Arden, the Archbishop of Canterbury and the Bishop of Winchester.
50. The six most recently created and hence junior United Kingdom barons on Chubb's list are given as follows: 'Glenlyon, A New Peer, later Lord of the Bedchamber . . . £1,000; Scarsdale, sons in the Army and Church . . . £2,400; Hopetown, Lord Lieut. of Linlithgowshire . . . £15,000; Lauderdale, A Retired Ambassador . . . £36,600; Fareham, Governor of the County of Cavan . . . £20,000; Loftus, Ely [*sic*], Governor of Fermanagh . . . £6,000'. (Hopetown and Lauderdale were Scottish earls who had recently received UK baronies.)
51. Perkin, *Origins, op. cit.*, pp. 271–339.
52. Sir Charles Trevelyan, main architect of the Northcote-Trevelyan reforms, noted in reply to objections made to him by Capt. H. H. O'Brien M.P. (sent to Gladstone on 11 January 1853) that 'Who are so successful in carrying off the prizes at competing scholarships, fellowships, etc. as the most expensively educated young men? Almost invariably, [they are] the sons of gentlemen, or those who by force of cultivation, good training and good society have acquired the feeling and habits of gentlemen. The tendency of the measure [i.e., the proposed reform] will, I am confident, be decidedly *aristocratic*, but it will be so in a good sense by securing for the public service those who are, in a true sense, . . . [of the governing class]. At present a mixed multitude is sent up, a large proportion of whom . . . are of an inferior rank of society . . . *and they are, in general, the least eligible of their respective ranks*': cited in Edward Hughes, 'Sir Charles Trevelyan and Civil Service Reform, 1853–5', *English Historical Review*, LXIV (1949), p. 72.

Earlier, speaking against the Reform Bill on 4 October 1831, the Earl of Harrowby protested against reforms 'by which the salaries of the great officers of the State have been reduced'. The Reform Bill, to Harrowby, was 'odiously aristocratical. By reducing the salaries . . . you leave the offices open only to the possessors of wealth; . . . you deprive the country of the power of calling into its service the most useful and the most brilliant talent which it possesses': *Hansard*, 3rd ser. VII, col. 1166 (4 Oct. 1831).
53. It must also be recognized that many of the costs of the unreformed system were exceedingly and prohibitively high. As is well known, the

Yorkshire election of 1807 may have cost its contestants over £250,000, while 'by 1830 a [borough] seat cost perhaps £1,200 to £1,800 a year, or £5,000–8,000 for the life of a parliament': Brock, *Great Reform Act*, *op. cit.*, p. 35. By 1832 what gains or rewards could compensate for such outlays?

54. See Rubinstein, *Men of Property*, *op. cit.*, Ch. 7; David Cannadine, 'The Landowner as Millionaire: The Finances of the Duke of Devonshire, c. 1800–c. 1926', *Agricultural History Review*, XXV (1977), XXVI (1978).

55. See the remarks in Greville's diary, 4 Dec. 1835, on the Whigs' perception of themselves as 'underdogs' in the patronage system: *The Greville Memoirs, 1814–1860*, ed. Lytton Strachey and Roger Fulford, 8 Vols. (London, 1938), Vol. III, pp. 264–5.

56. See Chapter 6.

57. Robert Southey told Lord Liverpool in 1817 that Cobbett's *Political Register* was 'read aloud in every alehouse': Brock, *Great Reform Act*, *op. cit.*, p. 17, citing Charles Duke Yonge, *Life and Administration of Robert Banks, Second Earl of Liverpool*, 3 Vols. (London, 1868), Vol. I, p. 298.

58. British radicalism has always included an important component of rationalism in all its dimensions—from anti-clericalism and the cult of the 'auto-didact' to the mechanics institute—which, though it predates the specific attack on Old Corruption, may well have found in its irrationalism a prime target. On this element in British radicalism, see, for example, Trygve R. Tholfsen, *Working Class Radicalism in Mid-Victorian England* (London, 1976), pp. 25–82, 243–57.

59. Patricia Hollis (ed.), *Class and Conflict in Nineteenth-Century England, 1815–1850* (London, 1973), pp. 4, 13–14, 214–23; Virginia Berridge, 'Popular Sunday Papers and Mid-Victorian Society', in George Boyce and James Curran (eds), *Newspaper History* (London, 1978), p. 259.

60. Berridge, *loc. cit.*, p. 259.

61. It is held among the Bentham MSS., University College, London, box 147. Cf. also his remarks on the 'suppression of places and pensions, without identifying the individuals who possessed them'.

62. David Roberts, 'Jeremy Bentham and the Victorian Administrative State', in Bhikhu Parekh (ed.), *Jeremy Bentham: Ten Critical Essays* (London, 1974), pp. 187, 189.

63. It might be suggested that *laissez-faire* in economics was advocated by Benthamites because it appeared to entail the most rational use of economic resources, according to political economics as it was understood at this time. More generally, and *pace* Dicey and his successors, the growth of rationality in government rather than the growth of *laissez-faire* might usefully be viewed as the central theme of British government between 1820 and 1880.

Recently L. J. Hume, in his *Bentham and Bureaucracy* (Cambridge, 1981), has also explicitly noted that 'Bentham's programme for government was an exercise in rational-legal authority in which every act, activity and office was legitimate only in so far as it was authorized by rules of law . . .' (p. 8).

64. Oliver MacDonagh's celebrated 'The Nineteenth-Century Revolution in Government: A Reappraisal', *Historical Journal*, I (1958), ought paradoxically to be read in this light.
65. See *ibid*.; Roberts, 'Jeremy Bentham and the Victorian Administrative State'; Henry Parris, 'The Nineteenth-Century Revolution in Government: A Reappraisal Reappraised', *Historical Journal*, III (1960); Jenifer Hart, 'Nineteenth-Century Social Reform: A Tory Interpretation of History', *Past and Present*, No. 31 (July 1965); L. J. Hume, 'Jeremy Bentham and the Nineteenth-Century Revolution in Government', *Historical Journal*, X (1967); William Thomas, *The Philosophical Radicals: Nine Studies in Theory and Practice, 1817–1841* (Oxford, 1979).

    The long persistence of the patronage system and government corruption must similarly have itself affected the attitudes of many in the direction of *laissez-faire* and against any extensions of government activity. It has been pointed out to me that Sydney Smith 'opposed the appointment of factory inspectors because he was sure that, if such were appointed, they would not inspect any factories'!
66. Louis Cazamian, *The Social Novel in England, 1830–1850: Dickens, Disraeli, Mrs Gaskell, Kingsley* (London, 1973), p. 121.
67. The 'dark side of Dickens' and his affinity with writers like Dostoyevsky and Kafka has apparently become a commonplace theme in Dickens criticism over the past thirty years, although to my knowledge no literary critic has yet linked this element in Dickens with Old Corruption or the pre-modern and irrational in an extended way. Useful recent works on Dickens include Alexander Welsh, *The City of Dickens* (Oxford, 1971) and F. S. Schwarzbach, *Dickens and the City* (London, 1979).

    The importance and credibility of Mayhew as an observer of the 'urban non-dynamic' aspect of London life is now widely recognized. Recent historical works which draw upon the Mayhew tradition include Gareth Stedman Jones, *Outcast London* (Oxford, 1971) and Raphael Samuel in several of his unpublished essays on the London working class, which emphasize the survival of the self-employed craftsman and artisan in old-fashioned, often bizarre trades rather than the modern and industrial side of London's economy. It is evident that the characteristics of this London have much in common with the German *Mittelstand*, at least those perceived in it by its German conservative apologists. One might further ask what the affinity is between Continental conservatives and the British tradition of 'radical patriotism' which embraced Cobbett, Dickens and Chesterton, who typically celebrated this element of London life.

    Among other writers of fiction after Dickens who worked in this tradition, one of the most notable and interesting was R. Austin Freeman (1862–1943), the creator of Dr Thorndyke, one of the immortals of classical detective fiction. Despite the fact that Thorndyke was the greatest 'scientific detective' and a supremely rational man, most of the Thorndyke stories are set in the urban non-dynamic areas of London (Covent Garden, Soho and the Inns of

Court), hero-worship the eccentric and self-employed craftsmen, especially in old and dying trades like clock-making and quality furniture building, and hinge upon irrational coincidences, utterly improbable plots, bizarre wills and the like. On Freeman, see Norman Donaldson, *In Search of Dr. Thorndyke* (Bowling Green, Ohio, 1971). It is probably not surprising to learn that Freeman was a notable figure in the eugenics movement and an evident right-winger whose stories are replete with unflattering references to 'foreign agitators'—generally Jews—and condemnations of mass society.

68. E. P. Thompson, 'The Peculiarities of the English', in his *The Poverty of Theory and Other Essays* (London, 1978), p. 52.

69. He states that 'Old Corruption has passed away, but a new and entirely different, predatory complex occupies the State . . . with its vast influence reaching into the Civil Service, the professions, and the trade union and labour movement itself . . .': *ibid.*, p. 56.

70. No doubt it is not in the light of day immediately obvious why, for example, a mastery of the literature of ancient Greece and Rome, demonstrated before the age of twenty-two, was considered the best possible training—indeed a *sine qua non*—for administering the Ministry of Fisheries, the Ministry of Aircraft Production, or of tropical colonies around the world, as it was for so long.

71. For a recent incisive work stressing the continuities, see, for example Wiener, *English Culture and the Decline of the Industrial Spirit, 1850–1980, op. cit.*

72. The main vehicle for this transformation was generally taken to be Christianity or, in Dickens, the 'good man' animated by Christianity or its morality. The resemblance at base of 'Victorianism' to socialism should also be clear.

73. In a subject marked by paradox nearly everywhere, two others might here be pointed out: France, which adopted the somewhat radical solution to its placemen and aristocratic parasites of decapitating them, did not industrialize or modernize until much later than Britain—which did so in the heyday of Old Corruption. Secondly, the typical aesthetic motif of the Georgian Age was the mannered, elegant and supremely civilized world of the later baroque, despite the underlying irrationality of its society, while the nineteenth century, successful at modernizing and rationalizing British society, was Romantic at heart.

10

Charles Dickens, R. Austin Freeman and the Spirit of London

'I am somewhat of an antiquity hunter, and am fond of exploring London in quest of relics of old times. These are principally to be found in the depths of the [C]ity, swallowed up and almost lost in a wilderness of brick and mortar . . .'

Washington Irving*

In this chapter I would like to suggest that a number of persistent notions about nineteenth-century London, its essential nature and ambiance found in many commentaries on Charles Dickens obscure the idiosyncratic and unique essence of London as a British city in the nineteenth century. This chapter will explore these unique features of London's evolution and attempt to show their importance for Dickens' writing; it will then turn to a much later and lesser-known writer, R. Austin Freeman (1862–1943) whose vision of London will help to specify these unique features and the implications they seemed to have several generations later. An understanding of these features, it will be further suggested, leads to a resituation of Dickens' politics: Dickens should in part be viewed as within the classical European conservative tradition. This understanding, furthermore, is important to coming to terms with several aspects of London's 'spirit'—its essential nature—which have been ill-explored or understated, but which are significant, in my view, in ways which go beyond the literary.

A number of perceptive literary critics, notably Alexander Welsh and F. S. Schwarzbach, have written extensively and, for the most part acutely on Dickens' perceptions of the city, and it is their view

---

* Washington Irving, 'London Antiquities', in *The Sketch-Book of Geoffrey Crayon, Gent.* (Irving's *Collected Works*, Vol. II, G. P. Putnam's Sons, New York, 1880 edn, p. 330)

of these which this chapter will examine and of which it will offer a critique.[1] By the 'city' these writers on Dickens of course mean London almost exclusively: 'Coketown' in the north and Rochester in the south are primarily minor appendages to Dickens' central vision of London, and to the importance in his writings of London as the primary exemplar of urban life. Dickens' vision of industrial 'Coketown', it will be suggested here, needs to be carefully contrasted with his perceptions of London, just as Britain's new industrial cities need to be contrasted in a variety of ways with London.

What such critics may be said to have in common is several related things: first, a failure to perceive the unique features of London's historical evolution and nature as a city and, secondly, a failure properly to distinguish these special characteristics of London from those of other large cities in Britain and Europe, especially from those genuinely new industrial and manufacturing towns which were growing up in the north of England, a category whose exemplar *par excellence* was Manchester. Allied with these misperceptions, though conceptually unrelated to them, is a near-blanket view of Dickens' image of London as virtually synonymous with death and degradation. To Welsh, for example, 'Death . . . is the common ground of the earthly city and of urban statistics in the nineteenth century'.[2] Schwarzbach's excellent study captures the ambiguous nature of Dickens' response to London to a far greater extent, perceptively noting Dickens' 'attraction of repulsion',[3] towards urban life, yet stating that 'the experience of the city was one of profound dislocation, of being cut off, physically and psychologically, from one's roots and one's community', and remarks that 'it is . . . by no means inappropriate to compare the experience of entering a life in the early nineteenth-century city in England to that of inmates of concentration camps in Germany . . .'.[4] Schwarzbach stresses the newness of London and its unparalleled expansion after 1800, and emphasizes 'how urban existence has become a new way of life, one in which traditional kinds of knowledge and customs no longer apply.'[5] London is 'the preeminently modern metropolis'.[6]

Such views, it will be argued here, seriously distort both the nature of London life and the complexities of Dickens' sensibility toward London. Nine salient elements, I should like to argue, were characteristic of nineteenth-century London and are essential both to coming to terms with Dickens' perceptions of London's special nature and of distinguishing London from other large British cities. In London, the old and antique—institutions and customs which had existed in many cases for centuries—survived and flourished to a *greater* extent than elsewhere in urban England: the old in all its aspects, including the old ruling class, older forms of capitalism and the professions, old institutions, old neighbourhoods and buildings, old trades. London was, in economic terms, the central city of the Empire—the 'Clearing-house of the World'—while lacking any substantial *factory* industries in the sense which delineated Manchester, Leeds or Newcastle. Indeed, London lacked a central and dominant industry—certainly in the sense that Manchester was synonymous with cotton, Leeds or Bradford with woollens, or Newcastle with colliery and engineering—although it was Britain's governmental centre, its financial/commercial capital, and the centre of wealth and display. London was chronically overpopulated, acting as a magnet for much of Britain's excess population, as it had since the seventeenth century or before.[7] This combination of an absence of manufacturing industry and overpopulation produced a *type* of working class and of poverty which was qualitatively different from that characteristic of the classical manufacturing towns in the northern cities.[8] In manufacturing areas working-class employment was marked by a cycle of periodical boom and bust, with most skilled and many unskilled workers knowing relative prosperity during the peaks of the trade cycle and the whole community knowing unemployment and universal hardship during depressions. London's working class, on the other hand, knew only chronic underemployment—a sort of urban Ireland—while London's economy was marked by the survival of small, preindustrial trades, sometimes seasonal in nature, small-scale and individual/familial, unmechanized, often, as depicted in Mayhew, eccentric, bizarre or hideously unpleasant, though *without* the routine, repetitive mass drudgery of the northern factories or the backbreaking dangers of the coal mines. Following from this, and as hinted at in Mayhew, the characteristic spirit and attitude of Londoners was one of individualism or eccentricity in behaviour, with antipathy to mass movements, and with mass working-class leadership, such as it was, characteristically provided by 'auto-didacts', shopkeepers, artisans, and what R. S. Neale has termed the 'middling classes'.[9] This individualism was mirrored by, and also reinforced by, London's enormous middle class and the individual/familial organization of most leading middle-class businesses (such as banks, merchant houses, and shops) and professions. Because of these characteristics, especially the lack of industrial capitalism and an organized *industrial* working class, London was supremely status conscious but it was seldom *class* conscious.[10] Because of this, too, London was divisible into a plethora of small and variegated social groupings. Similarly London was geographically divided into a formidable number of neighbourhoods, many of those in inner London old, settled and inward looking, and productive of a considerable local loyalty among their inhabitants. These represented an immensely wide scale of wealth and social status, from Mayfair to Jacob's Island, with every stratum in between (often resident side-by-side), and it is certainly inaccurate simply to bifurcate London into the rich and the poor, the latter consisting of the overwhelming majority, who were—to the wealthy or educated—barbaric, exotic and menacing. Finally, as Schwarzbach and others have pointed out, Dickens' attitude to London was extremely ambiguous—the 'attraction of repulsion'.[11] While this may rightly be linked to the extremes which London connoted in Dickens' own life, from Warren's Blacking Warehouse to his own Whittington-like rise to esteem and success, this attitude should also be linked to the inherent nature of London life and its *sui generis* features, of which, it need not be said, Dickens was in the main a wholly accurate observer and a writer uniquely sensitive to its peculiar essence.[12]

Of all the points made here, the most important and most misunderstood is the first. Those commentators on Dickens who emphasize the newness and extraordinary growth of London after 1800 miss the point that London was almost as populous, in relation to Britain's overall numbers, in 1700 as in 1850 and that, unlike Manchester or Birmingham, it was equally the most important city in Britain since William the Conqueror's time. Despite the 1666 Fire and relentless growth, central London comprised pre-existing housing, roads, neighbourhoods and memories which, rather than newness, were its most salient feature. Despite rapid mobility, families often lived in the same neighbourhood for generations, London neighbourhoods often possessing well-established reputations and persistent characteristics stemming in part from the fact that, before mass transport, workers had to live near their workplaces. Moreover, since inner London had not been built or developed as a unit, its neighbourhoods typically contained a patchwork of architectural styles dating from the medieval to the latest shops and jerry-built slums, dark, twisting, mysterious alleys, roadways, and riverside docks, and the absence of broad, straight avenues.

The old also survived in London by virtue of the fact that London was the seat of government which, until 1832, remained totally unreformed and which, even long after Reform, contained institutions of central importance (like the Inns of Court) which were—and even today are—unreformed. The ruling elite which largely governed unreformed Britain was one which used the existing institutions of the country for unparalleled rapacity and self-aggrandizement.[13] Although commonly depicted as a rural-based aristocracy and squirearchy—which of course in part it was— this elite was equally at home in, and dependent upon, Britain's older urban elite, the older professions and mercantile trades centred in London. Britain's ruling elite was also marked by a considerable degree of social mobility into the upper classes. Before it was broken by industrialization, the new movements for democracy and reform, and by the challenge of radicalism and resurgent nonconformity, perhaps the most striking feature of the English *ancien régime* was the uniformity of values, approaching a consensus, which it enjoyed throughout society, including London society, for most of the period, so much so that some historians have spoken of eighteenth-century Britain as a 'one-class society'.[14] An equally striking feature of the old regime and its institutions, and clearly of importance to Dickens' perceptions, was its irrationality in all spheres—whether in the unreformed constitution and the old laws or in the universality of nepotism, preferment and patronage rather than merit as the basis for employment and promotion— certainly anomalous in a country whose hallmarks were, it is often urged, an all-pervasive cash nexus and modernity in the Weberian sense.

Plainly, Dickens was centrally aware of these aspects of London (and English) society, and his sensibility was deeply affected by them. That he persistently returned to the theme of the antique and pre-modern nature of much of London society, and was both attracted by the quaintness and repelled by the inhumane and irrational side of the *ancien régime*, needs little reiteration.[15]

George Orwell and many other critics have drawn attention to the importance in Dickens' work of the old-fashioned 'London commercial bourgeoisie and their hangers-on—lawyers, clerks, tradesmen, innkeepers, small craftsmen and servants', and how 'in nearly all of his books one has a curious feeling that one is living in the first quarter of the nineteenth century'—that is, before Reform—even in works written many decades later.[16] As Harland S. Nelson has written in an extremely perceptive article, 'good places in Dickens are often old.' Nelson 'hear[s] a note of affection for the [Stagg] Gardeners', although 'it is not a very prepossessing spot'[17] consisting of (in Dickens' words) 'a little row of houses, with little squalid patches of ground before them, fenced off with old doors, barrel staves, scraps of tarpaulin,' etc.—an exceedingly typical Dickensian portrayal of 'dankness' and the 'urban non-dynamic' qualities we shall discuss below. Nelson cites Angus Wilson's description of 'a certain vague attachment to "old things" and "old buildings" ', but also notes Wilson's remark that Dickens suspected 'reverence for the past', and adds that Dickens was not attached to 'all old buildings, surely: not Tom-All-Alone's.'[18] Although both Wilson and Nelson are correct, they are, equally, far too diffident: Dickens was attached to 'old' things for the reasons suggested in Nelson's essay—the irregularity, diversity and humanity of the 'old-fashioned', and what he terms its 'plenitude, variety, unpredictable and delightful irregularity'.[19]

In Chapter 9 I termed the London world of survivals to which Dickens was particularly sensitive, as urban non-dynamic,[20] by which I meant the combination of irrationality, quaintness, dankness, pre-modernization and lack of full-scale industrial investment peculiarly characteristic of the London which Dickens knew. I would argue that these qualities, rather than growth, development, expansion and class divisions in the Marxist sense, are central to understanding the ambience of London between the early eighteenth century and around 1870. These qualities are, plainly, conceptually quite different, and linking them may seem difficult to justify, yet they are just those characteristics explicitly or implicitly connoted by the very term 'Dickensian'.

One element implicit in the urban non-dynamic is that London—especially central London—contains old-established and persisting communities relatively unaffected by London's growth. Dickens set much of Sketches by Boz, his earliest book and one of those most directly the product of his London youth, in such a community. 'Our parish, which, like all other parishes, is a little world of its own' is Dickens' comment on 'The Election for Beadle',[21] and other essays in the work describe various aspects of the life of what

appears to be a relatively settled and harmonious urban
community—the monthly loan society, practical jokes (in 'Our
Next-Door Neighbour') and, in the 'Scenes' section, 'apprentices
and shopmen ... busily engaged in cleaning and decking the
windows for the day', 'children waiting for the drawing of the first
bread' at bakers' shops, and 'goods in the shop-windows ...
invitingly arrayed.'[22] Doctors' Commons, the office of the old
ecclesiastical courts which had jurisdiction over probate and
divorces, and which is the subject of an essay in the same work, is
found by Dickens after 'crossing a quiet and shady court-yard,
paved with stone'. It is 'an old quaint-looking apartment, with
sunken windows, and black carved wainscoting, at the upper end of
which, seated at a raised platform, of semi-circular shape, were
about a dozen solemn-looking gentlemen in crimson gowns and
wigs.'[23]

   Dickens was equally well aware of the darker, more tragic, and
frightening depictions of London life which this work introduced as
a persistent theme in his writing—his famous sketch of 'Seven
Dials,' the notorious slum, the tragedy and pathos of London
streets at night, the scenes of urban decay—to the extent that many
believe that Dickens was employing the city as a general metaphor
for death. Such an interpretation is, in my view, misleading. There
can be little doubt that Dickens introduced to the standard
depictions of London life a new element of tragedy and realism but,
equally, Dickens saw the communities he knew and described as
long-established living entities, not merely as novel places of death.
A possible reason for this ambiguity is his well-known antipathy to
crowds and mobs, his surprising inability to depict or differentiate
members of the working class as individuals and, indeed, his general
lack of sympathy with or for the working classes. Orwell has
reminded us that the French 'revolutionaries appear to [Dickens]
simply as degraded savages—in fact, as lunatics',[24] while Anne
Humphreys has acutely compared 'Dickens' tendency to generalize
working-class life', his habit 'even when recounting the most
specific of his adventures, [of] project[ing] the overview rather than
the individual' adversely to Henry Mayhew's much more
individual depictions.[25] 'Dickens tends to distance himself from his
subject', while Mayhew's sketches are marked by a 'compulsive
search for details', an 'obsession with minutia', which 'particularize
the facts of slum life'[26]—qualities which, of course, are, to other
critics, virtually synonymous with Dickens' own literary style and

method. It may well be that readers of Dickens have inferred far too much about his general perceptions of London from this undoubted anomaly in his depiction of class.

Other contemporary observers of London life were also struck by its old-established and pre-existing communities, as well as its eccentric, individualistic occupational strata, and it would be useful to compare the impressions of two such writers, who viewed London contemporaneously with the young Dickens: Washington Irving, the famous American who lived in England in 1804–6 and 1815–22, and Charles Lamb, in his *Essays of Elia*. Irving's *Sketch-Book of Geoffrey Crayon, Gent.*, which appeared in 1820, contains a number of interesting essays, especially 'London Antiquities' and 'Little Britain', that focus on such neighbourhoods and on this aspect of London life. The two best-known pieces in the *Sketch-Book* are 'Rip Van Winkle' and 'The Legend of Sleepy Hollow', and it would be easy to dismiss Irving as an indulgent writer of whimsy, his impressions as those typical of many ingenuous American tourists then or since. Yet Irving was, beneath the surface, a hard-headed and even cynical observer who knew Tammany Hall from the inside and coined the phrase 'the almighty dollar' to describe America's 'great object of universal devotion', and his perceptions—with obvious and crucial differences—are rather similar to Dickens' own. Irving's essay 'Little Britain' begins by noting:

> In the centre of the great city of London lies a small neighborhood, consisting of a cluster of narrow streets and courts, of very venerable and debilitated houses, which goes by the name of Little Britain. Christ Church School and St. Bartholomew's Hospital bound it on the west; Smithfield and Long Lane on the north; Aldersgate Street, like an arm of the sea, divides it from the eastern part of the city. . . . Over this little territory . . . the great dome of St. Paul's . . . looks down with an air of motherly protection.[27]

After noting that long before 'rank and fashion rolled off to the west', Irving maintains:

> those thus fallen into decline Little Britain still bear traces of its former splendor. There are several houses ready to tumble down, the fronts of which are magnificently enriched with old oaken carvings of hideous faces, unknown birds, beasts, and fishes. . . . There are also, in Aldersgate Street, certain remains of what were once spacious and lordly family mansions, but which have in latter days been subdivided into several tenements.
> Here may often be found the family of a petty tradesman, with its

trumpery furniture, burrowing among the relics of antiquated finery, in great rambling time-stained apartments, with fretted ceilings, gilded cornices and enormous marble fireplaces.[28]

Irving observes that 'in this most venerable and sheltered little nest . . . I passed several quiet years of existence', the 'only independent gentleman of means of the neighbourhood', who 'managed to work my way into all the concerns and secrets of the place'.[29]

Little Britain may truly be called the heart's core of the city; the strong-hold of true John Bullism. It is a fragment of London as it was in its better days, with its antiquated folks and fashions. Here flourish in great preservation many of the holiday games and customs of yore. The inhabitants most religiously eat pancakes on Shrove Tuesday, hot-cross buns on Good Friday, and roast goose at Michaelmas; they send love-letters on Valentine's Day, burn the pope on the fifth of November, and kiss all the girls under the mistletoe at Christmas . . . They still believe in dreams and fortune-telling, and an old woman that lives in Bull-and-Mouth Street makes a tolerable subsistence by detecting stolen goods, and promising the girls good husbands. They are apt to be rendered uncomfortable by comets and eclipses; and if a dog howls dolefully at night, it is looked upon as a sure sign of death in the place. There are even many ghost stories current, particularly concerning the old mansion-houses; in several of which it is said strange sights are sometimes seen.[30]

Unlike both Dickens and Irving, Charles Lamb was a Londoner by birth and breeding, having been born in 1775 in Crown Office Row, Inner Temple, the son of a clerk to a member of Parliament. Lamb was educated at Christ's Hospital, then situated in the City of London, and worked for much of his career as a clerk in the East India Company's accounts department. Many of his celebrated *Essays of Elia*, especially the earlier ones in the series, written in 1820–21, describe the London which Lamb knew, the London of offices and clerks, with often eccentric and individualistic employees in a genteel but decaying environment; such essays were addressed to an audience to whom this milieu, though not necessarily its peculiarities, would have been familiar. The very first *Essay of Elia*, 'The South-Sea House', begins: 'Reader, in thy passage from the Bank—from which thou hast been receiving thy half-yearly dividends (supposing thou art a lean annuitant like myself) . . . didst thou never observe a melancholy looking, handsome brick and stone edifice to the left . . . South Sea house [?].'[31]

Although 'situated . . . in the very heart of stirring and living commerce', South Sea House has been bypassed by 'the hey-day of present prosperity' and, despite its location at the heart of the City, has been reduced to 'an indolence almost cloistral—which is delightful!'[32]

> With what reverence have I paced thy great bare rooms and courts at eventide! They spoke of the past:—the shade of some dead accountant. . . . But thy great dead tomes which scarce three degenerate clerks of the present day could lift from their enshrining shelves—with their old fantastic flourishes, and decorative rubic interlacings . . .[33]

At these offices remain 'stately porticos; imposing staircases . . . long worm-eaten tables, that have been mahogany, with tarnished gilt-leather coverings, supporting massy silver ink stands long since dry.'[34]

As to the clerks of South-Sea House ('which I remember . . . forty years back'): 'They generally partook of the genius of the place'.[35] Characteristically of the world of London's white-collar employees throughout the nineteenth century:

> They were mostly (for the establishment did not admit of superfluous salaries) bachelors. Generally (for they had not much to do) persons of a curious and speculative turn of mind. Old-fashioned, for a reason mentioned before. Humorists, for they were of all descriptions; and, not having been brought together in early life (which has a tendency to assimilate the members of corporate bodies to each other), but, for the most part, placed in this house in ripe or middle age, they necessarily carried into it their separate habits and oddities, unqualified, if I may so speak, as into a common stock. Hence they formed a sort of Noah's ark. Odd fish. A lay-monastery.[36]

In the case both of Irving and of Lamb, there is simply no hint that London was a place of death or degradation, but rather a world of innumerable small-scale localities and odd, eccentric individualists. To be sure, the purpose of entertainment is to entertain, and both Irving and Lamb may well have deliberately excluded any harrowing depiction of London's dark side which obviously existed and which both presumably knew existed well enough. On balance, however, one must surely acknowledge that Dickens' London has very much in common with that of Irving and Lamb, while, equally, differing markedly in sensibility from either.

Dickens, as critics like Schwarzbach have maintained, lacked a sense of the historical development of London—'It is precisely this awareness of the paradoxical continuity of ceaseless change in the city that marks Boz's urban observations. His city . . . is outside reference to traditional concepts of time and history'.[37] Most significantly, of course, Dickens added a new sense of realism virtually lacking in previous writers, certainly in Irving's complaisant description, introducing the elements of ugly and brutal poverty, death, and what I should like to term 'dankness', a quality pervasive throughout Dickens, crucial to our understanding of the *urban non-dynamic*, and much misunderstood.

By 'dankness' is meant the combination of squalidness, frowziness, dampness (often from river water), ramshakleness, seediness, decay, and the inappropriate and often repellent combination of the edible with wastes of all kinds (including human faeces) allied to the close proximity of incongruous occupations, tradesmen, smells and sights.* The qualities comprising dankness are the opposite of everything found in a twentieth-century suburban shopping centre, which is zoned, purpose-built, sanitized to the point of being anodyne, climate-controlled, lit by fluorescence. Dankness is also the opposite of the twentieth-century suburban ideal. Although it has its quaint, lively-vibrant, and hence attractive features it would, ultimately, be as repellent to twentieth-century Englishmen or Americans as a Bombay slum, and for many of the same reasons. Above all, dankness is repellent because of the lack of privacy and of adequate sanitation, particularly in the disguise and removal of human excrement. (Old Harmon, the wealthy dust contractor in *Our Mutual Friend*, though meant ironically, presents this facet of Dickens most directly.) Something of 'dankness' lingers, even today, in many English slums. A visit to a used clothing store, junk shop or second-hand dealer in a slum district will vividly recreate, at least in smell and sight, the repellent squalor which was pervasive in much of Dickens' London.

Descriptions of dankness run through most of Dickens' descriptions of London, from his earliest autobiographical memories to his considered later works. As Dickens became older and more fastidious, dankness became less and less a prominent part

* As with much else in coming to terms with Dickens' perceptions of London, it is difficult to be quite precise about what is meant. Often one must simply try to intuit what Dickens had in mind, as one term or mood linked together several things logically or conceptually separate (as in a dream).

of his imagery of London, possibly because he strove to develop a
new imagery of urban life, possibly because London itself had
changed. Plainly, dankness was deliberately used by Dickens to
describe, and as a metaphor for, scenes which he regarded as
especially unpleasant, like the vacant lots behind his childhood
house at Bayham Street, the 'frowzy fields, and cow-houses, and
dung hills, and dust heaps and ditches' near Mrs Toodle's Camden
Town home, or his famous description of the blacking warehouse of
odious memory, which

> was the last house on the left-hand side of the way, at old Hungerford
> Stairs. It was a crazy tumble-down old house, abutting of course on the
> river, and literally overun with rats. Its wainscotted rooms and its rotten
> floors and staircase . . . and the dirt and decay of the place, rise up visibly
> before me, as if I were there again.[38]

Although dankness and its associated metaphors are in large part
a deliberate literary contrivance, it is equally important to realize
that Dickens applied them only where he thought them realistically
appropriate, that is, to much of London. Because London slums are
characteristically and pre-eminently marked by the quality of
dankness, and Dickens was evidently fascinated by London slums,
it is easy to make one of two mistakes in approaching Dickens' use of
dankness: to assume that its qualities are a general description of *all*
urban slums, or that he was using it of all cities. In reality, the
characteristics of dankness were applied by Dickens especially to
the lower and lower-middle class world of the London he knew in
youth and middle age. But he occasionally thought dankness a
characteristic of upper-class London, when this London was pre-
modern and pre-technological. Equally, he confined dankness to
London's slums, *not* perceiving it in Coketown, whose slums were
ostensibly more miserable, poverty-stricken and jerry-built than
London's. Finally, dankness largely vanished with the coming of
artificially modern, large-scale investment and industrial
technological capitalism, whether in the form of a factory, a railway,
or even of public urban amenities.

Dankness among the London upper classes is found most
strikingly in *Dombey and Son* and (of course) *Bleak House*,
especially in its celebrated first chapter. Dombey and his wealth are,
in Schwarzbach's words 'a relic of the past . . . mercantile, placed
squarely in the eighteenth century'.[39] *Bleak House* is *ipso facto* a

description of the unreformed legal system, its delays and irrationality, such as existed at the time of Eldon. The riverside fog enveloping London still existed physically when *Hard Times* was published in 1852, but it had largely been dissipated by legal reform by then, in a metaphorical sense; in any case it is arguable whether many of the qualities we have ascribed to dankness-squalidness, frowziness, etc.—may properly be seen in Dickens' descriptions of the pre-Reform upper classes. The pervasive feeling implicit in Dickens' depictions of the pre-Reform legal world is fear—the fear of being caught up in a Kafkaesque world of irrational, obscurantist delay, pointless vexation, and ultimate injustice, which parallels Dickens' fear of lower-class mobs. When the element of dankness is not present, as in the Cheeryble warehouse's locale in the City, Dickens does depict, or at least hint at, the possibility of an Irving-like closed and comfortable organic neighbourhood.[40]

As in so much else, Dickens' attitude toward the old and unreformed is continuously one of ambiguity and even self-contradition. Possibly nowhere is this indicated more strikingly than in his attitude toward time. Dickens is pre-eminently the great English writer who cannot be compressed or made concise; indeed of all great writers, certainly of the Victorian period, Dickens is the one whose plots and characters appear to lose the most when sketched in thumbnail readers' guides and the like; he is, of course, *the* writer who cannot be skimmed or skipped. This is plainly deliberate artifice on Dickens part—his attitude here mirrors his attitude to life. Dickens would have fully agreed with G. K. Chesterton's adage that 'the heaviest chain ever tied to man is called a watch-chain', and his objections to time-discipline are perhaps similar to those suggested by E. P. Thompson.[41] Yet—paradoxically—Dickens could chomp loudly at the bit at the excessive and inhuman delay which accompanied Chancery suits or at the lengthy terms of imprisonment which occasionally and quite irrationally accompanied such suits or indebtedness. *Bleak House*, possibly Dickens' best work, is, of course, specifically about this theme, and had its origins in the actual punishments of the day. 'The Martyrs of Chancery', which appeared in *Household Words* in December 1850, and which may have influenced Dickens, depicts such victims of Chancery, then at Fleet Prison—for instance 'another miserable-looking object yonder-greasy, dirty and slovenly. He, too, is a Chancery prisoner. He has been so for twenty years. Why, he has not the slightest idea'.[42]

It must not, however, be supposed that Chancery never releases its
victims. We must be just to the laws of 'Equity'. There is actually a man
now in London whom they have positively let out of prison! They had,
however, prolonged his agonies during seventeen years. He was
committed for contempt in not paying certain costs, as he had been
ordered. He appealed from the order; but until his appeal was heard, he
had to remain in durance vile. The Court of Chancery, like all dignified
bodies, is never in a hurry . . .[43]

Dickens' soul revolted against this form of delay and this kind of
injustice.

That Coketown should be contrasted with pre-modern London
is controversial. Schwarzbach, for instance, has argued that 'the
vision of the city and the judgment of the urban experience in both
[*Hard Times* and *Bleak House*] are in fact strikingly similar.
Coketown is in a sense a direct extension of fogbound London'.[44]
This view is, I should like to suggest, inaccurate. There is no
question that Dickens vigorously disliked Coketown, as he disliked
the reality of Preston, Lancashire, which he visited briefly while
working on *Hard Times*. Clearly, it is a place of death and
degradation. But its essence is quite different from London's.
London's slums are a place of death because they are jungles where
only the strongest and most brutal survive; Coketown is a place
where men have become robots—the opposite, in fact, of Seven
Dials or Jacob's Island. 'Plenitude, variety, unpredictable and
delightful irregularity . . . the place where they are most directly
threatened is Coketown', Nelson has perceptively noted.[45]
Coketown

> contained several large streets all very like one another, and many small
> streets still more like one another, inhabited by people equally like one
> another, who all went in and out at the same hours, with the same sound
> upon the same pavements, to do the same work, and to whom every day
> was the same as yesterday and tomorrow, and every year the counterpart
> of the last and the next.[46]

In Coketown, machinery was king, not man:

> chimneys . . . were built in an immense variety of stunted and crooked
> shapes, as though every house put out a sign of the kind of people who
> might be expected to be born in it; among the multitude of Coketown,
> generically called 'the Hands'—a race who would have found more
> favour with some people, if Providence had seen fit to make them only
> hands, or, like the lower creatures of the seashore, only hands and
> stomachs . . .[47]

Coketown is dark and, indeed like London, full of a 'labyrinth of narrow courts upon courts',[48] but it is not *dank*. Its river is insalubrious, but this is because it 'ran purple with ill-smelling dye'[49]—the product of modern technology—just as its darkness is due, not to fog, but to its chimneys 'out of which interminable serpents of smoke trailed'.[50] Its misery in other words, is of an entirely new and different kind from London's.

There is considerable evidence, moreover, that Dickens had an extremely ambiguous attitude towards technology and mass industrialization. Nelson has noted Dickens' 1844 remark, written in Italy, that

> There are hundreds of parrots who will declaim to you in speech and print, by the hour together, on the degeneracy of the times in which a railroad is building across the water at Venice; instead of going down on their knees, the drivellers, and thanking Heaven that they live in a time when iron makes roads,instead of prison bars and engines for driving screws into the skulls of innocent men.[51]

There is little or nothing in Dickens' two co-authored, little-known, semi-factual portraits of industrial life, 'A Paper-Mill' and 'Plate Glass'—which appeared in 1850-1 in *Household Words*—to indicate any basic or ineradicable hostility to modern manufacturing industry *per se*.[52] In 'Plate Glass', indeed, Dickens includes a rather gratuitous panegyric to free trade and modern factory industry which would not have appeared out of place in the writings of McCulloch, Cobden or Bright.

> The manufacture of plate-glass adds another to the thousand and one instances of the advantages of unrestricted and unfettered trade. The great demand occasioned by the immediate fall in price consequent upon the New Tariff, produced this effect upon the Thames Plate Glass Works—They now manufacture as much plate-glass per week as was turned out in the days of Excise, in the same time, by all the works in the country put together. The Excise incubi clogged the operations of the workmen, and prevented every sort of improvement in the manufacture. . . . No improvement was according to [tariff] law, and the Exciseman put his veto upon every attempt of the sort. . . . Nor could plate glass ever have been used for transparent flooring or for door pannels [*sic*], or for a hundred other purposes, to which it is now advantageously and ornamentally applied.[53]

Dickens' use of the railway as a symbol of 'the dynamic and irresistible force of the future' in *Dombey and Son* has been commented upon perceptively by Schwarzbach and Nelson.[54] Nor did Dickens love the old for its own sake. As Nelson notes: 'Dickens was always ready to root out the obsolete growths of the past, whether the glacial bureaucracy of the Circumlocution Office or a legal labyrinth like Chancery; and the dreadful London slums . . . would have been pulled down if Dickens had had his way'.[55]

What factory and railway capitalism have in common is that they require a very great deal of capital investment, the widespread use of machinery and technology, and both a locale and a work-routine which is 'modern' in all senses—rational (in Weber's sense), scientific, independent of tradition or feudal bonds—and whose appearance and connotations are in all respects the opposite of the dankness of pre-modern London. Dickens, it should be reiterated, was by no means hostile to any of these. His attitude toward modern capital-intensive factory capitalism was ambiguous, just as it was to pre-modern London, but for opposite reasons. Dickens welcomed industrialization as a liberating, progressive force which would produce a higher standard of living for consumers and introduce rationality and simplicity into everyday life. He was appalled by the human cost of factory capitalism, the working-class automatons of 'Coketown' and forty other new manufacturing towns, as well, of course, as by the 'cash nexus' of Gradgrindism.[56] He loved the quaintness and eccentricity of pre-industrial London with its true human individuality. He both feared and was repelled by London's dankness and by the criminality of its perpetually underemployed proletariat, although, side-by-side with fear and repulsion, he was also plainly fascinated by the dark side of London. Dickens' reactions, it should be clear—however they are concealed and overlaid by his literary effects and devices—represent the feelings and emotions which any perceptive man of good will and humanitarianism might have toward these hallmarks of nineteenth-century England. Dickens' genius as a social commentator lay in recognizing and distinguishing these separate but overlapping spheres of Victorian life which were seldom evident to contemporary observers, while his goodness as a humanitarian lay in both his hatred of their evils, and his ability to discern their merits. How many of Dickens' contemporaries as social observers of Victorian England perceived all of these things? Arguably, none.

In the final analysis, Dickens, as it were, 'sided' with London against the north, because whereas both London and the north produced a poverty-stricken and miserable working class,

London's was a working class of individualists and eccentrics, while
the north's consisted of indistinguishable factory slaves whose
individuality had, like hope, been automatically abandoned upon
entering Coketown. Dickens was, of course, *par excellence* the
novelist of individualists, eccentrics and human oddities, above all
of individualists who are oblivious to the impression made by their
eccentricities upon others. Paradoxically, I should like to suggest,
this is also pre-eminently a London characteristic—paradoxically
because London was also the centre of status consciousness, that is,
of the judging and ranking of others according to their manners,
breeding, accent and behaviour. Despite this *caveat*, however, in
any stratum of society beneath the aristocracy and its imitators,
London was a city of individualists who *were* virtually oblivious to
one another. Its working classes, as we have seen, were disunited
and employed in small-scale trades and occupations rather than in
factories with their mass workforces. Equally, its middle classes
were employed as clerks in small offices—even the largest financial
and commercial institutions had surprisingly small office staffs—as
individual employees or business partners, in the free professions,
like the Law, which were organized on an individual basis—or as
freelance and generally struggling journalists, writers or artists and
the like. London contained, as well, thousands of the idle rich and
idle affluent with no occupations. It was the home of the English
eccentric, of clubland, of the bachelor existence and of the English
spinster, of people who talked chiefly to themselves. Dickens wrote,
moreover, of the era before the organization of business and
professional life had begun even to take the first steps toward
corporatism or the large-scale enterprise. The wealthiest London
merchant banks, on whose activities the economic fate of nations
often depended, had only a few dozen employees; even the Civil
Service departments, whose staff in this century is numbered in the
thousands, were at the time almost insignificantly small.

Finally, the period usually portrayed in Dickens' work—the first
quarter of the nineteenth century—was well before the era of late
Victorian and Edwardian pervasive middle-class conformity
produced in large measure by public-school attendance. Very few
middle-class sons below those with such immense wealth that the
father could actively contemplate withdrawal from business or
professional life to gentry status were sent to a public school before
about 1860 at the earliest. Prior to the reforms associated with
Thomas Arnold in the 1840s, moreover, public schools were

notorious centres of indiscipline, boy rebellions, brutality and lack
of supervision almost incomprehensible a generation later.[57] Once
again, Dickens may be best be seen as the mirror of his age.

II

Charles Dickens and his depiction of London are familiar from
childhood to every literate person in the world; it is safe to say that
the name and writings of R. Austin Freeman (1862–1943) are
unknown to the great majority of readers. If remembered at all,
Freeman is known as the creator of Dr Thorndyke, the scientific
detective, next to Sherlock Holmes probably the towering figure in
Edwardian detective fiction. Freeman also invented the 'inverted'
detective story, that is, one in which the culprit is known at the
outset and the plot revolves around his discovery and capture, not
around the identity of the villain.[58] Because of his important niche
in the annals of detective fiction Freeman is remembered, and his
works read, by anyone with a serious interest in this genre. Many of
his books are readily available in public libraries, and there is a
small, but dedicated and apparently growing Freeman cult
throughout the English-speaking world.[59] Two biographies of
Freeman have been published in recent decades.[60]

As an author, Freeman was neither more nor less than what he
purported to be, a good and lasting writer of Edwardian popular
fiction. He was not a great or distinguished writer in any sense:
except for Dr Thorndyke and Polton, Thorndyke's laboratory
assistant, his characters are two-dimensional; the range of emotion
and experience in his stories is stereotyped and limited; like most
Edwardian popular writers, he was unable to handle women or
sexual relationships, and his female characters are almost invariably
feeble examples of cardboard. Despite all of these qualifications,
there are a number of good reasons, as I hope to make clear, why it is
neither inappropriate nor misleading to compare and contrast
Freeman with Dickens. The depiction of London which occurs
again and again in the Thorndyke stories is, I believe, the foil and
natural outgrowth of the *urban non-dynamic* portrayal of London in
Dickens' works at seventy or eighty years' remove. So strikingly is
this the case that there seems little doubt that Freeman was actively
extending the vision of Dickens (whose writings he clearly knew
well)[61] in a way which is both original and, as it were, both

retrospectively illuminating of Dickens' endeavour and an important expression of the sensibility of London's unique spirit and ambience. The setting of his stories, the character of Dr Thorndyke, the bizarre and impossible nature of his plots, and the type of individual customarily found in his novels, it will be argued, are appropriate to coming to terms with the evolution of the *urban non-dynamic* since Dickens' time. Freeman's own extreme right-wing politics, his anti-semitic and racialist prejudices, and his long connexion with the eugenics movement are highly relevant as well, and must be discussed for their close connexion with the previous points.[62]

Central to understanding Freeman's relevance to this discussion is the locale in which must of his novels and stories are set.[63] Most are set, and 'habitually begin', in what Mayo has described as the 'quaint by-waters' of London 'which were destroyed by progress in his lifetime',[64] in the same *urban non-dynamic* areas of London—the Inns of Court, Soho, Bloomsbury and the City—which Dickens customarily portrayed. These give the Thorndyke stories much of their flavour, and Freeman—who continued to produce them until a year before his death—is most unusual, if not unique among his contemporaries, in portraying London in this manner rather than as a centre of the more typical urban qualities of perpetual motion, commerce, progress and modernity. Freeman freely admits these are survivals, hidden byways which survive by chance, but nonetheless they are of central importance in his perceptions of London. A few examples will suffice to indicate the nature of these:

> There is something almost uncanny in the transformation which falls upon the City of London when all the offices are closed and their denizens have departed to their suburban homes . . . [A] strange quiet descends upon the streets, and the silent, deserted by-ways take on the semblance of thoroughfares in some city of the dead.
>
> The mention of by-ways reminds me of another characteristic of this part of London. Modern, commonplace, and dull as is the aspect of the main streets, in the area behind them are hidden innumerable quaint and curious survivals from the past; antique taverns lurking in queer, crooked alleys and little scraps of ancient churchyards, green with the grass that sprang up afresh amidst the ashes of the Great Fire.[65]

> I walked on briskly up Fetter Lane until a narrow arched opening, bearing the superscription 'Nevill's Court', arrested my steps, and here I turned to encounter one of those surprises that lie in wait for the traveller in London by-ways. Expecting to find the grey squalor of the ordinary London court, I looked out from under the shadow of the arch

past a row of decent little shops through a vista full of light and colour—
a vista of ancient warm-toned roofs and walls relieved by sunlit foliage
. . . But if the court itself had been a surprise, this was a positive wonder,
a dream. Here, within earshot of the rumble of Fleet Street, I was in an
old-fashioned garden enclosed by high walls and, now that the gate was
shut, cut off from all sight and knowledge of the urban world that
seethed without . . . a grand old house, dark-eaved and venerable . . .[66]

Whenever my thoughts turn to that extraordinary case, there rises
before me the picture of a certain antique shop in a by-street of
Soho. . . . It was a queer little shop; an antique shop in both senses. For
not only were the goods that it contained one and all survivors from the
past, but the shop was an antique in itself. Indeed, it was probably a
more genuine museum piece than anything in its varied and venerable
stock, with its small-paned window bulging in a double curve . . . and
glazed with the original glass . . . I dated the shop at the first half of the
eighteenth century, basing my estimate on a pediment stone tablet at the
corner of the street; which set forth the name, 'Nassau Street in
Whetten's Buildings', and the date, 1734. It was a pleasant and friendly
shop, though dingy . . .[67]

Two features stand out even in a cursory view of Freeman's
depictions. First, whereas in Dickens' day nearly all of London,
apart from the wealthy West End and the outer suburbs, might be
seen as exhibiting the characteristics of the *urban non-dynamic*, the
quaint and antiquated, by the early part of this century[68] these had
definitely receded to a handful of hidden and forgotten areas in
central London often visible only after the crowd of office-workers
and shoppers had left for the suburbs. A few Thorndyke stories are
set in the slums of the East End, an area Freeman almost invariably
associates with charmless poverty, crime, socialist agitators and
unpleasant 'cosmopolitan' migrants. Freeman finds London's
eastern slums appealing only when they retain the small-scale
industries of skilled craftsmen, as the furniture makers of Curtain
Road and the Spitalfields silk weavers who were still, around 1930,
'working with the handloom as was done in the eighteenth
century'.[69] Secondly, to Freeman these survivals are hidden
treasures. Finding such an area, one stands in 'delighted
astonishment' before such 'a positive wonder, a dream'.[70] His
attitude, in other words, echoes Dickens' (and Irving's) own
essential delight at such survivals, but is entirely without Dickens'
sense of repulsion at their dankness—an element missing from
Freeman's perceptions—their criminality, or, naturally, their
strong association for Dickens with his childhood humiliations.

The small population remaining in such places, moreover, exhibits all of the pleasant and endearing qualities of Dickens' Londoners, especially eccentricity and individuality, but none of the unpleasant ones, especially criminality, which Dickens found.

It is obvious that Freeman was an arch-conservative whose vision of London was conservative not merely in the sense of prizing and admiring its quaint and old-fashioned survivals, but of possessing a conservative agenda behind his perceptions—conservative not only in the English Burkean sense, but in a way closely akin to Continental right-wing doctrines, desiderata, and hatreds. Freeman was, indeed, an explicit arch-conservative, and something ought to be said of his political ideas and their importance to his perceptions of London.

Of Freeman's early life surprisingly little is known. He was born in Soho, London, the son of a tailor. Remarkably, the place of his schooling was unknown even to his children and neither of his biographers has been able to trace it. Somehow Freeman was able to be educated as a physician at Middlesex Hospital, but was too poor to buy a practice and served, instead, as a physician to the British force in Ashanti from 1887 to 1891. He wrote an excellent book on his experiences,[71] and had a lifelong interest in eugenics and anthropology. Back in Britain, he began writing works of popular fiction as well as becoming increasingly involved in the eugenics movement.[72] It should be remarked that although he was both a physician and a well-known popular writer, he was always struggling and continued to write mainly to make money. He left only about £6,500 gross (£4,700 net) when he died in 1943.[73]

In 1921 Freeman published a considered work on eugenics and the 'racial' fate of mankind, entitled *Social Decay and Regeneration*. It contained an 'enthusiastic introduction'[74] by Havelock Ellis, and was widely reviewed. The eugenics movement, which had a wide following among intelligent men even in Britain, was centrally concerned with improving the quality of humanity by the selective breeding of 'superior' individuals and races, discouraging 'inferior' individuals and races from breeding, and the like. Freeman frequently made remarks in these writings which must strike us as simply repellent. No man of good will can, I believe, today read such statements of Freeman (or his fellow-eugenicists like Karl Pearson) as 'the shiploads of the sweepings of Eastern Europe that used to pour into the Port of London via Bremen and Rotterdam' or his division of the 'unfit' into two classes, the 'biologically unfit' (like deaf-mutes, who should be discouraged from marrying) and the 'socially unfit',[75] without thinking immediately of the extremes to which such sentiments were carried in Nazi Germany, an experience which has, of course, utterly discredited the eugenics movement. Nevertheless, it is important to realize that, prior to the 1930s, kindly and intelligent men and women—some, like the Webbs, on the left rather than the right—seriously debated the 'decline' of the European and British 'stock', suggesting remedies for this social ill without seeming to themselves or others to be lunatics or fringe extremists.[76]

Freeman was also a thoroughgoing racist and xenophobe. 'The negro race is admittedly far inferior to any white race', he wrote in *Social Decay and Regeneration*, and his Thorndyke stories are full of unflattering caricatures of many foreign groups, including Germans, Italians, Orientals and, above all, Jews. Although Freeman had no apparent contact with Jews,[77] and although stereotyped Jewish (and other foreign) characters were stocks-in-trade of Edwardian fiction, he appears to be simply obsessed by them, and Jewish characters gratuitously appear in nearly half of the Thorndyke stories.[78] Thorndyke's attitude to Jews was somewhat complex. Although one story concerns a 'Chicago–St Petersburg gang of anarchists' (!) and Jews appear throughout his stories as villains, they are also portrayed as victims and, occasionally and increasingly, as heroes. In one of his last (and best) novels, *Mr Polton Explains* (1940), Thorndyke's faithful laboratory assistant Polton is rescued at a crucial point by a solicitor named Cohen. Donaldson has speculated as to whether Freeman was making amends for his previous anti-semitism in the light of Hitler.[79] Like many essentially humane Englishmen who were anti-semites, Freeman was, apparently, cured of this disease when faced with endorsing Hitler's enormities.

Also central to Freeman's critique of society (in *Social Decay and Regeneration*) is what Mayo has termed his 'lament by a craftsman for his vision of the past. It provides an eloquent account of the tyranny of mechanism, and looks ahead to the evils of automation. Freeman . . . rejected collectivism . . . syndicalism and capitalism'.[80] Freeman continuously championed skilled and talented handcraftsmen, such as cabinetmakers, furniture artisans, old-fashioned clock and watchmakers, and the like, and the antique flavour of his fictional works is enhanced by his constant use of such craftsmen to indicate the vanishing urban communities of the past

'destroyed by progress in his lifetime'.[81] It is especially noteworthy
that Freeman invariably situates this lost or threatened utopia in
London, not in rural England. Whatever may have been the case
with Dickens, or with other analogous writers like Cobbett and
Chesterton, Freeman never considered rural England simply as an
earthly paradise, with the city as a metaphor for death. If anything,
it was London, especially central London, which almost alone
preserved these antiques traces of preindustrial craftsmanship and
skill.[82]

Freeman's vision and arguments—bizarre as they may often
seem—are fascinating and suggestive for a number of reasons which
cannot be explored here. They are clearly akin—given the obvious
cultural differences—to the ideas of the right-wing champions of
the German *Mittelstand*;[83] they must also be compared and
contrasted with the peculiarly British tradition of 'radical
patriotism', from Cobbett through to Orwell (and including
Dickens?). One would surely like to know to what extent Freeman
was *sui generis*.

What gives Freeman his primary relevance, however, is the
centrality he gives to London in his conservative perspective. In the
two generations separating Dickens from Freeman London had
undergone a profound transformation in every sense. The old
working classes of the West End and the City had moved eastward
and southward to the ever-spreading slums of south London and
the East End, where they developed, only from mid-century
onwards, the recognizable working-class institutions associated
with Cockney life.[84] Conversely, wealth and privilege, as well as the
middle business and professional classes, had moved westwards and
to London's new outer suburbs. The social classes became
increasingly divided in both economic and physical terms. More
importantly for this discussion of its ambience, London was
successfully and progressively modernized and rationalized in a
variety of key ways, ranging from greatly improved sewerage and
sanitation, the provision of board schools, reforms in local
government, and (perhaps centrally) a mass transit system based
upon railways, the underground, tramways and buses.[85] The
modernization of London was perhaps symbolized by the ruthless
destruction of many of the old courtyards, side-streets, disused
Inns of Court, and rookeries in the Covent Garden area—which
figure largely in the early Thorndyke stories—and by the
construction of Aldwych and Kingsway at the turn of the twentieth

century. London's builders and developers, both private and civic, were astonishingly brutal and uncaring in their treatment of the city's historic sites and neighbourhoods, often destroying the last remaining pre-Fire structures in an area without any sign of conscience at these gross acts of historical vandalism.[86]

One of the less mourned casualties of this process was 'dankness'. The social and physical reforms which transformed London, and which were part and parcel of Victorianism, had already begun in Dickens' lifetime. As the anonymous reviewer of the *Eclectic and Congregational Review* had discovered in 1865,

> Mr Dickens has now, to our knowledge, for sixteen years been haunted by a great Dust heap . . . he has been like a very Parisian chiffonier, industriously searching, with intense eye, among the sweepings, the odds and ends, and puddles of society. . . .
>
> Since the publication of ['Dust; or Ugliness Redeemed', *Household Words*, 1850] of course many of these heaps have been compelled to yield to that great Macadamizing spirit of change and progress, the railway line and station. The North London line now probably cuts right through the very region where stood Mr Boffin's Bower, and the vast heap of miserly old John Harmon.[87]

London had, in short, been increasingly purged of the characteristic features of dankness which Dickens found repellent (but which obsessed him), leaving only a benign, conservative residuum. The process which took place is something like that of a compound colour broken down and separated into its primary colour constituents, now distinct and apart, for previously London was perceived, and did contain, a jumble of often contradictory characteristics which existed side-by-side if not simultaneously.[88] Irving perceived London's *urban non-dynamic* as being composed of these elements a century before; by Freeman's time this aspect of London was not merely worthy of admiration, but was in many respects the embodiment of civilization's higher values now under attack from mass society, dangerous ideologies, and undesirable alien elements. Other writers of the period also perceived this element in London life. G. K. Chesterton of course comes readily to mind as a celebrated writer with a vision parallel to Freeman's in many ways, but Chesterton's endeavour was to conjure the extraordinary out of the ordinary, while Freeman's was to find the extraordinary alive and well.

A similar pattern of persistence and change had overtaken another distinctive feature of Dickens' London: the eccentricity and peculiarity of its individual characters. The oddity of Dickens' characters needs little amplification; this had a social basis in the occupations which typified Mayhew's London, albeit one which stemmed from the stark realities of London poverty. The characters in Freeman's novels were similarly eccentric, typically London bachelors (for example, one such typical creation, Daniel Penrose of *The Penrose Mystery* continually speaks in a mixture of puns and facetious allusions). Just as typically, they make bizarre and improbable wills, impossible to carry out, and mysteriously disappear. Finally, they are invariably upper-middle class in social status, living idly by virtue of a small inheritance or pension.[89] Although often annoying or infuriating in their eccentricity, these individualists are also viewed benignly, as lovable eccentrics. London—which was in fact the home of thousands of such eccentric, middle-class bachelors (and spinsters)[90]—has similarly been purged of any threatening element in these inhabitants. Poverty and crime there were, but these were confined to gangs, generally organized and led by foreigners and 'cosmopolitans' in the East End. The *urban non-dynamic* areas of central London were, by the twentieth century, lovingly quaint.

Freeman's depiction is symptomatic, too, of a bifurcation in the perception of London among writers of discernment which became increasingly evident from the mid-nineteenth century, with the ambiguities of Dickens' attitude replaced by a series of committed certainties. On the dark side, a long series of writers dwelt extensively and increasingly on the dark facets of London's life found by Welsh and Schwarzbach in Dickens, beginning, arguably and most strikingly, with James Thomson's great poem *The City of Dreadful Night* of 1874 and continuing through Gissing and a host of lesser portraitists of London slum degradation, like Arthur Morrison (in *A Child of the Jago*) and Israel Zangwill. On the other side there is even more: starting with innumerable popular writers, including nearly every writer of detective fiction, the focus is on London's imagined high life, as it is, of course, in whole or in part in the works of many important writers from Trollope through Arnold Bennett and far beyond. Dickens was writing arguably at the last historical moment before such a bifurcation became virtually a hallmark of writers on London, although London was probably not so strictly dichotomized as they believed—and as Freeman knew. More survived of the old and quaint in London than possible anywhere in England, although class-based spectacles made its identification increasingly difficult.

Dickens is, of course, customarily thought of as a radical in politics, and books have been written on this theme.[91] One of the more valuable results of viewing Freeman as, in some sense, the heir of one particular tendency in Dickens, is to question this virtual truism. Dickens was an extremely complex man, and cannot be readily fitted into any neat ideological category. Nevertheless, I should like to suggest that there is much in Dickens which should be seen as part of the classical European conservative tradition, rather than as a component of British radicalism. Russell Kirk, the American conservative theorist, listed among his 'six canons of conservative thought' the following general principles:

> 'Belief that . . . [p]olitical problems, at bottom, are religious and moral problems. A narrow rationality . . . cannot of itself satisfy human needs. . . . Affection for the proliferating variety and mystery of traditional life, as distinguished from the narrowing uniformity and equalitariansim and utilitarian aims of most radical systems. . . . Recognition that change and reform are not identical, and that innovation is a devouring conflagration more often than it is a torch of progress.[92]

It is difficult to think of a modern English writer to whom these principles might better apply. If Dickens was a conservative writer he was, of course, a highly *sui generis* one. Humphry House has recalled Lord Acton's remark that Dickens 'knows nothing of sin when it is not crime',[93] and it is this lack, as much as Dickens' ostensible radicalism, which separates him from, say, Hawthorne or Melville.

Dickens' affinity with much in the conservative tradition would have been recognized long ago, I believe, but for a number of important facts. First and most obviously, Dickens constantly espoused radical and reformist causes; he certainly felt no special affinity with the worst effects of pre-1832 Toryism. Secondly, and closely related to this, he seemed to have had a genuine feeling for the poor—at least through middle life and with the qualification that he loathed the mob. 'I have great faith in the poor . . . to the best of my ability I always endeavour to present them in a favourable light to the rich; and I shall never cease, I hope, until I die, to advocate their being made as happy and wise as the circumstances of their condition, in its utmost improvement, will admit of their becoming.'[94] It is important to realize, however, that never in any of his writings did Dickens offer a general, principled critique of

British society and its maldistribution of power and wealth or, still less, of private property as such. As the Mackenzies perceptively note, 'since childhood Dickens had been driven by a sense of unappeased grievance',[95] and much of his social criticism is highly specific to his own autobiography. Dickens obviously had no love for the pre-1832 Tory regime in Britain—which was largely based upon unequalled rapacity rather than Burkean principle[96]—but once its obvious abuses had been reformed (without revolution and often from within) Dickens' outrage gradually quieted. His own feelings for the poor must, moreover, be qualified. As the social historians Christopher Harvie, Graham Martin and Aaron Scharf have pointed out of the workhouse scenes in *Oliver Twist*:

> there is no attack on the personnel who run the institutions, nor are the inmates pictured as martyred saints, but as representatives of all conditions of distress, from honest poverty to downright criminality. It is on this lumping together, on this failure to use the workhouse as anything other than a social dustbin, that the attack is made.[97]

This particular 'lumping together' was at one, of course, with that in the Hungerford warehouse, and is based on Dickens' own experience as much as in his realism. His continuing attack on Manchester liberalism, utilitarianism and *laissez-faire* are fully consistent with classical conservatism, which was antipathetic to industrial capitalism and its consequences.[98] Unlike European socialists, who also attacked Manchester liberalism, Dickens offered not revolution but—as in *Hard Times*—'another world of Fancy, filled with fairy tale people of the circus, who come and go on the fringes of Coketown like wisps of imagination in the smoke'.[99]

There is evidence, moreover, that with maturity Dickens was losing whatever there had been of his youthful radicalism. He dedicated *Hard Times* to Thomas Carlyle. Carlyle is *sui generis* as much as is Dickens, but is frequently classified as in the mainstream of British and conservatism, attacking the 'cash-nexus' of *laissez-faire* society from a right-wing rather than a left-wing direction.[100] According to the Mackenzies, *Our Mutual Friend* 'laid the blame' for the rigour and maladministration of the Poor Laws 'at many doors—on parish guardians, misers, money lenders, speculators, political economists, lawyers, and politicans. But the connecting thread between them all was the curse of money'.[101] This is, I would suggest, as much as a right-wing as a left-wing indictment, and is strikingly similar to the anathemata of the continental extreme right at a slightly later date.[102] Within this context, Dickens' notably ambiguous attitude toward Jews as money-lenders, in *Oliver Twist* and *Our Mutual Friend*, is well known. Most tellingly, in 1865 Dickens sided with Carlyle, Tennyson and Ruskin against much of mid-Victorian liberal intelligentsia, including John Stuart Mill, Darwin and Huxley, in supporting Governor Eyre's suppression of a native revolt in Jamaica and the hanging of its leader. Dickens stated 'that platform-sympathy with the black—or the native, or the devil—afar off, and that platform indifference to our own countrymen at enormous odds in the midst of bloodshed and savagery, makes me stark wild'. Eyre's attackers in England 'badgered about New Zealanders and Hottentots, as if they were identical with men in clean shirts at Camberwell'.[103]

Dickens died at fifty-eight in 1870. Although unanswerable, it is worth considering the direction his thinking might have taken had he died at eighty-eight. He died just before the *fin-de-siècle* period of European culture which was hallmarked by nationalism, racism and anti-semitism, ever more strident national rivalries, pervasive social Darwinism, the 'scramble for Empire', and growing right- and left-wing attacks on bourgeois society, 'finance capital', and Europe's settled order. Crucially influenced by Germany's unification in 1871, the British phase of this period is often said to have begun with Disraeli's famous Crystal Palace speech of 1872. It is difficult to believe that Dickens would have remained wholly uninfluenced by these trends. By the time of his death he was, furthermore, a national institution virtually unique in British literary history. From relative youth Dickens had been freely compared to Shakespeare[104] and at the time of his death he occupied a position in the literary world roughly comparable to that held in the political sphere by Winston Churchill from 1940 to his death, a unique, almost superhuman living legend. Dickens was treated as virtual royalty when he set off for his second American tour in 1867;[105] he was 'the Queen's and the Prince of Wales' favourite novelist',[106] and would, it seems clear, inevitably have been offered a title—as with Tennyson's peerage—had he lived a few years longer. Dickens left £80,000 at his death—the equivalent of about £2 million in today's money—a remarkable sum for a writer, let alone one who rose from poverty and had no inherited means.

These facts would surely have affected Dickens' creative vision had he lived longer. One also suspects that the effluxion of time would have lent to the London of his youth, even to its formerly hateful characteristics, the glow of nostalgia.

There is, however, another reason why Dickens is rarely viewed as essentially a conservative, one more directly related to the main theme of this chapter, and the central point made by Welsh and Schwarzbach: Dickens' apparent hostility to the city and, in particular, his use of London as a general metaphor for death. If their views are correct, paradoxically this would seem only to add further weight to the situating of Dickens as in some sense in the European conservative tradition. Nineteenth-century conservatives are supposed to dislike cities as the locus and embodiment of modernity, tumult, revolutions, leftist agitators and so on, while preferring the preindustrial hierarchies of rural society as the embodiment of conservative values. Although Dickens is often seen as sharing this view, strangely this has not caused literary critics to view him as a conservative. Whatever his nostalgic perceptions of rural England, Dickens clearly did not prefer the preindustrial hierarchies of rural society and, rightly or wrongly, is strongly associated with reform and radicalism in Britain, apparently exhibiting compassion for the urban poor. This chapter has already touched upon the possibility that this perception, despite its ubiquity, is essentially mistaken.

More fundamental than this, however, is the possibility that the city, rather than the countryside, may be the locus of conservative ambience and sentiment. This view is, surely, an implausible and remote one in nineteenth-century Manchester or Leeds, but it is, perhaps, a novel and compelling way of viewing nineteenth-century London, whose evolution, unique characteristics, and special demographic circumstances marked it off as essentially different in nearly every way from the newer industrial cities of northern Britain. No one would wish to narrow Dickens' highly complex, individual and multi-faceted genius into a single cubicle, but it is to the special nature of London, with its age-old survivals and the simultaneous feelings of repulsion and nostalgia these were capable of engendering, that one must look in seeking to understand its most sensitive and perceptive observers.

NOTES

1. Welsh, *The City of Dickens, op. cit.*; Schwarzbach, *Dickens and the City, op. cit.* See also Christopher Hibbert, 'Dickens' London', in E. W. F. Tomlin (ed.), *Charles Dickens 1812–1870* (London, 1969),

and Anne Humphreys, 'Dickens and Mayhew on the London Poor', in Robert B. Partlow, Jr (ed.), *Dickens Studies Annual*, Vol. IV. (Carbondale, Ill., 1975). Hibbert's piece probably comes closest to perceiving Dickens' vision of London in the manner suggested in this chapter. Also interesting is John Greaves, 'Going Astray', in Robert B. Partlow, Jr (ed.), *Dickens Studies Annual*, Vol. III, (Carbondale, Ill., 1974).

2. Welsh, *The City*, *op. cit.*, p. 228.
3. Schwarzbach, *Dickens*, *op. cit.*, p. 23.
4. *Ibid.*, p. 10. Schwarzbach's unwonted and extreme analogy in my view is both offensive and nonsensical; this can be demonstrated clearly by asking oneself how many persons *voluntarily* migrated from the countryside to British cities in the nineteenth century and how many voluntarily entered a Nazi concentration camp.
5. *Ibid.*, p. 34.
6. *Ibid.*, p. 107.
7. E. A. Wrigley, 'A Simple Model of London's Importance in Changing English Society and Economy, 1650–1750', *Past and Present*, No. 327 (1967).
8. The best study of London poverty remains Stedman Jones, *Outcast London*, *op. cit.* See esp. pp. 19–51.
9. R. S. Neale, 'Class and Class Consciousness in Early Nineteenth-Century England: Three Classes or Five?', *Victorian Studies*, XII, No. 1 (1968).
10. See Chapter 3, esp. pp. 69–70.
11. Schwarzbach, *Dickens*, *op. cit.*, p. 23.
12. Obviously Dickens used metaphor, but literary critics have exaggerated the instances where Dickens' descriptions of contemporary London were intended as metaphor rather than as accurate observation. See, for instance, Alan R. Burke's remarks on London as 'labyrinth' or 'maze' in his interesting essay, 'The House of Chuzzlewit and The Architectural City', in *Dickens Studies Annual*, III, *op. cit.*
13. See Chapter 9, which should be read as a prelude to the arguments made here.
14. Laslett, *The World We Have Lost*, *op. cit.*, esp. pp. 23–41.
15. See, for instance, the very perceptive quotation from the critic Louis Cazamian cited in Chapter 9, p. 292.
16. George Orwell 'Charles Dickens' (1940) in *The Collected Essays, Journalism and Letters*, *op. cit.*, Vol I, pp. 456, 487.
17. Harland S. Nelson 'Stagg's Gardens: The Railways Through Dickens' World', in *Dickens Studies Annual*, Vol. III, p. 44.
18. *Ibid.* The Angus Wilson quote is from his *The World of Charles Dickens* (New York, 1970), p. 192.
19. Nelson, *loc. cit.*, p. 45.
20. See Chapter 9, p. 292.
21. Charles Dickens, *Sketches By Boz* (Oxford Illus. edn, 1957), p. 18.
22. 'The Streets—Morning'; *ibid.*, p. 51.
23. 'Doctor's Commons'; *ibid.*, p. 86.

24. Orwell, *loc. cit.*, p. 463.
25. Humphreys, *loc. cit.*, pp. 88, 87.
26. *Ibid.*, p. 78.
27. 'Little Britain', in *Collected Works*, *op. cit.*, Vol. II, p. 339.
28. *Ibid.*, p. 340.
29. *Ibid.*, p. 341.
30. *Ibid.*, pp. 342–3. Irving goes on to describe a neighbourhood rivalry somewhat similar to that in 'The Beadle' and others of the earlier *Sketches By Boz*.
31. 'The South-Sea House', in *The Complete Works and Letters of Charles Lamb* (Modern Library edn, New York, 1935), p. 3.
32. *Ibid.*, p. 4.
33. *Ibid.*
34. *Ibid.*, p. 3.
35. *Ibid.*, p. 4.
36. *Ibid.*, pp. 4–5.
37. Schwarzbach, *Dickens*, *op. cit.*, p. 35.
38. John Forster, *The Life of Charles Dickens*, 2 Vols. (Everyman edn, London, 1966) Vol. I, p. 21.
39. Schwarzbach, *Dickens*, *op. cit.*, p. 106.
40. *Nicholas Nickleby* (Oxford Illus. edn, 1950), p. 468.
41. E. P. Thompson, 'Time, Work-Discipline and Industrial Capitalism', *Past and Present*, No. 38 (1967). E. P. Thompson suggested that modern notions of time and scheduling emerged with industrial capitalism and were unknown before.
42. 'The Martyrs of Chancery', in A. E. Dyson (ed.), *Dickens: Bleak House, A Casebook* (London, 1969), p. 42.
43. *Ibid.*, p. 43. Note also Philip Hobsbaum's comments that 'the prototypes of this unending case [Jarndyce v. Jarndyce in *Bleak House*] are so numerous that even the legal historian, Sir William Holdsworth, declines to give examples. One instance, cited by Edgar Johnson, was the Day case, which at the time of Dickens' writing had been going on for seventeen years, and had involved at any given time between seventeen and forty lawyers, and had already incurred costs of £70,000. Even more long-drawn-out was the Jennings case, which crawled on throughout the nineteenth century, from seventeen years before Dickens's birth to forty-five years after he died, amassing as it went, costs of over £250,000! . . . the reason for such slowness of proceeding was that Chancery insisted on reviewing the whole of each case, no matter how trivial the point to be decided. Thus, the complexity of juridicial procedure bore no relation to the matter under discussion'. *A Reader's Guide to Charles Dickens* (New York, 1972), p. 163.
44. Schwarzbach, *Dickens*, *op. cit.*, p. 144.
45. Nelson, *loc. cit.*, p. 45.
46. *Hard Times* (Oxford Illus. edn, 1955), p. 22.
47. *Ibid.*, p. 63.
48. *Ibid.*
49. *Ibid.*, p. 22.
50. *Ibid.*

51. Cited in Nelson, *loc. cit.*, p. 44.

52. Harry Stone (ed.), *Charles Dickens' Uncollected Writings From Household Words 1850–1859*, 2 Vols., I (Bloomington, Ind., 1968) pp. 137–42 and 205–15. 'A Paper-Mill' was co-authored with Mark Lemon; 'Plate Glass' with W. H. Wills.

53. *Ibid.*, p. 214.

54. Schwarzbach, *Dickens*, *op. cit.*, p. 107; Nelson, *loc. cit.*

55. Nelson, *loc. cit.*, p. 43.

56. Both of the industrial sketches in *Household Words* were of factories located in (or just outside) Greater London (in Dartford and in Gravesend), not in the north. It is perhaps for this reason that Dickens did not encounter true mass factory capitalism of the kind he despised in *Hard Times*.

57. See, e.g. Gathorne-Hardy, *The Old School Tie*, *op. cit.*, pp. 37–68.

58. Probably one-half of today's television thrillers are in the 'inverted' format, and it is difficult to believe that no author ever wrote an 'inverted' detective story before Freeman's 'The Case of Oscar Brodsky' around 1912, but this is so.

59. *The Thorndyke File*, a quarterly journal on Freeman, has been published in America since 1976. In 1979 a suitable memorial was erected on Freeman's grave in Gravesend, Kent, by public subscription from among his enthusiasts. First editions of his rarer works fetch up to $1,800 on the American rare-book market.

60. Donaldson, *In Search of Dr Thorndyke*, *op. cit.*; Oliver Mayor, *The Anthropologist at Large* (Adelaide, 1980).

61. Mayo, *Anthropologist*, *op. cit.*, pp. 74, 123–5. Freeman once wrote a novel entitled *The Mystery of Angelina Frood* (!) attempting to solve the Drood case.

62. This chapter cannot, of course, discuss Freeman's merits or methods as a writer of detective stories. Nevertheless, something must be said of them. It is my opinion that Freeman was the best of all writers of the classical detective short story, superior to Conan Doyle and Chesterton. His stories are models of elegant dialogue and construction, and of truly astonishing deduction, and are warmly and charmingly written. His detective novels are not, in my view, generally as well-written and raise a set of problems which should be considered separately.

63. Nearly all of his stories are set in London or in nearby Kent, especially the Gravesend area. Those London stories not situated in the *urban non-dynamic* areas of inner London are generally set in Hampstead, which Freeman knew as a youth.

64. Mayo, *Anthropologist*, *op. cit.*, p. 15.

65. R. Austin Freeman, *Felo De Se?* (London, 1937), p. 11. The 'curious "hinterland"' in this novel is 'an area bounded by Cornhill, Gracechurch Street, Lombard Street, and Birchin Lane, and intersected by a maze of courts and alleys' (*ibid.*).

66. R. Austin Freeman, *The Eye of Osiris* (London, 1911), pp. 15–16. Nevill's Court was off Fetter Lane (near the Public Record Office) and was destroyed during the Blitz. See Michael G. Heeman and

Philip T. Asdell, 'On the Trails of Dr Freeman and Dr Thorndyke',
The Thorndyke File, No. 8 (Fall 1979).
67. R. Austin Freeman, *The Penrose Mystery*, (1936), p. 231, in *The
Stoneware Monkey and The Penrose Mystery: Two Dr Thorndyke
Novels* (Dover repr.; Intro. by E. F. Bleiler, New York, 1973). Both a
sign announcing 'Nassau Street in Wheetens Buildings' [*sic*] and the
place (though not the shop, of course) still exist. It is off Gerrard
Place, near Shaftesbury Avenue in London's 'Chinatown'. See David
Ian Chapman, 'Nassau Street in Whetten's Buildings', *The
Thorndyke File*, No. 13 (Spring 1982).
68 There are few clues in the Thorndyke stories as to precisely when they
are supposed to have occurred, but most certainly took place within a
long period from 1895 to 1930, i.e., a decade or so before they were
written.
69. Freeman, *The Stoneware Monkey*, *op. cit.*, (1939), p. 170. One must
also note that not one of the Thorndyke stories is set in the affluent
West End, and there is a total absence in Freeman of the 'body in the
library' country-house milieu so common during the classical period
of British detective fiction.
70. *Eye of Osiris*, *op. cit.*, p. 15.
71. *Travels and Life in Ashanti and Jaman* (London, 1898).
72. The biographical sketch here follows Mayo, *Anthropologist*, and
Donaldson, *Thorndyke*, both *op. cit.*
73. Mayo, *Anthropologist*, *op. cit.*, p. 169. The writing of detective fiction
was notoriously ill-paid during the inter-war period, even for the
Sayerses and Christies.
74. *Ibid.*, p. 110.
75. Cited *ibid.*, p. 111.
76. See for instance, Bernard Semmel, *Imperialism and Social Reform*
(London 1960) and G. R. Searle, *Eugenics and Politics in Britain:
1900–1914* (Leyden, 1976) for the pervasiveness of these ideas in
Edwardian England.
77. There has been some speculation that Freeman's father, a Soho tailor,
may have seen immigrant Jews as competitors.
78. In contrast, there is not a single Jewish character in the Sherlock
Holmes stories, which were written between 1891 and 1927.
79. Norman Donaldson, 'A Freeman Postscript', *Mystery and Detection
Annual, 1973*, p. 87.
80. Mayo, *Anthropologist*, *op. cit.*, p. 110.
81. Freeman's *Social Decay* also outlines an elaborate scheme for the
'superior classes' to form small communities and outbreed the
'inferior classes'. 'Superiority', it should be noted, was to be indicated
by possession of a skill or degree. It was not to be based upon race or
background. (Mayo, *Anthropologist*, *op. cit.*, p. 111–12).
82. There may thus be a conservative urban tradition in modern English
culture apart from the emphasis on rural England discussed, e.g., by
Martin Wiener in *English Culture*, *op. cit.* It should also be noted that
Thorndyke is the epitome of a 'scientific' detective. Freeman actively
supported science, so was not anti-science, as are many conservatives

who are anti-technology.
83. See David Blackbourn, 'The *Mittelstand* in German Society and Politics, 1871–1914', *Social History*, No. 4 (January 1977).
84. On London working classes see Stedman Jones, *Outcast London*, *op. cit.*
85. Francis Sheppard, *London 1808–70: The Infernal Wen* (London, 1971); T. C. Barker and Michael Robbins *A History of London Transport, I, The Nineteenth Century* (London, 1963); Nelson, *loc. cit.*; E. J. Hobsbawm, 'The Nineteenth-Century London Labour Market', in *Worlds of Labour: Further Studies in the History of Labour*, (London, 1984).
86. Hermione Hobhouse, *Lost London* (London, 1971) contains graphic pictorial evidence of this often wanton destruction.
87. [Anonymous] 'Mr Dickens' Romance of a Dust-heap', *Eclectic and Congregational Review*, (Nov. 1865); repr. in Philip Collins (ed.), *Dickens: The Critical Heritage*, (London, 1971), pp. 458–9.
88. This tendency is not unlike the 'rectification of ideology' described in Chapter 11.
89. Many Thorndyke novels also revolve around utterly improbable coincidences, i.e. two seemingly unconnected mysteries brought to Dr Thorndyke's attention are revealed as intimately connected. This and other irrational features of the Thorndyke stories should be contrasted with the supreme rationality of Dr Thorndyke, the 'scientific' detective.
90. In 1891 in the County of London there were 68,127 unmarried males aged 35 or over of a total male population (excluding widowers) aged 35 or over of 523,437; that is, 13.02 per cent. However, the percentage of bachelors aged 35 or over living in the middle-class areas of west and central London was higher: 16.69 per cent in the 12 middle-class districts of west and central London. It was highest in central London, rising to 29.36 per cent in the Strand district, 26.67 per cent in St Giles, 25.25 per cent in Westminster, and 18.67 per cent in the City, suggesting that Thorndyke (a bachelor living in rooms in King's Bench Walk in Inner Temple) and many of his clients conformed to a realistic model.
91. See, e.g. T. A. Jackson, *Charles Dickens: The Progress of a Radical* (1937; repr. New York, 1971).
92. Russell Kirk, *The Conservative Mind* (Chicago, 1960), pp. 7–8. Many other theorists of conservatism have made the same general point, e.g., Peter Viereck, *Conservatism from John Adams to Churchill* (New York, 1956).
93. Humphry House, 'The Macabre Dickens' (1947), in Stephen Wall (ed.), *Charles Dickens: A Critical Anthology* (Harmondsworth, 1970), p. 352.
94. Charles Dickens to James V. Staples, 3 April 1844, cited in Norman and Jeanne MacKenzie, *Dickens: A Life* (Oxford, 1979), p. 151.
95. *Ibid.*, p. 247. Dickens' attack on the evils of the Great Money System in *Our Mutual Friend* probably comes closest, but it is significant, and highly typical, that Dickens' conclusion is that money is no evil if

properly employed. 'It [*Our Mutual Friend*] is not a Marxist novel', Philip Hobsbaum remarks (*op. cit.*).

96. See Chapter 9.
97. Christopher Harvie, Graham Martin, Aron Scharf (eds), *Industrialisation and Culture, 1830–1914* (London, 1970), p. 122.
98. Viereck, *Conservatism, op. cit.*, esp. Ch. 1. Dickens of course differed from classical conservatives in a number of ways. For instance, he never accepted the British landed aristocracy as the natural and best rulers of society.
99. MacKenzie, *Dickens, op. cit.*, p. 264.
100. Viereck, *Conservatism, op. cit.*
101. MacKenzie, *Dickens, op. cit.*, p. 343.
102. On the German extreme right and its cultural values, see Fritz Stern, *The Politics of Cultural Despair* (Berkeley, Cal., 1961).
103. Dickens to William de Cerjat, 7 July 1865, cited in MacKenzie, *Dickens, op. cit.*, p. 346. On Dickens and Eyre, see Bernard Semmel, *The Governor Eyre Controversy* (London, 1962), pp. 114–15.
104. Collins, *Critical Heritage, op. cit.*, pp. 3–4.
105. *Ibid.*, p. 15.
106. *Ibid.*

11

British Radicalism and the 'Dark Side' of Populism

Comparative history is at once the most valuable and most dubious way of writing history: valuable because of the light which such comparisons uniquely shed on events and tendencies in one country by tracing the nature and development of similar patterns elsewhere, dubious for the equally compelling reason that all national histories are unique, and even societies which most closely resemble one another are essentially dissimilar in their fundamental bases and evolution—unfortunately for the historian in ways which are far from obvious. This chapter is an exercise in comparative history and is therefore open to the objection made here; hopefully the intrinsic value of the historical comparisons will in this case outweigh the disadvantages. The purpose of this chapter is to draw attention to the similarities and affinities between many aspects of English radical thought of the eighteenth and nineteenth centuries and what has come to be known as the 'dark side' of the populist movement as it existed in America between 1880 and 1914 and in Australia—where a very similar but lesser-known populist movement emerged—between about 1890 and the 1930s.

The concept of populism's 'dark side' will be familiar to most historians of the United States, for whom the notion and its rebuttals will be recognizable as the subject of a long-standing debate. For them and most others, the parallel development of a thoroughgoing populist movement in Australia with similar characteristics will surely be less familiar, while the perception of its analogue in Britain will probably be a novelty, and one must of course immediately begin the discussion by outlining what is meant by populism and its 'dark side'.[1] Before so doing, however, it is necessary to make a few general points and observations. First, it

should go without saying that few if any populists believed in or
illustrated all of the features which will be outlined below, any more
than all conservatives or Marxists, or adherents of any other
ideology or creed, profess belief in or demonstrate the
characteristics of its most full-blown doctrines. Secondly, to
reiterate a point made above, it is equally true that to claim a
commonality among any set of beliefs among individual writers and
political activists more than a century apart in different parts of the
world is likely to distort not so much the ideas of these men but the
societal and historical contexts in which they lived. Although this is
true, it is also true, as will be seen, that in this case at least the
historical and societal contexts in which these varieties of populism
arose were similar enough to make the comparison a useful one.
Thirdly, the discussion of populism here is limited to the three
English-speaking countries of Britain, North America and
Australia, and quite specifically excludes other manifestations of
what some historians and political scientists have also included as
instances of the term: the original populist movement in
nineteenth-century Russia from which the movement takes its
name, the activities of more recent movements and leaders like
Poujadism in France, Peronism in Argentina, or various Third
World Bonapartist dictators like Nkrumah and Sukarno.[2]
Additionally, this discussion is limited, within the three countries,
to the time-spans noted above, and also excludes leaders or
movements sometimes termed 'populist' from other eras—Huey
Long in the United States or Enoch Powell in Britain, for instance.

In my view, the type of populism which those historians who
perceive a 'dark side' identify has more than a dozen salient and
common characteristics and features which link together its
manifestations in America and Australia with a significant strand in
British radicalism seventy or one hundred years earlier. First, and
centrally, this strand of populism posits what might be and is
frequently termed a 'conspiracy theory' view both of history and of
the world today, in which, most centrally, a malign ruling elite
exploits and enslaves the 'ordinary people'.[3] This malign ruling
elite normally comprises the aristocracy and the leading financial
and banking magnates situated at a distance in the metropolis of that
country, or internationally and ultimately in a world metropolis
where central political and financial power is held. The key to the
domination of the ruling elite lies in its financial power. Both the
critique of the ruling elite offered by populism and the solution to

ruling elite oppression offered by populism revolve heavily around the banking and financial systems and their fundamental reform and restructuring. The ruling elite, according to populism, is thoroughly corrupt and parasitical, earning its wealth through financial manipulation, through unearned increments of usurious debt repayments or landed rents, or by open corruption.

Following from this, the main instrument of the ruling elite's control over the 'ordinary people' is often the debt system, which enslaves the majority of ordinary people either by charging usurious interest rates on personal debt repayment or indirectly by raising taxes, especially the taxes on the income and expenditure of the poor, to repay the national debt which is largely owed to the same elite of aristocrats and financial magnates. Populism is a movement of the debtor class and is especially attractive during periods of deflation. It is often associated with so-called 'under-consumptionist' theories of the economy and with 'funny money' notions of currency reform. Indeed, the currency in all its aspects is typically a central and ever-present concern of populist theory.

Populists are fond of personalizing and identifying the members of the ruling elite by name, often writing books with titles like *The History of the Great American Fortunes*, *The Sixty Rich Families Who Rule Australia*, and, as will be argued, *The Black Book, or Corruption Unmasked* which listed the names of thousands of government placemen and beneficiaries of 'Old Corruption' in early nineteenth-century Britain.

In the populist critique there is regularly a strong and evident element of anti-semitism, with 'Jewish money power' routinely posited as constituting a major portion of the malign financial elite responsible for exploiting and controlling the ordinary people. When other discernible groups or interests, such as Scotsmen, Quakers, the City of London, Wall Street, and the British aristocracy, rather than Jews, are perceived as central to this critique, they are credited with almost precisely the same evil characteristics which nineteenth-century anti-semites invariably ascribed to Jews—parasitism, usury, profiting from octopus-like control of governments and institutions, constituting a mysterious, all-powerful clique, knowing no national loyalties, and so on—in what might be termed an *ersatz* anti-semitism.

Further, there is usually a strong tinge of xenophobia and racism in other manifestations of populism, such as British radicalism's belief in the 'Saxon virtues' corrupted by the 'Norman yoke', or Australian populism's strong advocacy of an anti-Oriental 'White Australia' policy. Populism is not internationalist.

Notwithstanding any of these points, by definition populism advocates a radical democratic popular sovereignty in politics and therefore seems to constitute a radical left-wing attack on the oligarchy or aristocratic government, popular sovereignty based upon universal manhood suffrage being seen as the only source of political legitimacy. In the programme of American populism, democratic elections were to be extended by such measures as the initiative, referendum, and recall procedures. It must be stressed that one must believe in popular sovereignty and democratic electoral procedures to be termed a populist; those who merely hold, say, extreme right-wing attitudes associated with populism's 'dark side' cannot be properly situated in the populist tradition unless they are also advocates of radical popular sovereignty.

Populism is strongly associated with auto-didacticism and the self-taught 'ordinary man' and often regards the knowledge of 'experts' with suspicion. It is also strongly associated with eccentrics and faddists of various sorts, with believers in the weird and bizarre, with cranks and 'ratbags' with 'secret knowledge' and pseudo-scientific theories, individualistic religious beliefs and free thought.

Along with this is commonly what might be termed the 'cult of the whole man' in this strand of populist thought, a concept which normally embodies an opposition to the division of labour found in modern industrial societies, and an emphasis upon manual, creative work and a mistrust of most urban traders, merchants and bankers and of the products of modern mass society. Traditional rural society is often, but not always, said to be the main locus of the 'whole man'.

Thus far little has been said about the social classes or groups likely to be drawn to this strand of populism. It seems clear that, to a disproportionate extent, its appeal is to marginalized rural groups suffering perceived relative deprivation and economic distress during a period of rapid urbanization, combined with a depressed rural economy. Plainly this represents the social basis of much American populism, and is also parallelled both to some extent in the Australian case and in the case of many eighteenth-century British radicals including the most thoroughgoing radical of this stamp, William Cobbett. The rural social base of populism in itself goes a long way toward explaining some of the characteristics which have been noted—its central mistrust of the urban elite, its emphasis on the manual, creative 'whole man', even its concern with currency and debt. Nevertheless, it is simply untrue that populism is exclusively a rural movement. In none of the three countries was this so. In particular, the populist intelligentsia, if such a term is applicable, was certainly not rural-based but urban-based. In Australia and Britain populism took on an urban and even industrial profile at least as often as a rural one. In these societies it is likely that populism was to be found among marginalized urban groups made redundant by the growth of large-scale industrialization.

Although the social bases of populism were instrumental in determining its thrust and aims, other factors were just as significant. Populism was not, in my view, identical or even similar to any other recognizable modern ideology, although its obvious affinities with fascism have been noted by some historians. Nevertheless, it has clearly never been a form of fascism—to take one evident difference, populism believes in popular sovereignty and is neither elitist nor does it advocate a dictatorship. Nor is populism a form of Marxism, although there are again many features in common, especially with what is sometimes termed 'vulgar Marxism', for instance the propensity to identify by name the chief malefactors of great wealth. Populism lacks a consistent world-view and is largely lacking in the systematic element of the critique found in historical materialism. Finally, populism appears to constitute an extension of the radical democratic tradition; indeed, some would claim that it *is* the radical democratic tradition, and certainly British radicalism contained most of the seeds of the electoral reforms of the nineteenth century. Nevertheless, it is wrong in my view to see the 'dark side' of populism, with its racism and conspiracy theories, as anything but inimical to the libertarian tradition which has gone hand-in-hand with increasing democracy. It is also unclear whether populism should be seen as a precursor to welfare-state liberalism of the type which emerged in Britain and America, with its strong policies of centralization and incorporation of well-educated left-liberal opinion makers and bureaucrats into the governing elite.[4]

It is, I should suggest, the very difficulty of fitting populism neatly into the recognizable ideological spectrum which is the chief cause of the mystery which has surrounded it: populism simply

does not fit neatly into the familiar modern ideological spectrum of
Marxism/socialism/liberalism/conservatism/facism.[5] It is possibly
for this reason, too, that its relevance to understanding British
radicalism has been disguised for so long.

I would suggest that populism should be seen as associated with a
literate artisan, farming or skilled working class *lacking* in one of the
accepted and consistent ideological world-views and *outside* the
hegemonic knowledge/value system. It is for this reason that
populism is so heavily associated with auto-didacts and the self-
educated. Populism is *par excellence* the ideology of the talented,
self-taught scribbler, especially one with an inherent disrespect for
the learning or knowledge of experts or opinion-makers, or for the
authority of the ruling elite. It is as difficult to imagine an Oxford-
or Harvard-educated populist as to imagine one who was a Wall
Street stockbroker, and for similar reasons.

For these reasons, I would also suggest that populism all but
vanishes in the English-speaking world with increased education,
sophistication and modernity, and with the rise of a hegemonic
knowledge and value-system (which may take different forms) and
with the evolving role of 'intellectuals' in the English-speaking
world. Whatever remains of the populist tradition today may be
found, in my view, in the faddists of 'secret knowledge', the
underground of pseudo-science, secret historical facts, and extreme
libertarian beliefs, which flourish in near-complete obscurity,
ignored, it would seem, by the university-educated, their studies,
and their journals. Ideologically, in so far as this surviving populist
stream can be identified or situated, it seems clearly associated with
the political far right, although totally removed from the political
mainstream or from the public agenda of the contemporary
mainstream right. One must turn to the lunatic fringe of right-wing
movements and writings in the contemporary West to find whatever
exists of the contemporary populist genre.[6]

The last point, which follows from this, is that the problems of
populism, its origins, typical programme, and social bases, are
essentially questions in the sociology of knowledge rather than in
political ideology or the history of social classes. By this I mean that
the populist tradition might be seen as concerned rather more than
anything else with what is true knowledge and information and with
the dark elitist forces which keep this knowledge from becoming
generally known and commonly discussed. To populists, what the
ruling elite conspires to protect and conceal, above all else, is

knowledge of the true state of the world. Such a concealment is anterior to and necessary for the protection of its privileged position; as much as a conspiracy over money and finance the ruling elite is engaged in a conspiracy over history and the nature of political power.

Because it is so well-surveyed in recent American historiography, the debate about the 'dark side' of American populism will not be fully discussed here. As is generally known, from the 1950s an important and controversial school of interpretation about American populism arose which drew attention to those 'dark' features outlined above. Its major protagonist was the distinguished historian Richard Hofstadter, in works like *The Age of Reform* and *The Paranoid Style in American Politics and Other Essays*; Hofstadter was joined in his critique by other historians like Victor C. Ferkiss.[7] Centring on the anti-semitism of populist writers like 'Coin' Harvey, the movement's persistent anglophobia, anti-Wall Street and anti-finance capital streaks, and its pervasive anti-intellectuaism, as well as on its propensiy for 'crank' ideas in a variety of fields, these writers strongly contrasted populism with progressivism and New Deal liberalism, linking it with the extreme right of the political spectrum rather than the left. This interpretation contrasted with the older view of populism which saw it as a progressive and radical movement, and it was soon answered by other historians like Walker T. K. Nugent and Norman Pollack, who argued that the Hofstadter interpretation was exaggerated and misleading.[8] Apparently, here the matter rests and the debate—as is the inexplicable habit of such historiographical exchanges—has become somewhat *passé* during the past ten or fifteen years. As an outsider, it seems to me that the particular ambience and congruence of 'dark' attitudes pointed to by Hofstadter has not been successfully or persuasively refuted by its opponents' rejoinders, and that a strong case remains that Hofstadter was correct in the final analysis, although he may well have overemphasized particular features of American populism in a misleading way. It is the congruence and combination of the ideas and attitudes described above—a *gestalt*, if you will—which should be regarded as of crucial importance in identifying and distinguishing populism from other ideological movements.

Although the main outlines at least of American populism may be at least superficially familiar to most readers of this chapter, the fact that a parallel, largely urban and, from the perspective of its 'dark side' probably even more extreme, populist movement emerged in Australia at a slightly later date will be less well known, and populism's Australian echo should be considered before going on to Britain.[9] Australian history has its distinctive features which should be noted: Australia expanded enormously after the discovery of gold in rural Victoria near Melbourne in 1851 and experienced a boom lasting for forty years; the resultant mass migration of hundreds of thousands of Englishmen greatly expanded its cities (Melbourne's white population grew from zero in 1834 to over 500,000 by 1890) and its industrial and economic base, previously located almost exclusively in the export of wool.[10] With this expansion came the rise of trade unionism and of industries in the modern sense as well as of a self-conscious and independent agricultural workforce. Labour had always been relatively scarce in Australia (as it also was in the United States) and wages and living standards were, comparatively, much higher than in Britain from at least about 1850. The long post-gold boom ended with a major recession in the 1890s. This recession greatly helped to increase the electoral popularity of the Labour party, which was among the first social democratic parties to achieve electoral office. The ideology of the labour movement in Australia always centrally emphasized the maintenance of a continuing high standard of living by three related routes: the continuing spread of unionization and enforceable wage awards throughout the Australian economy; the deliberate use of tariff barriers—at a time when the commitment to free trade was all but ubiquitous in Britain—to encourage native Australian industries and to prevent the import of foreign goods; and, perhaps most importantly, the exclusion from Australia, and particularly from the Australian workforce, of cheap, non-white Oriental or Melanesian labour. Racism in Australia, directed mainly against Orientals and to a lesser extent against Pacific Islanders, was as pervasive as in the contemporary United States, a racism whose strength was reinforced by Australia's highly anomalous position as a thinly-populated white, European outpost close by Asia.

The attitude of Australian labour to Great Britain was ambiguous. Australian labour emphasized and reiterated a boisterous Australian nationalism, a search for national self-identity and a place in the sun, which plainly lay behind much of its economic and social desiderata. Yet the great majority of Australian workers were first- or second-generation Britons at the zenith of Empire (the others being mainly Catholic Irishmen, who were often at the forefront of both Australian nationalism and of the Labour movement). Nearly everyone looked to Britain, and especially to its navy, for protection from the Oriental hordes and other foreign threats. Nevertheless, much of Australian labour was highly antagonistic to the City of London's apparent continuing domination of Australian finance, and the Australian Labour Party's view of the malign control exercised by capitalist, especially British, finance—the theory of the 'Money Power'—became a major element in its ideology. Its spokesmen notably advocated nearly all of the strands in populism's 'dark side' discussed earlier, and the Australian Labour Party's ideology in this period was populist in the sense we mean perhaps even more certainly than was the ideology of the People's Party in the United States.[11]

The final element which helped to engender Australian populism and possibly the most difficult to specify precisely, is the Australian tradition of 'ratbags'—a glorious Australian term for an unpopular or unpleasant eccentric-rugged individualist with advanced or nonconformist ideas.[12] 'Ratbaggery' flourished in Australia as it did in Midwestern America of the same period, with much the same ambience and characteristics. Single-taxers, international socialists, White supremacists, sexual experimenters, health faddists, proponents of occultism and the like flourished with growing vigour. As in Midwestern America, Australia at this time was stifled by an all-embracing Babbitry and conformity in its official culture—the Australian term is 'wowserism'—largely derived from values shared by both Protestant nonconformity and Roman Catholicism. Unlike Britain, but again like Midwestern America, Australia lacked an official high culture, the equivalent of Oxbridge, or—as with Bloomsbury—a nonconformist culture of repute drawn from the same social and educational backgrounds as its official culture. In such an environment 'ratbaggery' became in effect the official opposition culture, indeed at its best virtually the only intellectual artefact of standing produced by Australia at this time.[13]

It was in this milieu that Australian populism grew up and became strong. Defined by Peter Love as 'a radical nationalism, which constructed a distinctive Australian identity in terms of class, race, and anti-imperialism',[14] it was almost exclusively the intellectual provenance of the Australian left and of organized labour, the conservative forces and the wealthy generally supporting Britain with loyalty and dedication, and reluctant to engender or advocate a separate Australian national identity or nationality.[15] To the left, however, radical nationalism

> invoked images of Australia as a virgin continent unsullied by the corruption, ignorance, and persecution of Europe. True Australians had the opportunity to build a new and better society in a land with a dead past . . .[16]

To Australian populism, 'Money Power' was invariably identified with the British aristocracy, the City of London and international Jewry, and was almost always attacked with what seemed superficially a radical rather than a conservative rhetoric. The Melbourne *Tocsin*, a populist labour journal, attacked Australian participation in the Boer War in the following highly typical terms, when commenting upon a British offensive in which 'only' seven Boers were killed:

> Only seven homes where the father will never return; seven groups of little ones stretching out appealing hands to God for him who will never see them; seven wives who will wait in vain for seven brave men, butchered to make a few soldiers peers and a few Johannesburg Jews millionaires.[17]

The most important and considered work of Australian populism is probably Frank Anstey's *The Kingdom of Shylock*, written during World War One. Anstey (1865–1940) was a prominent Australian Labour Party member of the Victorian Parliament for many years, and was actually Deputy-Leader of the national Australian Labour Party from 1922–7. The cover illustration of Anstey's work depicts a Shylock-like Jewish money-lender: 'Interest ish rishing—6 per shent to day, 7 per shent tomorrow', reads the sign on his window.[18] The chapter headings—'Lords of Lootery', 'The Clutching Hand'—about international Jewish finance, especially the Rothschilds—'The Australian Money Trust', 'The Profiteers' Programme', and so on—speak for themselves. The three persistent themes of the book are an attack on Jewish and City of London financiers, the war debt as an intolerable burden on Australian working men, and a lengthy call for currency reform and a thorough overhaul of the gold standard and paper currency systems—all obsessive features of populist thought down the ages.

Perhaps the most striking theme in the rhetoric and imagery of Australian populism was its flagrant anti-semitism, and a word might be in order here about Australian Jewry and anti-semitism.

There were only 15–20,000 Jews in Australia during the populist era, most of whom were English-speaking migrants from Britain rather than from eastern Europe, and most historians agree that there was little significant anti-semitism in Australia.[19] Although a tiny minority, Jews were extremely prominent in Australian public life including its highest places,[20] and, in general, met little hostility beyond social snobbery, and no *organized* anti-semitism. It should also be emphasized that Jews did not own or 'control' any significant portion of the Australian economy, and certainly not its major financial or commercial firms. Reflecting this, it is a notable feature of Australian populism's anti-semitism that *Australian* Jews were seldom if ever named or included in its critique of 'international finance', its odium being largely reserved for City of London, South African, or Wall Street men and dynasties. Precisely the same sort of anti-semitism (and anti-finance capital rhetoric aimed at non-Jewish bankers and magnates) has been observed by Hofstadter in American populism:

> It would be easy to misstate the character of Populist anti-Semitism or to exaggerate its intensity. For Populist anti-Semitism was entirely verbal. It was a mode of expression, a rhetorical style, not a tactic or a program. It did not lead to exclusion laws, much less to riots or pogroms. There were, after all, relatively few Jews in the United States in the late 1880s and early 1890s, most of them remote from areas of Populist strength. . . . Everyone remote and alien was distrusted and hated—even Americans, if they happened to be city people. The old agrarian conception of the city as the home of moral corruption reached a new pitch. Chicago was bad; New York, which housed the Wall Street bankers, was farther away and worse; London was still farther away and still worse.[21]

As with the case of American populism, in Australia unfamiliarity bred contempt, together with myths and the imaginings of sinister and wilful conspiracies.

The case of Australian populism has been dwelt upon here for a number of reasons—its unfamiliarity to most readers, the striking parallels, in a remote setting, with American populism, and to demonstrate populism's emergence full-blown in a British colony, inhabited almost entirely by *emigré* Britons outside and apart from the American context.[22] At first glance it may appear to strain the historical imagination to the limits of credulity to argue for any meaningful analogy between American and Australian populism and British radicalism of the late eighteenth and early nineteenth centuries. Before discounting any mooted suggestion, and indeed before exploring the affinities in a considered way, I would ask the reader what one is to make or how one is to categorize *Cobbett's Political Weekly*, opened virtually at random at any point in its history. On 17 June 1826, Cobbett tells us (cols 727–30):

> Gentlemen, a very large portion of taxes of this twenty pounds a year, paid by the weaver, is raised on account of the National Debt, and there are people who want us to believe that there has always been such a thing as a National Debt. That notion, Gentlemen, is exceedingly false. A National Debt has not been known to England only about one hundred and thirty-five years [*sic*]. Before that England knew no such degrading curse as a National Debt. . . . The debt, Gentleman, amounts to eight hundred millions of money. . . . Let me remark that this debt, this horrible and incredible parcel of money has been lent us; the fundholder, the money-broker; the stock-jobber, and Jews, and all the vermin of this description who prey on the vitals of the people, tell us that they lent us this money; lent us what? . . . Is it possible! What! the Jews to lend *us* ten times as much money as ever was in the world! Where did they get it? . . . [T]he Revolution has secured to us a national debt, that great curse which robs the weaver of his dinner and other comforts.—Gentlemen, this Parliament, which was to sit for seven years, made wars. The placemen and pensioners in it, acting contrary to the principles of the Revolution, in the first place continued to act for their own interest. They made wars because wars were profitable to themselves—but fearing that the people would not be so ready to hand them the money, they borrowed money for the purpose of carrying out the war.

It is common—indeed virtually invariable—to view British radicalism indulgently as wholly rational, progressive and liberal, and to those unfamiliar with Cobbett's writings I would venture to say that the effect of such an extract—and a hundred others would have done equally well if not better—will surely be somewhat startling. One must clearly reiterate that this extract is absolutely typical of Cobbett, as anyone who has read him will know, and only reasons of space preclude the reproduction of many others. The contents of Cobbett's writings are remarkable enough, but I would stress that the main point here is not simply his racial prejudice *or* the intensity of his anti-banking economic opinions and anti-aristocratic muck-raking, but the close resemblance *in the congruence of ideas* to the 'dark side' of American and Australian populism seventy years later. Perhaps four such elements predominate in virtually everything Cobbett ever wrote: his hostility to London, 'the great Wen', and admiration for the threatened rural values and virtues; his opposition to and contempt for the corrupt nature of the British aristocracy and the Establishment of the day (termed by Cobbett 'the Thing'); his group hostility to the curious and seemingly unrelated trio of Jews, Quakers and Scotsmen; and, centrally, his extraordinary obsession with the evils of paper money, the British national debt, the currency system, and with bankers and financiers, which his most recent and thorough biographer described thus: 'to the citizen of the twentieth century who has lived so long in the tiger's cage that he no longer fears the tiger, Cobbett's never-ending strictures on the public debt and paper money seem to be near-madness.'[23] Cobbett's anti-semitism, a pervasive and highly unpleasant feature of his writings, while often clearly what Hofstadter termed 'a mode of expression, a rhetorical style', with the term 'Jew' employed as a general, non-specific term of abuse for all money-lenders and financial exploiters, is also, equally often, aimed explicitly at Jews and employs traditional anti-Jewish imagery and stereotypes.[24] Similarly, the Quakers and the Scots were the recipients of Cobbett's venom for similiar reasons to the Jews—as parasitical financial exploiters and somehow alien to the proper ordering of English society.[25] On 4 February 1826 (col. 368) the *Weekly Register* describes Quakers indeed as 'worse than the Jews' for 'the devils [i.e. the Jews] do work sometimes', while Quakers are 'a whole sect not one of whom ever does any work'. Similarly the hateful paper money 'is of Scotch origin and has been upheld by Scotsmen, more than by any other men in the world' (28 Jan. 1826, col. 268). Paper money is also described by Cobbett as 'this Scotch, Jew, Quaker trap' (14 Jan. 1826, col. 132). It would belabour the point to add any more examples—Cobbett was the most prolific writer of his day, perhaps of the nineteenth century, but one has, in a sense, read everything he has ever written after a few random dips into the *Weekly Register*.

Cobbett is often and regularly described as a 'Tory radical' or in similar terms, and it may well be objected that he should not be situated within the English radical tradition. But the depiction of Cobbett as a Tory is, in my view, quite untrue: Cobbett was not a Tory but was specifically and continuously anti-Tory, and it is as misleading to describe Cobbett as a Tory (even a Tory radical) as it would be to describe the *New Stateman* as a Tory newspaper. Indeed, when the true direction of his critique is appreciated, it is virtually impossible to think of a figure of the day who might less accurately be described as a Tory. For most of his career, and in the context of his era, Cobbett was a thoroughgoing radical, probably the leading one of his time, whose whole endeavour was an attack upon 'the Thing'—the British Establishment of his age—and it is important to realize clearly what precisely was the target of Cobbett's wrath, as well as the wrath of many other radicals of the day who shared his view. They were attacking the union of greater landowners and landed aristocrats, many of new rather than old families and dynasties, and the City of London financial and mercantile magnates and interests, who together grew wealthy and monopolized power and status in Britain during the long years of Tory rule under Pitt and Liverpool. The burden of Cobbett's almost hysterical critique of 'paper money' lay, of course, in the enormous expansion of the national debt which accompanied the American Revolution and the Napoleonic wars and which in its wake created an enormously expanded class of public creditors— mainly, it would seem, financiers and aristocrats, who could be paid their interest only by taxes on the ordinary citizen. Although Cobbett is customarily depicted as a champion of small landowners and the traditional yeomen who were vanishing in the wake of Britain's economic expansion—a description which is accurate enough—it is equally important to realize that the object of his venom was the ruling elite of his day, itself landed and aristocratic at its core, and not industrial.

Against the notion of Cobbett as a Tory it is also necessary to insist that he was a genuine radical and to emphasize the radical component of his thought. Cobbett, of course, advocated a thorough reform of the unreformed parliamentary system and the borough-mongers who dominated it, and was an equally passionate defender of the liberties of Englishmen. To Cobbett,

> paper money enabled the war-people to carry on the [Napoleonic] war; it enabled them to keep a German army in the heart of England, and to flog Englishmen at the town of Ely under a guard of German bayonets; it enabled Pitt and Dundas, and the rest of them of that day, to suspend the Act of Habeas Corpus over and over again; it enabled them to pass a whole code of laws hostile to the liberty of the press; it enabled them, with the assistance of the Spanish patriots to restore the Inquisition, the Bourbons, and the Pope.[26]

John Foster claims in his important Marxist study of three industrial towns that the Lancashire cotton manufacturing centre of Oldham was, after 1832, effectively controlled by the working-

class majority of non-voters who heavily influenced the
'shopkeepers, publicans, and "farmers" (smallholders with a few
cows) who were all dependent on working-class custom for flour,
beer, and milk.'[27] According to Foster, this radical working-class
majority made the traders return Cobbett, a virtual folk-hero
among Britain's working classes, to Parliament by a tremendous
majority over his Tory opponent in 1832, despite the fact that he
had previously had little to do with the industrial north. In
Parliament, although very ill (he died in 1835), and an unsuccessful
debater, Cobbett was a tireless campaigner for further
parliamentary reform and against the New Poor Law.[28]

Although Cobbett was doubtless a unique figure, and bizarre and
extreme as his rhetoric often appears to be, the astonishing degree of
popularity and influence he enjoyed in the nation at large ought to
be emphasized. His *Weekly Register* for 2 November 1816 sold
44,000 copies, and a cheap reprint of an essay in that issue sold
200,000 copies in two months;[29] at the same date, *The Times* and
other London daily newspapers probably sold no more than 2,500
copies per issue.[30] Cobbett was quite arguably the most popular and
widely read journalist in Britain before the rise of Edward Lloyd in
mid-century and the Harmsworth press in the late Victorian period.
His public influence was also immense, extending to the financial
sphere, as for example when he advised note-holders of country
bank currency to convert their holdings to gold, his advice and
publicity being among the main causes of the bank panic in 1825
and the subsequent and far-reaching banking reforms.[31] His
influence on other radicals of the day was similarly enormous. 'It
was Cobbett who created this Radical intellectual culture', as E. P.
Thompson has summarized it.[32]

If Cobbett, influential as he was, were merely an English
eccentric with no real predecessors or progeny, he could perhaps be
dismissed, although even then it is clear that his, to us, hyperbolic
and often unpleasant rhetoric evidently struck an immensely
popular chord in English society. However it seems abundantly
clear that Cobbett followed in the wake of a long tradition of writers
and publicists who shared many of his central views. The originator
of this tradition seems clearly to have been that mysterious and
ambiguous figure Henry St John, first Viscount Bolingbroke
(1679–1751), while such key radical figures as Thomas Paine and
John Cartwright continued and added to key aspects of
Bolingbroke's ideology, which was also strongly associated with

aspects of the so-called 'country party' in eighteenth-century British politics.

What this tradition, begun by Bolingbroke and his circle[33] held and expressed, often in the most extreme language, was that the expansion of public credit and the national debt under Sir Robert Walpole had created a new ruling class of corrupt and avaricious financiers, centred in the City of London, closely allied to the ruling aristocracy who were themselves often from new rather than old families. These groups, together with the impact of the national debt, were responsible for the perilous decline of the smaller gentry, yeomanry and farming classes, the traditional backbone of English liberty and prosperity. This critique was extraordinarily pervasive throughout much of the 'opposition' in eighteenth-century politics. It was often expressed in language and rhetoric extreme even by the standards of the day. Consider, for example, this extract from *Cato's Letters*, written in 1724 by the 'Commonwealthmen' John Trenchard and Thomas Gordon:

> The resurrection of honesty and industry can never be hoped for while this sort of vermin is suffered to crawl about, tainting our air, and putting everything out of course, subsisting by lies, and practising vile tricks. . . . They are rogues of prey, they are stockjobbers. They are a conspiracy of stockjobbers! A name which carries along with it such a detestable image, that it exceeds all human invention to aggravate it. . . . Well, but monstrous as they are, what would you do with them? The answer is short and at hand, hang them.[34]

Along with this, and again an obvious element in Cobbett's rhetoric, was a surprisingly strong ingredient of anti-semitism, surprisingly strong because they were so few Jews in England—no more than 25,000 in 1815 and far fewer in the early eighteenth century—and surprising because there was virtually no significant tradition of Christian anti-semitism in Britain but considerable Protestant philo-semitism. Jews in no way dominated or controlled Britain's financial or commercial sector, while the values ascribed to Jews and the root cause of much hostility to them in many traditional societies, congruent with being bearers of modernity, rationality, and the cash nexus, arguably applied to the whole of English society, a society uniquely 'modern' and without surviving pre-modern atavisms. Yet throughout the writings of Bolingbroke and many of his followers there was a curiously strong and unexpected vein of anti-semitism, largely ignored by later historians.[35] For example, in Bolingbroke's newspaper *The Craftsman*, which in Kramnick's description primarily attacked the national debt, stockjobbers and monopoly trading companies,[36] there occurs a so-called 'Persian Letter' (No. 47 in the series) which Kramnick quotes as describing

> the existence among Christians of 'a peculiar sort called stockjobbers', men whom the Christians call Jews. They live and grow rich 'not by Traffick, nor by arts, or science, or industry, or labour, or mechanicks . . . or any other business of use or advantage of mankind'.[37]

Together with these elements went another very persistent strand in this tradition: the notion that Saxon England was genuinely pure, democratic and without corruption, and that both tyranny and corruption had been introduced by the Norman and their successors.[38] Bolingbroke cannot, however, by any stretch of the imagination be termed a radical as he held absolutely no belief in popular sovereignty or in a greater element of democracy as a solution to the disorders of his Britain, looking instead to a 'patriot king' to restore purity and liberty. The merger of Bolingbroke's critique of the financial and aristocratic elites and their depredations against the smaller landowners and common people, with a thoroughgoing belief in popular sovereignty and greater democracy, fully explicit in Cobbett, was gradually introduced into this 'country party' tradition by such radical thinkers as Thomas Paine and John Cartwright. Although Paine and Cartwright are primarily known for their radical and democratic critiques of Britain's hereditary system of government—Paine, of course, was a committed international revolutionary—it is important not to lose sight of the now-neglected fact that they also attacked the financial/aristocratic elites of their time, the great increase in national indebtedness, the new creditor class, and the harm this did to the 'ordinary man', in much the same terms as either Bolingbroke or Cobbett. In 1796 Paine wrote a highly popular attack on paper money in Britain and the enormous expansion of the national debt, *The Decline and Fall of the English System of Finance*, which caused Cobbett, previously Paine's bitter enemy, to mutate into one of his greatest champions; one bizarre result was that in 1819 Cobbett exhumed the bones of Paine, who had been buried in New Rochelle, New York in 1809, and brought them to England, much to the glee and amusement of his political enemies and Britain's satirical cartoonists. Paine also wrote at least two other pamphlets on the

Bank of England and on paper money, in 1786 and 1787, and was
among the first radicals of this period explicitly to attack Britain's
national finance in this way. Cartwright, who was probably the first
eighteenth-century radical seriously to advocate universal male
suffrage, was an even more clear-cut advocate of the viewpoint
originated by Bolingbroke and brought to full fruition by Cobbett.
In the words of his latest biographer, John W. Osborne:

> Hatred of finance capital, a desire for economy in government
> expenditures, parliament being summoned more frequently,
> resentment over the standing army and suspicion of foreigners
> represented a rich vein in English life . . . Cartwright was very much a
> part of this movement. We shall meet this spirit many times in his
> writings.[39]

In 1823, near the end of his long and active life, Cartwright
produced a 446-page work on English history and government,
described by Osborne as his 'chef d'oeuvre', The English Constitution
Produced and Illustrated. Most of it is devoted, in the familiar way,
to extolling the supposed liberties and virtues of the Anglo-Saxon
constitution. According to Osborne, Cartwright here set out his
belief that

> Jews were an unhealthy influence in the State. The aim of the book was
> to make the past a guide to the present and to prove that radical reform
> was not merely historically respectable but quite in line with the course
> of English development.[40]

It is also significant that Bolingbroke and his theories were widely
admired by such radicals as Richard Price, Horne Tooke and
Thomas Hollis who, together with Cartwright, formed the London
Society for Constitutional Information. Extracts from Bolingbroke
were frequently circulated to members, who used them as the bases
of several radical pamphlets. In 1771, for instance, Price too wrote
an essay on the national debt

> in which there is, woven into his lengthy prophecy of England's ruin
> from this monstrous burden, an attack on Walpole and praise for his
> 'Patriot' Opposition. Not only had Walpole raided the Sinking Fund,
> but he had also instituted the practice of using the fund and its offices to
> corrupt Parliament and the entire nation. Against these abuses
> Bolingbroke's patriots had appealed, Price wrote, but to no avail, and
> these evils still beset the nation.[41]

Taken both individually and as a bundle of congruent concepts and rhetoric, the close affinity between this strand in British radicalism and later American and Australian populism should be clear and obvious. There is in both the same attack on the 'conspiracy' of finance capital and the aristocracy, the same urging of the corruption of the independent and simple life, mainly rurally based, the same belief in popular sovereignty, and the same ambiguity on the political spectrum. With Cobbett, for instance, it is clear that his linking together of Jews, Quakers and Scotsmen is founded not only in religious and racial prejudice but in the fact that all three were known as successful commercial and financial minorities and were, in the context of Georgian England, bearers of radical modernity and modernizing values in Weber's sense. It is interesting to note that Cobbett's prejudices did not extend to Roman Catholics or Irishmen. Irishmen were regularly viewed as 'white niggers' by many English Tories and others, while Catholics were the victims of a widespread and pervasive hostility throughout Great Britain, founded both in religious fears and in national rivalries, at both the elite and popular levels. Cobbett noted that Catholics 'were a long-calumniated people; falsehood had been at work to depress, degrade, and oppress them for ages; I knew that my pen was capable of doing them ample justice'.[42] Cobbett's *History of the Protestant Reformation* was in part a hymn of praise for the Catholic England which existed before the Reformation. His group prejudices, in other words, were not general and were not necessarily those which were most widely shared. They were quite specific, aimed at groups which appeared to predominate in the financial and commercial elite,and which appeared to be the bearers of modern and rational values as opposed to those of rural and traditional England. The link between this and later populism seems plain, especially bearing in mind the very real democratic beliefs of Cobbett and his fellow radicals.

There are in addition many other affinities between the characteristic ambience of British radicalism and the features of populism which are familiar sixty or eighty years later. One of the most evident is the propensity for both to personalize and identify the ruling elite by name. Both the elite itself, and the evil influence of the elite, are largely equivalent to its individual members and their misdeeds; change them and the evil largely vanishes. The contrast here is strongly and evidently with sophisticated and 'scientific' Marxism, for which the individual members of the ruling elite of the day, their beliefs and actions, are themselves the products of broader underlying forces of history which are the base of every superstructure. In the long run the individual identities of the members of the ruling elite in a society are irrelevant before the broader current of history, and an exaggerated belief in their importance is assuredly a species of false consciousness. American populists had their muck-raking studies of tycoons and robber barons like *The History of Great American Fortunes*. Likewise, English radicalism of this period had book after book with titles like *The Black Book; Or Corruption Unmasked*, *The Red Book*, *A Peep at the Peers*, and so on. John Wade's *Extraordinary Black Book*, which appeared in various editions between 1820 and 1832, is probably the best known, most comprehensive and most typical. Normally, the format is to give the names of all substantial government placemen and office-holders, the annual value of their salaries, pensions and emoluments and, quite often, withering and sarcastic commentary on the rapacity or unfairness of the grossest or more irrational cases of mulcting and corruption. Additionally, Wade and other specialists in the genre added searching and accurate general essays about corruption and waste in a range of British institutions perceived as bound up in Old Corruption from the Church to the East India Company. These works were immensely popular, and did much to hasten the advent of Reform. So what? one might ask. The significance here is twofold. First, so far as I am aware, the radicals of Wade's day were the *only* radicals in modern British history who made lists of this type, and the genre simply vanishes with the Reform Bill.[43] There may have been several reasons for this—the stiff British libel laws are one—but when works enumerating the purported elite of wealth do appear in a later period, they are almost invariably hagiographic collective biographies by advocates of 'self-help' and sycophants of capitalism along the lines of Samuel Smiles. Radical critiques resembling *The Extraordinary Black Book* are, for instance, notably absent from Chartism, late Victorian radicalism, or the labour and socialist tradition, although by the late nineteenth century they were flourishing among populists and radicals in America and elsewhere.[44] It is also noteworthy that Wade's lists of placemen and their incomes are lists of the recipients of government money, state and state-related emoluments alone. They exclude the business incomes of leading businessmen, and the 'legitimate' landed incomes of landowners, and 'earned' income, even income from landed rentals, were exempt from at least the immediate thrust of their antipathy. On the other hand, in the main text of his work, Wade does clearly identify and attack the links between the government elite and London-based bankers, merchants and lawyers[45]—although never, significantly, its links with manufacturers or industrialists.

Another affinity between English radicalism of this period and later populism, and one which brings us closer to understanding one of the central reasons for these affinities, lies in the propensity for many of the chief figures in both movements to be what is known as 'auto-didacts'—the self-taught and normally self-educated with highly individual theories and distinct viewpoints not only on politics and political reform but frequently on a wide range of pursuits intellectual and otherwise, ranging from free thought and religion to sexuality to economic theories.[46] Many—arguably most—radicals of the day expended at least as much ink and effort on, say, deism, free thought and the attack on religious orthodoxy as on political reform. Similarly, the debate on currency, coinage and the Bank of England, whose best-known participants were Ricardo, Malthus and Cobbett, included dozens if not hundreds of pamphleteers and booklet writers now almost entirely forgotten.[47] A remarkable number of the leading radicals noticed in Baylen and Gossman's *Biographical Dictionary of British Radicals*[48] and similar modern sources were active in or often wrote books and pamphlets on unorthodox and unconventional subjects and movements ranging from the British Israelites to mesmerism, phrenology and occultism. Granting that orthodoxy and unorthodoxy are matters of opinion, and that the traditional certainties of religion were in a state of great flux while the later orthodoxy of science was not yet firmly established, there seems clearly to have been a strong affinity between 'crackpotism' of various kinds, especially involving self-realization or 'cosmic' understanding beyond the ordinary, and political radicalism of the Georgian (and perhaps later) vintage.[49] Much of the same ambience and propensity to 'crackpotism' of this sort was also found in American and Australian populism at the end of the nineteenth century. In the United States, perhaps the clearest example of this was the case of Ignatius Donnelly, author of the famous 1892 Platform of the People's Party, who in the words of Martin Gardner's exposé of pseudo-scientific theories,

> has been rightly dubbed the Prince of U.S. cranks. Usually the pseudo-scientist is obsessed with but one central topic, but Donnelly was

obsessed by three—the existence of Atlantis, a cipher message concealed in the play of Shakespeare (proving they were written by Francis Bacon), and the catastrophic effects upon the earth of a visiting comet.[50]

Although the propensity to unorthodoxy in the non-political realm seems clearly to be a part of the populist *gestalt*, both this unorthodoxy, and the political and economic beliefs typical of it, are the products of a wider explanation which is crucial to understanding the whole phenomenon. The wider bundle of populist attitudes are, in my view, apparently the most common and frequently encountered mentality of the class of politically literate auto-didacts, aware of the impress of political and economic power and the world's realities but outside the prevalent, hegemonic knowledge/value system—outside in the sense of not emerging from similar educational experiences and assumptions to the elite. Compelled to organize knowledge in their own way, in several widely differing political and cultural circumstances, these groupings, it seems, constructed similar ideologies which entailed, typically, the features discussed above, especially the combination of identifying an exploitative metropolitan aristocracy/financial elite as the central evil in society, the crucial importance of the currency and banking system, and democratic popular sovereignty.

If any identification between English radicalism and American/Australian populism is to be made by historians, it would seem most common to point to the similarity of their socio-economic circumstances—marginalized rural or working-class groups adopting a similar ideology at a time when all of these societies were rapidly urbanizing. Although clearly this similarity of circumstances is a valid and important consideration, my own view is that the apparent similarity of the belief systems and their progenitors, rather than the similarity of socio-economic circumstances, is more important to understanding why this ideology reappears so frequently in different guises. The alternative explanation—the similarity of the hard-pressed, marginalized, largely rural society (in England the lesser gentry and yeomanry, in America the Midwestern and Southern small farmers)—is, of course, up to a point highly significant. Cobbett was, after all, the author of *Rural Rides*, and many other radicals of his day had rural rather than chiefly urban links. However, this theory will surely not explain everything. In the first place, it would seem that much of what is here termed 'populism' and the typical populist critique was virtually ubiquitous in all shades of British radicalism from the

1780s to the 1830s and even beyond: to urban, industrial and artisan radicals as well as to rural radicals, and to occupational and sectional groups 'rising' as well as 'declining'. According to I. J. Prothero's very detailed study of the important trade union organizer John Gast, three extreme London radicals—Prothero terms them 'revolutionaries'—Watson, Preston and Thistlewood

> saw the people as exploited by the small number of persons who staffed the political system, and robbed and oppressed by unjust laws and taxation.[51]

This view was virtually pervasive among the urban artisanal radicals, it would seem. Patricia Hollis' important study of the radical press of this era bifurcates the unstamped press precisely into an 'old analysis' which attacked 'Old Corruption' and a 'new analysis' emphasizing more modern notions of labour exploitation and the labour theory of value. According to the 'old analysis', 'most wrongs would . . . be righted if taxes were greatly reduced, and this would come from radical reform and universal suffrage'.[52] Thomas Bewick, 'the foremost wood engraver of his day'[53] and a radical follower of Cobbett, routinely animadverted against Pitt and his government:

> This demo-oligarchy, cemented together by feelings of rapacious interests, in his hands was the best organized system of extorting money that had ever appeared in the world. They met together to tax-tax-tax; and under various pretexts to rob the people 'according to the law', and divide the spoil among themselves and their friends.[54]

Even radical periodicals which were not, as a rule, attached to the most squalid side of populist rhetoric occasionally indulged in it. For example, the *Black Dwarf* (1 July 1818) asked: 'who are they that cry money is scarce? Why the rich jew, or the rich jew christian, who want to buy two hundred pounds '.

Against the view that populism arose primarily from the marginalized rural classes might also be mentioned the fact that it had an urban as well as a rural locus: many English radicals lived or worked in urban areas, especially London, and even Cobbett, for example, wrote and lived for much of his career in London, despite loathing it and coining the term 'the great wen' to describe it. Australian populism was *primarily* urban and trade union based, although, as in America, it had a rural component as well.[55]

It can be argued, perhaps convincingly, that the populist stream

in English radicalism was replaced, in the wake of the 1832 Reform
Bill, by a newer type of radicalism emphasizing a more general
critique of capitalism and the exploitation of labour.[56] The
influence of Ricardo's economic analysis was important in this shift
of radical opinion, as were two other factors—the fact that Reform
had to a large extent broken the nexus which existed before 1832
between an entrenched and unrepresentative government (Old
Corruption) and the financial and commercial elite, and the sheer
increase in British industrialization and newer forms of working-
class employment. With railways joining cotton as Britain's 'lead
sector', northern and industrial capitalism increasingly became
central to any cogent critique of social class in Britain.[57] The first of
these two factors was probably as significant as the second: again
and again it seems clear that the fact that English—as opposed to
European—history continually has a 'happy ending' is due in no
small measure to the ascendancy of the post-1832 affluent Whig
aristocracy and the particular sorts of value which characterized
mid-Victorian middle-class liberalism.[58] But important as both
factors were, possibly the main reason for the near-disappearance of
'populism' lies, in my view, in what might be termed the
'rectification of ideology'—the increasing imposition of the modern
political ideologies, in their well-known order and schematism
(conservatism/liberalism/radicalism/socialism), upon all political
theorists. This had two important effects: doctrines or beliefs which
mixed elements of radical right-wing and left-wing ideologies (as
populism does) became perceived as increasingly eccentric and
inconsistent, while the new, 'pure' ideologies served as organizing
matrixes for all political thought, making deviant and eccentric
systems increasingly untenable. Some observers of populism who
have seen it as an ideology of delayed industrialization miss the
point that it was not industrialization which was delayed, but the
ideologies which are commonly associated with them: anti-
semitism is known to us as typically part of an extreme 'right-wing'
ideology, but why should this have been known to Cobbett?

It is not easy to point convincingly either to a compelling reason
for, or to a vehicle of, this process of 'the rectification of ideology'.
Certainly the modern ideologies in their familiar form grew largely
out of the French Revolution, and more broadly out of the
'democratic revolutions' of the eighteenth century, and were
extended by the response to industrialization.[59] English
conservatism, for example, of course largely began with Burke's

response to the French Revolution, and was added to by such figures as Coleridge and Disraeli to create an ideology in the modern sense, employing myths, a well-known litany of desiderata and anathemata, a golden age, a theory of history and so on. By, say, the time of Disraeli's Crystal Palace speech of 1872, this ideology was more or less completed, and politicians and writers who perceived themselves as situated in the conservative tradition have been marked by the stamp of this ideology which was enshrined as virtual gospel in the Conservative Party a century later. Neither the newness of this ideology nor its arguable unreality as an accurate description of the traditional British social structure and the British elite has had the slightest effect upon its retrospective canonization; in this the history of conservatism has largely resembled those of the other main ideologies, while its ubiquity as *the* ideology of the political right spared Britain from potential rivals during the 'era of tyrannies' like Mosley's. Significantly, the shift of conservatism's main bases of support from rural to urban Britain, and from the landed gentry to the middle classes from the 1870s onwards had little effect upon the ideology itself.

Even if this account is accurate, such a hardening of ideological assumptions cannot in my view fully account for the diminution of populist-style rhetoric in British politics since the 1830s, and doubtless other factors from educational and religious patterns to changed rates of social mobility and emigration were at work. For instance, the role of intellectuals altered greatly in Britain between the 1830s and the late Victorian period; possibly there were no 'intellectuals' in the sense of a separate and distinct class of social commentators before the Victorian period, and the one which emerged may have been truly Victorian in its sense of responsibility and lack of eccentricity in the old sense.[60] More importantly, the positing of the hardening of ideological assumptions as crucial to the near disappearance of populism must take account of the rise and decline of radical populist rhetoric in the three very different societies, the two latter manifestations of it discussed here having occurred *after* the milestones of the major modern ideologies had already been passed and after the major and recognizable ideologically-motivated political movements had begun fully to emerge—at least in Europe. In Midwestern America and in Australia it is at least arguable that the common European ideologies had little or no impact until they were widely taught and absorbed, while they grew out of dissimilar if not irrelevant political and economic circumstances.

It may well be that one can greatly exaggerate the extent to which either populism or the 'old analysis' disappeared from radical rhetoric in the 1830s, as Dr Prothero and Gareth Stedman Jones have suggested.[61] Much of the rhetoric of Chartism—often contrasted sharply with the older radicalism—resembled that of its predecessors in attacking parasitism, corruption, the aristocracy, unearned incomes, capitalist 'middlemen' and usury, as well as many of the other time-honoured targets of old-style radicalism; in his illuminating essay on this subject, Stedman Jones specifically links Chartism to the 'country party' ideology, as we have done with Cobbett and his school.[62] The *Northern Star* explained the emergence of Chartism in August 1838 as a response to 'making the working classes beasts of burden—hewers of wood and drawers of water—to the aristocracy, Jewocracy, Millocracy, Shopocracy, and every other Ocracy which feeds on human vitals'.[63] Perhaps the inclusion of the 'Millocracy' represents Chartism's original contribution to the rhetoric of populist radicalism. Half a century later still, Hobson, Chesterton and Blatchford are the most obvious examples in late Victorian and Edwardian times of a rhetoric and ideology which often bore a striking resemblance to Cobbett's. It is worth speculating whether some of the conditions of the Georgian period did not then recur, especially during the Boer War period—a seemingly unified and avaricious aristocratic/financial elite during a time of unpopular war and recession alongside an increasingly marginalized dissenting lower middle class; in the case of Chesterton, the debt to Cobbett was direct and gladly acknowledged, and it is also worth remembering that all of these figures, as well as most of their associates like Hilaire Belloc, were left-leaning Liberals or socialists, and not Tories. Even in this century it is possible to find more than a note of much the same spirit in—of all people—the George Orwell of *Coming Up For Air* and *The Lion and the Unicorn*, and the pre-*Animal Farm* Orwell is perhaps best seen as a successor to the tradition of Cobbett, Dickens and Chesterton rather than as something else.

It seems abundantly clear that this 'dark side' of populism was an important and possibly pervasive feature of English radicalism during the period associated with 'the making of the English working class' and arguably much later. Its importance and extent, it is fair to say, has been fairly systematically bowdlerized out of most accounts of British radicalism until very recently. There were probably two reasons for this: first, like other aspects of British history of the time, it was not 'right' and does not seem to belong to the proper Whig unfolding of modern English history, and hence many historians have simply not known what to make of it. Secondly there is the fact that much of populism was hyperbolic if not virtually lunatic, while other aspects of it—above all its racism—are shameful, and later partisans of Georgian radicalism have naturally been reluctant to expose this aspect of their ancestral ideology to too close an inspection. Even now, books are written about Cobbett which virtually ignore those central aspects of his writing discussed here,[64] while it is only in the very recent past that the link between English radicalism and populism has been explicitly drawn by historians, although no one, so far as I am aware, has systematically explored their affinities.[65] But the affinity is surely there, and anyone seeking his ideological ancestry in the radical response to early English industrialization must face the possibility that his family tree will include its share of family skeletons: illegitimacy, the bar sinister, and ideological miscegenation.[66]

NOTES

In preparing this chapter, I must acknowledge the helpful assistance of several people. My primary debt is to my post-graduate student Andrew A. Campbell, currently researching another topic in Australian history, whose seminar paper on Australian populism (based on his undergraduate thesis) delivered to Deakin University School of Social Sciences seminar in April 1984 reawakened my dormant but long-standing interest in this subject. I am grateful to him for his bibliographical suggestions and exchanges of ideas. I am also most grateful to Drs John Dinwiddy, I. J. Prothero, F. B. Smith, Ms Carole Taylor, and Mr Ray Duplain for their help and suggestions. An earlier draft of this chapter was read to the history seminars at Harvard, Johns Hopkins, and Princeton universities in November 1984, and I am most grateful for all the comments and criticisms made at the time. Malcolm Chase (University of Leeds), Dr David Sugarman (Middlesex Polytechnic), Dr John Stevenson (University of Sheffield), and Dr Michael Durey (Murdoch University, Western Australia) provided me with a series of valuable comments on this version of the chapter, only a few of which could be taken into account or commented on here.

1. General and intentional studies of populism include Ernest Gellner and I. Ionescu, *Populism: Its Meaning and National Characteristics* (London, 1969); Margaret Canovan, *Populism* (London, 1981), the

symposium 'To Define Populism', *Government and Opposition*, No. 3 (1968); James M. Youngdale, *Populism: A Psychohistorical Perspective* (Port Washington, N.Y., 1975); and V. Khoros, *Populism: Its Past, Present, and Future* (Moscow, 1984). Anthologies of writings and debates specifically on American populism abound, and normally include general introductory discussions of the subject, including the 'dark side' of populism analyzed here. These include Norman Pollack (ed.), *The Populist Mind* (Indianapolis, 1976); Theodore Saloutos (ed.), *Populism: Reaction or Reform?* (New York, 1968); and George Brown Tindall (ed.), *A Populist Reader: Selections From the Works of American Populist Leaders* (New York, 1966).

2. For a useful discussion of some of these points see A. James Gregor, *The Fascist Persuasion in Radical Politics* (Princeton, N.J., 1974).

3. On populist 'conspiracy theories' see D. McRae and D. Wiles, 'Populism As an Ideology: A Syndrome Not a Doctrine', in Gellner and Ionescu, *Populism, op. cit.*, pp. 157ff.; Edward Shils, 'The Fascination of Secrecy: The Conspiratorial Conception of Society', in *The Torment of Secrecy* (London, 1956), pp. 27–37; and Richard Hofstadter, *The Paranoid Style in American Politics and Other Essays* (New York, 1965), esp. pp. 3–40. My use of the term 'conspiracy theory', which may strike some as vulgar and superficial, follows numerous historians and sociologists of the subject, for instance Hofstadter.

4. Both American and Australian populists certainly wished to see an increase in the power and role of the state in the interests of the 'common people' against the oligarchy. Most historians of America, however, draw a distinction between populism and the subsequent Progressive movement—which was socially based largely in well-educated, often urban and eastern political reformers rather than in the rural South and Midwest. They view populism as socio-culturally the precursor to post-1932 New Deal-Fair Deal left-liberalism which rose to power with Franklin D. Roosevelt.

5. Nor do certain other political schools or movements which are similarly mysterious, for instance utilitarianism (see Chapter 9).

6. I have in mind especially the ideas and publications of the so-called Institute for Historical Review in California, notorious as an anti-semitic and neo-Nazi front organization, which exists to publish or publicize hidden or secret historical 'facts' which have been 'suppressed' by government and academic 'authorities'. The most important of these suppressed facts is that the Holocaust of European Jewry in World War Two was a hoax engineered by 'Zionists' and Marxists. Franklin Roosevelt's deliberate engineering of American involvement in that war, and Winston Churchill's 'war crimes', are two other familiar themes of its publications, which attempt to be well-documented works of historical scholarship, rather than the crude, obviously crackpot tracts one might expect. The so-called Institute is the culmination of a long-standing underground tradition in America which has occasionally involved mainstream figures like the historian Charles A. Beard.

A similar and related, but older, (and equally notorious) political group in Australia, the Australian League of Rights, has close links to Australian populism via its origins in the Douglas Social Credit movement, and distributes the same material (often originating from the so-called Institute) in Australia as well as works urging the view that international bankers control the world, Wall Street and the Kremlin are secretly linked, etc. On the League of Rights, see Ken Gott, *Voices of Hate* (Melbourne, 1965) and Andrew A. Campbell, *The Australian League of Rights* (Melbourne, 1978). Students of the contemporary Soviet scene will notice the affinities between this and the view found in many Soviet publications that the West is controlled by a conspiracy of Wall Street, the 'Zionists', and Freemasons. (On which see Howard Spier, 'Zionists and Freemasons: A New Element in the Soviet Propaganda Campaign Against Zionism', Institute of Jewish Affairs *Research Report*, London, Dec. 1978.) Even today, systematic doubt of the veracity of the commonly accepted sources of knowledge and information can appear as a major and underlying theme in the works of an author of international renown, often coming close to the systematic doubt of fringe figures; perhaps the best contemporary examples are the political writings of Noam Chomsky, for instance his work (co-authored with Edward S. Herman) on Indochina, *The Political Economy of Human Rights*, 2 Vols. (Sydney, 1980). On this aspect of Chomsky's work, see my 'Chomsky and the Neo-Nazis', *Quadrant*, XXV, No. 10 (Oct. 1981), the lengthy exchange between Chomsky, Robert Manne and myself in *Quadrant* (April 1982), and Geoffrey Sampson, 'Censoring Twentieth Century Culture: The Case of Noam Chomsky', *The New Criterion*, (Oct. 1984). (*Quadrant* is a Sydney monthly similar to *Encounter*.)

7. *The Age of Reform* (New York, 1955), *The Paranoid Style*, *op. cit.*, and *Anti-Intellectualism in American Life* (New York, 1963); Victor C. Ferkiss, 'Populist Influences in American Fascism', *Western Political Quarterly* X (June 1957).

8. Walter T. K. Nugent, *The Tolerant Populist* (Chicago, 1963), and Pollack, ed., *The Populist Mind*, *op. cit.* The literature of American populism is far too extensive to be summarized here. Some of the debate to the late 1960s may be found in Salutos (ed.), *Populism*, *op. cit.*

9. The best account of Australian populism and especially its Labour base, is Peter Love *Labour and the Money Power: Australian Labour Populism 1890–1950* (Melbourne, 1984). Despite the coverage accorded by Love, the ubiquity of populism's influence in many aspects of Australian life has not yet been fully discussed by historians. Other important works on the subject include Andrew A. Campbell, 'Australian Populism: From Periphery to Centre', (unpublished); Roger Coates, 'The Australian Labour Movement and Marx', *Australian Left Review* (Winter 1983); Peter Loveday, 'Anti-Political Political Thought', in Robert Cooksey (ed.), *The Great Depression in Australia* (Canberra, 1970), Ray Markey, 'Populist Politics', in Ann Curthoys and A. Markus (eds), *Who Are Our Enemies? Racism and the Working Class in Australia* (Sydney, 1978), and Humphrey McQueen,

A New Britannia? (Melbourne, 1978). The most important statement of the populist world-view by an Australian populist is Frank Anstey's *The Kingdom of Shylock* (Melbourne, 1917).

10. Good general introductions to Australian history include Frank Crowley (ed.), *A New History of Australia* (Melbourne, 1974); Gordon Greenwood (ed.), *Australia: A Social and Political History* (Sydney, 1955), and R. M. Younger, *Australia and the Australians* (Melbourne, 1982).

11. Love, *Labour and the Money Power, op. cit.*, esp. pp. 1–19.

12. On which see Keith Dunstan, *Ratbags* (Melbourne, 1979), John Clune, *Wild Men of Sydney* (Sydney, 1957), and Bruce Scates, ' "Wobblers": Single Taxers in the Labour Movement, Melbourne 1889–99', *Historical Studies*, Vol. 21, No. 88, (October 1984).

13. Such Australian cultural figures as made any international impact at this time, for instance the composer Percy Grainger and the artist Norman Lindsay, generally emerged from this milieu.

14. Love, *Labour and the Money Power, op. cit.*, p. 15. By 'anti-imperialism' Love means its hostility to British domination of Australia, not opposition to White control of Third World colonies.

15. As late as 1954, the great Australian conservative Prime Minister Robert Menzies claimed to be 'British to his bootstraps'. It was not until the 1960s or even later that purely Australian national identity became fully legitimate among its conservative forces, in the context, of course, of the near-total decline of Britain as a major power.

16. Love, *Labour and the Money Power, op. cit.*, p. 15.

17. Cited *ibid.*, p. 38. The precise date is not given.

18. Anti-semitic, racist, anti-finance capital, and anti-British aristocracy themes appeared frequently in Australian populist political cartoons. A typical one, reprinted in Love, *op. cit.*, p. 49, from *Labor Call* (4 May 1911) depicts a fat, cigar-smoking Jewish financier standing astride Australia, his pockets carrying papers reading 'Trusts', 'Combines', and 'Monopolies'. The anti-semitic caption—'The "Nose" Have It'— refers to the defeat of a Labour-backed national referendum in 1911 which would have permitted the Australian government to nationalize industrial monopolies. Similar cartoons depicting these persistent themes in populist propaganda are reprinted by Love on pp. 32, 39, 43, 54, 60, 66, 72, and elsewhere, and are only a small selection of those ubiquitous in the populist press at the time. Many attacked the 'Yellow Peril' posed by the rise of Japan and the importation of cheap Melanesian or Oriental labour, as well as the more familiar anti-British, anti-finance capital, and anti-semitic themes.

19. Hilary L. Rubinstein, *The Jews In Victoria 1835–1985* (Sydney, 1985), pp. 38–41, 84–94.

20. The two most notable Jews in Australian public life at the time were Sir John Monash (1865–1931), Commander-in-Chief of the Australian armies in Europe during World War One, and Sir Isaac Isaacs (1855–1948), successively Attorney-General, Chief Justice of the Australian High Court, and the first native-born Governor-General of Australia.

21. *The Age of Reform, op. cit.*, cited in Saloutos, *Populism, op. cit.*, p. 64. While generally agreeing with this, it seems impossible to dismiss Australian populism's anti-semitism as merely 'a mode of expression, a rhetorical style', given its wallowing in traditional anti-semitic stereotypes and imagery.

22. Populism also emerged in the western Canadian provinces at this time and spawned a social credit movement of some importance.

23. George Spater, *William Cobbett: The Poor Man's Friend* (Cambridge, 1982) Vol. I, p. 200.

24. For instance, in the *Weekly Register* of 23 November 1833 (col. 480) Cobbett reprints a letter from the *Newcastle Press* which condemns 'the pass[ing] of an act to declare that those who are descended from the murderers of Jesus Christ, and while they applaud the act, in what they have the impudence to call their religious ceremonies, are as fit to be judges and lord chancellors and privy-councillors and even lawmakers, as Christians are themselves'. Cobbett notes (col. 479) that Newcastle 'boasts of very few surpassing in either quality [talent and public-spiritedness] the author of this letter'. Cobbett's sentiments here should surely be contrasted with, for instance, the famous essay of 1831 by Macaulay, the archetypal early Victorian liberal, on 'The Civil Disability of the Jews'.

25. These three groups were also singled out and linked (and disliked) by other contemporary authors, for instance by Charles Lamb in his Elia essay 'Imperfect Sympathies', in *The Complete Works and Letters of Charles Lamb* (New York, 1935), pp. 51–6.

26. *Cobbett's Weekly Register*, 28 June 1823, col. 78–90.

27. John Foster, *Class Struggle and the Industrial Revolution* (London, 1974), p. 52.

28. *Ibid.*, pp. 69–71 and Spater, *William Cobbett, op. cit.*, Vol. II.

29. Lynne Lemrow, 'William Cobbett's Journalism for the Lower Orders', *Victorian Periodical Review*, XV, No. 1 (Spring 1982), p. 11, citing Richard Altick, *The English Common Reader* (Chicago, 1957), p. 382.

30. Chris Cook and Brendan Keith, *British Historical Facts, 1830–1900* (London, 1975), p. 215.

31. Frank William Fetter, *Development of British Monetary Orthodoxy, 1797–1875* (Fairfield, N. J., 1978) pp. 108, 111–18.

32. E. P. Thompson, *The Making of the English Working Class* (New York, 1966), p. 746.

33. Bolingbroke's links to Harrington have been traced by Quintin Skinner in 'The Principles and Practices of Opposition' in Neil McKendrick (ed.), *Historical Perspectives; Studies in English Thought and Society in Honour of J. H. Plumb* (London, 1974), pp. 113–24. I am grateful to Dr John Dinwiddy for this reference.

34. *Cato's Letters* (London, 1724), Vol. I, pp. 8 and 24, cited in Isaac Kramnick, *Bolingbroke and His Circle: The Politics of Nostalgia in the Age of Walpole* (Cambridge, Mass., 1968, p. 47). For a good treatment of English radicalism in the eighteenth century, focusing on the 'country party' ideology, see John Brewer, 'English Radicalism in the

Age of George III', in J. G. A. Pocock (ed.), *Three British Revolutions: 1641, 1688, 1776* (Princeton, N.J. 1980).

35. At the popular level there were periodic outbursts of anti-semitic rioting as over the 'Jew Bill' of 1753. See Thomas W. Perry, *Public Opinion, Propaganda, and Politics in Eighteenth-Century England: A Study of the Jew Bill of 1753* (Cambridge, Mass., 1962).

36. Kramnick, *Bolingbroke, op. cit.*, pp. 71–3.

37. *Ibid.*, p. 71.

38. *Ibid.*, pp. 177–81. This perennial theme has of course been traced for the seventeenth century by Christopher Hill in 'The Norman Yoke', in John Saville (ed.), *Democracy and the Labour Movement* (London, 1954) and is given its due and important place in late eighteenth-century radicalism in E. P. Thompson's *Making of the English Working Class*, Ch. 4, 'The Free-Born Englishman'.

39. John W. Osborne, *John Cartwright* (Cambridge, 1972), p. 14.

40. *Ibid.*, p. 149. The anti-semitic passages in Cartwright's work are at pp. xvii, 95, 99 and 399, according to Osborne (*ibid.*, n. 3).

41. Kramnick, *Bolingbroke, op. cit.*, p. 170.

42. *Cobbett's Weekly Register*, 31 Dec. 1825, cols. 28–9.

43. Malcolm Chase has, however, drawn my attention to later examples by Wade—like listings; for instance *The History and Mystery of the Civil List* (London, 1884?). The statement in the text should perhaps be confined to well-known radical movements of a later period, such as, say, Fabianism.

44. Arguably, no well-known work paralleling Wade appeared in England until Simon Haxey's *Tory M.P.*, published by the Left Book Club in 1939.

45. For example, [John Wade] *The Extraordinary Black Book* (London, 1832; repr. New York, 1970), pp. 286–333, 394–427 and 428–51 discuss, respectively, abuses in the law and law courts, the East India Company, and the Bank of England.

46. On aspects of the affinity to auto-didactism in Georgian Britain and their association with political reform see for instance Edward Royle (ed.), *The Infidel Tradition From Paine to Bradlaugh* (London, 1976), and *Radical Politics 1790–1900: Religion and Unbelief* (London, 1971); Fetter, *Development, op. cit., passim*, and Iain McCalman, 'Unrespectable Radicalism: Infidels and Pornography in Early Nineteenth-Century London', *Past and Present*, No. 104 (August 1984). E. P. Thompson's celebrated litany: 'the poor stockinger, the luddite cropper, the "obsolete" hand-loom weaver, the "utopian" artisan, and even the deluded follower of Joanna Southcott', (*Making, op. cit.*, p. 12) overlooked by the 'enormous condescension of posterity' certainly deserve 'rescue' and a searching examination by today's historians, so long as they can look what these people were actually saying, and its implications, squarely in the face.

47. But listed in full by the score in *The Catalogue of the Goldsmith Library*.

48. Joseph O. Baylen and Norbert J. Gossman, *Biographical Dictionary of Modern British Radicals, Vol. I, 1770–1830* (Brighton, Sussex, 1979).

49. Some examples (of very many): the famous radical William Carpenter

wrote (in 1872) *The Israelites Found in the Anglo-Saxons*; the radical
Julian Hibbert (1800–34) 'like many of his radical acquaintances . . .
experimented with mesmerism, Morrison's pills, temperance,
vegetarianism, and almost anything else that seemed to possess
curative powers'. (Joel H. Wiener in Baylen and Gossman,
Biographical Dictionary, op. cit.). Similarly the Owenite Charles Bray
(1811–84) 'theorized that the human body transmitted warmth and
that human thought existed in a kind of invisible reservoir which could
be tapped by clairvoyants'. (David de Guistino, *ibid.*). The connexion
between British radicalism and unorthodoxy over science and lifestyle
has continued to reappear ever since—throughout the Victorian
period; in the Fabian Society's emergence from the Fellowship of the
New Life; in the inter-war period, Orwell's celebrated strictures in *The
Road to Wigan Pier*; and its more recent manifestation during the
Vietnam and 'flower power' eras. (There is also an equally strong if not
stronger connexion on the extreme right.) Most of these later
manifestations of the radical/unorthodoxy connexion lack, however,
Georgian radicalism's central critique of the government's domination
by the aristocracy and finance capital and hence its affinity with
populism.

50. Martin Gardner, *Fads and Fallacies in the Name of Science* (New York,
    1957), p. 35. Beyond this, on the extreme right as well as the extreme
    left, and well into the realm of insanity, are the conspiracy theories of
    history, usually involving the 'Illuminati', the Freemasons, Jews, and
    Marxists, or some combination of all of these. For a recent work, not,
    apparently, by obvious lunatics and moreover linking all of these to
    UFOs and paranormal phenomena (!) see Anthony Roberts and Geoff
    Gilbertson, *The Dark Gods* (London, 1980). Historians are also
    coming to recognize the influence of such theories, involving
    occultism, conspiracies and 'secret knowledge', on the Nazis and their
    predecessors. See e.g., J. H. Brennan, *Occult Reich* (Aylesbury,
    Bucks., 1974).

51. I. J. Prothero, *Artisans and Politics in Early Nineteenth-Century
    London: John Gast and His Times* (Folkestone, Kent, 1979), p. 91.

52. Patricia Hollis, *The Pauper Press* (Oxford, 1970), p. 205.

53. Curtis W. Wood Jr. in Baylen and Gossman, *Biographical Dictionary,
    op. cit.*

54. Montague Weekly (ed.), *A Memoir of Thomas Bewick, Written by
    Himself* (London, 1961), p. 152.

55. See Ray C. Duplain, 'Seeds of Discord: Aspects of Rural Populism in
    the Wheat Belt of Victoria and N.S.W., 1895–1915', unpubl. Master of
    Arts dissertation, Monash University, Australia, 1976.

56. Hollis, *Pauper Press, op. cit.*, Ch. 7, pp. 220–58.

57. Presumably, too, a social class explanation of the disappearance of
    populism from radical rhetoric at this time would also focus on the
    squeezing-out of the 'middling class' along the lines suggested by R. S.
    Neale in 'Class and Class Consciousness in Early Nineteenth Century
    England: Three Classes or Five?', *Victorian Studies*, XII No. 1 (1968).

58. See Chapter 9, and the perceptive remarks of John Vincent and M.

Stenton: 'when one relates Dr Kenealy's [pro-Tichborne] victory at Stoke [in 1874] to other straws in the wind, indicative of undirected dissidence and polymorphic disaffection among the democratic electorate, unharnessed to official politics (the anti-vaccinationist movement, the Welsh and Irish anti-Jewish pogroms, the Sunday trading riots of 1855), one begins to see more of the full curiousness of working class history which makes it so hard to determine whether or not its central features are in some sense "progressive".' John Vincent and M. Stenton (eds), *McCalmont's Parliamentary Poll Book of All Elections 1832–1918* (Brighton, 1971), p. xii.

59. Robert A. Nisbet, *The Sociological Tradition* (London, 1967), pp. 21–8.

60. T. W. Heyck, *The Transformation of Intellectual Life in Victorian England* (London, 1982).

61. Prothero, *Artisans, op. cit.*, and 'Chartism in London', *Past and Present*, No. 44 (August 1969); Gareth Stedman Jones, 'Rethinking Chartism', in *Languages of Class: Studies in English Working-class History 1832–1982* (Cambridge, 1983), esp. pp. 134–8. See also Alfred Plummer, *Bronterre: A Political Biography of Bronterre O'Brien 1804–1864* (London, 1971), p. 65.

62. Stedman Jones, *loc. cit.*, p. 102.

63. Cited *ibid.*, p. 104.

64. For instance, Raymond Williams, *Cobbett* (Oxford, 1983).

65. Explicit use of the term 'populist' to describe those men and movements analyzed in this paper include Kramnick, *Bolingbroke, op. cit.*, pp. 60, 171; Craig Calhoun, *The Question of Class Struggle: Social Foundations of Popular Radicalism During the Industrial Revolution* (Oxford, 1982), esp. pp. 3–22; and Gertrude Himmelfarb, *The Idea of Poverty: England in the Early Industrial Age* (London, 1984), pp. 207–29. Himmelfarb is excellent on Cobbett—her chapter on 'Cobbett: Radical Populism' (*ibid.*) is probably the best recent short introduction to his attitudes—but she does not link him to the long tradition to which he clearly belongs. Himmelfarb is also excellent on Carlyle (pp. 191–206) who, of course, shared much in common with Cobbett but was not a believer in popular sovereignty or extended democracy and hence does not wholly belong to the populist tradition. Calhoun's challenging and important book does indeed describe the working-class radicals as 'populists' and 'reactionary radicals' (*ibid.*, p. 7) who were attempting to protect traditional community social bonds against industrialization. (This is an interesting and important thesis although one with which I cannot wholly agree), and 'populist' is used many times to describe their attitudes. Strangely, however—strange because Calhoun is an American sociologist who would be aware of American populism—the affinities with the 'dark side' of populism are not mentioned. One might ask whether this, too, is a case of conscious or unconscious bowdlerization. *Cf.*, too, Calhoun's remarks on the E. P. Thompson/Anderson and Nairn debate: 'Edward Thompson has been called a "populist socialist" by Perry Anderson and Tom Nairn. Thompson, with some justice, believes that his critics

use the phrase to refer to an idealization of chauvinistically English and atheoretically popular values; he has replied with some justified indignation that he is no such animal but rather is a "socialist internationalist" ' (*op. cit.*, p. 4).

66. Two other important matters cannot be covered in this chapter, given the limitations of space. The first is the influence of populist attitudes on literature, a thread which seems to run from Swift through Dickens to Chesterton and Orwell. On this see Kramnick, *Bolingbroke, op. cit.*, Ch. 8, 'The Nostalgia of the Georgian Poets', and Chapter 10 in this volume. Secondly there are the direct links between English radicalism and later populism, especially in Australia, which are often clear and direct, and on which see Love, *Labour, op. cit.*, John F. Finlay, *Social Credit: The English Origins* (Montreal, 1972), and in particular Michael Roe's important *Kenealy and the Tichborne Cause: A Study in Mid-Victorian Populism* (Melbourne, 1974), esp. pp. 163–97.

Index